# Whitehead at Harvard, 1924–1925

# Whitehead at Harvard, 1924–1925

Edited by Brian G. Henning and
Joseph Petek

EDINBURGH
University Press

Edinburgh University Press is one of the leading university presses in the UK. We publish academic books and journals in our selected subject areas across the humanities and social sciences, combining cutting-edge scholarship with high editorial and production values to produce academic works of lasting importance. For more information visit our website: edinburghuniversitypress.com

Edinburgh University Press Ltd
The Tun – Holyrood Road, 12(2f) Jackson's Entry, Edinburgh EH8 8PJ

First published in hardback by Edinburgh University Press 2020

Typeset in 10.5/13 Goudy Old Style by
IDSUK (DataConnection) Ltd, and
printed and bound by CPI Group (UK) Ltd,
Croydon, CR0 4YY

A CIP record for this book is available from the British Library

ISBN 978 1 4744 6135 1 (hardback)
ISBN 978 1 4744 5940 2 (paperback)
ISBN 978 1 4744 5942 6 (webready PDF)
ISBN 978 1 4744 5941 9 (epub)

# Contents

# Acknowledgements

This book's preface, introduction and Chapters 3, 5, 11, 13, 14, 15, 16 and 17 are based on papers originally delivered at the ninth international Whitehead Research Project Conference, 'Whitehead Revealed: Examining Whitehead's First Year of Harvard Lectures', in Claremont, CA, USA from November 30 to December 2, 2017.

Our gratitude to:

- George Whitehead, for trusting the Critical Edition of Whitehead editors with his grandfather's legacy.
- Frederick and Nancy Marcus, for unfailingly generous support to fund editorial staff and the conference out of which this volume grew.
- John Buchanan, for his continued financial support of the Whitehead Research Project and its conferences.
- Jenna Petsche, for help with matters editorial.

# Abbreviations

| | |
|---|---|
| AE | *The Aims of Education and Other Essays* (1929) |
| AI | *Adventures of Ideas* (1933) |
| CN | *The Concept of Nature* (1920) |
| ESP | *Essays in Science and Philosophy* (1948) |
| FR | *The Function of Reason* (1929) |
| HL1 | *The Harvard Lectures of Alfred North Whitehead, 1924–1925*, ed. Paul A. Bogaard and Jason Bell (2017) |
| IM | *An Introduction to Mathematics* (1911) |
| MT | *Modes of Thought* (1938) |
| OT | *The Organisation of Thought, Educational and Scientific* (1917) |
| PNK | *An Enquiry Concerning the Principles of Natural Knowledge* (1919) |
| PR | *Process and Reality: An Essay in Cosmology* (1929) |
| R | *The Principle of Relativity: With Applications to Physical Science* (1922) |
| RM | *Religion in the Making* (1926) |
| SMW | *Science and the Modern World* (1925) |

These abbreviations refer to works by Whitehead and not to any particular published edition. While there are several editions that share common pagination, there are some whose pagination differs between publishers. To find a specific reference, consult the relevant bibliographic list for the chapter in which the reference appears.

# Preface: A Brief History of the Critical Edition of Whitehead

*Brian G. Henning*

The first volume of the Edinburgh Critical Edition of the Complete Works of Alfred North Whitehead, *The Harvard Lectures of Alfred North Whitehead, 1924–1925*, was published in February 2017. But the story of the Whitehead Edition starts at least half a century earlier, in 1963 at Yale University. At the encouragement of Whitehead's former student, Paul Weiss, who was at that time a professor at Yale, the Graduate Philosophy Club started contacting Whitehead's former students to ask if they could transcribe and publish lecture notes from their time in Whitehead's class. According to the Yale students' account, the project was led initially by William Leon McBride[1] aided by Carl Vaught[2] and later led by John Bacon.[3] They ended up with six sets of notes taken in Whitehead's classes by George P. Conger, John L. Mothershead, Jr., A. H. Johnson, Edward Schouten Robinson, William K. Frankena and W. V. Quine.[4] Their first task was faithfully to transcribe the notes from handwritten pages to typescript generated on typewriters. The project involved nearly forty different typists transcribing different portions of the assembled notes. Tragically, a large portion of the originals of one set of notes, those of the Canadian A. H. Johnson, went missing.[5]

Unfortunately, this first 'Whitehead project' was not to be. After three years, in 1966, the Yale graduate students felt compelled to abandon the project with only two-thirds of the six sets transcribed, some verified, and none edited. Frankly, it is amazing that the graduate students kept at it as long as they did. In our case, even with graduate students collectively working thirty hours a week for more than five years and with all the benefits of modern word processing and graphic editing, it has been a herculean task to transcribe a bit more than half of the lecture notes we've collected. And, as Joe Petek and I are discovering as we edit volume two of the Edition, the 1925–27 Harvard lectures, the work of verifying those transcriptions is exceedingly painstaking and time consuming work. One can only imagine how difficult it would have been for these graduate students to try to transcribe handwritten notes using only typewriters. In the end, the students abandoned the project and deposited their unfinished manuscript in the Yale Library. And that is where we found it nearly a half-century later.

A quarter-century after the Yale students' failed attempt, an unrelated group decided it was time to work on a proper critical edition of the monographs (they had no intention of publishing the lecture notes). Inspired by Griffin and Sherburne's 1979 'corrected edition' of *Process and Reality*, in the early 1990s a team from the Center for Process Studies led by John Cobb applied for a Scholarly Editions and Translations grant from the US National Endowment for the Humanities (NEH) to fund the start of a critical edition of Whitehead. According to Cobb, they had even lined up individual scholars who would edit particular texts.[6] Unfortunately, their application was denied and the project was shelved indefinitely. The time for a Whitehead Edition had not yet come.

My own part of the story begins nearly a decade later in the late 1990s when I was myself a graduate student at Fordham University in New York City. One day I had gone to Fordham's Walsh Library to locate a copy of one of Whitehead's works, only to find that his various monographs were not all shelved together in the philosophy section. Instead, *Adventures of Ideas* was shelved with sociology, *Aims of Education* with education, and so on. I looked enviously at the thirty-odd volumes of the *Collected Works of Dewey*, with their handsome volumes all consecutively shelved. I thought what a great intellectual injustice it was that Whitehead didn't have a proper critical edition. It was little more than a passing thought at the time, but I resolved then to see what, if anything, could ever be done about it.

After defending my dissertation in late 2002 and graduating the next spring, I spent the first few years of my career rewriting my dissertation into a book, which was published in 2005 as *The Ethics of Creativity*. I then turned my attention to other scholarly projects. One of those was exploring the idea of the critical edition. Having learned that copyright issues had been a key problem in previous attempts, I first set about to learn what I could about copyright law and intellectual property.

When the Copyright Act was first enacted by the United States Congress in 1790, copyright protection only extended for fourteen years. Over the intervening centuries it has been extended again and again until today, *unpublished* works are copyrighted for seventy years from the author's death.[7] On the other hand, *published* works published before 1923 are already in the public domain in the United States. Thus, all of Whitehead's pre-Harvard published works are in the public domain, according to US copyright law.

However, registered works published *after* 1923 have continually had their copyright protection extended by successive acts of Congress. Why?

The unexpected answer has to do with Walt Disney and his first animated cartoon, Steamboat Willie. Every time this 1928 work has come close to entering the public domain, legions of Disney lawyers mount an all-out campaign to have the duration of copyright protection extended. The result? Because of a cartoon mouse steering a boat, most registered materials published in the United States after 1923 have copyright protection for ninety-five years from their publication date. That means that Steamboat Willie's copyright protection expires in just a few short years from the time of this publication (2024), but works published in 1923 have finally started entering public domain as of January 2019. As we approach 2023, when Steamboat Willie would become public, we will learn whether hordes of Disney corporation lawyers and lobbyists will once again emerge cicada-like to extend Willie's copyright. What we know now is that, if the law is not changed, Whitehead's post-London published works will start entering the public domain in 2020. And, to the extent that there are unpublished materials by Whitehead himself (for instance his personal correspondence), they entered the public domain in 2017, seventy years after his death in 1947.[8]

While doing this copyright research, around 2005–6, I contacted the then-new Executive Director of the Center for Process Studies, Roland Faber. Faber expressed interest in the Critical Edition, but asked if he could contact me a half-year later, as he was in the middle of moving, applying for tenure, and getting married. True to his word, Faber did contact me and, to my surprise, asked if I'd serve as the Director of Research and Publication for a new group that he had started the year before (2005) called the Whitehead Research Project.[9] I happily agreed, and the Critical Edition of Whitehead was begun, with me serving as its Founding Executive Editor.

Although I'd learned much about American copyright law, I was still having difficulty determining the exact intellectual property status of Whitehead's published works in particular, as this had been a matter of some dispute. My various searches brought me in 2008 to the process scholar Peter Farleigh in Australia, who was familiar with one of Whitehead's heirs, a certain Simon Whitehead, the great grandson of Alfred North. Simon is from the 'British side' of the family. Apparently A. N. Whitehead's son, T. North, remarried after his first wife died. The son of his first wife, Eric Arthur Whitehead, is Simon's father. Why it is considered the British side I will explain in more detail later on. With Farleigh's generous assistance, contact with Simon Whitehead proved fruitful, as he was able to put me in contact with the person who held the rights to Whitehead's estate and intellectual property, a certain George

Whitehead, who still lives in Cambridge, MA, not far from his grandfather's home at Radnor Hall.[10] As I will explain more fully later, George Whitehead is the son of T. North's second wife, Harriet, and the person who inherited the estate when his mother passed away. I was able to contact George Whitehead by email and then later by phone. He was very generous in his willingness to work with us. Indeed, Mr Whitehead wanted to 'do right' by his grandfather, agreeing to allow us to publish anything that was of scholarly significance.[11] I will return to Whitehead's heirs at the end of my comments.

As the scale of the project became more clear, I realised that we needed a senior scholar with extensive editing experience and exceptional knowledge of the history of Whitehead scholarship. I found the ideal partner in George Lucas, who generously agreed to join the Edition as its General Editor in 2010. The first phase of our work focused on officially securing copyright permission from George Whitehead, applying for funding from the NEH, constituting an Editorial Board, and, most especially, scouring internet archives for anything by Whitehead. In our first conversations, George Whitehead had confirmed the story long known to Whitehead scholars that his grandfather had indeed instructed the family to burn his effects upon his death. Thus, for decades there was concern that traditional *Nachlass* was lost forever. However, searches soon discovered an abundance of materials squirreled away in archives all over the United States, Canada, the United Kingdom and Europe.

It is hard to overstate the profound impact that the digitisation of libraries' archival holdings has had on this sort of research. The scale of the current project, with six projected volumes of Harvard lectures alone, simply could not have been possible without the advent of the internet and the digitisation of archival holdings. With the publishing of finding aids online it became possible for the first time to discover materials that had long lay hidden. WRP's holdings have now grown from several hundred items when we began to more than 1,300 items at present. It is important to not be too hard on those who were digging in the Whitehead mines before us. The robust shape and direction of the current Critical Edition was really only possible at this more mature stage of the internet and the electronic digitisation of archival holdings. Indeed, because this digitisation is an ongoing process, we have taken to doing an annual search of certain archives on the occasion of Whitehead's birthday in February of each year. And most every year something new comes to light.

Though we have had wonderful success in finding materials, we have had decidedly less success in securing US federal funding, with failed attempts at NEH grants in 2009, 2010, 2012, 2013 and 2016.[12] We came excruciatingly close in 2016 with all but one reviewer in strong support. Fortunately, starting in 2013, we were able to find a generous private donor who has provided ongoing financial support to allow us to hire graduate students at Claremont who could serve as Editorial Assistants to obtain, catalogue, digitise and transcribe materials. Without this generous donor, the Critical Edition of Whitehead simply would never have been. The first Editorial Assistant was Jeremy Fackenthal, followed by Nathan Greeley, John Becker, Joe Petek, Jason Taksony Hewitt, Rob MacDonald and Jenna Petsche. Richard Livingston, also a student, served as our technology consultant, ensuring best practices in terms of digitisation, storage and presentation, and helped to design our research database, the Whitehead Research Library. After years of countless invaluable contributions, Petek was invited to serve as the Edition's Chief Archivist and Assistant Editor.

As we proceeded to collect and transcribe materials, we became aware of two related projects which we hoped could be made part of the Whitehead Edition. One was by Nicholas Griffin at McMaster University and the Bertrand Russell Archives, who has long been working on the correspondence between Whitehead and Russell surrounding the writing of *Principia Mathematica*. Griffin was invited to have his planned volume of correspondence added to the Critical Edition of Whitehead and (in 2013) he agreed.

In a sense, the second project found us more than we it. It was prompted by Jason Bell's 2010 discovery of notes by a Winthrop Pickard Bell (no relation) in the archives at Mt. Allison University in New Brunswick, Canada. While working on another project concerning W. P. Bell's notes from his time with Husserl in Göttingen, Jason Bell had come upon notes that W. P. Bell had later taken of Whitehead's first year at Harvard (1924–25). To his credit, Jason Bell knew that he had discovered something special. Bell initially contacted his former undergraduate professor, Randall Auxier, for advice, and Auxier encouraged Bell to speak to the editor of *Process Studies*, Dan Dombrowski, who directed Bell to me.

At this point it was becoming clear that we needed to convene a meeting of the Editorial Board. With support from the Hocking-Cabot Fund for Systematic Philosophy, George Lucas and I hosted the first meeting of the Editorial Board at Harvard University in April of 2012.[13] Around this same time and while still trying to decide what to do about the Bell notes, George Lucas and I learned that, as luck would have it, there was already an eminent Whitehead scholar at Mt. Allison: none other than Paul Bogaard, who wrote his dissertation under the famed Ivor Leclerc at Emory University. In July of 2013, George Lucas and I made a pilgrimage to Canada's beautiful Maritimes to see the Bell notes and meet with Bogaard and Bell. By the end of our time together it was agreed that Bogaard and Bell would edit the first volume of the Edition, with W. P. Bell's notes as the centrepiece. What we needed was a publisher.

Contrary to the trend within critical edition scholarship and the preference of the NEH, our goal for the Critical Edition of Whitehead has always been to publish both print and electronic editions.[14] What we needed was a publisher who was willing to take on an enormous project that would likely run for decades. Years earlier (2009), in the process of trying to determine the copyright status of Whitehead's monographs, I had approached Free Press, which owns the publishing rights to Whitehead's post-London works, about the possibility of publishing a critical edition of Whitehead.[15] Unsurprisingly, the executive at Simon & Schuster said that their press was no longer interested in these sorts of projects.[16]

The search for a suitable publisher then led us to a British firm called Pickering & Chatto.[17] Negotiations began in 2010 and continued for several years. They tentatively agreed to publish the Edition and were even included in several NEH grant applications. However, they were slow to reply, and there was concern about whether they were in fact the right home for the project. In September of 2013, one of the members of our Editorial Board, Leemon McHenry,[18] contacted us regarding a conversation he had had with an editor, Carol MacDonald, at Edinburgh University Press. The connection proved fruitful. After a year of negotiations and a blind peer review of our series proposal, in March of 2014, George Lucas and I signed a contract, officially making the project the Edinburgh Critical Edition of the Complete Works of Alfred North Whitehead.

Confident that we had collected much of what was available in archives, we considered the first phase of the Edition completed and looked to proceed to the second phase: laying out the publishing of specific volumes. In a meeting at the Center for Process Studies in Claremont, California in January of 2015, Lucas, Petek and I planned out the first volumes of the Edition. And, with more support from the Hocking-Cabot Fund, later that year we held a second meeting at Harvard, this time with the scholars who would actively be editing volumes. This meeting concluded with a tentative agreement to publish five or six volumes of Harvard lectures, one volume of Cambridge lectures, and two volumes of correspondence, with the monographs following that in chronological order.

To bring this narrative up to the present and near to a close, I would like to relay the rather unforgettable experience that George Lucas and I shared in March of 2017 when we were invited to have tea with Whitehead's grandson, George Whitehead, at his home in Cambridge, MA. We came bearing gifts. In addition to presenting Mr Whitehead with an advance copy of the first volume of the Edition, George Lucas brought him facsimiles of some items we had discovered in the archives at Mt. Allison, including a picture of his half-brother, Eric Arthur Whitehead (Simon Whitehead's father, you will recall), and their father, T. North Whitehead, on a sail boat; a letter sent from T. North to W. P. Bell; and a picture of George Whitehead himself when he was about three years old. All of these items had been saved by W. P. Bell, who had become a friend of T. North's. I myself brought Mr Whitehead copies of the diaries of Charles Lindbergh[19] and of Anne Morrow Lindbergh,[20] which include rich accounts of the Lindbergh's visit with the Whiteheads in Cambridge, MA on 3 January 1940.

George Whitehead is a bright, amicable and hospitable man who warmly welcomed us into the sitting room of his lovely Cambridge home with fresh coffee and bagels. He appeared to be in his late sixties and in good health. He was quick to smile and welcomed us into his home with, 'Hello, I'm George Whitehead.' After pleasantries and the presentation of the various gifts, the Georges settled into arm chairs and I into a couch. The conversation lasted for approximately ninety minutes. The following are highlights of the discussion:

- According to George Whitehead: his grandmother, who lived in his home when he was young, pronounced her first name with a long 'e' as in Eve, rather than a short 'e' as in Ellen. Thus Alfred North's spouse pronounced her name Evelyn Wade Whitehead. We also learned that French was Evelyn's first language, even though she was English-Irish, because she grew up in a French convent.
- According to George Whitehead or, as he put it, 'according to Whitehead family lore', it may have been Evelyn who pushed A. N. to accept the position at Harvard. She believed that he was not sufficiently appreciated or sufficiently paid, given his stature within the intellectual community.
- According to George Whitehead: After the First World War, T. North married a war widow, Margot Schuster, who had two children, a boy and a girl, from a previous marriage: Roy and Sheila Dehn. Together Margot and T. North had Eric Arthur Whitehead, named after A. N.'s brother, Eric Whitehead, who died in the Great War. As we know, A. N. and Evelyn moved to America in 1924. T. North and his family continued to live in England until 1931, at which time they followed A. N. to America, taking up residence in Cambridge on the other side of the pond. T. North started teaching at the business school at Harvard and taught some of the first business courses for women at Radcliffe. When the Second World War started, T. North went back to England and was, according to his son, George Whitehead, 'reporting pretty directly to Churchill' in the foreign office. However, he had signed the official secrets act and dutifully refused to share details about what he did during

the war. T. North's first wife died just after the war of cancer. He remarried an American from Ohio. This was George Whitehead's mother,
Harriet. His father, T. North Whitehead, died in 1969 of complications
related to Parkinson's.

- According to George Whitehead: Roy and Sheila Dehn, T. North's adopted
  children, went to Bedales boarding school in Hampshire, England.[21] Sheila
  married a Harvard Professor, Myron Gilmore, and lived in Cambridge, MA
  for most of her life. She had two boys and two girls.

- According to George Whitehead: Eric Arthur Whitehead, George White-
  head's half-brother, finished Middle School at Shady Hill[22] in Cambridge,
  MA, but decided he wanted to go back to England and attended Bedales
  for the remainder of his education. After graduating he decided to stay in
  England, thus the 'English side' of the Whitehead family tree. Eric had two
  children, one of whom is Simon Whitehead, who lives today in Exeter,
  UK. Simon Whitehead himself has two children who would be A. N.
  Whitehead's great, great grandchildren.

- George Whitehead confirmed during our time together that his grandfather, A. N., did indeed direct Evelyn to destroy all of his personal papers
  upon his death. And he further added that, to his knowledge, this instruction was carried out not only by Evelyn, but that T. North 'inherited' this
  promise and dutifully destroyed any notes or manuscripts that he found,
  for instance after his mother, Evelyn, died. It turns out there is more to this
  story, as I will shortly explain.

- At the beginning of the war, T. North was in need of a warm coat, his pistol
  and some other items. Evelyn packaged them from Cambridge, MA and
  mailed them to him. However, they never arrived. Still needing the items,
  she bought new ones and got permission from Lloyd George to travel from
  the US to Paris where she stayed with Gertrude Stein and Alice Toklas.[23]
  During her time in Paris, Evelyn received several very personal letters
  from Alfred North. George Whitehead suggested that they reveal a side of
  A. N. that one does not normally see. They are overflowing with his love
  for Evelyn.

- According to George Whitehead, his grandparents, A. N. and Evelyn,
  were both cremated and there is no plaque marking where their ashes are
  interred. There is a record of their cremation at Mount Auburn Cemetery
  in Cambridge, MA.[24] There is, however, a plaque in his honour at Trinity
  College Chapel. Its Latin inscription reads:

  > This inscription commemorates Alfred North Whitehead, O.M., who
  > was Fellow of the College for fifty-seven years. He was for some time
  > Lecturer at Trinity and then Professor of Mathematics in London;

next he was Professor, and later Professor Emeritus, of Philosophy at Harvard University. Hence he could be said to have lived three lives in two countries, the first devoted to mathematics, the second to physics, and the third to metaphysics. He was a Fellow of both the Royal Society and the British Academy. A model of broad culture, if any man was, he died on 30th December 1947 at the age of eighty-seven.

As I've explained, and as all Whitehead scholars have known for more than seventy years, Alfred North Whitehead's papers and correspondence were burned or destroyed upon his death. What unknown materials were forever lost to the flame has been the source of speculation and disappointment. Were there unpublished manuscripts, such as volume four of *Principia Mathematica*? Were there early drafts of published works? With whom did he correspond and what did he say?

It is very likely that scholars came to have this story because it was the one shared by Whitehead's dutiful biographer, Victor Lowe, who had spent decades attempting to secure any and all materials relevant to Whitehead's biography.[25] In the opening pages of the first volume, Lowe writes:

> As he had requested, his widow destroyed (along with the letters he had received) his unpublished papers and drafts of books, and the manuscripts of the published writings. He idealized youth and wanted young thinkers to develop their own ideas, not spend their best years on a Nachlass.[26]

We now know that this narrative is largely, if not entirely, false. Although it seems that Whitehead himself took no efforts to preserve or even retain many items of philosophical interest (e.g., his work on volume four of *Principia*), of the things that Whitehead did keep, the family did not in fact destroy them, but rather dutifully stored them for seven decades. After getting to know us over a number of years and after seeing the quality of the work in the first volume of the Critical Edition, George Whitehead contacted us late in 2018 and shared the shocking news that he not only had a number of boxes of Whitehead's papers, but that he wanted to entrust them to the Critical Edition.

In the late fall of 2018, George Lucas arranged to collect what turns out to have been nine old file boxes of letters, pictures, contracts, off prints, legal documents, telegrams, course materials, manuscripts and other miscellaneous flotsam. Carefully packing them in an oversized suitcase, George flew them to Claremont in January of 2019 where he met with Petek and I to review the materials. At the time of this writing, it is not yet clear what has been received in this cache of materials, as it will take some time to carefully digitise and transcribe them. In unpacking a box, one could find stray business cards from various retailers, a telegram from a friend, a birthday note, and even a small box of seasickness pills (there are three doses still in their gel caps!). A narrow envelop with the word 'Will' written on it reveals Whitehead's legal will drafted in 1891, the year of his marriage to Evelyn – it is little more than a single handwritten page giving everything to her. (It most decidedly does not say anything about destroying his effects.)

So far, the single most significant discovery is a typed manuscript with the unassuming title 'First lecture. September, 1924'.[27] This manuscript, which is reproduced in this volume, is what Whitehead prepared in advance of his very first philosophy lecture in Harvard's Emerson Hall on 25 September 1924, the notes of which appear in the first volume of the Critical Edition.[28]

It is a new age of Whitehead research. Not only is the Critical Edition making available carefully edited materials previously unavailable or unknown to scholars, it is also upending long-held aspects of the intellectual history of Whitehead, his work and his life. We have always 'known' that Whitehead had his papers burned. Given the supposed absence of *Nachlass*, more than a few people questioned whether a critical edition of Whitehead would have anything worth publishing. What we now know is that many things we thought were certain fact were something else. What other gems we might unearth as we toil in the Whitehead mines is anyone's guess. It is surely an exciting time to be doing Whitehead scholarship.

## Notes

1. William McBride is Arthur G. Hansen Distinguished Professor at Purdue University <https://www.cla.purdue.edu/philosophy/directory/?p=William_McBride>
2. Carl Vaught died in 2005. He spent thirty-one years of his career at Pennsylvania State University but ultimately returned to his undergraduate alma mater, Baylor University, where he was Distinguished Professor of Philosophy <https://www.baylor.edu/mediacommunications/news.php?action=story&story=35770>
3. According to one obituary, John Bacon died in 2014: 'John Bacon was interested in philosophy, semantics and logic and held positions in faculties at the University of Texas, Austin, The Hebrew University in Jerusalem, Fordham University, City University in New York, Rutgers University, Pratt Institute in New York and the University of Sydney' <http://www.smh.com.au/comment/obituaries/john-bacon-a-philosophical-life-20140718-zuie8.html>
4. The editors of the Whitehead Edition have located several sets of the originals of these notes and may publish them in subsequent volumes of the Edition. In the case of Robinson, the partial transcripts from the Yale students are the only surviving record. The originals appear to have been discarded after his death.

5. In a letter dated 8 May 1965 from John Bacon to A. H. Johnson, he writes 'Thank you for graciously allowing us to keep your notes of Whitehead's lectures for six more weeks. I fear that you will find your generosity ill repaid: we have lost 58 pages of your notes . . . As of a week ago we had about finished transcribing the notes. On Thursday, April 29, I permitted a graduate student, Miss Susan Jones, to take the 58 pages in question together with the typescript to her dormitory room in order to proofread them with another girl's help. Miss Jones stayed up late Friday night working on the material while the other girl went to bed. Since Miss Jones planned to rise earlier, they agreed that she should slip the folder containing the notes under the other girl's door before leaving in the morning. However, the folder was too thick to pass under the door, so Miss Jones left the folder just outside, a procedure the girls frequently follow with lent books and other articles. Twenty to forty minutes later the other girl got up, and the notes were gone. We have searched and advertised for a week without finding anything . . .'.

6. Personal conversation, December 2017.

7. N.B. In the case of lecture notes, the author is the note-taker, e.g. Bell or Hocking or Heath, not the subject of the notes, Whitehead.

8. According to Whitehead's biographer, Victor Lowe, the primary copyright for Whitehead's works is held by Macmillan and secondary publishing rights are held by Cambridge University Press (Lowe, *Alfred North Whitehead, Volume II*, 180). We have not been able to independently confirm this.

9. Information about the Whitehead Research Project can be found at <http://whiteheadresearch.org>

10. See the picture of Radnor Hall in Petek's chapter (p. 16).

11. In a 22 June 2010 letter, Mr Whitehead wrote, 'As Alfred North Whitehead's grandson and the sole legal holder of the rights to his scholarly work, I write in full support of the Whitehead Research Project's goal to revitalize the scholarly study of my grandfather's work. As we have discussed, I am willing to give my permission to the Whitehead Research Project to publish A. N. Whitehead's writings that are of a clearly academic value to scholars.'

12. At the time of this writing we are once again preparing to submit a NEH grant application.

13. It is a wonderful thing that the money for this meeting came from the Hocking-Cabot Fund, named in honour of two of Whitehead's close associates, William Earnest Hocking and Dr Richard Cabot. As we see in the first volume of the Edition, Hocking attended Whitehead's class. In the 1925–27 Harvard Lectures, which are currently being edited, notes from Whitehead's guest lecture in Cabot's 'seminary' on 'Social Ethics' will likely appear.

14. Most edition projects in the United States are now exclusively digital.

15. Free Press, formerly Macmillan, was acquired by Simon & Schuster, which is itself a subsidiary of CBS. It is odd to think that CBS, the publisher of popular television shows such as 'The Big Bang Theory' and 'NCIS' is also the official publisher of Whitehead's *Process and Reality*.

16. Private email correspondence, Tom Dussell, 13 April 2009: '"Free Press" VP & Editor-in-Chief has decided not to take on this project, I'm afraid. Free Press now is a much more commercial publisher than it was in the past, and new editions of the Alfred North Whitehead books wouldn't fit with our current lines.'
17. Pickering & Chatto has since been acquired by Routledge.
18. At the time, McHenry was visiting as an American Philosophical Association fellow at the Institute for Advanced Studies in the Humanities in Edinburgh.
19. Charles Lindbergh, *The Wartime Journals of Charles A. Lindbergh*.
20. Anne Lindbergh, *War Within and Without*.
21. See a description of Bedale's here: <http://www.bedales.org.uk/home/history-bedales/history-overview>
22. More on Shady Hill here: <https://www.shs.org/page/about-us>
23. There is much more to be said about the relationship between the Whiteheads and Stein and Toklas than can be said here. Readers can consult Lowe's biography (*Alfred North Whitehead, Volume II*, 29–31) as well as Meyer, *Irresistible Dictation*. The Whitehead Research Project has collected approximately seventy letters from members of the Whitehead family to Stein and Toklas.
24. More about Mount Auburn Cemetery here: <http://mountauburn.org/about>
25. We do not presently have documentary evidence establishing where Victor Lowe got this story, but it is almost certainly the case that the source of the claim was Evelyn Whitehead herself, for reasons that we can only speculate. For one such speculation, see George Lucas's essay in this volume (p. 328).
26. Lowe, *Alfred North Whitehead, Volume I*, 7.
27. Some of the newly discovered materials have been made available through our online research tool the Whitehead Research Library <http://wrl.whiteheadresearch.org>
28. See Paul Bogaard's essay in this volume, examining the relationship between the prepared manuscript and what students recorded in that first lecture (p. 56).

## Bibliography

Bogaard, Paul, and Jason Bell (eds), *The Harvard Lectures of Alfred North Whitehead, 1924–1925: Philosophical Presuppositions of Science* (Edinburgh: Edinburgh University Press, 2017).

Boydston, Jo Ann (ed.), *The Collected Works of John Dewey, 1882–1953* (Carbondale: Southern Illinois University Press, 1969–1991).

Henning, Brian G., *The Ethics of Creativity: Beauty, Morality, and Nature in a Processive Cosmos* (Pittsburgh: University of Pittsburgh Press, 2005).

Lindbergh, Anne Morrow, *War Within and Without* (New York: Houghton Mifflin, 1980).

Lindbergh, Charles A., *The Wartime Journals of Charles A. Lindbergh* (New York: Harcourt Brace Jovanovich, 1970).

Lowe, Victor, *Alfred North Whitehead: The Man and His Work Volume I: 1861–1910* (Baltimore: Johns Hopkins University Press, 1985).

Lowe, Victor, *Alfred North Whitehead: The Man and His Work Volume II: 1910–1947* (Baltimore: Johns Hopkins University Press, 1990).

Meyer, Steven, *Irresistible Dictation* (Palo Alto: Stanford University Press, 2002).

*Steamboat Willie*, Directed by W. Disney. USA: Walt Disney Studios, 1928.

To Alfred North Whitehead's grandson,
George Whitehead

# Introduction: Tales from the Whitehead Mines – On Whitehead, His Students and the Challenges of Editing the Critical Edition

*Joseph Petek*

I was hired as a Whitehead Research Project Assistant in February 2013, and have now spent better than six years searching for, cataloguing, transcribing and editing thousands of pages of archival material related to Whitehead. Brian Henning has jokingly referred to this work as 'the Whitehead mines', from which I have derived the title of this paper.

My understanding of Whitehead's philosophy has, of course, grown in that time. On countless occasions I have been transcribing notes from Whitehead's classes and come across some particularly keen insight that I would then excitedly share with my colleagues at the Center for Process Studies (CPS). But I have also found myself fascinated by the people whose work we are collecting and editing, both Whitehead and his students, and the moments when they suddenly seem to come alive, usually from some funny story or odd connection that reminds me that there were real people behind the words on a page.

There is probably no better position in the world than the one I am in for getting a picture of Whitehead the man and his students and contemporaries. Of course, Victor Lowe wrote a two-volume biography that illuminated much about Whitehead that would otherwise have remained obscure, and it continues to be the best single source of information about Whitehead's life available. That said, over the years we have uncovered things that Lowe never saw, materials ranging from the profound to the inane.[1] As I am lucky enough to be at the centre of the Whitehead Research Project's acquisitions, it seemed entirely appropriate that I should begin this volume by painting a picture of Whitehead and his Harvard students as people, to provide the human context to the philosophical work. The people of eight decades ago can often seem remote, dead; even though we know intellectually that they were people like any others, it is all too easy for them to seem unreal and abstract. My ultimate goal in sharing the following stories and materials is to jolt the reader into a felt realisation of Whitehead and his students and contemporaries as living people, as I have been pleasantly jolted on various occasions in my work at WRP.

In a second section, I will also be touching (all too briefly, I am afraid) on the challenges involved in gathering and editing such materials. Approaching Whitehead's lectures through the notes of his students presents some unique difficulties that merit careful examination. For now I will content myself with a brief overview of these complexities, supplemented by a short case study. A more thorough discussion of these issues will appear in the introduction to the forthcoming second volume of Whitehead's Harvard lectures.

Lastly, I will provide short summaries of the sections and chapters of this volume to help orient the reader to the discussions that the publication of the first volume of the Harvard lectures has generated.

## Whitehead in England

I want to focus mainly on Whitehead in America and his students at Harvard and Radcliffe; nonetheless, I would like to lead off with a few recently discovered materials relating to Whitehead's life in England.

### Teenage Whitehead

I do not think I can begin anywhere other than with the recent discovery of various photos of Whitehead from his time at Sherborne School in Dorset. Brian Henning had contacted the school back in 2010 looking for any material they had related to Whitehead, but got little for his trouble. It was bad luck on his part, because less than a month after Brian contacted Sherborne, they hired an archivist named Rachel Hassall, who since her hiring has been working to raise Whitehead's profile at the school and highlight its connection to him. A chance conversation with a colleague at CPS led us to contact the school again in August 2018, leading to our discovery of five Whitehead photos taken between 1877 and 1879, when Whitehead would have been just 16–18 years old. It is rather shocking to see Whitehead with hair; the earliest photo I had previously seen was from 1898, when Whitehead would have been 37, and he was already bald.

Two of these photos show Whitehead with his class, while the other three are of Whitehead with the football (rugby) team, which he captained from 1879–80. Whitehead was apparently quite a good rugby player; an issue of the student magazine in 1880 called him 'the best forward the school has ever had'.[2]

Figure 1 Taken on 10 March 1877, this is the earliest known photo of Whitehead, and shows him with his Sherborne School Football (Rugby) team after winning the Interhouse Challenge Cup. Whitehead is in the second row, first on the left. He had just turned sixteen years old. Photo courtesy of Sherborne School Archives, with thanks to School Archivist Rachel Hassall.

Figure 2 Whitehead with the Football team, Christmas 1877. Whitehead is in the bottom row on far right. Photo courtesy of Sherborne School Archives, with thanks to School Archivist Rachel Hassall.

Figure 3  Whitehead with his '6th Form' (high school) classmates, Christmas 1877. Whitehead is in the second row, second from left. Photo courtesy of Sherborne School Archives, with thanks to School Archivist Rachel Hassall.

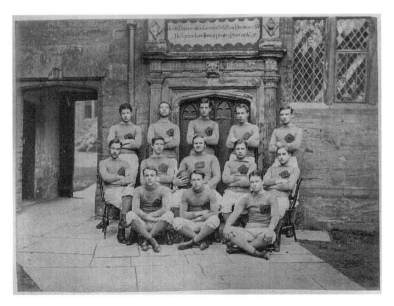

Figure 4  Whitehead with the Football team, Christmas 1878. Whitehead is in the middle row, second from right. Photo courtesy of Sherborne School Archives, with thanks to School Archivist Rachel Hassall.

Figure 5 Whitehead with his 6th Form classmates, Midsummer 1879. Whitehead is in the second row, fourth from right. Photo courtesy of Sherborne School Archives, with thanks to School Archivist Rachel Hassall.

## Whitehead's Servants

Just as we are unused to thinking about Whitehead playing sports, we are unused to really thinking about his style of living in England at the time, but I cannot be the only one to have watched the recent and wildly popular British period drama *Downton Abbey* and wondered, with a start, how many servants Whitehead may have employed, living in England as he did around the same time. As it turns out, Whitehead did, in fact, employ a number of servants during his time at Grantchester, where the Whiteheads lived from 1899–1907,[3] and which his son North recalls in amusing detail, and here I quote at length:

> Neither of my parents had any money. We lived on what my father earned, and the salaries of university dons were far from ample by any standard. Our house was a modest one, and many of our friends lived in a bigger way than we did . . . We had living in the house, besides my mother and father and three children, a cook, a maid, a children's nurse and, for much of the time, a governess. But we also had some help from the village – a daily girl, a 'tweeny' who seemed to do most of the work, chased around by the

others, who were 'learning her'. We also had a full-time gardener, who usually turned up drunk . . . Then an adolescent boy, 'the boots', used to clean
our boots every morning, and also clean the table knives . . . I think that
is all, except that we had mother Heffer once or twice a week . . . [who]
did the washing in the wash room beyond the kitchen, and a little rough
cleaning around the house.

So, in addition to the family, we had four people living in the house,
and four more on full or part time who slept in the village . . .[4]

It is interesting that people whom North describes as '[not having] any
money' still employed eight servants. It was a very different time, and a very
different social order. And even though North describes his parents' house-
hold as 'less formal than most', it was formal enough that meals were all tightly
scheduled and preceded by a gong, and for dinner, two gongs, with the first
'dressing' gong being sounded about twenty to thirty minutes before dinner.[5]
North described meals as having 'a formal, parade-like quality' that resembled
an army mess.[6]

Figure 6  This undated photo shows Whitehead rowing in the mill pond in front of
the Old Mill House in Grantchester with his son, North, and daughter, Jessie.

Unfortunately, there is very little information about the Whiteheads' home life and how it evolved throughout their later time in England and later in the United States, although a few scattered references confirm that they continued to employ a number of servants after their move to London.[7] We do know that during their time in America, they employed a full-time maid named Mary, who sailed with them from England, as was usual at the time for Americans with the Whiteheads' income.[8] Descriptions of graduate students helping to prepare refreshments during Sunday evening visits[9] suggest that they likely had few other servants during their time in America, although there is a reference to Whitehead having a chauffer to take him back and forth from his home to his classroom during his later years of teaching in the mid-1930s.[10]

## Moving to the United States

But now I will move on to discuss Whitehead in America, starting with his arrival. Whitehead's salary of $8,000[11] was, of course, donated in secret by Julia Isham Taylor and Henry Osborn Taylor, who were most anxious that he

Figure 7 Julia Isham Taylor, Henry Osborn Taylor, Whitehead, Lawrence J. Henderson, 8 October 1932.

should never know from whence the funds for his appointment came. In the course of Harvard extending Whitehead's appointment from five years to a permanent position, Lawrence J. Henderson wrote to President Lowell that he believed Whitehead had 'never suspected Taylor', and that 'even if [he] knew, it would be well to keep up the fiction of anonymity'.[12] Included with his salary was $1,000 for moving expenses; it was paid into a new American bank account for Whitehead rather than sent to England in order to avoid one third of it being taken as income tax.[13]

The Whiteheads' time in America differed from their time in England from the very moment they stepped onto the Boston Harbor dock on 27 August 1924.[14] Evelyn recalled that

> the immigration inspector inquired as to the purpose of their visit. "To lecture on Einstein and the theory of relativity," Whitehead replied, and the inspector asked: "Tell me, Professor, what is the theory of relativity?" Whereupon Whitehead commenced his first lecture, on the wharf. "That," said Mrs. Whitehead, "could only happen in America."[15]

There were other things that could only happen in America, such as Evelyn's introduction to a uniquely American plant during their first year. In a letter to his son North, Whitehead wrote that 'We picked a wonderfully decorative wildflower, like a gigantic wild mint. She crushed the leaves in her hands and put her face in it to smell.'[16] As Lowe wryly remarked, 'this was an English-woman's introduction to poison ivy'.[17]

## Whitehead at Harvard

During that first year, not many students were brave enough to take White-head's courses for credit. For his lecture courses, which took place on Tuesdays, Thursdays and Saturdays for about an hour, his grading notebook lists only ten names, six at Harvard and four at Radcliffe.[18] But this paltry number was not anywhere near the number of people who actually showed up, some as official auditors, some not. Whitehead wrote in his notebook that the total number of people attending his first semester of Harvard lectures was 'plus or minus 30'.[19] The second year was much the same; it was not until year three that the number of registered students suddenly jumped to more than forty,[20] and for most of his time at Harvard it appears that he had about forty to fifty students and/or visitors in the room for his lectures at any one time.[21]

Figure 8 Top Row (L-R): Clarence Lewis, Sinclair Kerby-Miller, Ralph M. Blake, Ralph Eaton, William Ernest Hocking. Front Row (L-R): Ralph Perry, Alfred North Whitehead, James Haughton Woods, James W. Miller, John Wild, Henry Sheffer. Photo courtesy of Bruce Kuklick from *The Rise of American Philosophy*, 1977.

## The Radcliffe Women

It is interesting to note also that not all of these visitors were men. Although Whitehead lectured at Radcliffe separately, the division was not always as sharp as might be thought, and sometimes Radcliffe students would sit in on the Harvard lectures, which Whitehead 'mildly disapproved of'.[22] Joseph Brennan tells an amusing story of one such occasion:

> One day a Radcliffe visitor installed herself in the first row right under his nose and sat smiling eagerly up at him. 'By the by', he mused plaintively, pausing to gaze out the nearest window, 'if there are any persons present who are not registered members of this course, perhaps they might sit another time toward the back of the room, where I cannot see them'.[23]

It is important to note that Whitehead's discomfort here almost assuredly had more to do with his desire to follow the rules, or at least not flaunt them quite so obviously, than it did with the women's presence per se. By all accounts we can find, Whitehead was on the right side of history in being an advocate for women's equality at a time when this was not always a popular cause or attitude. For instance, he was for degrees for women at Cambridge in 1896, when students were against it by almost four to one;[24] he also spoke at a meeting of the Cambridge Women's Suffrage Association on 6 November 1906, with his speech later being printed and distributed as a pamphlet.[25]

But Harvard at the time was not lacking in misogynists. In fact, in an email exchange I had with Stephen Kaiser – the son of Hillis Kaiser, one of Whitehead's teaching assistants in the early 1930s – he wrote that 'My father came out of Harvard as a misogynist and a true believer in the inferior position of women in society.' It was also, of course, rather difficult for women to gain high academic positions, and few managed it. Of Whitehead's students, Susanne Langer and Dorothy Emmet were two of the exceptions to this rule, and we luckily have some class notes from both. I was amused to discover from Langer's notes that she was apparently a great Harvard football fan; at the beginning of any of Whitehead's lectures that were also game days, she would write the name of Harvard's opponent, presumably as a reminder to herself to attend the game later that day.[26]

One woman's story stands out for me above the others. In the course of attempting to track down Whitehead's students in a bid to perhaps find more class notes for our project, I found myself contacting Dr Caroline Bynum, who is the daughter of Dr Merle Bernice Grubbs Walker, a Whitehead student from 1932–33.[27] Dr Bynum told me that she knew for a fact that none of her mother's notes from Whitehead's courses survived, because she had burned them when she gave up the academic career that she so craved. In her own words:

> When her second child was born and she decided to give up her job at Georgia State College for Women to do what she and my father both felt was right – stay home with the children – she burned all her notes from graduate school in a fierce and self-punishing act of renunciation. I grew up with a sense, learned partly from my father, that high-achieving women were peculiar and threatening, that there was something shameful about my mother's academic past. I also grew up with a sense, learned from her, that to be female is to make acts of sacrifice and self-denigration.[28]

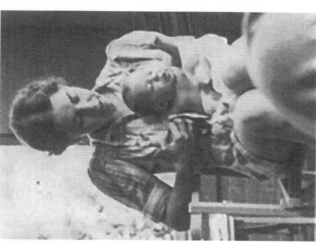

Figures 9–11  Merle G. Walker during 1930s, 1940s and 1970s respectively. Photos courtesy of Caroline Bynum.

It is perhaps some form of poetic justice that Dr Walker's daughter later became the first woman to be appointed University Professor at Columbia. I was also happy to be able to share with Dr Bynum that, according to Whitehead's gradebook, her mother was the only student in Whitehead's Radcliffe class that semester to earn an 'A+',[29] though in some ways this only compounds the tragedy of lost potential. Dr Walker's story strikes me as an important one to remember, representing as it does the stories of countless women from the early to mid 1900s who would be forced away from academia by the social prejudices of the time.

## Whitehead's Classroom

But let us move now to an account of Whitehead himself as seen by his students. What were these lectures actually like, and what did his students think of him?

Figure 12  Whitehead on the steps of Emerson Hall, Harvard University, 1936. Photo courtesy of George Whitehead.

First there was his look, of which we have all probably seen enough pictures to be familiar. Richard Buch described him as having an 'old-fashioned Victorian appearance',[30] and Lewis Feuer said he was 'adorned by clothes such as I had seen before only in nineteenth century prints'.[31] He wore a black suit of clerical cut, a high starched wing collar, a cravat ('often a rich blue'), and a Prince Albert frock coat.[32] Whitehead himself thought that he resembled the Dickens character Mr Pickwick.[33] As to his manner, he was often described by his students as seeming even a bit older than his years, walking slowly with his shoulders a little bent.[34] Despite this, he was not unenergetic. As described by Lewis Feuer, 'Though he looked physically like the oldest man in the world, I had never seen an adult radiate so much energy and enthusiasm.'[35] He would often sit at a desk on the lecture platform, but would rise from it either to draw a diagram on the blackboard, or simply to pace about energetically when there was some point he wanted to emphasise.[36]

Then there was his voice. There are no known audio recordings of Whitehead, but many students wrote about how he sounded. In general, his speech was slow, gentle and high-pitched.[37] Richard Buch described it as 'dulcet' and 'flute-like',[38] and Feuer said it contained a 'singsong soprano-like enthusiasm'.[39] We also know, as demonstrated by some amusing examples, that he had what might be considered a slight speech impediment, with his 'r's' often sounding like 'w's'.[40] The most spectacular example of this appears in the notes of W. V. O. Quine, who at one point recorded Whitehead as saying of Plato that 'He definitely denies a fwozen wöhld of evalahsting fixtyahs' (Fig. 13).[41]

We are lucky here that Quine was a bit mischievous, and undertook to record Whitehead's words exactly as he heard them. But apparently none of this kept Whitehead from occasionally correcting what he saw as mispronunciations by his students. One of Whitehead's teaching assistants in the 1930s, Hillis Kaiser, liked to tell of how 'Whitehead would often correct the pronunciation of Greek names or words by Greg Vlastos, a Greek student

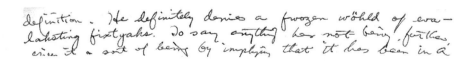

Figure 13 Quine, 'Cosmologies Ancient and Modern', page 10. Photo from MS 284, Victor Lowe Papers, Special Collections, Sheridan Libraries, Johns Hopkins University.

who grew up in Athens and graduated from college there, but hadn't studied Greek in England.'[42]

Whitehead was apparently quite witty when he wanted to be. He himself opined that students at Harvard 'are less witty, and less irreverently epigrammatic, than analogous Cambridge Undergraduates; but they greatly enjoy anything in that way which is put before them'.[43] Anne Morrow Lindbergh recalled that when she and her husband visited the Whiteheads in 1940, he had 'a saintlike quality that made his humor and sometimes even sardonic wit rather a shock when it came'.[44] He was apt to summarise his lectures with a humorous anecdote,[45] and punctuate his points with simple and humorous examples, such as that half a sheep is mutton (HL1, 414), or this discussion of the validity of scientific experiments:

> The invariable success of a proof of experiment does not mean that the description is necessarily the right one. Some peoples have thought that the setting sun was swallowed by a dragon, and to the end of saving the sun from destruction they performed certain religious rites. These ceremonials were <u>always</u> successful![46]

Whitehead's lecture courses tended to be straight lectures without much interruption or discussion. He did not often invite questions, nor were many offered.[47] He was also heard to say that although he prepared his lecture notes on the day he presented them, he found he needed to wait until the lecture itself to find the right phrasing.[48] And in finding that phrasing, he was often seen to stare out the window while he talked.[49] Harvey Potthoff wrote:

> How often in a lecture he has looked out the back window from his desk in the front of the room, and as he talked apparently become totally oblivious to those in the classroom as he has grappled with some great problem for which he almost seemed to have a solution.[50]

Ernest Hocking gives a similar account:

> He sometimes had notes, but, as I recall, seldom stuck to them; he gave the impression of a mind not repeating former results but winning anew the insights he had to convey – it was water from a living spring, not from a faucet. It was at times as if he were speaking to himself, wrapped in the movement of the thought and almost unaware of the group before him, they straining to hear the words which became less audible as his own wrestling became intense.[51]

Figure 14  Whitehead's classroom in Emerson Hall, April 2015.

But despite the fact that Whitehead preferred to lecture with little interruption from students, this is not to say that he was uninterested in hearing from them. Quite the contrary. It was his habit to wait a while after the lecture was concluded and talk with any students who wished to do so, which typically took about twenty to thirty minutes after the hour-long lecture.[52] And then, of course, there were his Friday 'seminaries' (as seminars were called at the time), which were much more discussion-based, and the famous Sunday evening get-togethers at Whitehead's home, at which Alfred and Evelyn would hold court for up to a hundred students and other friends, offering 'conversation, hot chocolate to drink, and cakes to nibble'.[53]

## The Seminaries

The Friday seminaries also took place at Whitehead's home, rather than in Emerson Hall; George Conger noted that they were usually held around the dining room table, and that almost everyone except Whitehead himself smoked, creating a rather thick cloud.[54] The students were as responsible

Figure 15  Exterior of Radnor Hall. Whitehead lived on the fifth floor from 1924–38.

for driving the discussion as Whitehead was, with two or three students making presentations each session. J. Robert Oppenheimer, the father of the atomic bomb, was one of Whitehead's students during his first Logic seminary in Spring 1925, and at one point wrote to a friend that 'I have got to debate with Whitehead at the Seminar next week, and I am already trembling.'[55] But Oppenheimer enjoyed his time in the seminary, saying that reading the *Principia* with Whitehead was 'an exciting time',[56] and that Whitehead was the perfect teacher because he was ten years removed from the *Principia* and had forgotten most of it, so that he was 'both master and student' as they worked through the text,[57] occasionally coming to a theorem that puzzled him and saying 'Well, that was one of Bertie's ideas.'[58] In case you're wondering, Whitehead awarded Oppenheimer a 'B' for his efforts in the course.[59]

Not everyone enjoyed Whitehead's seminaries. His biographer, Victor Lowe, has said that he found them rather boring, and that Whitehead 'seemed to assume that every seminar student was a genius'.[60] Lowe recalled sitting near the back of the room during these seminars and playing blindfold chess with a classmate during student presentations – i.e. playing chess without a board while keeping track of the game in his head – but he would perk up his ears whenever Whitehead spoke.[61]

## Whitehead the Diplomat

It is perhaps worthwhile to stop for a moment and discuss this comment that Whitehead thought that all of his seminar students were geniuses. While it is true that he did not seem to be a particularly difficult grader, awarding mainly A's and B's, the larger and more important point is that Whitehead was a generous thinker and a thoroughly nonconfrontational person. He was extremely patient of criticism of his own thought, but his criticisms of others were few and almost invariably gentle.[62] At times this could actually create problems. Paul Weiss recalled, for instance, that Whitehead was not a good dissertation director. As Weiss put it, 'He was quite amiable and friendly, but he never gave me any really sharp criticisms. When I presented my thesis, I thought I had his approval. The department turned it down. I hadn't realised that he hadn't altogether thought it was a good thing.'[63] Whitehead also effected what Joseph Brennan referred to as 'his celebrated air of modest ineffectuality', serving to disarm whoever he was conversing with.[64]

From all this one might conclude, as Weiss did, that Whitehead would have made a poor administrator.[65] But there is ample evidence that this is untrue, and not just arising from the time he spent in high administrative positions in England. As Russell put it, Whitehead had a 'shrewdness enabling him to get his way on committees in a manner astonishing to those who thought of him as abstract and unworldly'.[66] He made his genial and nonconfrontational manner work for him in a way that allowed him to steer groups in the direction that he wanted them to go, an ability illustrated in the following story relayed by Tressilian Nicholas, former bursar of Trinity:

It was at a College Meeting in 1913 . . . The question before the meeting was whether any pressure should be put upon undergraduates to attend services in the College Chapel, in those distant days a battleground between the "clerical" and "anticlerical" parties in the College. The discussion culminated in a particularly violent speech by the philosophy professor James Ward, denouncing a clerical Fellow which he considered cynical. I wondered what would happen next, when an elderly Fellow of benign appearance and mellifluous voice rose to his feet and began a miniature filibuster with a series of unexceptionable remarks having no obvious connexion with the resolution under discussion which he continued until passions died down. The resolution was at once put to a vote resulting in an overwhelming defeat for the clerical party and the matter has never been raised again. I recognized a junior mathematical Fellow and asked who it was who had saved the situation. He replied "Oh, don't you know that was A. N. Whitehead, the man who discovered what numbers mean?"[67]

## Letters

In fact, in assessing Whitehead's administrative abilities, Russell thought that he had only one weakness, which was an inability to answer letters.[68] Whitehead was rather famously bad at this, enough that when he took up his post at Harvard, many of his English friends claimed to have never heard from him again.[69]

One story about Whitehead's letter-writing across three different sources really brought this home for me. George Perrigo Conger, an assistant professor in philosophy at the University of Minnesota (and later its chair), spent the 1926–27 academic year attending every one of Whitehead's lectures and seminars that he possibly could. He wrote in his journal that on Friday, 18 March, at the last seminary meeting which he was to attend, Whitehead offered to write him letters of introduction to anyone he wished, and Conger sat by as Whitehead wrote out quick letters to J. J. Thomson of Trinity College, Bertrand Russell and George Santayana.[70]

Brian Henning later discovered a short letter from Santayana to Conger in a bound volume of Santayana's letters, dated a few months later, telling Conger that he would be happy to meet with him in either Rome or Paris, depending on the date. He also said that 'You might have introduced yourself without the intervention of Prof. Whitehead, but I am glad to have a word from him for other reasons.'[71]

Imagine my amusement, then, when I found the following in an article by another of Whitehead's students, Lewis Feuer: '[Evelyn] would gently rebuke Professor Whitehead in public for not answering his letters: "For months he's had a letter from Santayana on his desk; it would take but a page to reply, but he never writes it." Whitehead sat by meekly.'[72]

While I'm on the subject of letters, there is one recently discovered one that I cannot resist sharing a portion of. Sent to Henry Osborn Taylor on 21 August 1928, Whitehead briefly discusses his experience of delivering the Gifford lectures. He writes:

I think that the 'Giffords' went well. Some of the middle lectures were rather too closely reasoned for verbal delivery even to a Scotch audience – but on the other hand the last lecture was, in my judgment, the best that I have ever delivered, whatever be the worth of that level.[73]

While this does not precisely contradict J. M. Whittaker's famous account in Lowe's biography of Whitehead's audience dwindling from several hundred to only a half dozen,[74] it does seem to suggest that Whittaker may have been exaggerating. And it is interesting to see that Whitehead himself thought highly of what would become the last chapter of *Process and Reality*, which is so often held up by Whitehead scholars as some of his finest work.

## The Challenge of Uncovering and Editing Archival Whitehead Materials

But now I want to pivot and briefly discuss some of the difficulties involved in gathering and editing the archival materials on which the Critical Edition is based. It took about ten years for the Whitehead Research Project to produce the first volume, at least partly because of the difficulty in gathering materials. The Victor Lowe collection at Johns Hopkins certainly provided a good start, but Lowe could not and did not find everything, and even some of what he did find remains problematic for us as editors.

One example of problematic materials is the few notes we have from Edward Schouten Robinson, who attended Whitehead's first two years of lectures. Robinson sent 410 pages of his notes to the Yale Philosophy Club in the early 1960s, which were to be transcribed as part of the Club's Whitehead project.[75] However, they abandoned the effort in 1966 due to lack of resources and interest, and sent the notes back to Robinson having transcribed only seventy-seven pages of them, or less than 20 per cent. Two years later, in 1968,

Robinson was struck and killed by a car while crossing the street.[76] He had no immediate family, and the person who ended up being his heir – a distant cousin from Switzerland – seems to have disposed of the notes, not knowing their value. What we are left with is a partial transcription that, in the words of the Yale Philosophy Club itself, '[was] not proofread against the manuscripts', meaning that it is likely rife with errors.[77]

Besides having some manuscripts such as the one for Robinson which are not original, there are some others for which we *do* have the original, and yet encounter other difficulties that potentially limit their usefulness. One such collection of notes is the one by Victor Lowe from Fall 1929,[78] which uses a shorthand that is extremely brief and seemingly unique to him, making it rather a bear to decipher, and quite possibly impossible in places where we do not have other notes taken at the same time with which to compare them.

Another is the 1925–26 notes of Charles Hartshorne, which he discovered by chance in 1978 and then 'edited' before sending them on to the Center

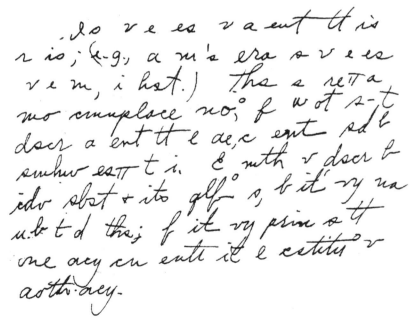

Figure 17  A selection from Victor Lowe's Fall 1929 notes for Whitehead's Philosophy 3b. Photo from MS 284, Victor Lowe Papers, Special Collections, Sheridan Libraries, Johns Hopkins University.

| ° | -tion, -sion | is | it is | -r | our |
|---|---|---|---|---|---|
| π | flex suffix | it | into | s | is, his |
| ππ | adverb suffix | k | know | t | to |
| a | a, an | -l | all | -t | at, out |
| b | be, by | m | must | tt | that |
| bf | before | mo | most | v | of |
| bt | but | mr | more | vy | very |
| c | can | mt | might | w | with |
| e | the | n | no, not | wd | would |
| e,y | theory | -n | on | wh | which |
| f | for | ng | thing | W'h | Whitehead |
| -f | of | nk | think | wo | world |
| fr | from | o | or | w,t | without |
| h | has, have | pm | problem | xp | experience |
| i | I, it, in | pn | upon | y | you |
| ia | idea | r | are, where | z | as |

*Partial key to Lowe's shorthand*

for Process Studies.[79] In doing this editing, the pages were rearranged into an order which we now know through a painstaking comparison with the notes of Fritz Jules Roethlisberger to be rather magnificently wrong.[80] Meanwhile, sometime between when Roland Faber transcribed the notes for *Process Studies* in 2001 and my arrival on the project in 2013, the original Hartshorne notes were lost, leaving us with four different photocopies of the notes that all have different page orders and different handwritten addendums and markings on them. How does one begin to sort out this kind of mess? Are such compromised materials even worth publishing?

An allied question to this one is how to handle multiple sets of notes from the same lectures. Though the first volume of the Critical Edition reproduced the full text of all three sets of notes we had available for Whitehead's first year — two rather different sets from Harvard and one from Radcliffe — at times we have more repetitious material than is feasible to publish in full. For instance, we have three full and one partial set of notes for the Harvard lectures of 1930–31. Is publishing all four really reasonable or helpful to the majority of Whitehead scholars who will be examining them?

I think, in fact, that in going forward with future Critical Edition volumes, we will be forced to make hard choices about which materials to include and which to exclude, at least as full, stand-alone texts. But I also think that it will be important to make as much use of the excluded material as we can to both corroborate and augment our chosen published text where appropriate. Most students are, after all, selective in their note-taking, and so will take detailed notes at one moment while taking few, if any, at another, and so the usefulness of having multiple sets can hardly be overestimated. At the very least they can be used, as already mentioned, to interpret difficult shorthand (as in Lowe's notes), and to re-order and properly date disorganised notes (such as Hartshorne's).

I now want to take a look at a few pages of a specific case study, a comparison of notes from Whitehead's Philosophy 3b in 1930–31 taken by W. V. O. Quine,[81] Charles D. Tenney[82] and Furman G. McLarty,[83] and a few of the surprising little ways in which having several sets of notes from the same class can shift interpretation, and how we might begin selecting one set to represent them all.[84]

In his lecture of 21 October 1930, Whitehead gave a chronology of major philosophical figures 'of the transitional period from the end of the Hellenic age to the middle ages',[85] starting with Plato and ending with Augustine, including birth and death dates. In discussing Augustine, Whitehead mentioned that 'the Vandals were about to sack the city in which he was living when he died'.[86]

And here comes the point of interest: the name of that city. Tenney mentions no specific city.[87] McLarty has it as 'Nola' (actually, he misspelled it as 'Nollo', but never mind that), but crossed this out and wrote 'Hippo'.[88] Meanwhile, Quine also had 'Nola', but crossed it out and wrote 'Thagaste'.[89] So, what exactly is going on here?

As luck would have it, McLarty clears most of this up for us at the beginning of his notes for October 28th. He writes: 'Erratum: Whitehead by slip of the mind asserted a few lectures back that Augustine died in Nola, N. Africa. He meant to say Hippo, N. Africa. Augustus Caesar died at Nola, S. Italy'.[90] This explains why McLarty had crossed out the 'Nola' in his earlier notes and written 'Hippo'. But why, then, does Quine have 'Thagaste'? Well, I have a theory about that, based partly on another difference between the three sets of notes within the very same lecture.

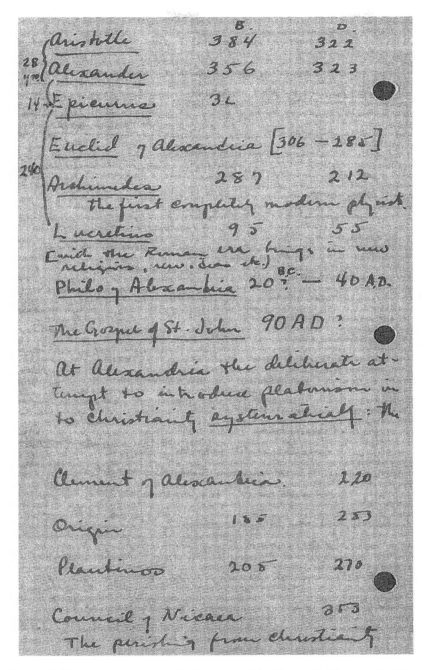

Figure 18  McLarty's notes, page 33. Courtesy of the Harvard University Archives.

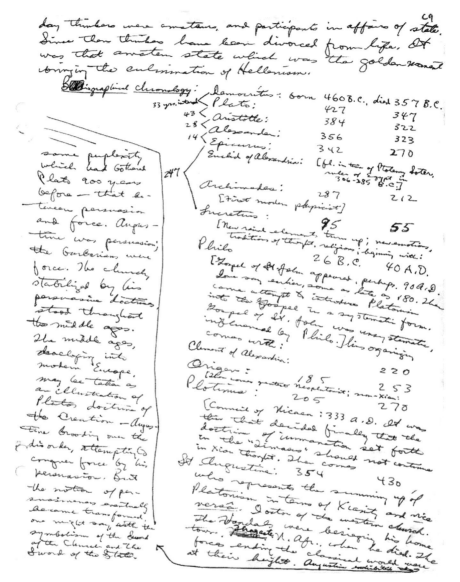

Figure 19  Quine's notes, page 20. Photo from MS 284, Victor Lowe Papers, Special Collections, Sheridan Libraries, Johns Hopkins University.

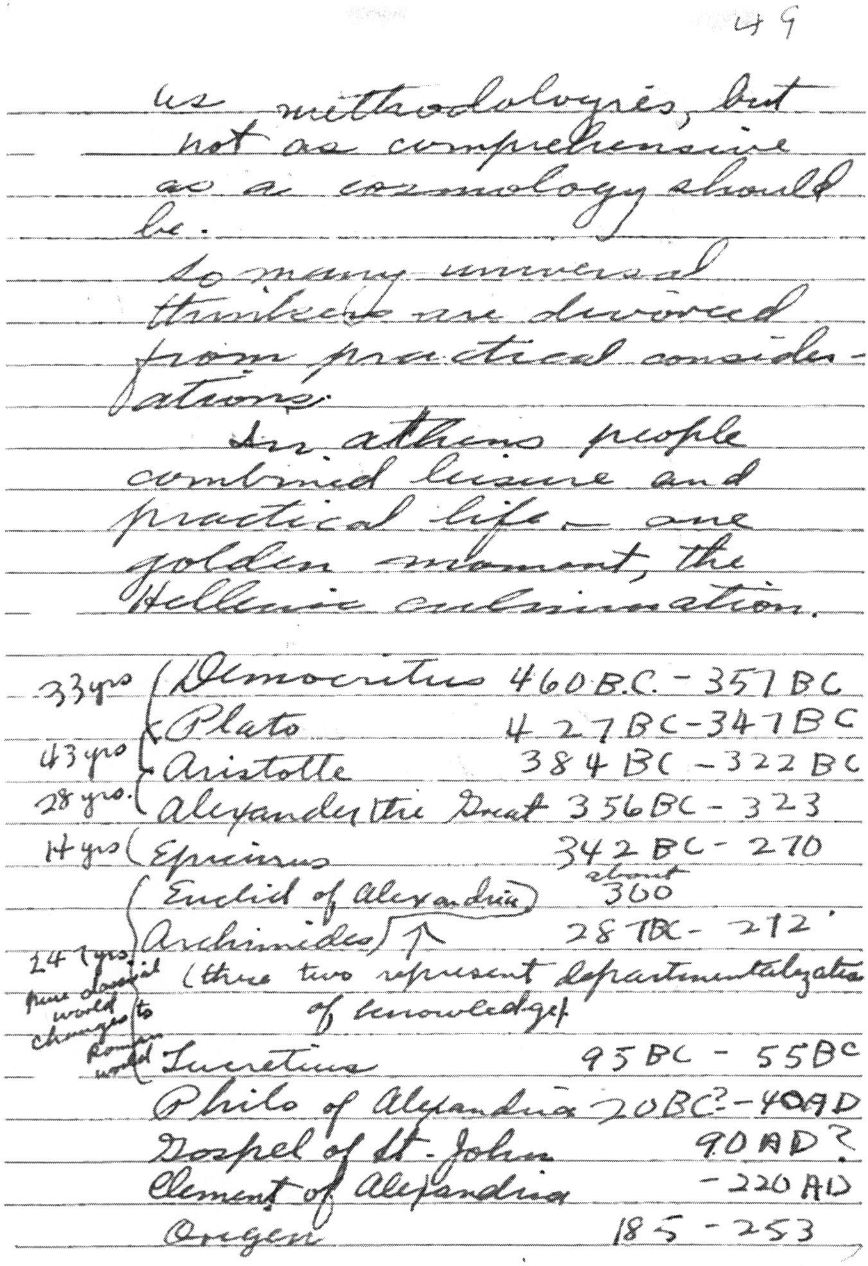

49

us methodologies, but not as comprehensive as a cosmology should be.

So many universal thinkers are divorced from practical considerations;

In athens people combined leisure and practical life — one golden moment, the Hellenic culmination.

| | | | |
|---|---|---|---|
| 33 yrs | (Democritus | 460 B.C. | - 357 BC |
| 43 yrs | (Plato | 427 BC | - 347 BC |
| 28 yrs | (Aristotle | 384 BC | - 322 BC |
| 14 yrs | (Alexander the Great | 356 BC | - 323 |
| | (Epicurus | 342 BC | - 270 |
| | (Euclid of alexandria) | about 360 | |
| 24 (yrs) | Archimides) ↑ | 287 BC | - 212 |

pure classical world to Roman world

(these two represent departmentalizatio of knowledge)

| | | |
|---|---|---|
| Lucretius | 95 BC | - 55 BC |
| Philo of Alexandria | 20 BC? | - 40 AD |
| Gospel of St. John | 90 AD? | |
| Clement of alexandria | | - 220 AD |
| Origen | 185 | - 253 |

Figure 20  Tenney's notes, page 97. Used by permission of Special Collections Research Center, Southern Illinois University Carbondale.

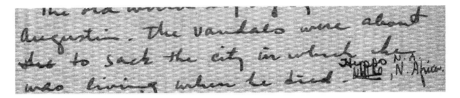

Figure 21  McLarty's notes, page 34. Courtesy of the Harvard University Archives.

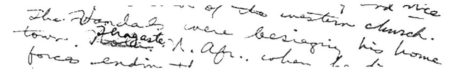

Figure 22  Quine's notes, page 20. Photo from MS 284, Victor Lowe Papers, Special Collections, Sheridan Libraries, Johns Hopkins University.

For the birth date of Philo, McLarty has '20 B.C.?' with a question mark,[91] while Quine has '26 B.C.' with no question mark.[92]

If we had just the two sets of notes, the most reasonable explanation would seem to be that McLarty was not sure if he had heard Whitehead correctly, while Quine *was* sure; hence, Quine's date is the one that Whitehead likely actually said. However, Tenney *also* has '20 B.C.?' with a question mark.[93]

That not one, but two of the three have a question mark is interesting. And suddenly the most reasonable explanation is very different: it seems now that it was Whitehead himself who was uncertain about the date, and that Quine filled in what he thought to be the proper date himself. Both 26 B.C. and 20 B.C. are dates that have been advanced by different historical scholars as estimations of Philo's date of birth; when Whitehead said he wasn't sure, McLarty and Tenney noted that fact, while Quine took it as permission to write in a date he happened to remember from a different source, both because he had a mind like a steel trap, and because he seemed to be a bit of a know-it-all. It seems like something Quine would do.

And I feel fairly certain that this is how 'Thagaste' ended up in Quine's notes as the city where Augustine died. He quickly realised that Whitehead was wrong when he said 'Nola', then crossed it out and wrote what he thought was the correct city based on the recollections of that steel-trap mind of his. As it happens, he was wrong. Thagaste was the place of Augustine's birth, but not his death.

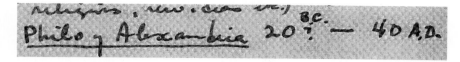

Figure 23 McLarty's notes, page 33. Courtesy of the Harvard University Archives.

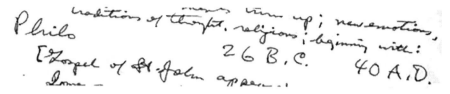

Figure 24 Quine's notes, page 20. Photo from MS 284, Victor Lowe Papers, Special Collections, Sheridan Libraries, Johns Hopkins University.

Figure 25 Tenney's notes, page 97. Used by permission of Special Collections Research Center, Southern Illinois University Carbondale.

After hearing all this, you might think that McLarty's notes would be the ideal set to use as a base, since he is the only one who caught all this detail, and then went back and made the proper correction. But of course these few examples do not tell the whole story, because McLarty's notes have their own deficiencies. He seemed to struggle more than the other two to keep up with the pace of the lecture, often leaving blanks to fill in information he had missed, blanks that ultimately stayed as blanks. In other cases, he marked things in a way that would be impossible to interpret without the other note sets.

Take the dates that Whitehead associated with Euclid. McLarty writes them as '[306–285]'.[94] What do the brackets mean? Quine has the answer: 'in time of Ptolemy Soter, ruler of Egypt in 306–285 B.C.'.[95] So the dates actually refer to Soter rather than Euclid, a fact that would be hard to discover based solely on McLarty's brackets. Meanwhile, Tenney did not bother to record the dates of Soter's rule, and instead wrote that Euclid was born 'about 300 B.C.'.[96] In another case, that of Epicurus, McLarty began to write his birth date, but never finished (he had just '34' followed by blanks), while both Tenney and Quine have '342–270'.[97]

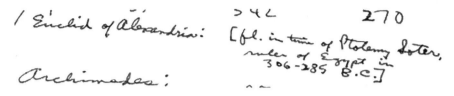

Figure 26  McLarty's notes, page 33. Courtesy of the Harvard University Archives.

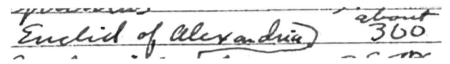

Figure 27  Quine's notes, page 20. Photo from MS 284, Victor Lowe Papers, Special Collections, Sheridan Libraries, Johns Hopkins University.

Figure 28  Tenney's notes, page 97. Used by permission of Special Collections Research Center, Southern Illinois University Carbondale.

Of course, it would be premature to extrapolate final conclusions about these three sets of notes and their authors based solely on these examples. But from this admittedly very preliminary look, it would appear that Quine was the most proficient and knowledgeable of the three, but was also the least conscientious – he rarely dated his notes, and, as I've shown, apparently did not feel much compunction about amending Whitehead's lectures without noting that he was doing so. McLarty may be the most conscientious note-taker of the three, but often struggled to keep up with the pace. Tenney seems somewhere in the middle. Anecdotally, Tenney's and McLarty's notes seem to match more closely than Quine's do with either of them. The irony here is that Quine's philosophic ability actually hindered the accuracy of his notes; while the other two were simply writing down what Whitehead said, Quine was evaluating it on the fly and making corrections and additions where he thought necessary.

If you're going to pick one of these sets to use as a base, which one do you pick? It's an interesting question, and not one easily answered. What's certain is that it is a very good thing indeed to have the luxury of multiple people covering the same material; without multiple authors, it is impossible to see many of the eccentricities of the note-takers themselves. Without McLarty, we would not know that some of things that Quine writes are not what Whitehead actually said. Without Quine, we would not know some of the things that McLarty and Tenney left vague or missed completely.

All of this is to say that we have rather a long road ahead of us as editors of the Critical Edition of Whitehead, and face many editorial challenges in bringing this new material to light in the most useful and beneficial possible form. But I'd like to think that we are up to the challenge. Indeed, the forthcoming second volume of the Critical Edition will make full use of the multiple sets of student notes available to us for 1925–27, augmenting our chosen primary account with expansions and clarifications from alternative sets of notes in a way that we believe will make it the best possible resource that it can be.

## Chapter Summaries

This volume is divided into six parts, as follows.

### I. The First Lecture

We lead off the volume with an exciting find: the typescript of Whitehead's first lecture at Harvard, originally delivered on 25 September 1924. This typescript was discovered in the papers donated to the Whitehead Research Project by Whitehead's grandson and heir in late 2018.[98] It is, of course, a little unfortunate that it was not discovered prior to the publication of the first volume of the Critical Edition, or else we surely would have included it along with the lecture notes of Bell, Hocking and Heath. But we include it here as an important supplement to the Critical Edition.

It should be noted at the outset, however, that this typescript is not exactly what Whitehead actually delivered at Harvard on that Thursday afternoon ninety-five years ago. As my characterisation of his lectures above shows, Whitehead was not one to stick completely to a script. We know through a comparison of this typescript with the notes of Bell and Heath in HL1 that when the day came to deliver his first lecture, Whitehead both added and subtracted from what appears here. Paul Bogaard's chapter immediately following Whitehead's lecture endeavours to compare it with Bell and Heath's notes and answer the question of exactly how closely it matches what Whitehead said in Emerson Hall.

### II. The Fitness of the Environment

One of the take-aways of the first volume of the Critical Edition is surely that Whitehead was more influenced by Lawrence J. Henderson in his first year at Harvard than anyone had previously realised. Though he is footnoted in

*Process and Reality* just once, this first year of lectures makes clear that Henderson's work was an important inspiration for Whitehead. The three essays in this section (which derives its title from Henderson's 1913 book of same name), discuss Whitehead's biological thought generally, and Henderson's influence specifically (among others).

Paul Bogaard leads off with a discussion of Whitehead's 'philosophy of evolution', tracing the concepts of organism, environment and evolution through the Harvard lectures and his published works, concluding that 'evolution' as a concept seems to fade in importance for Whitehead in subsequent years (somewhat surprisingly, given its prevalence in the lectures). Maria-Teresa Teixeira follows with an examination of evolution and time as they appear in the Harvard lectures and Whitehead's *The Function of Reason* five years later, noting Whitehead's influences and the ways in which his views shifted. Dennis Sölch's chapter finishes the section with a look at 'Whitehead's biological turn', in which Whitehead saw science undergoing a paradigm shift (especially given the confusion in the field of physics at the time), and hoped to bridge the physical and biological sciences and create a more unified concept of nature.

## III. Physics and Relativity

As just mentioned, the 1920s were a somewhat chaotic period in the history of physics. Gary Herstein's chapter on 'Quanta and Corpuscles' leads off this section with an account of this confusion, and examines a number of strands of Whitehead's response to it, including the centrality of continuity and 'Whitehead's refusal to surrender conceptual explanations in favour of mere mathematical cleverness'.[99] Following are two chapters by Ronny Desmet, the first focusing on a close reading of the first lecture and Whitehead's shift from continuous to atomic becoming from one semester to the next, while the second focuses on Whitehead's thoughts on quantum theory. The section concludes with short pieces by Desmet and Herstein commenting on one another's work, and noting some of their disagreements, including the status of Lewis Ford's temporal atomism thesis.

## IV. Whitehead's Philosophical Context

The three chapters in this section relate Whitehead to other philosophers. Jason Bell and Seshu Iyengar begin the section with a discussion of Whitehead and his complicated relationship to Kant, of whom he is highly critical in parts of the Harvard lectures, and yet with whom he also shares some common themes, including 'the limits of both empirical and cognitive investigations, and the role of the subject in generating mechanics'.[100] George Shields' chapter compares Whitehead's Harvard lectures to the philosophy of Charles Hartshorne, arguing that the two are united in defending the possibility of a 'transcendental project' and an 'ontological approach'. Finally, Aljoscha Berve examines Whitehead's relationship to Plato's philosophy in the Harvard lectures, arguing that the lectures clarify Plato's influence on Whitehead as one half of an idealised contrast with Aristotle, the mathematician as opposed to the biologist.

## V. Metaphysical Reflections

The two chapters in this section are deep dives into Whitehead's notoriously difficult yet evocative metaphysics. George Allan examines the use of diagrams and myths as abstract surrogates in Whitehead's lectures, and particularly the metaphor the 'shadow of truth' as giving us crucial insight into Whitehead's metaphysics. Jude Jones follows this with an analysis of the mirrored concepts of eternity and perishing, and how value and grief become two sides of the same coin, a paradox revealing the nature of ecstatic individuation.

## VI. Reinterpreting Whitehead

The final chapters might best be described as general overviews of how our views of Whitehead's thought are changed by the first volume of the Critical Edition of Whitehead. George Lucas' chapter begins with a discussion of all the ways in which he and others (including Victor Lowe and Lewis Ford) had misinterpreted aspects of Whitehead's life and thought throughout the years, owing in some cases to a lack of adequate information, and in others to a simple lack of adequately attentive scholarship, both of which this first collection and the first volume of the Critical Edition help to correct. Brian Henning's chapter ends the volume. Henning takes a close look at numerous key passages that shift our understanding of Whitehead (including, for instance, the influence of C. D. Broad as a philosophical foil), and, just as importantly, notes the subjects and terms missing from this first year of lectures which we might have expected to find, including God and even (mostly) creativity.

## Concluding Thoughts

As Brian Henning notes in his preface, the Critical Edition of Whitehead project has been a long time in the making. In one sense, it was started more than fifty years ago by a group of students in the Yale Philosophy Club, who after three years of work discovered that they had bitten off more than they could chew. As the person primarily responsible for cataloguing and transcribing thousands of pages of archival materials for the project over the past six years, I can identify with their feeling of being overwhelmed. But we are finally seeing the first real fruits of all those years of effort, and so my sense of being overwhelmed is now more than matched by my excitement for the discoveries ahead. This anthology explores just a few of the ways in which Whitehead can never be read in quite the same way again, and this from only the first year of Whitehead's Harvard lectures. Who knows what else we will discover in the years to come?

## Notes

1. This includes a collection of Whitehead's papers recently given to us by Whitehead's grandson (see Henning's preface to this volume), which contains not only such exciting finds as the manuscript of Whitehead's first lecture printed in this volume (see Chapter 1), but also unused seasickness pills from the Whiteheads' 1924 voyage across the Atlantic.
2. Sherborne School, 'Characters of the Fifteen', 318. Whitehead would later use rugby as a metaphor for 'the Real' in a private conversation with Ernest Hocking: 'being tackled at Rugby, there is the Real. Nobody who hasn't been knocked down has the slightest notion of what the Real is . . . I used to play in the middle of the scrum. They used to hack at your shins to make you surrender the ball, a compulsory element – but the question was How you took it – your own self-creation. Freedom lies in summoning up a mentality which transforms the situation, as against letting organic reactions take their course' (Hocking, 'Whitehead as I Knew Him', 512).
3. Lowe, Alfred North Whitehead, Volume I, 202.
4. T. North Whitehead, 'Now I am an American', 13–14.
5. T. North Whitehead, 'Now I am an American', 15.
6. T. North Whitehead, 'Now I am an American', 14.
7. A family friend recollected Evelyn saying in March 1913 that 'the servants are all out for the afternoon . . .'. See Lowe, Alfred North Whitehead, Volume II, 22.
8. Lowe, Alfred North Whitehead, Volume II, 136; Johnson, 'Whitehead as Teacher and Philosopher', 351; T. North Whitehead, 'Now I am an American', 107.
9. Price, Dialogues of Alfred North Whitehead, 15.
10. Brennan, 'Alfred North Whitehead: Plato's Lost Dialogue', 524.
11. Adjusted for the 2.86% inflation rate over this period, Whitehead's $8,000 salary would be approximately $116,000 in 2018 dollars.
12. Henderson, Letter from Lawrence J. Henderson to A. Lawrence Lowell, 15 December 1926. Whitehead and Henderson would become fast friends, with the latter being more influential on Whitehead's thought than anyone had realised before the publication of HL1. See in this volume especially Bogaard's chapter on 'Whitehead and his Philosophical Evolution', and Sölch's 'Whitehead's Biological Turn'.

13. Lowe, *Alfred North Whitehead, Volume II*, 135.
14. Lowe, *Alfred North Whitehead, Volume II*, 136.
15. Feuer, 'Recollections of Alfred North Whitehead', 534–5.
16. Lowe, *Alfred North Whitehead, Volume II*, 153.
17. Lowe, *Alfred North Whitehead, Volume II*, 153.
18. Whitehead, 'Student Record Book', 3.
19. Whitehead, 'Student Record Book', 7.
20. Whitehead, 'Student Record Book', 20.
21. Brennan, 'Plato's Lost Dialogue', 517.
22. Brennan, 'Plato's Lost Dialogue', 517.
23. Brennan, 'Plato's Lost Dialogue', 517.
24. Lowe, *Alfred North Whitehead, Volume I*, 214–17.
25. Whitehead, 'Liberty and the Enfranchisement of Women', 37–9.
26. Langer, 'Notes on Whitehead's Course on Philosophy of Nature'.
27. Whitehead, 'Student Record Book', 169.
28. Bynum, 'Curriculum Vitae: An Authorial Aside', 10.
29. Whitehead, 'Student Record Book', 169.
30. Buch, '"Fair Harvard's" Intellectual Giants', 119.
31. Feuer, 'Recollections of Alfred North Whitehead', 530.
32. Buch, '"Fair Harvard's" Intellectual Giants', 119; Brennan, 'Plato's Lost Dialogue', 515.
33. Brennan, 'Plato's Lost Dialogue', 515.
34. Brennan, 'Plato's Lost Dialogue', 515; Johnson, *Whitehead and His Philosophy*, 1.
35. Feuer, 'Recollections of Alfred North Whitehead', 530.
36. Johnson, *Whitehead and His Philosophy*, 1; Potthoff, 'Alfred North Whitehead', 2.
37. Brennan, 'Plato's Lost Dialogue', 515; Johnson, *Whitehead and His Philosophy*, 1.
38. Buch, '"Fair Harvard's" Intellectual Giants', 119.
39. Feuer, 'Recollections of Alfred North Whitehead', 530.
40. Buch, '"Fair Harvard's" Intellectual Giants', 120.
41. Quine, 'Cosmologies Ancient and Modern', 10.
42. Morgan, *Memories*, 54.
43. Lowe, *Alfred North Whitehead, Volume II*, 293.
44. Lindbergh, *War Within and Without*, 74.
45. Johnson, *Whitehead and His Philosophy*, 1.
46. McLarty, 'Philosophy 3b: Philosophy and the Sciences', 56.
47. Johnson, *Whitehead and His Philosophy*, 2.
48. Potthoff, 'Alfred North Whitehead', 2.
49. Brennan, 'Plato's Lost Dialogue', 515.
50. Potthoff, 'Alfred North Whitehead', 2.
51. Hocking, 'Whitehead As I Knew Him', 513–14.
52. Lowe, *Alfred North Whitehead, Volume II*, 295; Potthoff, 'Alfred North Whitehead', 4; Johnson, *Whitehead and His Philosophy*, 2.
53. Price, *Dialogues of Alfred North Whitehead*, 15. It is interesting to note that no one who actually knew Whitehead personally seems to have thought much of Price's

*Dialogues*, which recounts some of the conversations that took place during these Sunday evening gatherings. Paul Weiss called the book 'terrible', and said that Evelyn was of the same opinion (Weiss, 'Recollections of Alfred North Whitehead', 46); George Conger wrote that 'while it brings back many things and much atmosphere to me, [it] leaves me with mixed feelings as regards its taste, if not sometimes its accuracy' (Conger, 'Diary Entry', 3).

54. Conger, 'Diary Entry', 2.
55. Hunner, *J. Robert Oppenheimer, the Cold War, and the Atomic West*, 27.
56. Thorpe, *Oppenheimer: The Tragic Intellect*, 37.
57. Monk, *Robert Oppenheimer: A Life Inside the Center*, 84.
58. Lowe, *Alfred North Whitehead, Volume II*, 147.
59. Whitehead, 'Student Record Book', 5.
60. Brennan, 'Plato's Lost Dialogue', 519.
61. Brennan, 'Plato's Lost Dialogue', 519.
62. From Conger, 'Diary Entry', 2: 'When one day I quoted something about mathematics from Wildon Carr, Whitehead said, gently, "I think anything that Wildon Carr writes about mathematics you may safely neglect." Even more gentle was the comment he made to someone concerning Alexander's *Space Time and Deity* – "I'm afraid the dear man doesn't know enough mathematics."' Of course, he was not *always* gentle; in a letter to Henry Leonard, Whitehead wrote that 'Wittgenstein annoys me intensely. He is a complete example of the saying "I am Master of this College, What I know not, is not knowledge"' (Whitehead, Letter from Whitehead to Leonard, 10 January 1936).
63. Weiss, 'Recollections of Alfred North Whitehead', 48.
64. Brennan, 'Plato's Lost Dialogue', 517.
65. Weiss, 'Recollections of Alfred North Whitehead', 52.
66. Brennan, 'Plato's Lost Dialogue', 517.
67. Brennan, 'Plato's Lost Dialogue', 517.
68. Weiss, 'Recollections of Alfred North Whitehead', 52.
69. Jacyna, *Medicine and Modernism: A Biography of Henry Head*, 268.
70. Conger, 'Diary Entry', 3; Whitehead, Letter from Whitehead to Russell, 18 March 1927.
71. Santayana, *The Works of George Santayana*, Vol. 5, Book 3, 329.
72. Feuer, 'Recollections of Alfred North Whitehead', 538.
73. Whitehead, Letter from Whitehead to Taylor, 21 August 1928.
74. Lowe, *Alfred North Whitehead, Volume II*, 250.
75. Graduate Philosophy Club of Yale University, 'Notes from the Lectures of Alfred North', 1. See Henning's preface for a discussion of the Yale Philosophy Club's efforts.
76. Email with exchange with Richard De George, 1 February 2016.
77. Graduate Philosophy Club of Yale University, 'Notes from the Lectures of Alfred North Whitehead', v.
78. Lowe, 'Whitehead Lecture Notes'.
79. Faber, 'Introduction: Charles Hartshorne's Handwritten Notes', 289.

80. A version of these notes that has now been put back into proper order is available at the Whitehead Research Library at wrl.whiteheadresearch.org.
81. Quine, 'Cosmologies Ancient and Modern'.
82. Tenney, 'Philosophy 3b: Cosmology'.
83. McLarty, 'Philosophy 3b: Philosophy and the Sciences'.
84. We hope to publish these notes in a fourth volume of student notes covering the years 1930–33.
85. McLarty, 'Philosophy 3b: Philosophy and the Sciences,' 32.
86. McLarty, 'Philosophy 3b: Philosophy and the Sciences', 34.
87. Tenney, 'Philosophy 3b: Cosmology', 98.
88. McLarty, 'Philosophy 3b: Philosophy and the Sciences', 34.
89. Quine, 'Cosmologies Ancient and Modern', 21.
90. McLarty, 'Philosophy 3b: Philosophy and the Sciences', 44.
91. McLarty, 'Philosophy 3b: Philosophy and the Sciences', 33.
92. Quine, 'Cosmologies Ancient and Modern', 21.
93. Tenney, 'Philosophy 3b: Cosmology', 97.
94. McLarty, 'Philosophy 3b: Philosophy and the Sciences', 33.
95. Quine, 'Cosmologies Ancient and Modern', 21.
96. Tenney, 'Philosophy 3b: Cosmology', 97.
97. Quine, 'Cosmologies Ancient and Modern', 21; Tenney, 'Philosophy 3b: Cosmology', 97; McLarty, 'Philosophy 3b: Philosophy and the Sciences', 33.
98. See Henning's preface to this volume.
99. Herstein, 'Quanta and Corpuscles', below p. 122.
100. Bell and Iyengar, 'Whitehead and Kant at Copenhagen', below p. 222.

## Bibliography

Bogaard, Paul and Jason Bell (eds), *The Harvard Lectures of Alfred North Whitehead, 1924–1925: Philosophical Presuppositions of Science* (Edinburgh: Edinburgh University Press, 2017).

Brennan, Joseph Gerard, 'Alfred North Whitehead: Plato's Lost Dialogue', *The American Scholar*, 47:4 (1978), 515–24.

Buch, Richard P., '"Fair Harvard's" Intellectual Giants of the Early 1930s', *Modern Age*, 32:2 (1988), 113–21.

Bynum, Caroline Walker, 'Curriculum Vitae: An Authorial Aside', *Common Knowledge*, 9:1 (2003), 1–12.

Conger, George Perrigo, 'Diary Entry', Mss020, George Perrigo Conger autographs and papers, Box 4, Notes on Whitehead's class lectures at Harvard University, 1926–1927, University of Minnesota Archives and Special Collections <http://archives.lib.umn.edu/repositories/16/resources/349>

Faber, Roland, 'Introduction: Charles Hartshorne's Handwritten Notes on A. N. Whitehead's Harvard-Lectures 1925–26', *Process Studies*, 30:2 (2001), 289–300.

Feuer, Lewis S., 'Recollections of Alfred North Whitehead in the Harvard Setting (1931–1937)', *Yale Review*, 76:4 (1987), 530–50.

Graduate Philosophy Club of Yale University, 'Notes from the Lectures of Alfred North Whitehead at Harvard University, 1926–37', MS 644, Philosophy and Social Sciences Manuscript Collection, 'Alfred North Whitehead' <http://hdl.handle.net/10079/fa/mssa.ms.0644>

Henderson, Lawrence J., 'Letter from Lawrence J. Henderson to A. Lawrence Lowell', 15 December 1926, UAI 5.160, Records of the President of Harvard University, Abbott Lawrence Lowell, Box 306, Folder 970, Harvard University Archives <http://oasis.lib.harvard.edu/oasis/deliver/~hua03003>

Hocking, William Ernest, 'Whitehead As I Knew Him', *The Journal of Philosophy*, 58:19 (1961), 505–16.

Hunner, Jon, *J. Robert Oppenheimer, the Cold War, and the Atomic West* (Norman: University of Oklahoma Press, 2009).

Jacyna, L. S., *Medicine and Modernism: A Biography of Henry Head* (London: Pickering & Chatto, 2008).

Johnson, A. H., 'Whitehead as Teacher and Philosopher', *Philosophy and Phenomenological Research*, 29:3 (March 1969), 351–76.

Johnson, A. H., *Whitehead and His Philosophy* (Lanham: University Press of America, 1983).

Langer, Susanne K. 'Notes on Whitehead's Course on Philosophy of Nature', 1927. MS Am 3110, Susanne Langer papers, Box 5, Houghton Library, Harvard University <http://id.lib.harvard.edu/aleph/008605615/catalog>

Lindbergh, Anne Morrow, *War Within and Without* (New York: Harcourt Brace Jovanovich, 1980).

Lowe, Victor, 'Whitehead Lecture Notes: Philosophy 3b, Fall 1929', Ms. 284, Victor Lowe Papers, Johns Hopkins University Archives.

Lowe, Victor, *Alfred North Whitehead: The Man and His Work, Volume I: 1861–1910* (Baltimore: Johns Hopkins University Press, 1985).

Lowe, Victor, *Alfred North Whitehead: The Man and His Work, Volume II: 1910–1947* (Baltimore: Johns Hopkins University Press, 1990).

McLarty, Furman G., 'Philosophy 3b: Philosophy and the Sciences', HUC 8930.402, Student notes and papers for philosophy courses, 1930–1932, Harvard University Archives.

Monk, Ray, *Robert Oppenheimer: A Life Inside the Center* (New York: Anchor Books, 2012).

Morgan, Kenneth W. *Memories* (2007) <https://www.dropbox.com/s/ugus2k8fuao316u/Memories%20-%20Kenneth%20W%20Morgan%202007.pdf?dl=1>

Potthoff, Harvey H., 'Alfred North Whitehead', Iliff 3-F-12, Harvey H. Potthoff Papers, Series VII-G: Subject Files – Alfred North Whitehead, Iliff School of Theology.

Price, Lucien, *Dialogues of Alfred North Whitehead* (New York: Mentor Books, 1956).

Quine, W. V. O., 'Cosmologies Ancient and Modern', Ms. 284, Victor Lowe Papers, Johns Hopkins University Archives.

Santayana, George, *The Works of George Santayana: The Letters of George Santayana, 1921–1927*, Vol. 5, Book 3 (Cambridge, MA: MIT Press, 2002).

Sherborne School, 'Characters of the Fifteen', *The Shirburnian*, IX:LXXXIII (1880), 318–19 <http://oldshirburnian.org.uk/wp-content/uploads/2015/07/1880-April.pdf>

Tenney, Charles Dewey, 'Philosophy 3b: Cosmology', Charles Dewey Tenney Papers, Series 4, Sub-Series 1, Box 6, Folder 23, Southern Illinois University Carbondale <http://archives.lib.siu.edu/?p=collections/controlcard&id=3195>

Thorpe, Charles, *Oppenheimer: The Tragic Intellect* (Chicago: University of Chicago Press, 2006).

Weiss, Paul, 'Recollections of Alfred North Whitehead', *Process Studies*, 10:1–2 (1980), 44–56.

Whitehead, Alfred North, 'Letter from Alfred North Whitehead to Bertrand Russell', March 18, 1927, *Bertrand Russell Archives*, Box 5.54 710.057486, McMaster University.

Whitehead, Alfred North, 'Letter from Alfred North Whitehead to Henry Osborn Taylor', 21 August 1928, Whitehead Research Library, LET661 <http://wrl.whiteheadresearch.org/items/show/1094>

Whitehead, Alfred North, 'Letter from Alfred North Whitehead to Henry S. Leonard', 10 January 1936, Bertrand Russell Archives, Rec. Acq. 1386, McMaster University.

Whitehead, Alfred North, 'Liberty and the Enfranchisement of Women', *Process Studies*, 7:1 (Spring 1977), 37–9.

Whitehead, Alfred North, 'Student Record Book for Harvard and Radcliffe Classes', HUG 4877.10, Papers of Alfred North Whitehead, 1924–1947, Harvard University Archives <http://oasis.lib.harvard.edu/oasis/deliver/~hua10017>

Whitehead, T. North, 'Now I am an American: Habit and Change' (Unpublished manuscript, 1966).

# Part I

# The First Lecture

# 1

# First Lecture: September, 1924

## Alfred North Whitehead[1]

|1|[2] My first words in this university will be expressive of personal feeling. I can discern in myself many strains of intense emotion. Among them there are two feelings to which I must give explicit expression. One of them is my sense of the honour you have conferred by your invitation to occupy a chair of philosophy in a University which, throughout its centuries of existence, has been continuously occupied with the deepest topic which can fill the mind of man: a University whose foundations were laid amidst debate on the meta-physical mysteries of Puritan theology, –

> [They] reasoned high
> Of providence, foreknowledge, will, and fate,
> Fixed fate, free will, foreknowledge absolute;
> And found no end, in wand'ring mazes lost.–:[3]

A University which studied Berkeley's doctrines before their full impor-tance was recognised in Europe: And, to come at once to recent times, a University in which the senior portion of my audience will have listened to William James, to Hugo Munsterberg and to Josiah Royce. A man would be dull indeed who in this position did not feel emotion.

My other feeling is one of immense responsibility. I cherish to the full the implications of that ancient phrase 'Divine Philosophy'. The Faculty of Philosophy in a great University exists to foster and to make explicit the ultimate meanings which underlie all rational activities, crafts and sciences and arts alike.

There is a meaning in things, and perplexities <u>can</u> be unraveled – dimly, slowly, patiently. It is not given to one man, to one nation, to one age of history, or to one school of thought, to exhaust the |2| depth and the full-ness of reality, of all that has been, and can be, and is. I have an immense distrust of all-inclusive neat systems which profess to finish up the philosophical problem in well-chosen explanations. I hold that every system of philosophy, if it be properly expounded, should show on the face of it that it is dealing with a few aspects of a limitless interplay of relations. It is for this reason that the philosophy of any age is so intensely characteristic of the inward motives and outlook of that age. It emphasises[4] those relations of things which fill the mind of the age. The philosophy prevalent during a period of history is the autobiography of its Time-Spirit.

At the present time, if philosophy is to remain true to its task of revealing and rationalising the inner preoccupations of humanity, one strain of philosophy must start from the analysis of the presuppositions of science. In the Graeco-Roman period of civilisation an analogous position was held by ethics; and accordingly the Stoics and the Epicureans and others started with an analysis of ethical meanings. Of course they also took account of science, and we also take account of ethics. But in our day a dominant emphasis may be claimed for Science; and until we can feel our way towards a rationalisation of scientific thought, we cannot lie easy in our philosophic beds.

Now every philosophy is dominated by some type of difficulty which is in the mind of those who put forward the system. A philosophy is a solution of some ultimate problem which is crying aloud for explanation. There is some wonder, some puzzle which disturbs the rationality of thought and demands the evolution of a point of view capable of reintroducing harmony. It is useless to expound philosophy to |3| those who have never wondered, or to those who are exclusively occupied with other aspects of the great mystery of things. Conversely, from the point of view of those who enter upon an examination of a system of philosophy, the first question to ask is, What are the peculiar difficulties of everyday thought which this philosophy is designed to resolve? Every philosophy is a riddle until that question has been answered. Accordingly in this lecture I propose to touch upon some of the philosophical difficulties which immediately press upon us when we consider those aspects of knowledge which are systematised in science. Of course, I cannot touch upon them all, nor can I consider them in detail. But what I can say will, as I hope, serve to lay bare the sort of difficulties which are perplexing my mind and are guiding my development of the philosophical problem. Conversely[5] in my next lecture I desire to illustrate how philosophical considerations may guide us in our search for that urgent necessity, namely a re-constitution of a coherent system of assumptions for physical science. This second lecture will be more purely scientific than is usual, or even proper, for a philosophical lecture. But I think that it will illustrate the possibilities of philosophy in an age when the fundamental conceptions of science are in process of re-constitution. I have planned the two lectures together so that they may jointly illustrate the practical bearing of science upon philosophy, and of philosophy upon science.

In this lecture we want to elucidate what science is in itself. We ask what is the true character of this great unexpected movement of human thought issuing in modern science. How does it arise, and what is it now that it has arisen? I call the movement 'unexpected' |4| because it seems impossible that men in the remote civilisations which flourished over two thousand years ago can have had the most remote anticipation that the course of history was finally to be controlled by this outgrowth of man's curiosity.

We might take our start from an examination of the chief motives of scientific activity as they exist in the constitution of the human spirit. We should thus enter upon the subject along that line of thought which first considers how men came to think of science – having regard to what human nature is –, and thence proceed to the further consideration of what are the general characters which bind together the various strains of scientific thought.

In this lecture my starting point will be different from that of human psychology. I ask what is there in the nature of things which necessitates that science should have the general type of character which in fact it does have. The psychological starting point would propound the question, What is there in human nature which leads mankind to think of science: I ask, What is there in the nature of things which leads there to be any science – such as there in fact is – for men to think about? I start from experience, and consider what is the general character of things experienced which leads science to be what in outline it is.

Such a discussion can be initiated by touching upon some general relations of metaphysics, theology and science. As we all know, Theology has been warned off the scientific premises. About a hundred years later Metaphysics shared the same fate. As to dates, we may put the departure of Theology at the year 1600 A.D., and that of Metaphysics at the year 1700 A.D. Of course you |5| will not construe these dates too pedantically. But up to and including the sixteenth century Theology was influencing the development of scientific thought, and during the eighteenth and nineteenth centuries metaphysics did not seriously affect scientific progress.

I am not counting the external collision between Science and Theology due to the current interpretations of certain chapters in the Bible; nor am I counting the unconscious metaphysical assumptions which influenced scientific hypotheses.

The reason for this assertion of the autonomy of Science, is, I think, to be found in this consideration. There must be complete freedom for scientific hypothesis. Any hypothesis which will work on a sufficient scale must be given its fair trial. This is the first condition of scientific progress. We could illustrate this necessity of freedom by examples of, the repudiation of the claims of one branch of Science to control other branches. But exactly the same considerations hold as between natural science in general and Theology or Metaphysics. Though we are seeking for a rational systematisation of our beliefs, we must not be over-anxious about its smooth completeness. The complexity of things is beyond our powers to cope with it. We must resign ourselves to rough edges of thought, if we are not arbitrarily to exclude inconvenient facts. I have always been struck by the extreme crudity in appearance which is characteristic of some new ideas. They may look silly, because they do not fit into our inherited system of thought. We are not used to the nomenclature which they impose.

But when we have said everything about freedom of hypothesis and the autonomy of natural science and of |6| its branches, we must come back to the fundamental fact that it is a rational synthesis that we are seeking. The unity of science over-rides all the autonomies. The autonomy of science, or of sciences, is merely a practical expedient to secure the progress of knowledge, having regard to the way human nature works. If we look to the nature of things, the truth is that all things are interconnected. There are no autonomous entities or groups of entities. If the human body is composed of compounds of carbon, it will behave as compounds of carbon do behave; and we must call in the chemist to inform us upon that question.

In conformity with this principle of unity, we must hold that Philosophy and even Theology are capable of rendering services very necessary for Natural Science, insofar as those two sciences have themselves arrived at any formulations which are sufficiently true. Furthermore, there is some cause to believe that even medieval Western Theology, obstructive as it has been over details, has in a general way in the past rendered incalculable service in fostering the scientific spirit. At the present time, there is in every country a corps of eager scientific workers. Our present epoch is a stage of utilisation, which issues in our general support of science, and in our keen sense of its importance. But this attitude is very recent.

It is true that, wherever men are civilised, there is the stage of wonder, of romance. But how does romance pass into precise investigation, and thus generate science. The spur to this transition is the unconquerable belief that there are great simple truths dominating the complexity of appearance. Without such a belief, what is the good of precise investigation? |7| It would be natural to believe that things happen one way one day, and another way another day, and that all the order there is lies on the surface of things, such as the succession of the seasons. In the great civilisations of Eastern Asia, civilisations older and more continuous than ours, when men wondered they retired to mountains and to monasteries, and continued to wonder. There was nothing else to be done.

Again even the Greeks, and the peoples of the Eastern Mediterranean, from the death of Aristotle to the irruption of the Tartars and Turks in the fourteenth century, had a period of about fifteen hundred years during which under various forms of government a high civilisation prevailed generally. They were distracted by no disturbances worse than those in Europe during the seventeenth century. Yet in that one century in Europe the foundations of modern science were laid; whereas in the fifteen centuries of Levantine prosperity subsequent to the death of Aristotle, some things indeed were added to science, but very little outside mathematics.

I ask, what was the spirit, the outlook, which had gradually been acquiring strength in Western Europe, so that at the appointed moment it burst its bounds and founded modern Science.

The Chinese are at least as patient and observant as the Europeans; why did not they do it in the course of two thousand years?

The pursuit of science presumes that the nature of things is adjusted in every detail with inflexible rationality. For example, we know something of the molecular nature of chemical elements, and we observe the complexity of the lines in the spectra due |8| to light from these elements. Throughout Europe and America our spectroscopists are searching with the most detailed analysis to discover the correlations between the characteristic atom of a sub-stance and the characteristic spectrum it emits. But why should there be any such correlation to be discovered. We do in fact believe that there is one, simply and solely because we believe that there is in every detail a rational adjustment in the properties of connected things. If a thing behaves one way at one time, and another way at another time, we believe that there are other determinate factors, which we have overlooked, to which the variation is due. Now there can be no justification for this ultimate motive towards scientific investigation, except our knowledge of something in the very nature of reality which justifies it. It is the weakness of Hume's philosophy and of its modern derivatives that it gives no such justification. Furthermore, it gives no reason to believe that, because scientific generalisations have been discovered in the past, there are any more to be discovered in the future. Nor does this philoso-phy even give any reason to suppose that the generalisations which worked in the past will continue to work in the future.

The motive towards science must include an intimate conviction in the ultimate rationality of things in their minutest detail. A Cambridge mathematician once expressed this to me by the outburst – 'I assume that there is a fundamental decency of things.' Speaking generally the men of Asia generated but little science because they had a weak hold upon this fundamental decency of things. Their Theology presented them with a God either too arbitrary or too inert to make the Universe safe for decency. The |9| men of Western Europe in the sixteenth and seventeenth centuries inherited from the middle ages the impression of scholastic theology with its insistence upon the rationality of the nature of God. Indeed it was over-impressed upon them, so that they thought that they could deduce the motions of the planets from their knowledge of that nature, a knowledge which they sadly over-estimated. But as soon as it was realised that there was no substitute for looking at the facts, modern science was generated by this union of the method of observation with unquestioned belief in the decency of the Universe. Without Scholastic Theology it is not likely that, so far as science is concerned, Western Europe would have surpassed Eastern China. It all depended on the habit of mind which came from a belief in an active rational God who attends personally to every detail.

We are, most of us, not in a mood to receive our ideas of Providence from Scholastic Theology. But our trust in science demands a metaphysic which equally supports this belief in the coherent rationality of things.

It is one of the many great merits of Immanuel Kant as a Philosopher that, being also a Scientist, he realised that metaphysics has to satisfy this condition. You will not ask me, in an aside in this lecture, to explain the general character of the Kantian solution.

The principle on which he proceeded was to ascribe to our process of cognition, a function analogous to that exercised by Mrs. Grundy[6] over morals in the social world and by the late Mr. Bowdler in his edition of Shakespeare.[7] According to Kant we |10| never know the real things, but only an édition de luxe which has been expurgated into rationality.

But although nobody, so far as I am aware, takes seriously Kant's exact theory of things in themselves, I cannot understand how anyone who lays emphasis on the problem which he set himself to solve, can doubt but that his work forms a turning point in the progress of metaphysics. The process of cognition is merely one type of relationship between things which occurs in the general becoming of reality. The becoming of relationships between things requires that the things which become related should be such as to be capable of these relations. Accordingly the fact of any particular entity forming an element in a united Universe which is in the process of becoming, imposes upon that Universe the obligation of being patient of it. Thus every particular entity, by reason of what we may call its relational essence, imposes upon the rest of things a certain systematic character whereby they tolerate its possibility of reality. Kant worked out this theory for the particular case of an entity capable of the relation of cognisance in the capacity of cognisant. He asked, How is cognisance possible? I suggest to you the more general question, How is any particular, entity possible having regard to the relationships which it presupposes? It is along this line of thought that – at least in my opinion – metaphysics will be able to deal with another, and very analogous, problem for which science looks to metaphysics for explanation; I mean the problem of Inductive Logic.

Why are the generalisations of Inductive Logic sensible procedures? I do not mean what are the particular precautions to be taken in order that these generalisations may carry the greatest weight. This |11| latter problem was discussed by Mill in the famous second volume of his Logic and also by Venn in his Inductive Logic, and later by statisticians such as Karl Pearson. The problem which I am thinking of is the more fundamental one, Why should these generalisations carry any probability whatsoever, however carefully they are conducted? I have no doubt but that they ought to carry about the amount of probability which all men in practice ascribe to them. It follows therefore that a metaphysical description of the nature of things must account for the fact that inductive reasoning can give knowledge respecting the Universe.

The point is this:– How can our knowledge of one fact A give us any knowledge of another fact B which is not included in fact A? As Hume points out, it is no good protesting that no cautious reasoner does depend for his induction on one fact only. In the first place, if the one fact A can give no information of any kind as to fact B, it is quite obvious that 100 facts, $A_1$, $A_2$,. . . . $A_{100}$, each of which separately has no bearing at all upon B, cannot in conjunction afford any information as to B. Hume affirms this position, and I cannot see any escape from it. Accordingly, the consideration as to how to generalise with comparative safety from a large number of particular facts – the sort of consideration which was undertaken by Bacon, and Mill, and Karl Pearson – affords no answer to this problem. We have got first to solve the preliminary problem, as to how one particular fact can afford information, however slight, about any particular fact. When we have settled this point, there can be no difficulty in understanding that 100 relevant facts can afford much more information when properly analysed. But the root question is, |12| How can one fact be relevant to another fact which is not included in it? Science collapses if you once admit an independent atomicity of facts.

In the second place, you do not get out of the difficulty by introducing probability. If fact A is entirely irrelevant to fact B, it can make nothing probable as to B. You can never get rid of your question, as to how particulars can be relevant to other particulars.

Thirdly, you do not get rid of the difficulty by saying that in practice nobody doubts it. We are all agreed there. We are only asking that a metaphysical description of the general nature of the Universe should account for this procedure, which is essential to science, and which is such that nobody doubts it.

Fourthly, no help is to be got by basing your trust on past experience. You can in this way explain – as Hume explained – your habit of making these generalisations. But when you are convinced of the truth of this explanation of the habit, you ought to find your belief in its rationality rather weakened than otherwise. Apparently there has been a run of luck, and the human race has slid into indefensible habits of thought. Furthermore, if the present is irrelevant to the future, the past was irrelevant to the present. Accordingly, our memory, which is a present fact, is merely delusive if we take it as giving knowledge of the past. You cannot evade accounting for the relevance of a particular fact A to another particular fact B. The answer which I would give in outline is that the becomingness of reality is a process of exhibiting the togetherness of things, and that this togetherness is essential. Accordingly, | 13 | any one entity X which is realised requires of the rest of reality a patience of the entry of X into that togetherness. From the point of view of X, I call this the significance of X, and from the point of view of the rest of the Universe, I call it the patience of reality for X. Now a fact A is a complex of many inter-related entities $X_1. \ldots .X_n$ together with their relatedness in A. Thus in some way or other, such a complex entity as A has significance as to the constitution of all reality, and in particular, may well have important significance as to the possible constitution of some other fact B.

The Togetherness of Things. I wish to make it evident that the first step in the Philosophy of Science is the consideration of the togetherness of things. As we look around – either in perception or thought – we do not find things in isolation. For example, we do not find one horse, out of time and out of space, disjoined from the rest of creation. Zoology does not take its start from the examination of such isolated entities. There could not even be a horse without time and space. The very idea of a non-temporal, non-spatial horse is nonsense. It is not wrong; because it has no meaning at all, and cannot arrive at the dignity of rightness or wrongness. What we mean by an individual horse requires time and space in order to show its points.

But time and space simply exhibit aspects of the way in which things are together with each other. Thus, to say that a non-temporal, non-spatial horse is an unmeaning collection of ideas, is merely another way of saying that there can be no such thing as a horse apart from its togetherness with other things. I am not talking of where a horse will be happiest, or survive longest, but of the general character of the togetherness |14| which is necessary for the very being of a horse. For example, a horse is happy when galloping over grass downs, it could exist for a few seconds under water at the bottom of the English Channel, and for a very small fraction of a second somewhere between the Sun and Sirius, even if those two stars were blotted out. But, apart from its systematic togetherness with the electromagnetic field required by its electrons, there can be no horse even for a billion billionth of a second. A certain systematic type of togetherness is required for the very being of a horse. Apart from that, it cannot even proceed to die. The happiness of the horse, producing its continued survival, issues from conditions of reality which retain the horse as a realised value in the system of things. It is in this sense that I call every individual entity 'abstract'. Because every such entity presupposes a definite togetherness with other things. This togetherness must have a certain general systematic character in order that there may be such an entity at all – for example, a horse requires spatial and temporal relations with other things. But also in every particular instance, the togetherness will have accidental characters which might be otherwise, though they must be definite. For example, a definite horse at the present moment is either in London in the Strand opposite Charing Cross, or in South America, or on the surface of the moon, or somewhere else. It must have definite relations to other things in time and space; and what those other things are is somewhat accidental, though there is usually a historical explanation.

When we consider an entity by itself, we ignore this togetherness except those aspects of its general systematic character which are necessary to give meaning to our thoughts. But no definite horse at a definite |15| moment is living indefinitely in 'any environment'. There is no such thing as 'any environment'. The definite horse requires a definite environment. We ignore that, though it must be there. I am elaborating an obvious idea. For the idea is obvious, if I have expressed myself with any clearness, though the history of the philosophy of science shows that it is very necessary to elaborate it. The brilliant, and deserved, success of the Aristotelian system of classification has in the past somewhat obscured this essential togetherness of things. Classification directs attention to an entity in isolation. The entity is cross-examined as to its predicates, which are its own peculiar property, and is then assigned to its proper genus and species. Thus the procedure of classification ignores the primary consideration of togetherness. Half the difficulties of philosophy result from an exaggerated emphasis on the abstract entity as though it were capable of independent reality. The predicates of an entity are in general merely a one-sided way of expressing its relation to its environment. These predicates belong to the environment just as much as to the entity. For example, the grass is not green apart from its environment: since the light in the environment is required for this greenness. Accordingly classification, by ignoring the environment, has badly misled philosophy.

Classification does not express the origin of science in the very nature of things. The predication of qualities and the resulting classification are very useful and highly technical devices, but they cloak the fundamental idea which lies at the base of science. This idea is that every entity must be studied in its environment; and that this environment has partly a |16| systematic character required by the very essence of the entity, and partly an accidental character, which must be determinate, but which is not determined by the mere consideration of the entity. The togetherness of an entity with the accidental items of its determinate environment is what we mean by the experience of the entity. [By experience I do not mean cognition]. The total environment of an entity can be discriminated into a fluent environment of changing parts. The way the entity is connected with the succession of its partial experiences is what we mean by the behaviour of the entity. It is one purpose of science to determine general truths concerning the behaviour of entities as their partial experiences succeed each other. It is another purpose of science to determine the systematic characters of the types of togetherness required by various types of entities.

The Process of Realisation. This togetherness of things takes the form of a process of realisation. Reality is not static: it is a process of becoming. This fluent character of the togetherness of things was already emphasised in Greek philosophy: All things flow, said Heraclitus. Indeed the fact is too obvious to escape notice. But unfortunately things which are too obvious often escape receiving their due emphasis. The result is that there has been a tendency to give an account of reality which omits this essential processional character of the togetherness of things. It is then held that what is processional cannot be real. The fluent togetherness of things is then given a lower place as mere appearance, and we are left with a world in which the appearance which passes is contrasted with the |17| reality in the background, exempt from passage.

This train of metaphysical thought has the unfortunate effect of separating philosophy from science. For science is concerned with our experience of the passage of things in their fluent togetherness. Whereas, on this metaphysical theory, philosophy is concerned with the ultimately real which lies behind the superficialities which lie within the scope of science.

According to the view which I am putting before you there is nothing behind the veil of the procession of becomingness, though there is much pictured on that veil and essential to it which our dim consciousness does not readily decipher. Indeed the metaphor of a <u>veil</u> of appearance is wholly wrong. Reality is nothing else than the process of becomingness, of which we are dimly conscious. Every detail of the process is open for consciousness, though in fact our individual consciousness is only aware of a very small fragment of what is there for knowledge.

<u>Relativity</u>. The process of becoming real is a process of making real the togetherness of things. It follows that there are degrees of reality according to the completeness of realisation of togetherness. It is the connections which are realised. In a sense the idea of reality does not apply absolutely to the things thus connected, but only relatively. Thus by reason of the realisation of a type of togetherness between A and B, A is real for B and B is real for A. But it is nonsense to speak of A as absolutely real in itself, or of B as absolutely real in itself. A and B are individual existents with a relative reality each for the other. This relative reality of B for A is the becoming of B for A: namely B becomes a reality for A: that is to say, | 18 | the individual quality of B – what B is in itself – becomes significant for A, and affects the character of A's experience: thus the Universe is what it is for A because of the realisation for it of B's individual character. Thus realisation means at bottom the making real of value. It is the achievement of valuation, and valuation is a one-sided view of realisation. The process of becoming from the standard-point of A is the breaking in of B's character upon A. Then A is real because it is a term in this process and so is B. But the true reality is the achievement of this relation between A and B. There are stages of reality and degrees of reality of an entity A, according to the completeness with which A's individual character has ejected itself into the entities of its environment, and according to the completeness with which A on its side has received the injection of the characters of those entities. A mere absence of any such transfusion of character – value spells nonentity. Every existence is somehow envisaged from the standpoint of reality, and to that extent has some element of reality in its basic individual existence. But, an existent is not fully absorbed into the becomingness of reality unless the realised valuation is reciprocal, so that its mere formal experience has gained a realised significance for it.

This is the doctrine of the complete relativity of reality – at least, it is a doctrine of relativity, expressed from a realist standpoint in philosophy. An

entity is not merely abstract by reason of its general requirements of togetherness with other entities; this is its formal experience. But in the fluent becomingness of reality, even the intrinsic essence or character of an entity is not for
itself alone: it becomes a value for other entities. Otherwise, this transition
|19| of individual essence into value for others constitutes the relative char-
acter of reality. It is here that contingence arises, and we meet the last problem
to which I shall draw your attention in this lecture.

An entity enjoys all the formal experience which its significance requires.
This is the basis of the necessity which reigns throughout nature. But its real
experience, its experience of the becomingness of value, has for us an air of
contingence.

Why are we all here in the exact way we are, immersed in this special
realisation of the becomingness of real values? Or to put the matter in a more
limited special form, Why have the events of today followed those of yesterday
in the exact way in which in fact they have? Why not in other ways? Cannot
we discern some ground for the determination of the process?

Science seeks to discover what are the factors in the present which determine the direction of this process of achievement.

Now the present reality can be analysed into valuation as display, which
is the realisation of the intrinsic character of the sense-data, such as colour,
sound, bodily feelings, and into valuation as directive, i.e., into a distribution
of character directive of display. This character distribution is what may be
termed the physical field. It is the electromagnetic field of electrons, protons,
and the field of activity which they stand for. This directive field is intertwined
from the present to the future; so that the present being what it is, the future
is thereby determined to be what it will be. Whereas the field of display in the
present can be definitely determined as that display in the present without ref-
erence to the future. The physical field on the other hand is |20| nothing but
the way in which in the present the foundations of the future are being laid.
The display in the present can be definitely expressed in terms of the physical
field in the present: but the physical field in the present cannot be adequately
analysed except in terms of what it transmits into the future. For example,
the theory of the retarded potential exhibits an electron nothing else than a
process of transmission into the future.

Thus the display of the present is connected with the display of the future,
by means of the connection of the display of the present with the physical field
of the present, and the connection of the physical field of the present with
the physical field of the future, and the connection of the physical field of the
future with the display of the future.

But – and here is one great problem –, is not this physical field a mere myth, based on no knowledge? I do not believe in this mythical theory. It is difficult to understand how the scientific machinery of thought ever arose, if there is no direct discernment of the physical field. It is a clear fact of scientific history that the machinery arose from a gradual making precise of objects which mankind has always imagined itself to have direct immediate knowledge of: I mean chairs, trees, stones, and other objects of perception.

If mankind does in any real sense observe such objects, then the scientific objects merely claim to be merely a more precise rendering of perceptual objects which are somewhat vaguely observed. But if no such perceptual objects are really observed, and if the so-called perceptual objects are merely our ways of recollecting classes of sense-data, then the scientific |21| physical field is based upon no direct knowledge and must be treated as a useful mythical method of expressing somewhat complicated relations which hold directly between sense-data. For example, when you see a cricket ball coming swiftly towards you, and you catch it, and it stings your hands, the introduction of the ball is mere myth on this latter theory. There is a dot of colour in the sky approaching you, and this is succeeded by a sort of bumpy feeling, and this by a tingling stinging feeling; these various sense-data having certain definite spatial relations.

This account seems to me to be very unconvincing. If you are a school-boy with an important catch coming your way, it is not the colour you ever think of: it is the object exhibiting the colour. These objects are the most insistent things in our experience. They are vague in definition, but insistent for apprehension. You may forget the colour of the ball, but the ball imprints itself on your memory. Why on earth does one worry about the myth? How account for its vividness and universality?

One theory as to the status of the perceptual object – for example, of the cricket ball – is that such an object is merely the class of its appearances. There is a certain flux of sense-data, such as, patches of colour, sensations of touch, and other experiences, all associated with the various locations of the ball. These sense-data – it is said – are all we know of the ball, and are in fact the ball itself when we have added to them the sense-data which might have been observed but which in fact have escaped notice. This is the class-theory of the status of a perceptual object. The theory has been advocated by Bertrand Russell, and was put forward by him |22| in his Lowell lectures on Our Knowledge of the External World. It is a theory with strong reasons on its side, and I will examine it with more care in subsequent lectures. But I am growing increasingly sceptical of it.

The class theory would make the school-boy, in the agony of catching, have his mind occupied with a class of sense-data such as the redness of the ball when it was a new ball at the beginning of the match. Whereas such a thought never enters into his mind. He is thinking of the ball as a unique entity which is the control of display, but he does not classify the display which in its main outlines is not interesting him.

According to the alternative theory – I mean the control theory – the perceptual object is a persistent character inherent in the flux of reality which expresses the selective control by which a definite process is achieved. There is an element of display even in this character, since its individual reality breaks in upon us, and we have a discernment of it. This discernment is insistent and in a sense vivid, yet it is vague. In the endeavour to cure this vagueness science introduces its molecules, its atoms, its electrons and its protons. This procedure of science is entirely analogous to the analysis of the total volume of sound in a concert hall into definite notes, and each note into its fundamental tone with its harmonic overtones.

Both lines of thought, the class-theory and the control-theory present great difficulties and secure certain philosophical advantages. I cannot at this final stage of my lecture consider them further.

I will conclude with one reflection. Neither in Science nor in Philosophy, nor in any branch of human achievement do we reach finality. The data of crude |23| evidence upon which Philosophy works is provided by the general state of civilised thought at the epoch in question. In one sense Philosophy does nothing. It merely satisfies the entirely impractical craving to probe and adjust ideas which have been found adequate each in its special sphere of use.

In the same way the ocean tides do nothing. Twice daily they beat upon the cliffs of continents and then retire. But have patience and look deeper; and you find that in the end whole continents of thought have been submerged by philosophic tides, and have been rebuilt in the depths awaiting emergence. The fate of humanity depends upon the ultimate continental faith by which it shapes its action, and this faith is in the end shaped by philosophy.

## Notes

1. This chapter previously appeared in *Process Studies*, 48:2 (2019).
2. Denotes Whitehead's original page breaks.
3. Milton's *Paradise Lost*, Book II, lines 558–61.
4. Authorial interlineations have been placed in their intended locations and marked with carets, following the convention used in volume one of the Critical Edition.

5. The text from this point until the end of the paragraph was marked with a brace in the left margin.

6. An unseen character introduced in Thomas Morton's 1798 play *Speed the Plough*, the name became an English figure of speech for a conventional or priggish person.

7. Thomas Bowdler famously edited Shakespeare's plays to remove content he deemed inappropriate for women and children, publishing the result as *The Family Shakespeare* in 1807.

# 2

# Examining Whitehead's 'First Lecture: September, 1924'

*Paul A. Bogaard[1]*

In early January 2019, George Lucas sent an exciting note: 'I am going through the three boxes of hitherto unknown papers that I picked up from George Whitehead on the way home.'[2] As General Editor for the *Edinburgh Critical Edition of the Complete Works of Alfred North Whitehead*, George Lucas had been keeping in close touch with Alfred North Whitehead's grandson, as the key person to ensure the family was aware of and comfortable with this long-term project moving ahead. Those relations have warmed and strengthened over recent years, and George Whitehead was pleased to see that the first volume of *The Harvard Lectures* for this series had been published.

On his previous visit, Whitehead's grandson had asked George if there might be interest in three boxes of papers. For many years, the story has been that Alfred North Whitehead's remaining papers were destroyed after his death in 1947. It turns out that this was not entirely the case. Having edited the first volume, devoted to Whitehead's first course of lectures at Harvard, including his inaugural lecture, I was as surprised and excited as George Lucas's email, and it was particularly thrilling to be told that amongst 'several handwritten and typed drafts of various talks by Whitehead . . . one is entitled "First Lecture, September 1924." It is 23 typewritten pages.'[3]

Immediately, speculation flew between George, myself, Brian Henning and Joseph Petek by email: could this item actually be a typescript of Whitehead's inaugural lecture, and what could we discern from it? It was Joe Petek who quickly but carefully completed a page-for-page and line-for-line transcript of this curious document. And I agreed to draft an essay from these discussions, plus what I could determine from a close comparison with the lecture notes we had already published in HL1. Both Winthrop Bell, as one of Whitehead's young colleagues at Harvard, and Louise Heath, a graduate student at Radcliffe, had taken notes on what appears to be the same lecture (or portions of it), and these will form the basis of the following comparisons.[4]

Figure 29  The title page of Whitehead's manuscript

My first words in this University will be
expressive of personal feeling.  I can discern in
myself many strains of intense emotion.  Among them
there are two feelings to which I must give explicit
expression.  One of them is my sense of the honour
you have conferred by your invitation to occupy a
chair of philosophy in a University which, throughout
its centuries of existence, has been continuously
occupied with the deepest topic which can fill the mind
of man:  a University whose foundations were laid
amidst debate on the metaphysical mysteries of Puritan
theology, -

[They] reasoned high
Of providence, foreknowledge, will, and fate,
Fixed fate, free will, foreknowledge absolute;
And found no end, in wand'ring mazes lost.-:
A University which studied Berkeley's doctrines before
their full importance was recognised in Europe:  And,
to come at once to recent times, a University in which
the senior portion of my audience will have listened
to William James, to Hugo Munsterberg and to Josiah
Royce.  A man would be dull indeed who in this position
did not feel emotion.

My other feeling is one of immense responsibility.  I cherish to the full the implications of that
ancient phrase 'Divine Philosophy'.  The Faculty of
Philosophy in a great University exists to foster and
to make explicit the ultimate meanings which underlie
all rational activities, crafts and sciences and arts
alike.

There is a meaning in things, and perplexities
can be unravelled - dimly, slowly, patiently.  It is
not given to one man, to one nation, to one age of
history, or to one school of thought, to exhaust the

1.

Figure 30  The first page of Whitehead's lecture

## Physical Features

Before turning to a direct comparison with what we know from these other sources, let me review what can be said about the twenty-three pages themselves. First and most obviously, they are a typescript, and so far as we know, Whitehead himself did not type. (There would, of course, have been a handwritten draft, but none has been found amongst the other handwritten manuscripts in these three boxes.) Whether he had it typed up before or after the Whiteheads arrived in New England, in late August of 1924, is not known. There is no indication on these typescript pages of who typed them, nor when they were typed. The typescript is quite clean, with only a very few uninformative marks someone made in the left margin.

The type shows as light blue, rather than black, and we have puzzled over whether this might indicate that the typist used that colour of ribbon, whether it is a carbon copy, or whether it was even one of the multiple copies that might have been made at the time. The fingertips of others have reported there is some dimpling of the type that comes through to the back side, but not very much, and not consistently. That suggests that what we have is not the original typed copy. Neither does it support the idea that it is one of an early duplicating process, which also would have made it likely that other copies survived. So, while we cannot be certain, it seems what we have is what it most looks like, a carbon copy.

The paper on which it was typed – or at least this carbon copy – is an odd size. It measures just about 8″ wide and 12.75″ long. The paper used was neither the North American standard letter size (8.5″ x 11″) nor our so-called legal size (8.5″ x 14″) and makes us think more of the A4 that is standard in Britain. Mind you, it is not quite A4 dimensions (8.27″ x 11.69″) either, and for that matter these sizes were apparently not standardised for another decade after Whitehead had it typed. Nevertheless, on balance we think it more likely it was already typed up on British paper, and before Whitehead brought it with him from England in late August of 1924.

Lowe's biography suggests[5] that Whitehead would have had time to write his lecture after he arrived (there would have been about four weeks), but he also reveals that Whitehead had received the offer from Harvard many months previously, had accepted the offer by April, and had already been invited to give the Lowell lectures. This had given Whitehead time to consider what he might do for this series of public lectures; he had suggested a title, conferred with Woods (Head of the Department of Philosophy), and had time to change his mind about that title and send materials for later announcements at Harvard, all before leaving England.[6] So, he had plenty of time to be anticipating what he might do for this his first course of lectures in philosophy, and would surely have been thinking it through. Just when he first composed what he wanted to say, and when he had this draft typed up, is probably less important than our appreciating that he had a full typescript in hand, and prior to the occasion of his inaugural.

## The Typescript vs. Recorded Notes

We can forgive Lowe for concluding almost thirty years ago that 'there does not seem to be any transcript', when he reported on what was known of Whitehead's inaugural lecture.[7] He had certainly appreciated that it was quite an occasion. As Winthrop Bell recorded in his daily Diary: 'all the grandees were there' (HL1, 3). Apparently, they responded to the occasion in quite a variety of ways. This only makes it the more remarkable that, of all lectures, Whitehead's inaugural lecture at Harvard is one that has surfaced. Whether it was the script he read from on that occasion, or a draft later revised, that is a question on which we hope to shed some light.

We now know there are at least two other sources we can draw upon. And we should warn at the outset that we will need to proceed with some care, because the two sets of notes we have do not quite match this typescript. They do echo the typescript for a good deal of their content, enough to be confident that this was the lecture from which they were taking notes. But neither set of notes begins the way Whitehead's typescript does, the endings are completely different, and there are major gaps in between. There are ways to account for many of these divergences, but that will require a closer look. Happily, in some of these differences we can glimpse Whitehead thinking his way through issues that mattered to him, at this important transition in his thinking.

The two sources, as mentioned above, are two of the three main sources recorded in 1924–25 and presented in HL1. Winthrop Bell's notes on Whitehead's first course of lectures given in Emerson Hall are reproduced beginning on HL1, 3, and Louise Heath's notes at Radcliffe begin on HL1, 411. (The other set of notes that appear in HL1 are from William Ernest Hocking, but he does not seem to have begun attending Whitehead's course until 21 October.) Comparisons will be made quite closely between the Bell and Heath notes and the first lecture transcript, and for the latter reference will be made to the page numbers that appear at the bottom, centre (hereafter $|\#|$), which have been taken directly from the typescript itself, and are not to be confused with the page numbers of HL1 or this collection of essays. These original page numbers have also been retained in this format in the version of the typescript reproduced in this volume.

The first thing one notices is that Bell's notes begin with the first line of the last paragraph on |2|. Thereafter, Bell's notes capture not just the themes found in Whitehead's draft, but his notes include whole phrases, sometimes full sentences, most often word for word from Whitehead's typescript. It is a reminder, as considered in HL1, that Bell often captured the very words Whitehead used in a lecture, whereas Hocking's notes echo the same flow, the same sequence, and occasionally explicit phrases, but he usually noted down his own consideration of what has been said in the lecture. Bell's objective, throughout most of the lectures, seems to have been to provide a 'transcript' of Whitehead's lecture, made even more evident by his having included the asides, the jokes, and the comments about what is being sketched on the blackboard. Now we have the extraordinary opportunity to gauge what Bell has captured against Whitehead's own typescript.

There is more that needs to be said about this (for example, can we really take Bell to be capturing all of Whitehead's words?), but for the moment: what can one say about the first five paragraphs that Bell skips entirely? One consideration that will be haunting us throughout this comparison is how difficult it is to determine whether Bell has skipped something Whitehead delivered, or whether Whitehead skipped something written in his typescript, but which he later decided (or even at the time decided) no longer expressed his current thinking or was simply too long for this occasion.

In the case of the first two or three paragraphs, Whitehead was taking the occasion to express his gratitude to the 'grandees' who had assembled to hear his inaugural address, but who would for the most part not be attending the subsequent course of lectures. He wanted to express, as he said, the honour they had conferred upon him, and the responsibility he felt to speak not just as a mathematical physicist, but to the philosophical import of science. Lowe later reported that Whitehead began by saying 'what an honour it was . . .'[8] and there seems no reason to doubt he did express these feelings, and that Bell felt no compunction to record them in his notes. As Whitehead thereafter began focusing his remarks on the analysis from which philosophy must start, on the presuppositions of science, Bell no doubt picked up his pen and began to record.

By comparison, when Heath recorded what Whitehead delivered at Radcliffe two days later, it seems to be in the main the same lecture. But her first note was 'General Introduction', which could indicate that Whitehead repeated some of his introductory remarks or simply that she characterised his opening remarks in this way. Interestingly, she then began with remarks found in the typescript in the two paragraphs leading up to the first sentence Bell had recorded, i.e. the middle paragraph on |2| and the sentences above.

And so, we have the first of many such puzzles: Did Whitehead include these at Radcliffe but not at Emerson Hall? Did Whitehead use them in both presentations, but Bell did not bother to record them? That seems to me more likely, somehow, but provides an early caution that Bell's notes are not a full transcript of the lecture, as presented. We will see other occasions where this is the implication.

Before we turn to more detailed comparisons, it should be highlighted that on |3| Whitehead explicitly referred to what he will consider in his 'next Lecture'. In his search for 'a coherent system of assumptions for physical science' – reflecting directly the title he had set out for this course of lectures – he warned that the 'second lecture will be more purely scientific than is usual, or even proper, for a philosophic lecture'. Neither Bell nor Heath record this, but Whitehead actually confirms that he 'planned the two lectures together'. We know from Bell's notes that the lecture Whitehead gave two days later certainly threw his philosophy students into the deep end. The third and fourth lectures as well were devoted to features of the applied mathematics that had been prompted by experimentation into a new mode of subatomic physics, with repeated references to quantum theory. The students must have wondered if they had stepped into the correct lecture room.

And Whitehead clearly knew this was where he was heading. He had planned this, at least as early as he arranged for the typescript of his inaugural lecture. There is no known typescript for the 'next lecture' (at least none that has been found, to date), just as there has never surfaced any course syllabus or outline for what Whitehead was planning for 1924–25. But here, and occasionally elsewhere in his course of lectures, Whitehead does point to the plans he has made. Whether or not he knew in September of 1924 just where his thoughts would lead him throughout the next eight months, he seems to have already decided what his first two or three steps were going to be.

For the next nine pages or so, following |3|, we find Bell's notes picking out passages and whole sentences that Heath recorded as well, both of them word for word. These are interspersed with sentences one of them records, but the other not. Neither of them, it would seem, provides what could be considered a complete record of the lecture. But they do follow along the same sequence of thoughts and arguments, sometimes skipping a little of the material we find in the typescript, sometimes quite a lot, but they never stray from the sequence of points made in the typescript. If Whitehead at some point edited what we find in the typescript, shortened it perhaps, what we do not find is his having changed the flow and sequence of what he had decided to say.

For the remaining pages of the typescript, beginning with |13| to |14|, there are not just sentences and whole paragraphs that neither Bell nor Heath recorded, but whole pages. Both pick up on what Whitehead has to say on |15| and |17| to |18|, but thereafter nothing of the remaining pages was recorded. Whitehead provided a quite striking image for the conclusion of his first lecture in the existing typescript, but in both Bell and Heath there is recorded a quite different ending, which does not appear in the typescript at all. We will look more closely at some examples below, but it will be useful to say already at this point that what we can learn by comparisons between Bell-Heath and the typescript, and between Bell and Heath, does not remain constant throughout. After his expressions of gratitude, and the sense of responsibility captured in the early paragraphs, and some hints at planning out his approach to this course of lectures, Whitehead seems to have kept fairly closely to about the first half of his prepared text, as witnessed by our two sets of notes. From that point one begins to suspect that Whitehead does not deliver each paragraph nor each page as drafted. Whether he has edited this draft before he begins the inaugural is hard to say. There is no indication on the typescript pages themselves. He might have decided to skip portions at the occasion, worried about the time he had. Some portions he seems to have decided would be better left for later lectures, and some of the ideas he had drafted he may have decided to drop. (Again, we will consider some examples below.) But there can be little doubt about his concluding remarks. He had to have changed his mind completely about these.

There are then three features of Whitehead's first lecture I think we can underscore already at this point. One is to repeat, as was suggested above, that whatever portions were or were not recorded by these two note-takers, they both recorded the same sequence of Whitehead's thoughts, the same sequence as one finds in the typescript. About the flow of his arguments, Whitehead had no change of mind. A second consideration is that, despite their differences, what Bell recorded from the Emerson Hall lecture and what Heath recorded from the Radcliffe lecture two days later, were the same lecture. Whatever Whitehead decided to drop or change, it seems to have been the same for both occasions. And that seems to argue against the possibility that Whitehead was making these changes on the fly.

This last point we will return to at the end, but there is something more we can say about Whitehead's delivery. In HL1 I argued that, despite a widespread image of Whitehead sitting and reading his prepared text, the record of notes taken throughout the academic year suggests a different image. It must have been the case that Whitehead was often on his feet, often at the blackboard, often commenting out to his class. He seems quite capable of thinking on his feet, and re-thinking what he was trying to say as the academic year moved along. Having a full typescript for the first lecture he delivered at Harvard has not changed my mind about that. As an inaugural lecture, it makes sense that he would have wanted to work out quite carefully what he would say, but we can already see he changed his mind about what to include. What he did deliver, as we see from similarities between the two sets of notes, seems to have kept quite closely to his prepared text. But this still does not suggest a senior professor recently arrived at Harvard sitting at a table mumbling into his typescript. The reactions to Whitehead's inaugural were, as we have acknowledged, quite varied, but none were disappointed by the delivery on this occasion, nor the personality that shone through.

## What Can Be Gleaned About Content

Enough has already been said about Whitehead's introductory remarks, and what Whitehead had planned for the course of lectures this first one inaugurated. We'll turn, now, to teasing out what can be found by making direct comparisons in more detail. Beginning on |4| we find this typical pattern: each paragraph begun on this page is captured in both Bell and Heath. In each paragraph they record the same phrase or sentence. Perhaps this is not so surprising, since when Whitehead asked 'what is there in the nature of things which necessitates' what we find in science, this was clearly the main point he was raising. Similarly, in the next paragraph, when Whitehead turned to the 'general relations of metaphysics, theology, and science', that should have been enough for anyone listening to lean forward. As this interrelation is unpacked, through the centuries, only Bell recorded a full sentence here and there, but both note-takers were following the same narrative. On the following page, |6|, we have a particularly striking case of Bell and Heath each having recorded part or all of the same five sentences (out of about sixteen), with only one instance in which each of them recorded a phrase or a sentence the other did not. In other words, over half the sentences on that page were recorded by neither. We can only assume Whitehead delivered these lines as well, but they had not added much to the points he was making.

Another kind of question that becomes relevant here is where else do we find Whitehead presenting similar narratives? For example, the historical narrative that unfolds on |5|–|7| is similar to what becomes a central feature of *Science and the Modern World* (SMW), namely that the seventeenth century is 'that one century in Europe [when] the foundations of modern science were laid'. Both this historical unfolding and the cross-cultural comparisons (with, for example, the Chinese) are major considerations in SMW, published later in 1925, and therefore in the Lowell lectures given in February 1925, but they were not central to the course of lectures Whitehead gave through this academic year.[9] In the next couple pages of the typescript, and in bits and snatches captured by both Bell and Heath, Whitehead focused his attention on Hume and, thereafter, Kant. Both of these receive repeated attention throughout the subsequent course of lectures. By way of contrast, Whitehead gave the impression he was quite smitten by a Cambridge colleague who had insisted there is a fundamental 'decency' to things. However, this manner of expressing the point seems never to appear again within the lecture series, nor in SMW. In a similar vein, Whitehead attempts to capture the role Kant ascribes to 'cognition' by comparing it to Mrs Gundy's view of morals and to Mr Bowdler's Shakespeare. So far as I can determine, he never tries to use those comparisons again. Did he find these references too British for this New England audience?

Consideration of these philosophical antecedents led Whitehead to formulate what he took from Kant to be the problem of cognition, and from Hume the problem of induction. Readers will recognise these as two philosophical conundrums that haunted Whitehead throughout these lectures, through SMW, and through much of his remaining career. They appear as central issues Whitehead raised in his lectures at both Emerson Hall and at Radcliffe. Bell's notes suggest that (as in the transcript) Whitehead delineated how these problems are encountered in the work of Mill, Pearson and Bacon, whereas the absence of any of these in Heath's notes suggests she either was not at all familiar with these names, or Whitehead did not include them at Radcliffe. In this it suggests a difference between his two deliveries of this lecture we do not see elsewhere – that is, not elsewhere in this first lecture, whereas there are many differences to be found throughout the full course of lectures.

How one fact can be relevant to another fact, the 'root' question of |12|, is found in both Bell and Heath and using exactly the same wordings, for the most part, including 'the togetherness of things' that is the 'first step in the Philosophy of Science', as are Whitehead's suggestions for how these conundrums need to be addressed. But following |13|, the notes of both Bell and Heath fail to record much of what is found in the typescript. This seems to be a sort of turning point, though there are some useful examples we can tease out at this juncture:

The illustration Whitehead used to demonstrate the 'togetherness of things' was that of a horse. A horse cannot be found outside its own place in time and in space. It cannot have meaning outside its environment. These are deeply important concerns Whitehead introduced here, and which he pursued throughout that year's course of lectures and into his publications thereafter, but not by riding this example. The horse example is mentioned, briefly, by both Bell and Heath, but not again that year. Whitehead used the term at least seventeen times within two pages of the typescript. He was trying hard to make this illustration work. But, apparently, he must not have thought it worked very well.

I will reach ahead for a counter-example: on pages |20| to |22|, nearing the end of his 'First Lecture' (at least in the typescript), Whitehead tried out another illustration. Here he asked his audience to imagine a boy attempting to catch a cricket ball. And he did not just mention this in passing, as it consumes two full pages of the typescript, and is meant to help us appreciate his concern about the prevalence of relying upon 'sense-data' to understand how we observe the world around us. While he indicated his scepticism of Bertrand Russell's suggestion for dealing with this conundrum in his Lowell lectures given in 1914,[10] Whitehead only mentions that he has an alternative theory of his own, but does not pursue it further here. He does say 'I will examine it with more care in subsequent lectures', which is almost an understatement. It comes up time and again in subsequent lectures[11] as Whitehead attempts to refine this illustration and make it more effective. So, we find some illustrations continue to be used, while others are tried but then dropped.

Another kind of example arises on pages |14| and |16|. From Whitehead's text on |14| almost nothing makes its way into the notes of either Bell or Heath. Their notes are filled, thereafter, with much of |15|, where Whitehead returned to the theme of togetherness and the danger of its being missed in our appreciation of environment. But on the previous page he had introduced the notion of an 'abstract entity', which was noted in both Bell and Heath, though only briefly and only once. It is worth pointing out, however, that Whitehead was introducing here a concept which would blossom into significance for him going forward. This is a central theme that arises in at least twenty of his subsequent lectures.

A parallel example appears on |16|, where the 'togetherness of things takes the form of a process of realisation'. Both Bell and Heath caught this one, as well, on two occasions of its use by Whitehead, whereas the typescript reveals at least nine occasions of its use. And that is, of course, just the tip of the iceberg! Fully half of his course of lectures deals with this topic, including every lecture from 66 to the end, and that simply presaged how important it would become for Whitehead up to and including *Process and Reality*.

Given that so little of these hugely important themes is evident in our two sets of notes – perhaps one or two single references from out of several pages of typescript – and despite our knowing how important these themes would become, it seems to be the very opposite of Whitehead trying out an example or the wording of an unfamiliar concept, and then subsequently leaving it behind. These are introductions by him of ideas and formulations that become fundamental. Since he must have anticipated that, as with the problems surrounding sense-data, Whitehead clearly alerts his audience that these will be examined 'with more care in subsequent lectures'. Perhaps for that reason they were only introduced here. They may have been fleshed out with some initial care, as we read in the typescript, but what Bell and Heath recorded suggests Whitehead may have pulled back on his treatment of them in this initial lecture.

As mentioned above, when Whitehead returned to his thoughts about 'environment' on |15| and the process of becoming real on |17| and |18|, Bell and Heath were both busy taking extensive notes, often capturing the very same sentences or phrases, with Bell recording a bit more (especially from |17| through |18|), down to Whitehead's 'doctrine of the complete relativity of reality'. There are some key ideas they missed as well, like the peculiarly Whiteheadian notions of 'significance' and 'patience' introduced on |13|, with significance reappearing on |18|. These are not to be found in either Bell's or Heath's notes, and since they receive considerable attention in later lectures,[12] it would suggest these were candidates for Whitehead simply to leave out of his first lectures at Emerson Hall and Radcliffe, to be saved for later.

On |18| we also find the opposite, that is, Whitehead must have inserted references to Spinoza at the bottom of this typescript page, because this historical figure is not only recorded in both Bell's and Heath's notes (at exactly the same juncture), but they also both captured a claim Whitehead would make later on, that he found Spinoza 'the most suggestive of Modern Philosophers'.[13] We have not found many instances of Whitehead clearly adding to his inaugural lecture elements not there in the typescript we have been examining, but here his having done so is especially evident.

At the top of |19| Whitehead's typescript turns to 'the last problem to which I will draw your attention in this lecture'. Nevertheless, he must have decided not to draw his audience's attention to this last problem at all. The typescript suggests that our experience of the world seems to be contingent, whereas the underlying physical processes do not. Perhaps this underlying 'physical field' is just a myth, or is it our seemingly immediate experience of the objects of perception? This appears in the typescript and remained for Whitehead a major problem. He introduced the notion of 'contingence', and of the 'physical field' as opposed to the 'field of display'. But none of these make an appearance in the notes taken either at Emerson Hall or at

Radcliffe. In fact, nothing from |19| or |20| was recorded. And the same is true for |21| and |22|. The latter pages of the typescript are where White-head worked up his example of catching a cricket ball, but, as we saw earlier, this did not find its way into the inaugural lecture as presented.

And then one final missing metaphor: The typescript has Whitehead say-ing he 'will conclude with one reflection', that neither science nor philosophy reach 'finality'. Like the ocean tides, philosophy seems to do nothing. It only probes and adjusts ideas. 'But have patience and look deeper, and you find that in the end whole continents of thought have been submerged by philo-sophic tides and have been rebuilt in the depths awaiting emergence.' Many of us have been waiting for the continents of thought rebuilt by Whitehead to emerge from the depths. But so powerful a metaphor makes no appearance at either Emerson Hall or Radcliffe. They would not have both missed it, if it had been spoken.

Instead, we find in both Bell and Heath Whitehead's insistence that metaphysical philosophy is not merely the handmaiden of science, but that it 'stands as near to poetry as to science, and needs them both'. Another power-ful image, and one that for some reason Whitehead decided would be a more appropriate way to end his inaugural lecture than the ending found in the typescript.

## Summary Thoughts

We have considered three interrelated comparisons: Whitehead's typescript recently found allows us to compare this text directly with the notes recorded by Bell and by Heath. Along the way, this has also highlighted similarities and differences between these two sets of notes. And then, we distinguished those cases where Whitehead took up some of these same ideas in later lectures and publications from those cases where it seems he did not. This comparison with later work in particular awaits a much more thorough examination.

One conclusion seems inescapable: the typescript of Whitehead's 'First Lecture' is not simply the script he delivered at his inaugural lecture given in Emerson Hall on 25 September 1924, nor the lecture he repeated two days later at Radcliffe. If one focuses exclusively on the pages of the transcript where both Bell and Heath seem to follow along quite closely, as if that was the whole of the typescript, then one might be justified in concluding that the typescript was the script from which those two presentations were delivered. That Whitehead's introductory remarks were not recorded need not dissuade us from this simple conclusion, but the absence of any notes from several of the later pages, plus the complete change of his final reflection, should make

us suspicious. That we should draw a more cautious and complex set of conclusions just makes this challenge more interesting and offers us more to learn
about what Whitehead was thinking at this stage.

Where Bell and Heath did record what Whitehead presented quite closely –
and this seems to be the case for about fourteen of the twenty-three pages of
the typescript – even then they were noting down less than half of the material found on each typescript page. That already raises questions about how
thoroughly they had each recorded Whitehead's lecture (and the differences
between what each decided to record support the presumption that he delivered it all, at least on those pages), but it also leads to another conclusion,
that we might expect the notes to provide less than half of the words found on
that portion of the transcript. However, the complete typescript contains just
over 6,630 words, and Bell's notes for the first lecture contain just over 1,180.
That's only 1/6 the number of Whitehead's words, which in itself strongly suggests he did not deliver everything we find in the typescript.

It is hard to say conclusively, but we might ask whether Whitehead could
have read the complete transcript on each of these two occasions. Whitehead
confirms in a letter to his son, North, that his lecture periods were fifty minutes.[14] And I confess I have known colleagues who could spin through 6,600
words in an hour, but I neither considered that very effective nor what I would
have expected of Whitehead, now sixty-three. Bell's recording of later lectures
during the course of the academic year – also fifty minutes – were somewhat
longer, averaging 1,500 to 1,900 words. But in one telling example, late in
the year when Whitehead delivers to his class a paper he had written on the
history of mathematics, it takes him two full lecture classes (and took Bell
almost 3,000 words to record them.)[15] I'm not sure how compelling all these
comparative word counts are, but they certainly point in the same direction:
that Whitehead chose to deliver something less than the full typescript we
now have of his first lecture.

It seems quite possible that when the time came, he found his script too
long. And we have even more definitive evidence for which passages he
decided to leave out, since they did not appear in either Bell's or Heath's
notes. Of course, as note-takers, they only record some key sentences, but we
found that when they are following closely, they never skip a full paragraph.
Where whole paragraphs are missing from their notes, or as becomes increasingly the case, whole pages, we have reason to believe these passages were not
delivered. In some cases, this material reappears in later lectures, and Whitehead said explicitly in the typescript that this was what he was going to do.
Other times material drafted for the typescript seems never to have been used.
Where it does appear later we have tried to indicate where.

Just when Whitehead decided to edit and pare down the typescript we now have is difficult to say. But we can say with much more confidence that he did not skip passages when at the podium, where he might have had second thoughts or felt the pressure of time. I think we can conclude this because of the striking similarity between the two sets of notes. With very few exceptions, we have found both Bell and Heath include the same material, often word for word the same. Where paragraphs and whole pages are missing from their notes, they are the same ones, and when Whitehead adds in a reference to Spinoza, or switches to a quite different ending, they are the same. This could only happen if Whitehead had sat down with his typescript, and chosen passages, whole paragraphs or whole pages to either delete or save for later lectures. He must have jotted down 'Spinoza', rewritten the ending, gauged whether it was now an appropriate length, and stuck to this newly edited script through both presentations. We can even say that he did not feel the need to shift any of his earlier draft material around, because the sequence we find in both sets of notes and in the typescript remains the same. Would it not be grand to have found that edited version, with all the marks indicating passages for deletion, for reduction or rewording, and/or for considering in later lectures! What we do have is a carbon copy of the version he drafted earlier, and not the original he edited sometime later that he then used for delivery, and on both occasions.

We can draw such a conclusion because of how closely both Bell and Heath, on two separate occasions, managed to record just what is found in this typescript. That is, we can see how accurately they recorded what was in the typescript, after it had been edited. Without the typescript having been found, and the comparisons that has made possible, we would not know how reliable these notes in fact are. As confident as we were with the three sets of notes we transcribed for HL1, it is most heartening that in the case of this one lecture, our confidence seems to have been fully justified.

Two final comments that each reflect how I have myself been struck by this examination. The first is to underscore that it has been just as interesting to ponder those illustrations and formulations that were drafted, initially, and then set aside, as it has been to follow those that later grew in importance. We have mentioned, for example, the fairly concrete case of an illustration – that any one horse cannot simply be in any environment, let alone no environment – which having tried, Whitehead seems to drop. He certainly did not drop the general point he was trying to make but, rather, doing so on the back of a horse. And there are other instances not yet mentioned. There is his historical note about spectroscopy as significant experimental work that motivated some of the revolutionary changes in physics during his lifetime (see |8|), whereas this is at best only brushed past in his later lectures. Of more philosophic interest is his exploring what he took to be the instantiation of 'value', an important idea for Whitehead, both here, in his later lectures, and in later publications. Associated with this, we find another formulation he seems to have been trying out: 'valuation' – on |18| and |19|– but so far as I can determine 'value' survives into his later work, whereas 'valuation' is never used again. One last example already noted above is when Whitehead considered whether philosophy, in the end, does nothing. This seems to have been deleted from what was delivered at both Emerson Hall and Radcliffe (one can hardly imagine such a claim being missed), but it is picked up for further consideration in at least ten later lectures, all of them in the second term. In the typescript, however, he draws this out into the tidal metaphor quoted above, which seems never to have been used in either his inaugural or thereafter.

And my final comment: I do hope other readers will find the transcription of Whitehead's 'First Lecture' as informative as I have. I have found it more informative even than the abbreviated version of Lecture 1 from the notes we transcribed in HL1. The topics and ideas are recorded in the two sets of notes taken from this inaugural lecture, but too little was revealed of what Whitehead planned for his lectures, and of where he was going or what motivated some of the moves he made. The full typescript provides a more complete sense of what Whitehead had in mind, and why. That has been unexpectedly informative and something I cherish. Perhaps, for these reasons, I should be grateful it is the unedited carbon copy of his earlier draft that has been preserved, and not the edited version I wished for, above.

## Notes

1. This chapter previously appeared in *Process Studies*, 48:2 (2019).
2. Email from George Lucas to Paul Bogaard, 5 January 2019.
3. Same email as above. Within a month, George Lucas had also secured full custody and ownership of these materials.
4. For a detailed account of these two note-takers, and Whitehead's first course of lectures, see my Introduction to HL1, xxv–lii. We also relied upon notes taken by Whitehead's senior colleague, William Ernest Hocking, but no notes of his survive from the inaugural lecture.
5. Lowe, *Alfred North Whitehead, Volume II*, 139.
6. Lowe, *Alfred North Whitehead, Volume II*, 157–8.
7. Lowe, *Alfred North Whitehead, Volume II*, 141–3. Just as we can forgive him for getting the date wrong; it was 25 September.
8. Lowe, *Alfred North Whitehead, Volume II*, 141.

9. As argued in the Introduction to HL1 (see xlv), Whitehead's first course of lectures and his Lowell lectures were not organised in the same way.

10. Whitehead mentions this in Lecture 8 (HL1, 31), where we footnoted that Russell delivered his Lowell lectures at Harvard in March–April of 1914, and later that year they were published as *Our Knowledge of the External World: As a Field for Scientific Method in Philosophy* by Open Court.

11. Explicitly in Lectures 7 and 8, and then again in Lectures 68 and 71; and the conundrum this catching-a-cricket-ball example illustrates is even more widely addressed. It does not seem to have survived into SMW.

12. 'Patience' resurfaces in Lectures 58, 76, 83 and 84, as well as in SMW; and 'significance' (in his special sense) in Lectures 43, 45, 56, 63, 64, 70 and 72.

13. This is from our transcription of Bell's notes (HL1, 5), whereas Heath records: 'most significant of modern philosophers' (HL1, 413).

14. See his letter to North for 9 November 1924 in Lowe, *Alfred North Whitehead, Volume II*, 294.

15. These are Lectures 81 and 82 in HL1, in which Whitehead delivered a paper he had been asked to present at Brown University. It became the basis of his Chapter II in SMW. Chapter II is not much longer than the typescript of Whitehead's 'First Lecture'.

## Bibliography

Bogaard, Paul and Jason Bell (eds), *The Harvard Lectures of Alfred North Whitehead, 1924–1925: Philosophical Presuppositions of Science* (Edinburgh: Edinburgh University Press, 2017).

Lowe, Victor, *Alfred North Whitehead: The Man and His Work, Volume II: 1910–1947* (Baltimore: Johns Hopkins University Press, 1990).

Whitehead, Alfred North, *Science and the Modern World* (New York: The Free Press, [1925] 1967).

# Part II

# The Fitness of the Environment

# 3

# Whitehead and His Philosophy of Evolution

*Paul A. Bogaard*

Already in his third Harvard lecture on 30 September 1924, Whitehead warns that the next advances most needed are to be made in the life sciences. We might well suppose that what this portends is his *Process and Reality*, which declares itself from the outset and all throughout in terms of 'Organism'. In the first sentences of PR's Preface, Whitehead said: 'The Philosophic scheme which they [these Gifford lectures] endeavour to explain is termed the "Philosophy of Organism"' (PR, v).

In Part II of PR a chapter is devoted to 'Organisms and Environment', which brings in a correlative concept we will investigate further in this essay, and about which he here said: 'the character of an organism depends on that of its environment . . . the sum of the characters of the various societies of actual entities which jointly constitute that environment' (PR, 168).[1]

No one familiar with Whitehead's published work will be surprised that Whitehead was determined to displace the mechanistic philosophy that had dominated since the seventeenth century, nor that his alternative is characterised as a Philosophy of Organism. How he deploys the correlative notion of 'environment' may not be so obvious, as it gets only minimal play in PR, and seems quickly to be displaced by the language of societies of societies.

What becomes clear in the Harvard lectures of 1924, however, is (or was for me) the quite unexpected declaration that his alternative to materialism would be a 'Philosophy of Evolution'. How he understood 'evolution' by December of 1924, how he interwove this concept with 'organism' and 'environment', and what we can say about the close attention paid to evolution within six or eight of these lectures, are my topics for this essay. Not the least reason for this is George Lucas's warning, in 1989,[2] that, for a process philosopher, discussions of 'evolution' are curiously lacking in Whitehead's published works.

The lectures of 1924–25 are so obviously placed between Whitehead's earlier career devoted almost exclusively to mathematics and mathematical physics, and the metaphysical declarations of his *Science and the Modern World* and *Process and Reality*, that even for those who knew little or had only partial glimpses of these, his first philosophical lectures, one might expect that they were pivotal. This was Lewis Ford's point in his *The Emergence of Whitehead's Metaphysics: 1925–1929*, although as the first volume of the Critical Edition shows, he had only limited access to these lectures. One immediately wonders what aspects, if any, of PR and SMW are already to be found there. Or, are these lectures largely a summarising of positions Whitehead had already begun to work out in the *Principles of Natural Knowledge* and *The Concept of Nature*, perhaps even in his *Principle of Relativity*, all published within the five years prior to his appointment at Harvard (and the basis, presumably, of their hiring him into the Department of Philosophy).

So, I would like, *first*, to begin by reviewing, if briefly, how these particular concepts – organism, environment and evolution – are situated within Whitehead's published works. From there, *secondly*, I will consider the people upon whom Whitehead must have relied. He had no formal training in the life sciences, after all. But then, as he points out in his own autobiographical comments, he had no formal training in philosophy, either. Are these seemingly parallel cases similar? Are his thoughts about an early philosophy of biology as subtle and insightful as his engagement with his favourite sources from the history of philosophy? And then, *finally*, I will to turn to a closer reading of how he makes use of these three interrelated concepts, especially in Lectures 31–39, and what we might make of the close attention he pays here to 'evolution', before it fades away in favour of his use of 'organism'.

## At What Point Do These Biological Concepts Take on Metaphysical Import?

A beginning point can be established quite readily: the concept of organism is absent from the *Concept of Nature*, and evolution is used there only incidentally (in two instances), nor are they evident in his *Principle of Relativity*. In the *Principles of Natural Knowledge*, from 1919, the term 'organism' is used two or three times, but only in the usual biological sense, with little philosophical import. And 'evolution' does not appear (much as George Lucas had pointed out thirty years ago). It would be difficult to say anything other than: these biological concepts were already known to Whitehead, but they do not seem as yet to have struck a philosophical note. There is no evidence that they had as yet offered any sort of philosophical alternative, and this despite Whitehead's already making clear that mechanical philosophy – the assumptions that had figured in his own teaching for decades – was based on an assumption of simple location, and a fallacy of misplaced concreteness.

We will likely never know the chronology of this story as one might like, but by the beginning of his lectures at Harvard, during which he spends the first month and more in reviewing the revolutionary challenges presented by physics, he is already suggesting that inspiration is more likely from the life sciences. That was 1924, and to look ahead, by the time he composed the Gifford lectures that comprise PR (published in 1929, but the lectures were already in place during 1927) his convictions concerning a philosophy of organism must already have taken root.

Can we focus this transition any more tightly? *Science and the Modern World* is published in the Fall of 1925. But the manuscript was already sent in early July of 1925. And, of course, most chapters in SMW were presented in his Lowell lectures, given during the month of February in 1925 and composed (Whitehead tells his son[3]) in the two months leading up to their presentation. So, the timing here is important, and seems to be quite narrow.

What does he say in these Lowell lectures? In the century by century outline, as we have it in SMW, he said: 'My purpose is to trace the philosophic outlook, derived from science and presupposed by science, and to estimate some of its effects on the general climate of each age' (SMW, 41). This matches the objective of his 1924 lectures, I think we can say, although the lectures to his students were neither organised nor presented in this historical review. In the chronology of SMW:

> The scientific philosophy [of the seventeenth century] was dominated by physics. [Unfortunately, it left us with] concepts very unsuited to biology, and set for it an insoluble problem of matter and life and organism . . . But the science of living organism is only now coming to a growth adequate to impress its conceptions upon philosophy. (SMW, 41)

Whitehead concluded his review of the eighteenth century by calling for a 'provisional realism, . . . a complex of prehensive unifications . . . Thus [seeing] Nature [as] a structure of evolving processes' (SMW, 72). The nineteenth century sets the stage for the contrast between mechanism and organism:

> The doctrine I am maintaining is that the whole concept of materialism only applies to very abstract entities . . . The concrete enduring entities are organisms, [where] the plan of the whole influences the very characters of the various subordinate organisms which enter into it . . . until the ultimate smallest organisms, such as electrons, are reached. (SMW, 79)

While the phrase 'philosophy of organism' does not appear in SMW, the intent of drawing upon these insights from the life sciences is quite evident, including Whitehead's applying them to inanimate physical entities. More generally, he said, at this stage:

> One all-pervasive fact, inherent in the very character of what is real is the transition of things, the passage one to another . . . The general aspect of nature is that of *evolutionary expansiveness* . . . [Events] are the emergence into actuality of something. (SMW, 93; emphasis added)

With this emphasis on evolutionary expansiveness, he seems to echo from just a month or two earlier his declaration of a 'philosophy of evolution'. But the closest we find anywhere in SMW is: 'Nature exhibits itself as exemplifying a philosophy of the evolution of organisms subject to determinate conditions' (SMW, 93). This phrase 'philosophy of the evolution of organisms' makes it sound rather like, by February of 1925, Whitehead was firmly convinced of the efficacy of these biological concepts but is not declaring one over the other. This is a point I will want to examine more closely, in my final section.

So, to review: by 1925 Whitehead was determined to impress the key conceptions of biology onto philosophy. In 1919 he had made no mention of organism or evolution as philosophically relevant, and his 1920 and 1922 books mention these concepts not at all. However, by the end of 1924 in his first year of Harvard lectures he has declared: 'The key to nature is that of organism, not that of matter' (HL1, 153).

## What Influences on Whitehead Seem Most Likely?

Something shifted in Whitehead's thinking in 1924, and it would be most useful to know from what sources. Who and whose writings might have influenced him? Victor Lowe tells us that the inaugural lecture was met with the charge that it was 'pure Bergsonianism'. And in the lectures that followed, Whitehead did assign to his students readings from *Creative Evolution* (particularly Chapter IV). He also assigned readings from C. Lloyd Morgan's *Emergent Evolution* and acknowledges his influence, amongst others. So, these are obvious candidates. One might also credit his decades-long acquaintance with D'Arcy Thompson, a friendship established when they were students together at Trinity College, Cambridge. Whitehead tells us in his autobiographical comments provided for the Schilpp volume dedicated to him in 1941[4] how much he had learned through these friendships, accounting for much of his education outside the classroom in his Cambridge years. He even mentions a friendship with W. Bateson, who had been a neighbour while living in Grantchester. He mentions those he got to know through the Aristotelian Society, as well, later in his London years. And then there is his well-known friendship with Lord Haldane – not himself steeped in the life sciences, but his brother was – and Jack Haldane (J. B. S. Haldane was Lord Haldane's nephew) is mentioned in the lectures as another source to be read. And finally there is Lawrence J. Henderson, a name not known to me before working on these lectures, but who Whitehead directly credited, and who I shall argue is a particularly relevant source.

Through friendships such as these, Whitehead was clearly aware of how far biology had come in the preceding seventy years. During those decades a rich field of theoretical concepts had arisen from what had otherwise been for so long an observational field. D'Arcy Thompson had actually been in contact with Darwin.[5] Discussions about natural selection had become commonplace, and while contentious, had come to be melded into the emerging field of genetics in the hands of pioneer scientists like Bateson and the Haldanes. Darwin's conception of evolution had already been folded into broader philosophic stands by Spencer, Bergson and Lloyd Morgan. Whitehead knew and studied their writings; Bergson he had entertained in his home.

So, that this lifelong mathematical physicist, with no formal training in biology, was well aware of the conceptual array made available from the life sciences should not be surprising. It may prove more difficult to determine from whom he had drawn his key inspirations for what appears in these lectures, and especially since (as George Lucas pointed out many years ago) the concept of evolution seems little evident in Whitehead's own writings; except, it would seem, for these lectures.

Whitehead acknowledged openly that he was not the first to impress concepts from biology upon philosophy. The debates prompted by Darwin's theory of evolution had always been at least partly philosophical. Spencer is cited in these Harvard lectures, and Whitehead is comfortable enough within the debates about natural selection to criticise those like Spencer who narrowed their conception of it to competition (Spencer had coined the phrase 'Survival of the Fittest'). And he acknowledged the encouragement he had drawn from Lloyd Morgan's *Emergent Evolution*.[6] However, the similarities in their metaphysical stances is much more evident in what each says about the *emergence* of new levels within reality than in what one finds about the process of evolution.

Turning to Chapter IV of Bergson's *Creative Evolution*,[7] which Whitehead assigned to his students, we find explicit criticism of the 'mechanistic illusion' (in Bergson's phrase).[8] Whitehead also acknowledged he owed much to Bergson's emphasis on duration and his sense of the creativity needed to account for the continuity of life and the discontinuity of evolution's products. But I would suggest (much as I've said about Lloyd Morgan), that while each of them had a common purpose in constructing their broad views of the natural order within the frame of evolution, there is not so much in either of these sources that delineates what evolution permits or implies, at least not in any detailed sense we find Whitehead exploring, even when he does so in these lectures.

It may be that Whitehead shared with Russell some of the latter's resistance to Bergson's insistence upon the primary role of intuition.[9] And, in any case, I find myself aligning with Victor Lowe's warning that the influence of Bergson, especially in the positions Whitehead takes up from 1925 on, has been much overrated.

For a more nuanced sense of how the biological concept of evolution can be employed, and particularly in terms of organisms interacting with their environments, we must turn to L. J. Henderson. Henderson is quite explicitly the source Whitehead credited, when in the mid-December Lecture 31 he turned to what could be drawn from these biological concepts:

> The environment gives <u>its</u> contribution – at least as important as contribution of <u>other</u> elements. Big question (Whitehead put on to it by L. J. Henderson's *Fitness of the Environment*). (Later his *Order of Nature*) Each organism to some extent creates its own environment – Previous life of organism has stamped itself somehow on whole present environment. (HL1, 135)[10]

The 'fitness of the environment' had been Henderson's way of grabbing the attention of those in his new field – so new it was not yet called biochemistry – and the attention of the wider public. It is not just that organisms evolve by becoming more 'fit' in the seemingly static environment in which they find themselves; they do, but not without influencing that environment in the process. Environments evolve along with organisms. And insofar as the environment is comprised of other organisms, we are very close, here, to the insights debated amongst evolutionary biologists and philosophers of biology in recent decades. We have come to recognise mutualism as well as competition; we have come to appreciate that much of evolution is co-evolution. And Henderson, along with Whitehead, was wading into these interesting conceptual thickets a century ago.[11]

Although Henderson knew of Whitehead, and apparently had a role to play in Harvard's invitation to him,[12] they presumably met only after Whitehead had crossed the Atlantic. They did become friends, and with Whitehead's interest in what can be made from these key concepts in biology, and Henderson interested in the implications between scientific fields, and with philosophy (he was a member of the Royce Club), they must have had much to discuss, and for Whitehead at a most fruitful period. Whitehead seems to have read Henderson's *Fitness of the Environment* (published in 1913) – they had been presented first as Henderson's own Lowell lectures in 1912 – and *Order of Nature* (published in 1917), but it may well be that he had not read them until they met in Harvard Square.

Henderson had started with mathematics and physics when he studied at Harvard College, before turning to physical chemistry and then biological chemistry. He may even have attended some Royce seminars. After time at the University of Strasbourg, Henderson returned to Harvard in 1904, and had become full Professor by 1919. So, while younger than Whitehead by sixteen years, Henderson was well beyond being a junior colleague.

Whitehead and Henderson shared a keen interest in the advantages of broader education rather than narrow specialisation, and Henderson from his own vantage point also taught courses in the history of science. They both worked closely on projects like the formation of a Society of Junior Fellows at Harvard. Henderson had indicated that it was institutions like Trinity College, Cambridge that had served as a model. Later in their years together at Harvard, in 1934, Henderson was given an honorary degree by Cambridge. These bits and pieces lead, I acknowledge, at best to supposition (they are based on the careful memoir presented to the National Academy of Science in 1943, the year after Henderson died), but there can be little doubt of the influence, or at least, reassurances provided by what the NAS Memoir calls Henderson's 'thoughtful consideration of the relations of organisms to their surroundings'.[13]

Henderson's proposal that the environment itself was particularly 'fit' for living organisms and their evolution did not mean that some sort of inorganic natural selection was at work, but that the elements upon which he focused – particularly the principal components of organic compounds, namely, hydrogen, carbon and oxygen – and the properties of water and carbonic acid (simply carbon dioxide in water) were conducive to life. And perhaps something stronger: their prevalence and typical properties were just what they needed to be in order to be conducive of life. Henderson, we might say, was promoting an early example of what we've come to call the 'anthropic principle': that somehow the characteristics of the physical world are just what they need to be, within a

surprisingly narrow margin, for the promotion of life and its evolutionary unfold-
ing. For Henderson this suggested a teleological principle at work.

While Whitehead may have been comfortable with such a suggestion, we
know that he comes to view the divine element in our world, and the eternal
objects evident in all realisations, in somewhat different terms. They also had
in common a critique of 'vitalism' – as being far too content with a mechanistic view of the universe – and both criticised Herbert Spencer's extension of
evolution in terms of competition. And perhaps most fruitfully, Henderson's
more detailed biochemistry could have helped justify Whitehead's conviction that the principles underlying the physical sciences – instead of requiring
some extra-physical influence to engender life (and consciousness), implying
all the ills of nature's bifurcation – should be capable of bringing biological
insights down into the physical realm, such that the physico-chemical realm
would then seem fully capable of the emergence of living organisms.

## How Are These Concepts Marshalled in Whitehead's First Harvard Lectures?

In the Introduction to his *Order of Nature*, Henderson had said: 'the organism
and the environment each fits and is fitted by the other'.[14] Whitehead saw significant possibilities in exploring this role for the environment. At this crucial
juncture it seems to have allowed him to forge a pathway that would take him
further than either the concepts of organism or evolution on their own.

In Lecture 35, when he openly declared that 'The key to nature is that of
organism, not that of matter', he proceeded to argue that 'The organism [is] in
itself [an] environmental concept'; and, 'Apropos of Environment and Evolution. Progress of latter is essentially a problem of procuring a favorable Environment' (HL1, 155). 'The advantage of this point of view', he said in Lecture 39
as the teaching term picked up again in January, 'is that it admits of no jump
whatever in principle as between living and inanimate' (HL1, 172). Within the
world of living organisms, natural selection depicts how the organism becomes
fitted to its environment. But the environment will have been impacted as well.
And in the physico-chemical world, without access to the selection of the fitter,
generation by generation, it is the fitness of the environment itself, in Henderson's arresting phrase, which Whitehead seems to have found suggestive.

The 'Point of <u>evolutionary philosophy</u>', he had suggested in Lecture
33, was that the 'Order of Nature must be looked on as itself an emergent mode – having the processional, transitional character' (HL1, 143).
That a processional, transitional character provides the outlook Whitehead
favoured will not surprise us, but in this transitional period of Whitehead's

own philosophical development I think we need to see how the point of this evolutionary philosophy provides a possible solution to the challenge he had set for himself in these lectures and keep in abeyance whether this had yet developed into the objectives he sets for *Process and Reality*.

I suggested in my Introduction to HL1 that, in fairly broad terms, White-head from the very outset described the challenge as he saw it. The inaugural lecture had already introduced the alternative conceptualisations of a world characterised by continuity, and that undergirded by atomism. As he makes clear in his lectures through the Fall, we are not forced here to make a choice between what appear to be two radical alternatives, but challenged to unpack their underlying assumptions and articulate them within a metaphysical syn-thesis that enables a balance between both of them.

I would go further, today, and suggest it was not yet temporal atomism which enabled Whitehead to turn his metaphysical preferences towards some kind of coherence during 1924–25 (this had been Lewis Ford's surmise),[15] but rather the concept of evolution, broadened as with Henderson into a scope which embraces all of Nature. Just how his conceptualising of temporal atom-ism, admittedly crucial, is embedded in his metaphysics, seems to me the chal-lenge that required the full scope of PR to work out. But in 1924–25, as we follow Whitehead thinking new possibilities aloud in front of his Harvard stu-dents, it was his unpacking of the possibilities of organism, within a changing environment, across an evolutionary scale that convinced him there is a path for metaphysics to move forward.

He was trying, as he introduced Lecture 32 (in mid-December):

> to <u>embed</u> order of Nature in a more general metaphysical background. Two ways of looking at Nature which give you two rather extreme lines . . . Either your attention caught by the enormous permanences and make <u>this</u> the keynote of your thought – the mountains, atoms, electrons etc. [where the] Trouble for <u>this</u> Metaphysics is time. (HL1, 139)

The alternative, he went on to suggest, is to start from the very idea of change:

> . . . Change. That ultimate Entity in its own Essence is Transition, <u>both</u> internally and externally . . . So not independent of environment. All Concrete Things taken out of Environment are Abstraction – They're only concrete in environment . . . The man starting from Change and try-ing to be simply pluralistic <u>must</u> be in a muddle. The order of Nature is for us the unity of such transitional Ultimates. So we have exactly opposite difficulty – rather bothered with the Permanence.
> (HL1, 140)

How can Whitehead have supposed that a broadened conception of evolution, even with a renewed sense of the interactive role of the environment, will provide a pathway towards a stable order of nature without bifurcation? The scenario Whitehead suggested is this (I am paraphrasing from the middle paragraphs of Lecture 32, HL1, 140):

- The order of Nature has to take as its basis certain physical facts
- Three dimensions in space and one in time
- The electromagnetic field is at first mere flashes in the pan, achieving no endurance
- Then gradually self-propagating entities emerge, those with basis for endurance
- These entities are gradually evolving a more favourable environment . . . It is endurance itself which is evolved . . . the slow steady evolution of 'Environment'
- By comparison, in Darwinian evolution (discovered sixty years ago) the environment was thought of as fixed . . . Now environment is both given, and plastic!

So, Whitehead is not just speaking here of what we recognise as organic things. This mode of evolution also accounts for the enormous number of electrons (and other basic entities), and the evolution of similar things, which endure for tremendous periods of time.

From these emerge higher types, the ninety-two elements . . . and eventually living organisms and people with cognisance.

The underlying assumption, therefore, and the point (as he said) of evolutionary philosophy, is that the 'Order of Nature must be looked on as itself an emergent mode – having the processional, transitional character'. This clearly relies upon a broadened sense of evolution, such as one might expect in a process philosopher. And while I suspect Henderson may have reassured Whitehead of the legitimacy of broadening evolution in this way, more specifically he encouraged Whitehead to think of organisms and their environment mutually influencing each other, a sense of interdependency to which Whitehead was deeply attached. In his applying the biological concept of fitness to the physico-chemical environment, Henderson may have been a catalyst in Whitehead's thinking of how biological concepts can pervade the whole physical universe. This offered him a key for addressing the challenge of continuity or atomism; rephrased as, whether to start with stability and permanence or start from evolution and transition. From the latter, he might also be able to account for the former:

How to account for <u>enormous</u> stability of Electrons etc . . .

by survival of fittest. You go back to where within order of Nature you had fitful stretches of emergent enduring entities. We've finally got an order of Nature dominated by those entities which created an environment favorable not only to themselves but to production of other entities of same kind. An Environment i.e. created by a <u>Society</u> of entities producing an Environment favourable to existence of them all. <u>Environment</u> has evolved <u>as</u> an Environment which secures selection of definite types. The plasticity of the Environment is the <u>Key</u> to the Evolutionary problem and that of Permanence. (HL1, 135)[16]

Of course, the conditions that Whitehead is suggesting arise through change in the environment itself, which is what allows for the actualisation of 'organisms' such as electrons, and eventually those of living organisms, and finally those whose cognitive abilities we recognise as consciousness. And this process of actualisation of any one organism, and then another, and another generating whole societies, will require a vast metaphysical analysis we do not see until PR.

Before that daunting challenge could be taken on, however, Whitehead had to convince himself that there was some way of embracing all that the life sciences teach us, and psychology too, but without losing touch with the extraordinary understory the physical sciences had revealed. He needed a sense of how the process of a cosmic evolution could provide for life without leap-frogging over physics and chemistry. Part of this was embracing the idea that electrons, too, must be thought of as organisms, where one must take into account the whole before concluding what we say about the component. Another part was embracing the idea that there is a broader sense of evolution underlying our order of nature than Darwinian evolution, one nevertheless consonant with it and making it possible. But the key, he was now saying, for embracing both permanence and change, both atomism and continuity, was recognising that the environment is itself plastic.

When first encountering these middle lectures on the philosophy of evolution, I had thought they represented a stage along Whitehead's philosophical trajectory, and expected to find indications of why he later rejected the idea of a philosophy of evolution in favour of a philosophy of organism. This would account for both the confidence with which he announces a philosophy of organism, and why we find him speaking so little about a philosophy of evolution hereafter. Instead, I have come to understand his turning to these conceptions from the life sciences as more in tune with his conviction that we need not force a choice between temporal continuity and mechanical atomism, but must seek out some balance, some accommodation between them that substantiates them both. I no longer see Whitehead as struggling to choose between a philosophy of organism and a philosophy of evolution, but as turning to evolution as his way of framing an assumption capable of allowing him to avoid the bifurcation of nature. And the pathway to that resolution rests on the role of the environment, a pathway that opened up at this crucial juncture, and that he explored for a time with his Harvard colleague, L. J. Henderson.

Whitehead felt the need, in the midst of process and transition, for stability, and came to see in the midst of Lecture 32, literally thinking this through as these lectures developed, that 'Evolution towards Stability is on the whole an Evolution in which the modification of the Environment is the important thing' (HL1, 141), and that the environment itself can be seen as 'an enduring and stability attaining <u>organism</u> which is being evolved' (HL1, 142). 'Evolutionary process as far as we can observe it – takes place at an Edge between two Environments – between two fair stabilities and just enough Instability' (HL1, 141). What a wonderfully evocative phrase, and how remarkably contemporary, to think of evolutionary process as taking place at an edge between two environments.

As these lectures for his students resolved themselves into the Lowell lectures and then SMW, the call for a new 'philosophy of evolution' (late in 1924) becomes a 'philosophy of the evolution of organisms' (in 1925). No longer such a clarion call. When it reasserts itself in PR, the term 'evolution' has been dropped. And that seems puzzling. To remake it into a clarion call, did he simplify it into philosophy of organism, perhaps? Does the need for this systematic metaphysical analysis of actual occasions and of societies, each organisms in their way, elbow aside the need to reaffirm the underlying evolutionary process? To what extent does Whitehead intend for societies of societies to take a back seat to actual occasions?

The only place in all of PR where Henderson gets a footnote is in the section on 'The Order of Nature'. And many of the themes we have explored here are echoed there, but neither so clearly nor strongly. Whitehead stills says things like: 'The doctrine that every society requires a wide social environment leads to a distinction that a society may be more or less "stabilized" in reference to certain sorts of changes in that environment' (PR, 153). There is even a recognition of at least the possibility of cosmic epochs here. But without the express notion of evolution, it has all become rather cautionary. Evolution just doesn't seem like the centre of the story any longer.

# Notes

1. The preceding chapter in PR on 'The Order of Nature' suggests: 'Every society must be considered with its background of a wider environment of actual entities ... [itself] a larger society' (PR, 138).

2. Lucas, *The Rehabilitation of Whitehead*.

3. See his letter to North for 21 December 1924 in Lowe, *Alfred North Whitehead*, Volume II, 301.

4. Schilpp, *The Philosophy of Alfred North Whitehead*, 3–14.

5. Lowe mentions Darwin's interest in a translation Thompson had completed and for which he had written a 'preface'; see Lowe, *Alfred North Whitehead*, Volume I, 82.

6. Lloyd Morgan's *Emergent Evolution*, published in 1923, was first presented as his Gifford lectures in 1922.

7. Bergson's *Creative Evolution* had been published in 1907.

8. The phrase 'mechanistic illusion' appears in Bergson's header to *Creative Evolution*, Chapter IV, p. 287, the chapter Whitehead had assigned to his students at the outset of Lecture 19.

9. Russell published 'The Philosophy of Bergson' in *The Monist* in 1912.

10. See B. Henning's discussion of a similar point concerning the abandoned 'principle of the environment' in his chapter for this volume, 'Whitehead in Class'.

11. See D. Sölch's chapter in this volume, 'Whitehead's Biological Turn', which goes further than I have in identifying how what Whitehead seems to be introducing in these lectures is so redolent of debates active in the philosophy of biology today. Even as recently as 2018 Oxford has published the anthology by Nicholson and Dupre, *Everything Flows*, which takes its inspiration from Whitehead and also from Waddington. Sölch also provides more detail on the issues rippling through theoretical biology in Whitehead's own day.

12. See Lowe's many references to Henderson at Harvard in his *Alfred North Whitehead*, Volume II, and especially 132–3 for the occasion of Whitehead's appointment.

13. Much of what is known about Henderson and his publications can be found in Cannon, 'Lawrence Joseph Henderson'.

14. Henderson, *The Order of Nature*, 3.

15. For an analysis of Whitehead's first course of lectures that continues to hold, as did Lewis Ford, that there is a shift in Whitehead's thinking toward temporal atomism, see R. Desmet's chapter in this volume, 'From Physics to Philosophy, and from Continuity to Atomism'. Desmet does not seem to hold out for as sharp a turn as had Ford's assessment from thirty years ago, but he still insists upon a clear shift from the beginning of Whitehead's first term to the last two months of his second term. I do not disagree that there was a development in Whitehead's thinking through the course of these lectures, but I am focusing on different motives and adjustments. Desmet's bringing out of Whitehead's position in the publications that preceded 1924 is especially strong, but while

he notes Whitehead's rapidly growing interest in the life sciences, he does not attend to the role I would contend they play in the middle lectures from December and January.

16. Lecture 31 is the first instance within the lectures of Whitehead referring to a 'society' of entities. See M. T. Teixeira's essay in this volume, 'Some Clarifications on Evolution and Time', which is especially good at extrapolating what Whitehead continues to say about evolution in *The Function of Reason*, and appreciates how significant is the rise of Whitehead's concept of 'society'.

## Bibliography

Bergson, Henri, *Creative Evolution*, trans. Arthur Mitchell (London: Macmillan, 1922).

Bogaard, Paul and Jason Bell (eds), *The Harvard Lectures of Alfred North Whitehead, 1924–1925: Philosophical Presuppositions of Science* (Edinburgh: Edinburgh University Press, 2017).

Cannon, Walter B., 'Lawrence Joseph Henderson, 1878–1942', *Biographical Memoirs of the National Academy of Sciences*, 23 (1943), 31–58.

Henderson, Lawrence J., *The Order of Nature* (Cambridge, MA: Harvard University Press, 1917) <https://archive.org/details/cu31924012262030>

Lowe, Victor, *Alfred North Whitehead: The Man and His Work, Volume I: 1861–1910* (Baltimore: Johns Hopkins University Press, 1985).

Lowe, Victor, *Alfred North Whitehead: The Man and His Work, Volume II: 1910–1947* (Baltimore: Johns Hopkins University Press, 1990).

Lucas, George, *The Rehabilitation of Whitehead: An Analytic and Historical Assessment of Process Philosophy* (New York: State University of New York Press, 1989).

Morgan, C. Lloyd, *Emergent Evolution* (London: Williams and Norgate, 1923).

Nicholson, Daniel J., and John Dupre (eds), *Everything Flows: Towards a Processual Philosophy of Biology* (Oxford: Oxford University Press, 2018).

Russell, Bertrand, 'The Philosophy of Bergson', *The Monist*, 22 (1912), 321–47.

Schilpp, Paul, *The Philosophy of Alfred North Whitehead* (La Salle: Open Court, 1941).

Whitehead, Alfred North, *Science and the Modern World* (New York: The Free Press, [1925] 1967).

Whitehead, Alfred North, *Process and Reality: An Essay in Cosmology* (New York: The Free Press, [1929] 1978).

# 4

# Some Clarifications on Evolution and Time

## Maria-Teresa Teixeira

In the Harvard lectures, Whitehead's notion of evolution is sometimes comparable to the idea of change.[1] Transition opposes permanence. Endurance is important for the understanding of time. 'Endurance is essentially the evolution of societies, i.e. evolution of entities which create a favourable environment for similar entities' (HL1, 461).

These statements on permanence and endurance clarify the notion of a society – which seems to have its origin in the Harvard lectures – and highlight the role of the environment in the emergence of societies. Plasticity of the environment becomes a key concept.

It is important to keep in mind that the Harvard lectures are comprised of student notes taken down as Whitehead lectured, and not a polished monograph; they must not be considered as incorporated in Whitehead's works. Many times he was thinking out loud as he spoke before his audience in Harvard, though this was certainly an important preliminary exercise that facilitated his later written work, the writings that came to be considered his philosophical oeuvre. Through his Harvard classes and lectures, Whitehead was able to dwell on many philosophical issues and questions that he never would have explored had he not been appointed for this job.

Whitehead's discourse is sometimes tentative; sometimes he does not make clear judgements about certain theories, such as the doctrine of the survival of the fittest in Evolution Theory, which he later rejects in *The Function of Reason*. On the other hand, he sometimes seems to anticipate some of his statements in *Process and Reality* or *The Function of Reason*. Given this tentativeness, his Harvard lectures provided a good opportunity to test his philosophical theories before an audience.

Whitehead's theory of evolution – if he really had one – can be found mainly in *The Function of Reason*. He does make some references to it in *Process and Reality* and *Modes of Thought*, but the first pages of *The Function of Reason* seem to synthesise his thought on this subject. In the Harvard lectures he makes many references to evolution and uses the concept more freely and broadly. He is clearly trying to mould his thought and seeing where it might lead him.

Before examining what the Harvard lectures have to tell us about this topic, let us examine the first pages of *The Function of Reason*.

In the introductory summary, Whitehead underlines two tendencies in nature: 'slow decay' – which leads to 'degradation of energy' – and 'renewal' – 'the upward course of biological evolution'. He also considers reason the only element capable of introducing 'self-discipline' into reality.

Whitehead underlines several problems with the theory of evolution. Firstly he points out 'the evolutionist fallacy suggested by the phrase "the survival of the fittest"'. Whitehead holds that the struggle for survival as eliminating the less fit and allowing for the success of the fittest explains nothing. Life itself is 'deficient in survival value' (FR, 4). Persistence through time is associated with dead matter. Complex organisms like human beings have evolved with very little survival power, and that poses a very difficult question: how can fragile species emerge as complex, successful and organised beings? In Whitehead's analysis, it is the neglect of time which leads to the explanatory failure of most theories of evolution (FR, 5).

Ignoring time and focusing on the fact that there are various 'levels' of life misses out the importance of the continued progress of existence (FR, 6). The very idea of evolution requires a temporal framework.

However, Whitehead's main concern has to do with a different way of interpreting evolution, which takes time into consideration. In broad terms, the classical theory states that species and individuals disappear due to some kind of maladjustment to their environment. The problem with these doctrines is that one never gets to know about the cause that led to the dying out of the species; one never gets to know about the nature of the struggle. The disappearance of a certain species *per se* is no proof of maladjustment (FR, 6). Whitehead says we hardly know about the causes at the root of the struggle that may have led to the disappearance of a species. It may be that the species disappeared for no reason related to maladjustment to its environment. The struggle of the fittest is thus a concept which does not clarify why a certain species became extinct.

The trend of evolution is upwards. The physical world, however, has a tendency towards decay and degradation. Not so with evolution, which is a tendency in the direction of renewal; every novel trend invites the appearance of new elements in the complex progress of existence. Evolution develops in time. However, this temporal development cannot be explained by the idea that species adapt to the environment or that of the struggle and success of the fittest (FR, 7). Whitehead rejects the idea of animals adapting to their environment. Mankind is an important illustration of this reluctance to adapt to the surrounding milieu. Human beings have championed modifying the environment. They have led a true attack on the environment (FR, 8). Thus, evolution – which takes place within a certain lapse of time – is not explained by the idea of adaption to the environment, neither is it clarified by the narrative of the struggle of the fittest.

Whitehead thinks that the important factor resides in the fact that beings adapt the environment to themselves. It is not a question of taking a given milieu into which several individuals, or a particular species as whole, have to integrate and become successful elements in the pre-set biological system. Living individuals and living species are not simply inserted in a static biological framework so that they adapt to those pre-existing conditions. They evolve with their surroundings, and their environment evolves with them.

Living beings transform their environments; they change it and mould it, in accordance with their needs and ways of living. 'Even the more intimate actions of animals are activities modifying the environment. The simplest living things let their food swim into them. The higher animals chase their food, catch it, and masticate it. In so acting they are transforming the environment for their own purposes' (FR, 8).

Purpose is an essential element in understanding the theory of evolution. Much depends on the capacity of anticipation. In the theory of evolution, different species can only be characterised if a final end is taken into account. However, final causation is usually not taken into consideration. Each occasion of experience reflects its own purposes (FR, 31). Although the common belief amongst scientists is that nature is purposeless, Whitehead holds that purpose is essential for the understanding of life and especially for the understanding of evolution. The existence of physical and chemical laws should not rule out the fact that animals are sustained by purposes. 'There is clear evidence that certain operations of certain animal bodies depend upon the foresight of an end and the purpose to attain it' (FR, 16).

Reality becomes absurd if there is no value attached to it. The very fact of existence represents the attainment of an end. 'This is the doctrine that each actuality is an occasion of experience, the outcome of its purposes' (FR, 31). The process of coming into existence is self-determining and self-defining. Every actual entity is the outcome of self-constitution in accordance with one's subjective aim.

If final causation is not taken into account, then efficient causation cannot be explained. For Whitehead, the incorporation of antecedent data in a novel actual entity is the outcome of efficient causation. But it is final causation that introduces novelty, because it introduces value. In other words, purpose introduces value into reality. Subjective forms in every actual entity include purpose and valuation. 'The components in the concrescence are thus "values" contributory to the "satisfaction"' (PR, 84–5). Evolution relates directly to value and purpose. Evolving beings need purposes in their evolving processes, and these are possible because value is introduced as novelty emerges and actual entities constitute themselves, thus modifying their surrounding milieu.

Thus, 'the higher forms of life are actively engaged in modifying their environment. In the case of mankind this active attack on the environment is the most prominent fact in his existence' (FR, 8). The tendency upwards is a positive one according to Whitehead, and so is this transformation of the environment.

Of course, this theory should be examined within a restricted framework, that of a Whiteheadian theory of evolution. Today this 'active attack on the environment' by mankind does not have an upward tendency, but is instead a suicidal undertaking.

Whitehead associates evolutional development with the use of reason. The environment is acted upon through reason. Reason scrutinises its surroundings and makes its own judgements; it tracks down final causation as it searches for the purpose of action.

Reason is a very active factor in the composition of reality, introducing novelty into the world. Physical activity does not explain evolution, because it is governed by the laws of inorganic matter. In looking for final causation, reason introduces purpose into the world, thus explaining the upward trend of evolution and clarifying why living beings adapt to their environment.

Reason is frequently seen as 'the operation of theoretical realization . . . exemplifying of a theoretical system' (FR, 9). 'Reason is the godlike faculty which surveys, judges and understands' (FR, 9). But this concept of reason cannot be complete, especially when temporality is brought into the discussion as an important element. 'In the newer controversy Reason is one of the items of operation implicated in the welter of the process' (FR, 9). The search for purpose in the course of events is an instance of the way time influences and constitutes novel reality. Reason in some way regulates reality. The prime role of reason is thus to enhance the final causes and direct the aims towards their purposes. It is a pragmatic undertaking, and it leads living beings towards the upward trend in evolution.

'Reason is the self-discipline of the originative element in history. Apart from the operations of Reason, this element is anarchic' (FR, introductory summary). For Whitehead

> The lowest form of mental experience is blind urge towards a *form of* experience, that is to say, an urge towards a *form for* realization . . . The higher forms of intellectual experience only arise when there are complex integrations, and reintegrations, of mental and physical experience. Reason then appears as a criticism of appetitions. It is a second-order type of mentality. It is the appetition of appetitions . . .
>
> Mental experience is the organ of novelty, the urge beyond. It seeks to vivify the massive physical fact, which is repetitive, with the novelties which beckon. Thus mental experience contains in itself a factor of anarchy. We can understand order, because in the recesses of our experience there is a contrasting element which is anarchic. (FR, 32–3, emphasis in original)

This is the pragmatic function of reason that seeks speedy undertakings and legitimises final causes; final aims are the real motivations that can always be found amongst living things. Reason can but enlighten the upward trend of evolution. There is no arbitrary path in nature. Rationality emerges as a fundamental and basic element in reality. This is the reason to be found 'in the welter of process' (FR, 9).

However, pragmatic reason regulating the development of evolving, temporal beings has to be combined with speculative reason for a thorough understanding of reality. Whitehead considers the latter to be 'Reason, asserting itself above the world', whereas pragmatic reason 'is Reason as one of many factors within the world' (FR, 10). Speculative reason 'is the flight after the unattainable' (FR, 65), because it aims at generalisation and clearness. Final causation contradicts the physical tendency towards decay.

'In our experience, we find Reason and speculative imagination' (FR, 89). This kind of reason is vague, but it is directed towards final causation; when it aims at ideal ends it becomes speculative reason.

Whitehead's speculative reason is creative; like the flight of an airplane, it aims at an enlargement of reality and at our grasp of it. Generalisation is not reduction; it is the growth of an ever-vaster reality. It is our grasping of reality, getting greater and greater.

Reason thus rejects the tendency towards decay and fosters the upward trend leading us to speculative imagination and growing generalisation. This is how Whitehead explains evolution in his 1929 *The Function of Reason*.

In the Harvard lectures of 1924–25, Whitehead is fairly concerned with the theory of evolution and the concept of environment. He is conscious of Darwin's idea of the survival of the fittest, and seems also to have been familiar with Herbert Spencer's ideas on evolution. The ideas he expresses on evolution are not wholly identical with the ideas he expresses in *The Function of Reason* and *Process and Reality*. But they appear to be a first emergence of his evolution theory, and they are coherent with what comes later.

Value and emergence are in some way introductory to evolution. 'To ask how anything is real is to ask for the unity of all things. "Emerged by reason of itself, by exclusion of irrelevance" for itself – (hence value?) Emergence of value' (HL1, 121). Individuality and self-determination are patent in this excerpt of Hocking's notes. Value emerges because coming into being is possible, because actual entities are self-determining and unique. Their individuation creates value. And it excludes irrelevance by way of self-creation.

According to Bell's notes, the emergence of value is the outcome of a process of selection that excludes what is irrelevant to process. The emergence of individuality thus requires the emergence of value. Selection is a 'determinative' that works as the conditioning of the future (HL1, 120). Again, the outcome is an individual that brings value into the world. Selection determines and conditions future reality.

Metaphysics should focus on the order of nature. Nothing really new can be said about it unless we take the path of Whiteheadian generalisation, which is able to unveil an ever-vaster reality. But that is not to be found immediately around us. The permanence of matter in some way builds up evolution, change and progress. Unity of pattern is found in actual potentiality, the path to individuality. As entities emerge, a historical route can be found which has unity and identity of pattern. But pattern is really an abstraction. Concreteness is needed in the real world; realisation is not attained through a simple route. 'Mere route in itself has no survival unity (of pattern) in it' (HL1, 134). Emergence of a certain entity comes with endurance; the permanence of pattern is completed by the re-emergence of pattern, but that also enables actuality and its very own survival. Survival is no more than re-emergence. The historical route is built up as the pattern repeats itself in concrete re-emergence. 'The value being realised is such as, when passes into actual effectiveness, to reproduce its own pattern along the continuous route' (HL1, 134–135). The environment is an element in this process of emergence. 'Each organism to some extent creates its own environment – Previous life of organism has stamped itself somehow on whole present environment' (HL1, 135). Re-emergence is re-invention; it introduces novelty into the world, and in so doing somehow creates it. But pattern and stability are also important elements in this process, laying the necessary foundations for creation. Creatures are not isolated from the world in which they emerge.

The environment is thus an element in the process of becoming. It is not a pre-given frame, where living creatures are placed in order to transform themselves, in accordance with the already formed features of the surroundings.

The classical theory of evolution holds that the environment is given and that living beings have to adapt themselves to it. But Whitehead sees it quite differently. Organisms create their own surroundings so that the environment can favour them: 'think of Brazilian Forest – No individual tree could have grown without its environment. They produced an environment favourable to each other. That's really the Key! Those animals die out which passively fit themselves to environment. The great lizards e.g. [It's the restless ones that survive]' (HL1, 135). Only 'isolated or feeble groups of entities' can be considered within the classical viewpoint of a being adapted to the environment. Ordinary organisms work as societies. Higher beings are the result of these societies.

The concept of 'societies' seems to originate in the Harvard lectures. It is a crucial concept in *Process and Reality*. Notwithstanding, societies *per se* are not included in the categories of existence; instead we have nexüs (plural of nexus). 'A society is a nexus with social order; and an "enduring object" or "enduring creature" is a society whose social order has taken the special form of "personal order"' (PR, 34). But the term 'society' also has to do with the order of nature, because a society is a nexus of 'actual entities, which are "ordered" among themselves' (PR, 89). A society is much more than a mathematical concept that can be identified as a set. It is 'self-sustaining' and 'its own reason' (PR, 89). Its members bear a close resemblance, but their common character – by forcing itself on the members of the society – leads to the likeness that exists among its members. In other words, a society has a specified character common to every one of its members; but that specified character is the outcome of an environment that results from the society itself (PR, 89).

> Thus a society is, for each of its members, an environment with some element of order in it, persisting by reason of the genetic relations between its own members. Such an element of order is the order prevalent in the society.
>
> But there is no society in isolation. Every society must be considered with its background of a wider environment of actual entities. (PR, 90)

In the Harvard lectures, one can find the following statement: 'The plasticity of the environment is the Key to the Evolutionary problem and that of Permanence' (HL1, 135). The idea of a symbiosis between the environment and the evolving creatures that generate it and need it in order to exist seems to have given rise to the concept of societies; the environment is certainly the necessary setting for societies to emerge. But it does not precede them; it comes about with societies. In the same way, evolving beings are not preceded by a container-like environment which pre-exists their appearance. Both evolving beings and the environment come about at the same time and co-exist in a spontaneous symbiotic process. The plasticity of the environment is also the ultimate reason for the permanence that can be found in reality. As the environment adapts to the beings that originate it, it endures. It is always there, but it exhibits transformations and changes which are the outcome of its adaptation to the beings that cause it to exist. This intermingling of evolving beings and the environment that they adapt to themselves is inextricable, and one cannot live without the other. But it also reveals time in its different views. Permanence is one of those aspects; endurance is another. These two concepts may have some common characteristics, but in Whiteheadian philosophy they are not equivalents. Permanence relates to the repetition of patterns and forms and to the permanency of things in the world, like mountains or stones, whereas endurance is connected with the continued maintenance of a being in a temporal framework. Permanence is the cause of order (PR, 238). It is an element in the flux, and there is no flux without permanence (PR, 337). Endurance is associated with change (PR, 136).

This temporal context is highly relevant for societies and also for evolution. But we cannot help noticing that the mould behind the explanation of evolution and the mould behind societies is the same; societies in some way end up translating what is a light philosophical concept and also a biological one into an ontological construct, which relates to the introduction of value in reality. Thus we get back to emergence as a self-determining and self-defining process. What emerges, emerges by reason of itself, by exclusion of irrelevance, by inclusion of value into itself and into the world. This is true for actual entities, which re-arrange themselves into societies, also providing the background environment for societies to become true societies. If we take the ontological standpoint, we realise that existence requires the emergence of value, and it also requires permanence in order to survive. Survival is a re-invention and a re-emergence. From a more ontological point of view, it is progress and change. It represents what Whitehead called later an upward trend. The upward trend is related to evolution when this word takes the meaning of a positive, advancing progression towards a worthy objective. It does not consider, as such, regression

and downward, downgrading experiences. This Whiteheadian concept of evolution is somehow optimistic. Change and evolution seem to be positive and
part of an advancing progress. This is only possible due to permanence. Entities
emerge as part of a historical route. There is a permanence of pattern, and pattern keeps re-emerging. But emergence cannot be dissociated from endurance;
the permanence of pattern that keeps reappearing leads to actuality. The re-
emerging actual entity is keeping up with its very own survival. And the plasticity of the environment is an important element in this process of re-emerging
emergence, which is really a process of self-creation and creation of the world.
Stability enables progress and change.

Louise R. Heath's notes taken at Radcliffe College are also very interesting when considering the question of evolution. In these lectures, the relation between evolution and time seems to be more obvious. The main idea,
that of the adaptation of the environment to organism, is also prominent
(HL1, 459). Interestingly it is followed by a reference to the evolution of the
laws of nature: 'Very laws of nature may be considered the product of a gradual
evolution' (HL1, 459). The laws governing societies only arise because of the
character similarity of actual entities. And the 'arbitrary . . . elements in the
laws of nature warn us that we are in a special cosmic epoch. Here the phrase
"cosmic epoch" is used to mean that widest society of actual entities whose
immediate relevance to ourselves is traceable' (PR, 91). Societies emerge in
virtue of the background environment that enhances the relationships and
kinship amongst themselves. Evolution can then be described as the evolving
symbiosis between societies and their environment.

The advance of nature is not a linear one; time is not linear either. Only
expansion expresses the way the world evolves. 'In order to get around the
notion that in modern science linear quality of time was rather thrown over &
get expansiveness. Then whole spatio-temporal point of view may be considered an evolution, i.e. other forms of issue, or transition lying behind space-
time' (HL1, 460–1).

Space-time is no container-like milieu where entities are placed and
moved. It is a 'field of action' (HL1, 461). Space-time evolves just like any
other element in the universe. The past does not vanish as is depicted in classical theories of time. The past is in the present. The concept of endurance
seems to coincide with the evolution of societies, 'which create a favourable
environment for similar entities. Not of one species but of an association of
2 or 3 species. Also differentiation within species' (HL1, 461). Evolution is a
certain process of differentiation pertaining to a certain unity. The presence
of the past in the present is thus essential for the evolution of societies and
is at the root of endurance. The creation of a 'favourable environment' is

not arbitrary; it is the outcome of a field of action described as space-time. Whitehead 'suspects that real space-time is an evolution i.e. a certain differentiation between fundamental unity' (HL1, 461).

Heath also states that Whitehead refers to the Darwinian concept of ruthless competition, which should be replaced by that of 'mutual aid' as suggested by Prince Kropotkin. Mutual aid[2] is as true an element in evolution as competition. Her notes capture a significant limitation of evolution, which is usually disregarded: 'there is a great deal of environment that you can't alter, ex. – Absolute untameableness of the sea' (HL1, 461). This last comment underlines the importance of permanence. But this time it is not a re-emergence of form or pattern, but an unavoidable matter of fact that presents itself beyond any possibility of evolution. It is a very interesting idea that Whitehead does not develop in his subsequent work.

Louise Heath thus shows how Whitehead was concerned with different viewpoints on evolution that were being disseminated at the time he was lecturing at Harvard. His wide perspective on evolution – not restricted merely to Darwin's theory – led him to an original theory of evolution that emphasised time, the dialectical symbiosis between beings and their environment, and the overall importance of the environment. His evolutionary doctrine emphasised that beings adapt the environment to their needs, and dismissed the idea that beings necessarily adapt to their surroundings. It was indeed a very bold idea which is still largely ignored today.

The idea that beings adapt the environment to themselves rather than adapting to their surroundings is preserved in Whitehead's philosophical oeuvre. The concept of societies in *Process and Reality* also seems to emerge from these preliminary investigations. However, in the Harvard lectures, reason is not yet associated with evolution, and it certainly is not presented as its guiding force. Reason does not yet act upon the environment in order to scrutinise its surroundings, tracking down final causation and the aims of action.

In the Harvard lectures, Whitehead mainly explores the symbiotic relationships between beings and their environment, enhancing the importance and the power of creatures that adapt the environment to their needs and evolutional process. It is indeed a very important, unorthodox and fresh idea.

## Notes

1. Cf. Paul A. Bogaard's chapter in this volume, 'Whitehead and His Philosophy of Evolution'.
2. Cf. Brian Henning's chapter in this volume, 'Whitehead in Class'.

# Bibliography

Bogaard, Paul and Jason Bell (eds), *The Harvard Lectures of Alfred North Whitehead, 1924–1925: Philosophical Presuppositions of Science* (Edinburgh: Edinburgh University Press, 2017).

Whitehead, Alfred North, *The Concept of Nature* (Cambridge: Cambridge University Press, [1920] 2000).

Whitehead, Alfred North, *Science and the Modern World* (New York: The Free Press, [1925] 1967).

Whitehead, Alfred North, *The Function of Reason* (Boston: Beacon Press, [1929] 1958).

Whitehead, Alfred North, *Process and Reality: An Essay in Cosmology* (New York: The Free Press, [1929] 1978).

Whitehead, Alfred North, *Adventures of Ideas* (New York: The Free Press, [1933] 1967).

Whitehead, Alfred North, *Modes of Thought* (New York: Free Press, [1938] 1966).

# 5

# Whitehead's Biological Turn

*Dennis Sölch*

In recent years, the individual sciences have increasingly drawn on the concept of process as a fundamental heuristic category. Today, there is a large and growing number of sub-disciplines with a process label, as for example process physics, process linguistics, process theology, or process psychology, to name only a few. This development is by no means limited to the humanities, and insofar as both various natural sciences and disciplines within the humanities are using process ontologies for a critical reflection and partial revision of their basic concepts, one may justifiably speak of a *processual turn*. Biology has come to be the domain to which process ontology is most fruitfully applied. Fundamental biological concepts such as 'cells', 'environment' or 'species' are increasingly regarded as oversimplified abstractions that have played an important role during the phase of the increasing mathematisation and formalisation of biology and chemistry, but appear to be rather deficient in the full light of today's empirical findings and theoretical developments. Such notions, originally derived from physics, fail to do justice to the essential interdependence of a living being and its environment, and are inadequate for a coherent description of both human and nonhuman organisms, because they are taken to be part of a bottom-up hierarchy. Molecules and macromolecules, such as DNA, are conceived of as primitive elements that combine to form organisational levels of higher complexity, as for example tissue or an individual organism. Since more complex structures provide novel properties not displayed by the more primitive elements, this generally leaves us with a rather unsatisfactory form of supervenience. What is more, the hierarchical order with its more or less static constituents tends to brush aside the enormous diversity and complexity of the observed phenomena, especially including the inescapable relationality of the entities in question. In this sense, as Dupré stresses, biology rests on 'a naïve conception of the organism'[1] that calls for a problematisation of the very idea of molecules and cells as basic constituents of life.

This problematisation has given rise to process biology, which aims at developing an alternative biological framework that is inclusive of non-mechanistic and non-reductive explanations of relationality or final causation. Pioneering works by Dupré or Koutroufinis seek to redefine or replace the relatively static ontology with discrete individuals underlying current biological theories with more dynamic and holistic concepts. In both cases, Whitehead's philosophy serves as a point of departure, if not of continuous orientation. For Koutroufinis, Whitehead's metaphysics offers itself as a valuable conceptual resource, because a successful overcoming of the theoretical limitations of biology's notion of organism seems to require 'a philosophically elaborate concept of "process"',[2] informed but not determined by the scientific practice. Recourse to an elaborate vocabulary for precise descriptions of processual micro- and macrostructures appears to be particularly helpful, since every attempt at describing the autonomy of organisms with regard to aspects of growth or regeneration in a formal language that is based on strictly quantitative relations reveals the 'principal limits of contemporary biological causal mechanisms'.[3] Dupré, on the other hand, in one of his most recent publications rather sees himself as someone who stands in the tradition of the biological organicists inspired by Whiteheadian process philosophy. While acknowledging Whitehead's criticism of philosophical abstractions and his historical importance for the development of process thinking, Dupré (and his co-author Nicholson) wish to distance themselves 'from the association with Whitehead's metaphysics'.[4] Although the reasons for this distancing – the 'unconventional meanings to familiar concepts', 'a number of neologisms' and 'idiosyncratic technical terms'[5] in *Process and Reality* – strike me as somewhat artificial, the process biological trajectory is similar to that in Koutroufinis: process philosophy (has) provided a paradigm shift from mechanist materialism to processual organicism that theoretical biologists adopt(ed) for a more coherent framing of their own views.

One of the ideas to be addressed critically in the philosophy of biology is that of an organism as essentially determined through its morphological structure, which in turn allows for particular functions. As Dupré has pointed out, it is indeed extremely difficult to clearly separate morphological elements and to ascribe specific functions to them. Genes, cells and complex organisms rather appear to be 'static abstractions from life processes, and different abstractions provide different perspectives on these processes'.[6] The same holds true for the distinction between a living being and its environment, which is not fixed, and which cannot be determined by recourse to given and experimentally definable parameters. Instead, biological organisms in each situation contribute to the definition of what their actual environment consists in, so that organisms and their respective environment mutually and continuously constitute each other.

Process metaphysics, especially that of Whiteheadian provenance, provides the platform and linguistic tools for a critical transformation of biological theory.[7] Process biology, as the most fruitful proponent of various process ontologies and process-oriented sub-domains of the individual sciences, thus appears to be an application of a more comprehensive process metaphysics. Historically or chronologically, then, Whitehead's philosophy comes before the revolutionary development in theoretical biology and can be said to have at least contributed to that development.

The recently published notes of Whitehead's lectures on the *Philosophical Presuppositions of Science*, however, paint a somewhat different picture. Whitehead himself, as can be seen in the manuscripts, was heavily indebted to theoretical biology. While his interest in questions of metaphysics and epistemology began with his work in the fields of physics and mathematics, biological concepts and categories became influential for Whitehead at a crucial stage of his philosophical development. According to his student Louise Heath, Whitehead referred to the modern era of science as the 'biological age' (HL1, 463) in his Radcliffe lectures – a statement that is particularly striking, if one takes seriously the fact that Whitehead refers to his own ontology as a 'philosophy of organism', and that he repeatedly refers to contemporary biologists in his published work, including his Harvard colleagues Lawrence Henderson and William Morton Wheeler. In short, there is a lot of evidence to suggest that while modern process biology can to a large extent be regarded as an application of process metaphysics, the genesis of Whitehead's own process metaphysics is inextricably linked to the development of theoretical biology. As Henderson remarked in his almost unnoticed 1926 review of *Science and the Modern World*, 'the main affinities of Whitehead's central hypothesis are biological'.[8] What is more, the turn to biology is not only of philosophical significance, but, according to Whitehead, is also meant to come to the rescue of physics, which seemed to have reached a dead end in the early twentieth century. Hence, a detailed assessment of the first volume of the Critical Edition promises to shed light on the extent to which Whitehead was indebted to biology and the biologists of his time.

## Dead End Streets in Physics

Whitehead's early philosophical work, up to *The Concept of Nature*, is an attempt at unifying the philosophic presuppositions of the natural sciences. It seeks to set physics on a firmer basis in the sense of fleshing out a coherent and viable concept of nature that avoids a bifurcation into primary and secondary qualities and leaves out metaphysics – including the question as to 'the "why" of knowledge' (CN, 32) – as much as possible. Whitehead's aim here is to explicate the status of the concepts indispensable to physics against the background of the fullness of our sense perception. In contrast to classical physics, it emphasises the fundamental relatedness of events and objects as opposed to the disconnectedness of independent entities localised in space and time. Yet, while in *The Concept of Nature* he is already conceiving of events as 'the ultimate fact for sense-awareness' (CN, 15), the focus is still on 'material entities in space and time' (CN, 16) as the subject matter of science in general. The subsequent exposition of space and time as an interconnection of events draws on the analogy to the concept of electromagnetic fields. The notion of science meant to form the starting point for the philosophical inquiry is largely that of physics.

Half a decade later, in *Science and the Modern World*, the picture has become much more encompassing. 'Science is taking on a new aspect which is neither purely physical, nor purely biological. It is becoming the study of organisms' (SMW, 103). With the dawn of the twentieth century, Whitehead sees science in the midst of a paradigm shift, and the book is a narrative of the scientific development up to that shift. The great merit of *Science and the Modern World* does not consist in its contribution to the history of science so much as in its endeavour to explicate the metaphysical or cosmological assumptions hovering in the background of all the scientific theories of a given period. Its object is not science, but the implicit presuppositions of each scientific outlook dominant during a particular historical epoch. Crucially, the implicit presuppositions of all the dominant scientific outlooks since the seventeenth century rest on the same kinds of abstraction, namely the idea of matter as a passive bearer of properties, including the distinction between primary and secondary qualities, and the idea that matter can be unequivocally defined by reference to a location in space and time. The natural sciences in general, on this analysis, are pervaded by the fallacy of simple location, because they all take for granted the abstractions at work in classical physics.

The Harvard lectures on the *Philosophical Presuppositions of Science* spell out many of the details that are lost in the grand panorama of *Science and the Modern World*. They lack almost completely the historical or genealogical dimension that provides a narrative structure and makes the published work a nice piece of literature. Instead, they come right to the heart of the matter, which in Whitehead's case is twofold: First, the philosophical critique of scientific abstractions concerns the search for coherence. In this sense, the lectures continue the earlier studies in the philosophy of nature and aim at a coherent epistemological account of the unity of the objective world underlying the pluralism of phenomena and divergent theoretical descriptions. Second, the philosophical presuppositions of science are shown to be highly relevant for science itself, particularly for the field of physics. The argument unfolded through many of the lectures in the first half of the course is that physics has reached a dead end. Its further progress seems to be restricted to details and minor problems, while the theoretical foundation 'shakes and rattles' – to borrow Emerson's expression – in the face of irreconcilable data. These, Whitehead indicates, might hopefully be overcome by a philosophical modification of the underlying paradigmatic assumptions of physics.

The first dilemma encountered by physics is having to explain the equal validity of two conflicting theories of light. In the context of quantum theory, the corpuscular theory of light and the wave theory appear to be equally feasible. The state of science, Whitehead remarks, has hardly changed over the previous forty years. We have to use the wave theory on Monday, Wednesday and Friday, leaving the corpuscular theory for Tuesday, Thursday and Saturday (HL1, 12). The two models are '[u]tterly contradictory and yet each explains one enormous mass of phenomena, which the other doesn't; and vice versa' (HL1, 12). As long as there is no unifying theory which would allow us to decide in advance when to use which theoretical approach, physics has to cope with a degree of contingency that obstructs further progress, because we are forced to resort to the method of trial and error with regard to the feasibility of the respective theoretical models.

The second obstacle encountered by physics, Whitehead indicates, is due to the 'habit of thinking [of the] Electron as much more concrete than it really is' (HL1, 26). An electron is treated as a subatomic particle with a certain radius, and although the electron is regarded as punctate, the electron radius is a standard constant in physical formulas. The concept of electrons as concrete particles akin to bits of matter here turns out to be at odds with the concept of electromagnetic fields, in which the effect is spread out across three dimensions. Whitehead stresses, as the quotation marks in Winthrop Bell's lecture notes certainly indicate, that instead of an electronic particle all he sees is a "little spot of mist" (HL1, 26). Regarding an electron as a corpuscular entity thus means committing the fallacy of misplaced concreteness:

All you really want of the Electron is a sort of structural or imposed character with a focal centre in the sphere we call the Electron. That type of vibration with that focal location. Electrons would be, then, highly abstract in relation to concrete fact of Electro-magnetic field. (HL1, 26)

An electron, hence, may on the one hand be considered as a particle with an extension in space, even though this extension might be minute, and on the other hand it is a structured field with a focal centre and blurry edges. Experimental observation, theoretical interpretation and mathematical formalisation do not form a coherent picture.

Physics, Whitehead makes clear, is entangled in problems that it cannot seem to solve, because a possible solution would hinge on the same paradigms that have caused the problems in the first place. The 'progress in science has now reached a turning point' (HL1, 28), where physics will either manage to successfully revise its fundamental concepts so as to avoid theoretical dead ends or become a mere orthodoxy with an increasingly smaller explanatory power. Philosophy has so far provided no alternative framework. Metaphysics had taken the path of Cartesian dualism, with two different types of substances to be described by recourse to incompatible paradigms, and was now finding itself in problems similar to those encountered in physics. Accordingly, it was time to look out for alternative approaches to reshape both physics and metaphysics in order to turn them into adequate and coherent theories once again. Fortunately, this alternative approach was just being developed in the field of biology.

## Theoretical Biology

While physics, according to Whitehead, seemed to have reached the boundaries of its conceptual inventory, biology was experiencing a phase of rapid theoretical and experimental progress, with which the conceptual apparatus could not always keep up. Three biologists in particular were eagerly working on fleshing out the new theoretical framework and developing the corresponding conceptual tools. Two of them were Whitehead's colleagues at Harvard, namely Lawrence Joseph Henderson, professor of biochemistry and chemistry from 1919 to 1942,[9] and William Morton Wheeler, professor of applied biology from 1908 until 1937. The third pioneer was John Scott Haldane, reader in physiology at Oxford, who was awarded an honorary professorship at Birmingham in 1923.

The time when Whitehead was beginning to teach in Harvard coincides with the culmination of a development that had been going on for almost a century. At its core lay the question as to the nature of life. Beginning with the Cartesian separation of the body, characterised by its mere physical extension in space, from an active and living mind, mechanism was fuelled by the mathematisation of science in the seventeenth century. Extended matter was taken to be the subject-matter of science in general, leaving biology faced with

the problem of accounting for the phenomenon of life in some of these material bodies. Until around the end of the nineteenth century, the lines in the
'perennial battle between Mechanism and Vitalism' (HL1: 153) regarding the
explanation of life, especially consciousness and voluntary action, were rather
sharply drawn, with reductive materialism or mechanism on the one hand,
and vitalism on the other hand as the two explanatory paradigms.

As a distinctly biological theory, materialism had gained momentum in the
early nineteenth century, with Helmholtz, Schleiden and Du Bois-Reymond
seeking to explain physiological activity by recourse to the principles of mathematical physics. Despite the undeniable progress in measurement and classification afforded by the early mechanist school, the underlying philosophy 'was
quite naïve'.[10] For example, in his study on the fundamental limits of human
knowledge of nature, Du Bois-Reymond insisted that scientific explanations
consist in 'the reduction of all changes in the physical world to movements
of atoms',[11] i.e. in breaking up natural processes into a mechanism of atoms.
Mechanics seemed to involve the same apodictic certainty as mathematics,
requiring nothing more of a causal explanation than describing the effects
of the potential and kinetic energy of atoms in organic bodies. The ensuing
impossibility of a coherent philosophy of nature capable of integrating mind
and nature was explicitly accepted. The demand for an adequate and coherent explanation not only could not be fulfilled, but, as Cassirer succinctly
stresses, it could not even be raised in a sensible way.[12] Neither the nature of
matter and force, nor the connection between mental activity and its material
conditions, according the Du Bois-Reymond, can ever be understood. 'And so
will it ever be.'[13]

Vitalism, which had evolved as a countermovement to the reductive materialism, was apt at pointing out the flaws in mechanistic explanations of life.
Yet, it failed to offer a convincing alternative that could be scientifically utilised. The vitalists' criticism had an impeccable logic in advancing 'a number
of perfectly valid refutations'[14] of mechanism, but their own theories generally amounted to the mere stipulation of a living force required on top of the
Cartesian materialism. In general agreement with Bergson, Whitehead rejects
vitalist thinking as fundamentally short-sighted, insofar as its methodology is
at odds with the whole endeavour of modern science without providing an
adequate account of the interrelation between final and efficient causation
(HL1, 159).

This stalemate situation ended at the beginning of the twentieth century
with the emergence of an organismic paradigm. Confronted with the complexity of chemical and physiological coordination that proved to be incapable
of a mechanical explanation in agreement with Newtonian physics, the study

of living organisms was seen to require a new foundation. The description of isolable physical or chemical phenomena began to be replaced by the idea of an integrated coordination. This more holistic perspective found expression in the concept of an organism as a self-regulating system which maintains a dynamic equilibrium and continually adapts to changing circumstances. 'An organism', according to Wheeler, 'is a complex, definitely coördinated and therefore individualised system of activities, which are primarily directed to obtaining and assimilating substances from an environment, to producing other similar systems, known as offspring, and to protecting the system itself and usually also its offspring from disturbances emanating from the environment.'[15] The organism does not stand for a unit with neatly defined limits, but is defined as a process bent on preserving coherence while interacting with its dynamic surroundings. In this sense, Wheeler 'intentionally blurs the clear distinction between an organism and its environment'.[16] The role of the environment thus shifts dramatically. Instead of forming a mere setting for the struggles of individual plants and animals, it becomes an integral constituent of the organism itself.

The significance of the environment as an essential factor in the maintenance of an organism as an organism is elaborated by Lawrence Henderson, whom Whitehead in *Process and Reality* explicitly credits with having provided a foundation for any discussion on the issue of the order of nature (PR, 89n). For Henderson, biological fitness is not simply a one-way relation, but a reciprocal relationship between organism and environment. The physico-chemical environment itself is not considered a self-evident given, but as crucial to the very idea of fitness. Fitness, as Henderson explains, had previously been treated as an independent variable. 'Yet fitness there must be, in the environment as well as in the organism.'[17] Fitness is not only a property of living matter, but also refers to the physical elements and the cosmos as a whole. As a result of his detailed study of the specific properties of water and carbon, Henderson concludes that they are uniquely fitted to allow for the development and maintenance of living systems. Considering the complexity of life and the ideal balance of the physical and chemical preconditions for its existence, he rejects the idea of chance association of inorganic molecules in the course of evolution.[18] Rather, the close interdependence of living organisms and their specific environments should be seen as an intricate organisational unit. This paradigmatic shift from the environment as a mere variable to something constitutive of the organism as such receives further differentiation. Henderson distinguishes between, on the one hand, an external environment with a high degree of stability allowing the organism to endure and, on the other hand, an internal environment in complex organisms that provides further protection to safeguard from quick changes in the external environment.[19]

One of the earliest statements that explicitly comment on this paradigm change in our understanding of nature was made by John Scott Haldane, who in 1908 predicted: 'That a meeting-point between biology and physical science may at some time be found, there is no reason for doubting. But we may confidently predict that when that meeting-point is found, and one of the two sciences is swallowed up, that one will not be biology.'[20] The rise in importance of biology was almost a scientific commonplace in the early twentieth century. Yet, few went as far as Haldane in seeing physics swallowed up by biology, and hardly anybody would even think of spelling out what physics might look like when digested by biology – or maybe rather when cooked after a recipe written in biological vocabulary. Whitehead is the exception, and the Harvard lectures provide a look into the laboratory in which the attempt was being made to put physics and metaphysics on a new foundation.

## Whitehead's Biological Turn

The rapid development in biology did not go unnoticed. Particularly the new vistas opened up by genetics and molecular biology seized the attention of scientists and philosophers, especially those with speculative inclinations, who sought to spell out their practical applications and long-term consequences in social, economic and political matters. The most prominent example among the scientific utopians was Haldane's son, John Burdon Sanderson Haldane, who later became known mainly as one of the founders of population genetics. His famous essay *Daedalus, or Science and the Future*, published one year before Whitehead's Harvard lectures, predicts an enormous, unprecedented impact of natural science on civilised life over the next generations. According to the essay, the chief value of physics and chemistry, having reached the peak of their theoretical development, lies in industrial and commercial applications, the effect of their respective research being primarily a question of quantitative advances. Biology, in contrast, would provide revolutionary breakthroughs, for example in the field of experimental genetics. As a consequence, the younger Haldane foresees the 'invasion and destruction' of mathematical physics by physiology.[21] Bertrand Russell, who was always quick at popularising new tendencies in the sciences and presenting them in an easily accessible language, replied to Haldane's book with his technology assessment *Icarus, or The Future of Science*. Despite his sceptical view of politics and the ensuing applications of science, Russell fully agrees with Haldane's account of the importance and the future prospects of biology, musing for example on the possibilities of eugenics or of 'controlling the emotional life through secretions of the ductless glands'.[22] Biology, it seems, was increasingly affecting the scientific and philosophical outlook and affirming its far-reaching independence from physics. Whitehead recommended that his students read both books, whose publication marked the beginning of 'a physiological-biological age' (HL1, 149) in which the scientific ideas based on Cartesian dualism and Newtonian physics were breaking down.

And yet, in spite of the increasing attention given to biology, John Scott Haldane justifiably commented that 'the significance of biological science in philosophical survey of our experience [had] hitherto received only scant recognition by philosophical writers'.[23] Theoretical philosophers steeped in a tradition of Newtonian physics were slow to recognise the revolutionary nature of the organismic paradigm. This is particularly true of Russell, who in his survey of *Human Knowledge*, published as late as 1948, completely rejected the idea that 'organism' should be regarded as a fundamental concept in biology. The notion of organism as a functional unit, according to Russell, was part of a dated Aristotelian heritage and stood in the way of scientific progress. 'It is therefore in any case prudent to adopt the mechanistic view as a working hypothesis.'[24] But Russell was not the only one oblivious to the enormous dynamics that had been initiated by theoretical biology and were starting to find their way into metaphysics. Even Haldane's son, the younger Haldane, had difficulties grasping the conceptual novelties that were largely at odds with both materialist and vitalist presuppositions, and in his *Daedalus* suggested that 'the basic metaphysical working hypothesis of science and practical life will . . . be something like Bergsonian activism'.[25] Considering that Bergson's theory of creative evolution effectively remained within the dichotomy of materialism and vitalism by introducing the *élan vital* as the agent responsible solely for future developments of organic life while retaining the materialist framework for the study of existing organic structures, Haldane's reflections simply miss the essential point of the new biological theory. His father, Haldane the elder, as Whitehead recalls, drily judged his son's book to be 'full of bad physiology' (HL1, 149), which in this regard was not the only unsuccessful attempt at understanding the metaphysical implications of Henderson's, Wheeler's and Haldane's works. Indeed, Whitehead was probably the first to fully understand the ground-breaking potential of the new organismic biology for a reinvigoration of physics and metaphysics.

With the stable foundations of physics breaking up, the Harvard lectures, more emphatically even than *Science and the Modern World*, show a straightforward embrace of biology as the science with the greatest prospect for radical innovations. The '[n]ext great advance in Physics [is] to

be made in <u>realm</u> of Biology' (HL1,12), with the underlining of the word
'great' in Bell's lecture notes probably indicating the emphasis of Whitehead's words. It is noteworthy that Whitehead does not speak of the next
scientific advance in general to be expected from biology, but rather that
biology is expected to contribute to the science of physics. The quotation
sounds very much like a prophecy. Biology is expected to both disentangle
itself from the paradigmatic presuppositions in classical physics and in turn
to contribute to a re-evaluation and modification of the foundational concepts in physics itself, allowing for a new unified cosmological perspective.
The biological conception of the organism as an enduring process turns out
to be essential beyond the domain of physiology, if molecules and electrons
are construed as 'another exhibition of organism' (HL1, 153). Following
Henderson, Whitehead appropriates the idea of the integral function of the
environment for the constitution of an organism and significantly extends
the field of its application in a passage worth quoting in full.

> The environment gives <u>its</u> contribution – at least as important as contri-
> bution of <u>other</u> elements. Big question (Whitehead put on to it by L. J.
> Henderson's *Fitness of the Environment*). . . . Each organism to some extent
> creates its own environment – Previous life of organism has stamped itself
> somehow on whole present environment. How to account for <u>enormous</u>
> stability of Electrons etc. and for evolution of things in this order of Nature?
> Whitehead says by survival of fittest. You go back to where within order of
> Nature you had fitful stretches of emergent enduring entities. We've finally
> got an order of Nature dominated by those entities which created an envi-
> ronment favorable not only to themselves but to production of other enti-
> ties of same kind. An Environment i.e. created by a <u>Society</u> of entities
> producing an Environment favourable to existence of them all. <u>Environ-
> ment</u> has evolved <u>as</u> an Environment which secures selection of definite
> types. The plasticity of the Environment is the <u>Key</u> to the Evolutionary
> problem and that of Permanence. (HL1, 135)

Whitehead's enthusiasm shines through the notes taken by Winthrop Bell.
Both in the world of living matter and in the realm of physical objects, an
environment is never a mere background for events, but always a particular environment for a particular organism which it helped to bring forth.
This environment, in turn, is modified by the organism in order to produce stable conditions favourable to the organism's future existence.[26] With
regard to the dichotomy of the electron as a particle and electromagnetic
fields, the individual entity here must be conceived as taking account of the

field it is embedded in and vice versa: 'The Entity then isn't the Entity in itself alone but in interaction with [its] Environment' (HL1, 93). Instead of having to choose between a particle theory and a field theory, both of which yield correct results within certain limits, the two aspects should be seen as mutually dependent factors within an organic process. For the physicist, the relational dimension of an organism's embeddedness in an environment 'can be expressed in Spatio-temporal terms' (HL1, 113). The notion of the particular location of an electron loses its sense, if it is considered as a mere particle apart from the field. At the same time, the field or environment forms the necessary background against which it becomes possible to talk about individuality or particularity: An entity considered in isolation does not refer to a concrete individual (HL1, 115), but only to an abstract pattern, since concreteness implies the embeddedness in a specific environment. The structure of the whole context in which an entity is situated influences the character of the individual organism, so that the scope and validity of the theory of materialism is limited to the discussion of abstract patterns or formulas. The lectures thus constitute a first approach to one of the central aspects of Whitehead's magnum opus *Process and Reality*, in which the seeming dichotomy between particularity and universality finds expression in the mutual dependence of actual entities and eternal objects.

The transference of the biological and physiological conception of the organism to the domain of physics has a bearing on the concept of evolution, too. Anticipating the critique of the simplified interpretations of evolutionary theory in *The Function of Reason*, Whitehead not only rejects the notion of a one-sided adaptation of an organism to an environment as early as in the 1924 lectures, but also elaborates on the idea of the duration of societies of organisms. An entity may not be identical with a particular pattern, but due to its embedded nature it necessarily goes along with a pattern favourable to its own duration through time. Illustrating the quintessential role of the environment for an individual entity and for entities of the same type by the example of the Brazilian rainforest (HL1, 135; SMW, 206), Whitehead once again extends the scope of Henderson's work, this time by taking up the distinction between interior and exterior milieu: the production of a supportive environment that 'takes care' of an object accounts for endurance and leads to the conception of increasingly stable societies and species. When it comes to higher, i.e. more complex objects, an organism can be seen as an ingredient of other objects. A molecule that is part of the human body, like an electron existing in that molecule, is what it is by being part of the whole body with its peculiar structural pattern. However, that does not mean that the physicist or

the biological chemist would always have to deal with a totality (HL1, 174):
The whole is always exemplified in the concrete, and at the same time the
most concrete elements of our experience contain the most general characteristics of the world.

## Conclusion

While Henderson, almost immediately after the publication of *Science and the
Modern World* – the condensed outcome of Whitehead's Harvard lectures –
commented that 'to the biologists, this book is so important that we may not
yet venture to estimate its importance',[27] the astonishing biological dimension
of the philosophy of organism did for a long time become quite forgotten.
Thus, the late Dorothy Emmet, in her reminiscences of her philosophical life,
remarks that, having listened to Whitehead's Lowell lectures at Harvard, she
had hoped 'he was going to work out a general theory of organism which
might bridge the physical and biological sciences',[28] which, according to her
impression, he did not accomplish. Even earlier, in 1931, John Haldane, while
agreeing with Whitehead on the necessity of formulating a new metaphysical theory that is apt to account for biological principles, critically declares
that Whitehead 'is somewhat confused through attempting to conceive an
organism apart from its environment'.[29] Yet, the new volume of *The Harvard
Lectures* clearly shows that both Haldane's and Emmet's critical comments
are mistaken.

   In the course of his lectures on the philosophical presuppositions of science, Whitehead time and again stresses that an organism can only be adequately understood in its entanglement with its environment. An organism
is characterised through its emergence from a particular environment, its
dependence on the environment and its active contribution to that environment. Events, occasions or actual entities are not detached from their
surroundings, but intrinsically related to them. And yet, pace Haldane, it is
sometimes tremendously helpful to speak of organisms as atomic – as Whitehead does in *Process and Reality* – since otherwise we would be left with environment only, unable to accommodate human subjectivity or to give account
of causality. As we have seen, neither the physicist nor the biological chemist
is supposed to refer to a mere totality, insofar as this totality is exemplified in
the concrete object. Moreover, pace Emmet, Whitehead does indeed bridge
the physical and biological sciences. The path illustrated by the course of his
lectures leads from dilemmas encountered in the domain of physics to the
field of biology in order to develop a theory 'which is neither purely physical,
nor purely biological' (SWM, 129). It applies biological concepts both to the

theoretical foundations of physics, and, for that matter, to the ontological presuppositions of science in general. The new physics as well as the new metaphysics that finally emerge may justifiably be said to have made a giant leap towards a more unified concept of nature.

## Notes

1. Dupré, *Processes of Life*, 91.
2. Koutroufinis, 'Organism, Machine, Process', 21.
3. Koutroufinis, 'Organism, Machine, Process', 32.
4. Dupré and Nicholson, 'Manifesto for a Processual Philosophy', 6.
5. Dupré and Nicholson, 'Manifesto for a Processual Philosophy', 7.
6. Dupré, *Processes of Life*, 85.
7. Cf. the collection of essays in Henning and Scarfe, *Beyond Mechanism*, and in Nicholson and Dupré, *Everything Flows*.
8. Henderson, 'Philosophical Interpretation of Nature', 293.
9. Paul A. Bogaard's article on Whitehead's philosophy of evolution, also published in this volume, not only elaborates on various aspects of Henderson's thought only hinted at in my essay, but also provides helpful information on the biographical connections between Whitehead and Henderson (cf. pp. 80–2).
10. Mayr, *This is Biology*, 6.
11. Du Bois-Reymond, 'Limits of Our Knowledge', 17.
12. Cf. Cassirer, *Determinism and Indeterminism*, 5.
13. Du Bois-Reymond, 'Limits of Our Knowledge', 29.
14. Mayr, *This is Biology*, 12.
15. Wheeler, 'Ant-Colony as Organism', 308.
16. Sölch, 'Wheeler and Whitehead', 498.
17. Henderson, *Fitness of the Environment*, 6.
18. Cf. Fry, 'Biological Significance', 180.
19. Cf. Henderson, *Fitness of the Environment*, 32f.
20. Haldane, 'Relation of Physiology', 696.
21. Cf. Haldane, *Daedalus*, 16.
22. Russell, *Icarus*, 53.
23. Haldane, *Philosophy of a Biologist*, 30.
24. Russell, *Human Knowledge*, 36.
25. Haldane, *Daedalus*, 16.
26. Maria-Teresa Teixeira, in her article in this volume on the concept of evolution in Whitehead's Harvard lectures, speaks of 'a symbiosis between the environment and the evolving creatures' (p. 96).
27. Henderson, 'Philosophical Interpretation of Nature', 293f.
28. Emmet, 'Whitehead in Cambridge', 41.
29. Haldane, *The Philosophical Basis of Biology*, 35.

# Bibliography

Bogaard, Paul and Jason Bell (eds), *The Harvard Lectures of Alfred North Whitehead, 1924–1925: Philosophical Presuppositions of Science* (Edinburgh: Edinburgh University Press, 2017).

Cassirer, Ernst, *Determinism and Indeterminism in Modern Physics: Historical and Systematic Studies of the Problem of Causality* (Orig. *Determinismus und Indeterminismus in der modernen Physik*), trans. O. Theodor Benfey (New Haven: Yale University Press, 1966).

Du Bois-Reymond, Emil Heinrich, 'The Limits of Our Knowledge of Nature' (Orig. 'Über die Grenzen des Naturerkennens'), trans. J. Fitzgerald, *The Popular Science Monthly*, 5 (1874), 17–32.

Dupré, John, *Processes of Life. Essays in the Philosophy of Biology* (Oxford: Oxford University Press, 2012).

Dupré, John, and Daniel J. Nicholson, 'A Manifesto for a Processual Philosophy of Biology', in Daniel J. Nicholson and John Dupré (eds), *Everything Flows: Towards a Processual Philosophy of Biology* (Oxford: Oxford University Press, 2018), 3–45.

Emmet, Dorothy, 'A. N. Whitehead in Cambridge, Mass.', in *Philosophers and Friends: Reminiscences of Seventy Years in Philosophy* (Basingstoke: Macmillan Press, 1996), 34–49.

Fry, Iris, 'On the Biological Significance of the Properties of Matter: L. J. Henderson's Theory of the Fitness of the Environment', *Journal of the History of Biology*, 29:2 (1996), 155–96.

Haldane, John Burdon Sanderson, *Daedalus, or the Future of Science* (New York: E. Dutton, 1924).

Haldane, John Scott, 'The Relation of Physiology to Physics and Chemistry', *The British Medical Journal* (1908), 693–6.

Haldane, John Scott, *The Philosophical Basis of Biology* (New York: Doubleday, Doran & Company, 1931).

Haldane, John Scott, *The Philosophy of a Biologist* (Oxford: Clarendon Press, 1936).

Henderson, Lawrence Joseph, *The Fitness of the Environment* (Boston: Beacon Press, [1913] 1958).

Henderson, Lawrence Joseph, 'A Philosophical Interpretation of Nature. A Review of *Science and the Modern World: Lowell Lectures*, 1925, by Alfred North Whitehead', *The Quarterly Review of Biology*, 1:2 (1926), 289–94.

Henning, Brian, and Adam C. Scarfe (eds), *Beyond Mechanism: Putting Life Back into Biology* (Lanham: Lexington Books, 2013).

Koutroufinis, Spyridon, 'Organism, Machine, Process: Towards a Process Ontology for Organismic Dynamics', *Organisms. Journal of Biological Sciences*, 1:1 (2017), 19–40.

Mayr, Ernst, *This is Biology: The Science of the Living World* (Cambridge, MA: The Belknap Press of Harvard University Press, 1997).

Nicholson, Daniel J., and John Dupré (eds), *Everything Flows: Towards a Processual Philosophy of Biology* (Oxford: Oxford University Press, 2018).

Russell, Bertrand, *Icarus, or the Future of Science* (Nottingham: Spokesman Books, [1924] 2005).

Russell, Bertrand, *Human Knowledge: Its Scope and Limits* (London and New York: Routledge, [1948] 2009).

Sölch, Dennis, 'Wheeler and Whitehead: Process Biology and Process Philosophy in the Early Twentieth Century', *Journal of the History of Ideas*, 77:3 (2016), 489–507.

Wheeler, William Morton, 'The Ant-Colony as an Organism', *Journal of Morphology*, 22 (1911), 307–25.

Whitehead, Alfred North, *The Concept of Nature* (Cambridge: Cambridge University Press, 1920).

Whitehead, Alfred North, *Science and the Modern World* (New York: The Free Press, [1925] 1967).

Whitehead, Alfred North, *Process and Reality: An Essay in Cosmology* (New York: The Free Press, [1929] 1978).

# Part III

# Physics and Relativity

# 6

# Quanta and Corpuscles: The Influence of Quantum Mechanical Ideas on Whitehead's Transitional Philosophy in Light of *The Harvard Lectures*

*Gary L. Herstein*

Whitehead scholars have invested a great deal of time and *speculative* energy in guessing at the position which quantum mechanical physics occupies in his later metaphysical thought. This has led to various confusions about *applying* Whitehead's process metaphysics *to* the interpretation of quantum mechanics, versus imposing quantum mechanics upon Whitehead's process metaphysics as somehow determining the latter.[1] In a recent book, Auxier and Herstein argued quite forcefully against this latter move,[2] but their argument was still limited by the somewhat speculative nature of interpreting Whitehead's texts. This interpretation was supplemented with some important recent contributions to the history of the quantum theory, but it nevertheless remained speculative, given the paucity of supporting texts (notes, commentaries, etc.) from Whitehead himself.

With the publication of *The Harvard Lectures* (HL1) a significant part of this gap has been filled. One can scarcely offer praise enough to the editors, especially the front-line team of Bogaard and Bell, for their extraordinary work here. But we are not here to praise B&B; rather we're here to analyse Whitehead from the perspective of this marvellous new tool that has been put into our hands.

No small part of this analysis requires that we back away from earlier attempts to marry Whitehead's process metaphysics to the still emerging science of quantum mechanics, especially given the nascent, confused and disorganised state that science found itself in, in the years prior to Whitehead's metaphysical writings. The Auxier and Herstein critique of such moves was predicated upon a close reading of Whitehead's extant texts, such as were available at the time. But they did not have access to anything like Whitehead's own notes, or his transitional thoughts on the subject. With the detailed materials in HL1, we can now turn to Whitehead himself, as reported by his students.

Our first step in this process will involve a brief visit to the actual state of quantum mechanics in the years leading up to, and immediately following, 1925, the completion of Whitehead's first year of lectures at Harvard. Our purchase for this examination will be the historical survey of the fifth Solvay conference on quantum mechanics, which took place in Brussels in October of 1927.

## The Nasty Bump

'Then later another nasty bump in the Quantum Theory' (HL1, 7). This is how Bell reports Whitehead's description of the history leading up to the contemporary scene in quantum mechanics. Given the struggles the quantum brought onto the scientific scene, this phrase betrays no small measure of Victorian dry humour. Describing the scene in physics at the time as 'rampant chaos' would not be exceeding the bounds of historical accuracy. This becomes apparent when we examine the scene of the fifth Solvay conference, which took place in Brussels a full two years *after* Whitehead's first academic year of lecturing. We now have a much better picture of just how chaotic that scene was, even in 1927, than has been previously available.[3]

The conference series first began in 1912, funded by the Belgian industrialist Ernest Solvay.[4] These conferences were thoroughly disrupted by the First World War, and even in the aftermath of that conflict, several years passed before they once again regained their full international stature (which is to say, before Germans were invited to attend). The first of the fully functional conferences was the fifth, which in many ways took on the appearance of a three-ring circus, with no one knowing exactly what was happening in any of the rings. Quite aside from the struggle of bringing people together in the aftermath of the war, important new results from experiments continued to emerge even as the conference was being planned, requiring an ongoing rewrite of the conference programme.

But incorporating the new information into the conference was scarcely the hardest part of the project – rather, *making any sense* of that new information was the real hurdle. There were multiple approaches, multiple mathematical techniques (matrix algebra or wave equations?), seemingly contradictory experimental results, and so on. As Bacciagaluppi and Valenti note (quoting Langevin), 'the Solvay meeting in 1927 was the conference where "the confusion of ideas reached its peak"'.[5] At the end of the conference, the famous physicist Paul Ehrenfest went to the blackboard and wrote out the tale of the Tower of Babel, citing Genesis 11:3–7, to characterise the level of confusion which had been the dominant feature of the conference. (This was recorded as, 'And they said one to another: Go to, let us build us a tower whose top may reach unto heaven; and let us make us a name. And the Lord said: go to, let us go down and there confound their language, that they may not understand one another's speech.'[6])

The point being this: the disruption that the discovery of quantum phenomena introduced into physics was a 'nasty bump' in much the same way that *Thelma and Louise* speeding off the rim of the Grand Canyon was a dip in the road.[7] Scientists were at a compete loss as to how to deal with these new discoveries. The degree of this confusion has largely been washed out of the picture with the popular treatments and histories of the science of the quantum, a fact which in turn was facilitated by the ways in which Niels Bohr and his followers imposed the 'Copenhagen interpretation' upon the data. But despite the ham-fisted methods of Bohr and others to impose their version, many scientists, historians and philosophers have come to the 'realisation that alternative ideas may have been dismissed or unfairly disparaged',[8] a situation many Whiteheadians are themselves well aware of.[9]

What made the quantum theory so disruptive was the introduction of discrete units into phenomena that had previously been taken to be perfectly continuous. Whitehead's response to these puzzles will be discussed shortly, but his ideas on the subject were largely unknown to physicists of the day, who had almost entirely ceased attending to Whitehead's work after he failed to 'bend the knee'[10] before the altar of general relativity. No, their concerns were more narrowly and – sadly enough for all of us – more dogmatically focused. The result was the so-called Copenhagen interpretation[11] of quantum mechanics. A great deal of mythology has arisen about how this interpretation came about, specifically around the debates between Niels Bohr and Albert Einstein, most of it wrong.[12] Much could be said on this subject, but it suffices to note just two things here: One, the 'triumph' of the Copenhagen interpretation was predicated upon a complete misrepresentation of what occurred between Einstein and Bohr at Solvay. This *fact* is not a secret among philosophers and historians of physics, but gatekeepers such as Stephen Hawking have used their position to legislate *ex cathedra* that no attention is to be paid to such scholars due to their failure to 'bend the knee' to orthodoxy.[13] But, secondly, this dogma is itself the ultimate source of the half-joking (if even *half*-joking) command to young and up and coming physicists that they drop all their worries about the foundations of physics, and just 'shut up and calculate'.[14]

This is the context that *emerged* from the period when Whitehead was delivering his 1924–25 lectures. The intellectual chaos that led up to the Solvay conference did not vanish simply because physicists were instructed to ignore it. Whitehead, of course, refused to ignore it, and never embraced the 'shut up and calculate' mentality either before or after it was explicitly formulated. We turn now to the lectures, to get some sense of how Whitehead's thinking in the academic year of 1924–25 can inform our thinking today.

## Whitehead's Lectures: Three Strands to Note

The scholarly significance of the Whitehead lectures are almost impossible to summarise, but within the specific agenda of this essay three general lines of significance can be held up for closer attention. The first of these is also the most important, and can be seen as the root from which the other two branch off. This strand might best be described as the centrality of continuity. Whitehead's emphasis upon modes of continuity dominates the pages of HL1, while still accounting for forms of discrete effects and phenomena. The focus here, however, will remain broadly philosophical in its concern.

The second strand – or, if you prefer, the first branch from the above root – is Whitehead's refusal to surrender conceptual explanations in favour of mere mathematical cleverness. One sees this in *Process and Reality*, of course, but the development there has moved away from direct application *to physics* (even as examples from physics are still mentioned) towards the broader arena of *metaphysics*, or what he himself often called 'speculative philosophy'. But 'speculative philosophy' is a different programme from *conceptual physics*, and it is the latter that stands out in HL1. The conceptual aspect presents a solution to the hand-waving abandonment of fundamental questions which characterises Bohr's 'Copenhagen interpretation'. Central to this conceptual approach is the emphasis upon continuity that will be brought up in the first strand. Only this time, the focus will be more exclusively physical in its emphasis.

The third strand/second branch will be more narrowly philosophical in character, turning this time exclusively to aspects of Whitehead scholarship that have dominated much of contemporary discourse. This will cover two aspects of the contemporary scene: the first will be to put a stake through the heart of Lewis Ford's 'temporal atomism' thesis. The second will be to emphasise the need for achieving a certain minimal degree of facility with mathematical concepts in order to properly track Whitehead's own modes of thinking.

Throughout all three of the above strands, but especially in the first two, the use of the term 'corpuscle', and its various cognates, will be highlighted as indicating the trend of Whitehead's thought whenever the emphasis is upon physical or 'material' particles; the term 'quantum' (and *its* various cognates) *begins* to move towards a different collection of meanings. With that said, let us turn to the first strand.

## The Centrality of Continuity

One of the first steps in appreciating the role of continuity in Whitehead's thought is understanding how critical James Clerk Maxwell's formalisation of electromagnetic phenomena was in Whitehead's understanding of the world. Quite aside from the fact that it was central in Whitehead's own professional career from his earliest days as a Cambridge undergraduate, Maxwell's work (and its irreconcilable conflicts with Newtonian mechanics) was a, if not *the*, primary factor in driving the development of the theory of relativity.[15] In addition, Maxwell's work provided a leading edge of inquiry that itself contributed significantly to the development of the 'quantum revolution'.[16]

One does not have to go far to find Maxwell and his electromagnetic field equations arise in HL1. On page 7, Bell parenthetically notes regarding electromagnetic theory: 'Clerk Maxwell All modern theory just a modification of Maxwell.' (I'll not make any effort to correct or 'sic' grammatical or punctuation issues when quoting form HL1. These are notes, not polished essays.) Ronny Desmet, in his detailed chapters in this volume, concurs on the centrality of Clerk Maxwell in Whitehead's thought. Quoting Desmet: 'I hold, and HL1 confirms, that it is Maxwell's theory that influenced him most.'[17] This comes up again in an especially apposite quote that Desmet chooses from *The Organisation of Thought* (OT, 184–5). Thus, speaking of the corpuscular emphasis that such notions are typically given, Desmet says, 'If you take the isolated charge as the most concrete thing, you abstract from the relatedness.'[18]

Bell (following Whitehead) remains absolutely correct on this point, even today. References to Maxwell are all over the first fifteen to twenty pages of all three note-takers' collections, then peter out as the discussion moves on. But their essential contribution is in establishing the key aspect of continuity in the discussion. For, as Bell notes, 'the goings-on of the electro-magnetic field. That represented . . . a sort of continuity without slightest hint of <u>Atomicity</u>' (HL1, 7). Whitehead has opened this early lecture by insisting that the true contrast to continuity is with atomicity, while at the same time distancing the concept of continuity that he is developing from the related but more simplistic one employed in formal mathematics (HL1, 6). We must rely on Bell's notes for these particular points, as Hocking did not attend the earliest lectures. In addition, once Hocking's notes do become available, they are composed with a different agenda in mind than Bell's. As the editors note,

'Hocking's first set of notes already demonstrate his intention to organise Whitehead's content in his own way' (HL1, 45, n1). In any event, Whitehead continues to insist that any notion of discontinuity of space-time, as somehow mandated by the quantum theory, is 'nonsense' (HL1, 10), and that 'there's nothing in the Quantum Theory that makes it necessary for you to assume any discontinuity whatsoever' (HL1, 17).

Whitehead's use of the term 'atomicity' as a contrast to continuity bears some attention. Whitehead does not seem to use this term to refer a standardised material unit (the high-school physics book's 'atom'), but rather for a generalised unitary whole. Thus, Bell records Whitehead as saying, 'Let us suppose physical field consists ultimately not only of Waves but also "primates" – an *atomic structure of Vibrations* with a definite frequency' (HL1, 12, emphasis added). (Desmet also points out that 'the primate is "an atomic structure of vibrations"').

Notice that it is not a vibrating atom, but an 'atomic' *structure of vibrations*. Whitehead frequently uses terms like 'atomic structure', while it is comparatively rare that he uses any cognate of 'atom' in the traditionally material sense (one exception is HL1, 22, where he speaks of the differences in atomic weight that led to the discovery of argon). Whitehead goes on to say that the 'Inmost character of realisation is this *atomic character of the individuality* – achieved by structural limitation and definition expressing itself within this unbounded transition' (HL1, 22, emphasis added). This usage by Whitehead, as recorded by Bell, seems to confirm the argument in Auxier and Herstein, cited above, that Whitehead meant the term and its cognates in the classical Greek sense of 'uncut whole'.

On the other hand, when Whitehead does wish to speak of individual, physical units, the term he leans towards is 'corpuscle'. This term makes its first appearance at HL1, 12, in the context of Newton's theory of light, and is chosen precisely because of its standard usage in a large part of the physics literature. (Whitehead also introduces the very non-orthodox term 'primate' here, which he will go on to use quite extensively both in the lectures and in the chapter on quantum theory in the soon to be published *Science and the Modern World*. However, we'll not be discussing that here. Ronny Desmet's chapters in this book survey the use of 'primate' in substantial detail.) And while the number of times the word is used is not that great, those uses are all particularly telling. For unlike the word 'particle', which Whitehead uses throughout to designate any *material* unit of scientific interest – including entire planets and the earth (HL1, 190, in the context of his discussion of Newton and Galileo) – corpuscles are more fundamental, equivalent to, or only a single step of organisation above that of a primate. As Heath records this in her Radcliffe notes: 'That both electrons & protons are built up of ultimate corpuscles which he will call primates. A vibratory structure of one definite frequency' (HL1, 419). Thus a corpuscle, unlike a material 'particle', is not treated as a substantive 'thing' or bit of 'stuff', but rather a functional centre of rhythmic activity.[19] This functionally centred system of uniform vibration within a continuum provides us with a segue to our next section.

## Conceptual Physics

Whitehead never uses the phrase 'wave/particle duality', although we know from the lecture notes that he is well aware of the concept. It is worth quoting this section of the lectures at a little more length, as it sets up our discussion in this section very nicely, provides some interesting (and seldom mentioned!) history to Bohr's 'Copenhagen interpretation', and reveals one of those rare moments of 'twinkle' in Whitehead's character when his humour is allowed to slip into his formal presentations. The Whitehead quote begins with Whitehead himself quoting Sir William Henry Bragg:

> 'State of science now just as though on M.W.F. we had to use Wave theory of light and on Tu, Th, Sat had to use the Corpuscular.' Utterly contradictory and yet each explains one enormous mass of phenomena, which the other doesn't; and vice versa.
>
> There's a set of scientific Bolshevists that is inclined to acquiesce in that view. Whitehead is too much of a rationalist to acquiesce in that. (HL1, 12)

'Scientific Bolshevists' is a term we need to spread more widely in both philosophical and popular literature. But aside from that rather evocative image, what is so notable in the Bragg portion of the quote is that it has essentially summed up the 'Copenhagen interpretation', which Bohr supposedly 'invented' in response to Einstein's questioning at Solvay. This response, whether gladly embraced by Bohr at Solvay two years after the Harvard lectures, or woefully proclaimed by Bragg three years earlier, remains the basis for the 'shut up and calculate' standard of contemporary physics. One might as well snarl, 'Shut up and drink your gin.'[20]

'Whitehead is too much of a rationalist to acquiesce in that' – yet another line that bears repeating until the lesson is learned. Whitehead had, in earlier work, rued that 'it certainly is a nuisance for philosophers to be worried with applied mathematics, and for mathematicians to be saddled with philosophy' (R, 4). But he never denied either nuisance, a nuisance that becomes more necessary as we turn our eyes to the contemporary scene. Even as model centrists like Stephen Hawking declare, *ex cathedra*, that all the problems of quantum mechanics have been solved, and that doing philosophy is of no value (while doing philosophy himself, and doing it badly), conceptual approaches to physics continue to be brushed aside in favour of empirically vacuous, but marvellously clever, mathematical models. *Conceptual* approaches to physics are more desperately needed now than they have ever been. Whitehead's lectures provide us with rich insights into just such conceptual approaches, as well as how one ought to approach them.

As we have already noted, one of the most striking of Whitehead's insights is that the real issue in physics and quantum mechanics is *not* between waves and particles, but between *continuity and atomicity*. Nowhere else, not even in *Science and the Modern World*, does Whitehead set out this distinction with such clarity and force as it appears in the Harvard lectures. It is this clarity which shows the conceptual failure – a less forgiving sort might even say, the conceptual cowardice – of so much of contemporary physics.

Physics cannot merely content itself with clever mathematical formulae, a point Whitehead had already gone on record to emphasise. When it does – as it has, in point of fact, long since done – physics loses its connection to the reality it is supposed to be about. One ends up with 'string theories' which cannot be reconciled one with another, and are entirely devoid of empirical content in any event, and standard models of gravitational cosmology that have had so many additional parameters added to the model that they are no longer subject to any possibility of genuine test.[21]

Conceptual physics is the answer to such recondite formalism. The use of the term 'recondite' is deliberate here: Whitehead contrasts 'recondite' ideas with 'abstract' ones in his various educational essays, noting that recondite ideas are 'of highly special application and rarely influence thought' (AE, 78). Abstract ideas, on the other hand, while not concrete, nevertheless exemplify the real relations binding concrete factors of reality together. The importance of scientific and mathematical intuition, when properly cultivated, is that it allows us to focus upon the abstract, rather than distracting us with the merely recondite.[22] So, for example, no mathematical formula by itself, no matter how well 'verified' by test and observation, ever 'maps' *itself* onto the world; that connection must be generated by human inquirers who know what they *intend* those symbols to mean; it must be an expression of their intuitions of the abstract rendered, as it were, more concrete. Thus, a sequence such as

$ ! b ^ c0#–c

might be completely meaningless, or it might simply be a different way of writing

$$F = 1/2mv^2.$$

It is only on the basis of their cultivated intuitions that scientists have any notion of what *kinds* of questions they should be asking. It is for this reason that established theories can be so difficult to dislodge, because the intuitions that those scientists have spent so much time and effort cultivating do not offer much (if any) room for modification, much less rejection.

This is where an instrument such as *The Harvard Lectures* becomes so particularly important. Unlike *Science in the Modern World* – which was being written at much the same time as the lectures – these lectures were being delivered to students with the express purpose of serving as a teaching tool. The narrative structure of a book, even one as well written as SMW, will almost always take on a more formal air than an in-person lecture. This is a point that Whitehead himself made on numerous occasions, often regretting the fact that scholarly books and research could not always have that more personal touch, much less go the extra step to become a genuine dialogue. (There is an irony here, of course, in that the only reason we have these lecture notes is because persons other than Whitehead saved them.)

For scientists and other scholars looking for a different path than just 'shut up and calculate', HL1 is a guided tour into Whitehead's ideas about science that is primarily designed for those who are making their first substantive entry into the subject. Here is a door opening upon a new system of cultivated intuitions that remains fully grounded in the science.

## Whitehead Scholarship

The days are now past when Lewis Ford's purely hypothetical notions about Whitehead and 'temporal atomism' exercised the hegemonic domination of the field of Whitehead scholarship that they once did.[23] But having enjoyed such domination for something on the order of twenty-five to thirty years, they still require some commentary. Ford's thesis is well enough known that I'll not trouble to summarise it here, beyond just saying that Ford argues that time, for Whitehead, comes 'chunky style', in discrete, 'atomic' bits, where Ford doesn't even follow Whitehead's own meaning of the word 'atomic'; which is to say, as *a-tomos*, uncut, as a comprehensive and comprehending whole.[24]

Ford read into Whitehead's text this idea of 'temporal atomism', a term that appears nowhere in any of Whitehead's texts, by applying methods of 'compositional analysis', employed by some theologians in interpreting mil-lennia-old fragments, to Whitehead's texts, justifying this move on the basis that Whitehead's own papers were burned upon his death in accord with the wishes in his will.[25] This is a profoundly questionable method to apply, even to fragments of papyri that are thousands of years old. Yet when brought to bear on complete texts that are less than a century old, it is far from obvious what the justification for such an approach is supposed to be.[26] It is certainly the case that there is no trace of such a notion to be found *anywhere* in the Harvard lectures; indeed, throughout the lectures Whitehead unqualifiedly rejects any discontinuity of *either* space *or* time. Even in the absence of the lectures, it is difficult to imagine a legitimate reason for imposing such a method willy-nilly beyond the primary texts, when those texts are complete, less than a century old, and carry no reference to – or even tangential sug-gestion of – the thing one wishes to insist is central to the very possibility of reading those texts. George Lucas, in this volume, shares with me a less than charitable view of Ford's thesis.[27] The Harvard lectures offer us yet another reminder of why we should stick to the primary texts: just because we haven't found the lecture notes *yet*, does not prove that they are not there to be found.

Another lesson for Whitehead scholars from the Harvard lectures is that, nuisance or not, learning a bit of mathematics is not an optional extra when it comes to Whitehead's work. Whitehead spent almost forty years of his professional life as a mathematician, yet many scholars act as though this was a purely side issue when it comes to understanding his philosophical texts, as though it was no more relevant than his favourite colour or preferred cologne. Mathematical inquiry uniquely informs one's patterns of thought, and can no more be eliminated from consideration out of groundless 'math phobia' than it can be reduced to numerical calculation (IM, 48). To employ an analogy I have used elsewhere, one might as reasonably proclaim oneself an expert in Greek philosophy while disdaining to learn the Greek language.[28]

Whitehead himself certainly didn't hesitate to bring such mathematical materials explicitly to the fore in his lectures, lectures that were presented almost exclusively to *philosophy* students. The amount of mathematical exposure is hardly extreme – no one is deriving theorems in linear algebra or differential geometry. Nevertheless, the ideas must be glossed in order to show what they *genuinely* imply, discontinuity being notably *absent* from that list.

And speaking of notable absences, one of the most important is one that Whitehead gives only the slightest mention to, very early on in the lectures. Specifically, and recalling the quote above, the notion of continuity he is arguing for is related to, but different from, that which is commonly presented in mathematical contexts. This is such a casually mentioned fact, and so quickly moved past, that its essential character can easily be missed: How can one hope to understand the concept of continuity that Whitehead is pressing for *if one does not also know* the mathematical concept he means to *differentiate* it from? One must first know *what* the 'epsilon-delta' method is before one can understand *that* Whitehead's continuity is more than that. More generally, the only way one can ever hope to really get 'inside' Whitehead's thinking is by first achieving some minimal facility with what the 'inside' of mathematical thinking, broadly and in general, looks like.

And one cannot simply cleave Whitehead in twain, as Solomon threatened with the disputed baby, and pretend there is the 'science' Whitehead in one bloody, ruined half, and the 'metaphysical' Whitehead in the other. Whitehead never walked away from the thematic interests that drove his inquiries from the beginning, even as his attention turned to more philosophically 'ultimate' matters.[29] Whitehead the mathematician is every bit as present in his discussions of the primordial nature of God as he is in his discussions of the ideal point at infinity. One might as well pretend Plato wrote in English as skip over this fact.

## Conclusion

The central roll of continuity in our interpretations of reality is certainly one of the stand-out facts of Whitehead's thinking. At the same time, the structure of corpuscles as centred vibratory sources of action within physical reality is brought to the fore as a limiting principle within Whitehead's broader *philosophical* theory of nature. Thus Whitehead nowhere challenges the corpuscular facts of physical reality, but he does refuse to set these facts in the manner of a 'Hegel-like' (my term) dialectic of contradictory opposites with wave phenomena. Rather, a corpuscle is a concentrated focal point of activity within the 'ether of events' (R, 38; HL1, 415) that is the complete field of physical action.

Yet this is only one of the many aspects of Whitehead's thought that the Harvard lectures now make explicit to us. In the light of these lectures, much older scholarship needs to be revised or discarded. But at the same time, newer scholarship is now invited to enter the foreground, especially in the physical sciences where a revivified conceptual physics is so desperately needed to take the field.

# Notes

1. An exception to this is Epperson and Zafiris, *Foundations*.
2. Auxier and Herstein, *The Quantum of Explanation*.
3. See Bacciagaluppi and Valenti, *Quantum Theory*.
4. Bacciagaluppi and Valenti, *Quantum Theory*, 3ff.
5. Bacciagaluppi and Valenti, *Quantum Theory*, vii.
6. Bacciagaluppi and Valenti, *Quantum Theory*, vii.
7. *Thelma and Louise*, Metro-Goldwyn-Mayer, 1991.
8. Bacciagaluppi and Valenti, *Quantum Theory*, viii.
9. See, for example Herstein, *Measurement Problem*.
10. The phrase is from the fantasy story *Game of Thrones*, referring to the act (or the person who has performed the act) of swearing absolute fealty to a sovereign, even unto death.
11. *Stanford Encyclopedia*, 'Copenhagen Interpretation'.
12. Bacciagaluppi and Valenti, *Quantum Theory*, especially chapter 12.
13. See Auxier and Herstein, *The Quantum of Explanation*, chapter 10, for details Hawking's shameful dismissal of philosophy.
14. This last is such a commonplace in physics that offering a citation would be meaningless.
15. Holton, *Thematic Origins*, 268–9.
16. Mahon, Basil, *The Man Who Changed Everything*.
17. See below, p. 156.
18. See below, p. 165.
19. Recall the final chapter of Whitehead's PNK, 195–200.
20. One of Fagin's lines from the play/movie *Oliver!* (it does not appear in Dickens' text.) Auxier and Herstein refer to such an attitude as 'model centrism'.
21. Auxier and Herstein, *The Quantum of Explanation*, especially chapters 6 and 10.
22. See, for example, Desmet, *Intuition in Mathematics*.
23. Ford, *The Emergence of Whitehead's Metaphysics*.
24. Auxier and Herstein, *The Quantum of Explanation*, throughout.
25. Long after this essay, and basically everything in the entire body of Whiteheadian secondary literature, was written, it was discovered that a significant body of Whitehead's original papers *did still exist*. These have only recently been handed over to the Whitehead Project, and have only just begun to be analysed. Absent such detailed analysis (which will likely take years to complete), I allow the assumption that all such papers were destroyed to stand without further comment in the remainder of this essay, with the understanding that this will require subsequent revision and modification.
26. As recently as 2009 Ford continued to insist that his temporal atomism thesis was essential to reading Whitehead. See Ford, 'Indispensability'.
27. See below, p. 329.
28. Auxier and Herstein, *The Quantum of Explanation*, 84.
29. Herstein, 'Whitehead', *Internet Encyclopedia*.

# Bibliography

Auxier, Randy, and Gary Herstein, *The Quantum of Explanation: Whitehead's Radical Empiricism* (New York: Routledge, 2016).

Bacciagaluppi, Guido, and Antony Valenti, *Quantum Theory at the Crossroads: Reconsidering the 1927 Solvay Conference* (Cambridge: Cambridge University Press, 2009).

Bogaard, Paul and Jason Bell (eds), *The Harvard Lectures of Alfred North Whitehead, 1924–1925: Philosophical Presuppositions of Science* (Edinburgh: Edinburgh University Press, 2017).

Desmet, Ronny (ed.), *Intuition in Mathematics & Physics* (Anoka, NY: Process Century Press, 2016).

Epperson, Michael, and Elias Zafiris, *Foundations of Relational Realism* (Lanham, MD: Lexington Books, 2013).

Ford, Lewis, *The Emergence of Whitehead's Metaphysics: 1925–1929* (Albany: SUNY, 1984).

Ford, Lewis, 'The Indispensability of Temporal Atomism', *Process Studies*, 38:2 (2009), 279–303.

Herstein, Gary, *Whitehead and the Measurement Problem of Cosmology* (Frankfurt: Ontos-Verlag (now DeGruyter), 2006).

Herstein, Gary, 'Alfred North Whitehead', *The Internet Encyclopedia of Philosophy* <https://www.iep.utm.edu/whitehed/#SH2a>

Holton, Gerald, *Thematic Origins of Scientific Thought: Kepler to Einstein* (Cambridge, MA: Harvard University Press, 1980).

Mahon, Basil, *The Man Who Changed Everything* (New York: John Wiley and Sons, 2003).

*The Stanford Encyclopedia of Philosophy*, 'Copenhagen Interpretation of Quantum Mechanics' <https://plato.stanford.edu/entries/qm-copenhagen>

Whitehead, Alfred North, *An Introduction to Mathematics* (London: Oxford University Press, [1911] 1948).

Whitehead, Alfred North, *The Organisation of Thought, Educational and Scientific* (London: Williams & Norgate, 1917).

Whitehead, Alfred North, *The Principle of Relativity: With Applications to Physical Science* (Cambridge: Cambridge University Press, [1922] 2011).

Whitehead, Alfred North, *The Aims of Education and Other Essays* (New York: The Free Press, [1929] 1967).

# 7

# From Physics to Philosophy, and from Continuity to Atomicity

*Ronny Desmet*

*The Harvard Lectures of Alfred North Whitehead, 1924–1925* provide White-head's readers with a wealth of information to better understand not only all of Whitehead's published thoughts, but also the development of his thought in between the publication in 1922 of *The Principle of Relativity* and the publication in 1925 of *Science and the Modern World*, a period that coincides with Whitehead's professional transition from British mathematical physicist to American speculative philosopher.

Whitehead's 'flight of imaginative generalization' (PR, 5) started from the ground of a particular example of a particular theory in physics – the electron as exemplifying Maxwell's electromagnetic field theory – but aimed at a 'synoptic vision', adequate not only with respect to physics, but also with respect to all other fields of knowledge: biology, psychology, aesthetics, ethics, theology (HL1, 79, 82, 449; PR, 5). So Whitehead invoked paradigms beyond physics – the enduring organism of biology and the specious present of psychology – and yet he never lost sight of the origin of his speculative philosophy in physics. All this is revealed by Whitehead's Harvard lectures, but they also reveal that the American philosopher did not simply apply and gradually unfold a set of ideas acquired by the British physicist beyond their original scope. His speculative philosophy is critical philosophy as well ('Every science deals in a field of abstractions. It is for philosophy to criticize those abstractions' (HL1, 226)), and it avoids the trap of scientism ('Philosophy ought to cut across lines and get new points of view – get things together in a new way and thus get a new and illuminating abstraction' (HL1, 81)). Consequently, his ideas are subject to change. For example, in the course of HL1, Whitehead changes his mind with respect to the concept of the process of becoming, and conceives of it as atomic instead of continuous. However, when new insights prompt Whitehead to change his tentative metaphysical synthesis – each such synthesis is tentative, none is the ultimate synoptic vision – he does not simply turn his back on his preliminary design, but starts redesigning; he does not burn down his provisional conceptual framework, but performs a careful reconceptualisation to take into account what's new without loss of what already proved adequate ('Real change is gain in richness' (HL1, 416)). And finally, there is another thread running through HL1: Whitehead's persistent refusal to abandon common sense, or better, his obstinate refusal to follow scientists and philosophers who want to establish 'a common world of thought . . . apart from a common world of sense' (HL1, 339).

It would take a whole book to substantiate all the above claims. The aim of this chapter is more modest. It is to illustrate some of these claims – the synthetic and critical and common sense character of Whitehead's philosophy by focusing on his first Harvard lecture (§1), and the change from continuous to atomic becoming by comparison of first with second semester lectures (§2).

## §1 The First Lecture

Late September 1924, Whitehead opens his Emerson Hall and parallel Radcliffe College Lectures (resp. HL1, 3 and HL1, 411) on the 'Philosophical Presuppositions of Science' by saying that every age of philosophy is dominated by some fundamental problem, which it aims at solving. According to Whitehead, the root question animating early twentieth-century philosophy, including his own, is the 'question of unifying into a coherent whole the presuppositions of science' (HL1, 3). And he immediately highlights the first presupposition of science by looking at 'its ultimate motive' to find 'a rational synthesis', and at its ultimate belief 'that there's something in the fundamental nature of things' that accounts for the 'regularities' of science, for its 'rationality' (HL1, 4). Of course, Whitehead knows and highlights that the founding fathers of modern science (in Western Europe in the sixteenth and seventeenth centuries) inherited this belief from the medieval scholastic belief in a rational God (HL1, 4, 412), but that does not lead him to saying that a rational God is the first presupposition of science. Instead, he says that the first presupposition of science is 'the essential togetherness of things' (HL1, 413).

Whitehead does not hold fast to a God imposing regularities on a world of externally related things, as some of the founding fathers of science did. His secular point of departure is a world of internally related events. Later in HL1, it will become clear that this starting point is inspired by his interpretation of the electromagnetic field as a field of internally related happenings, and that his notion of the electromagnetic field is in line with the notions of organic environment in biology and psychological field in psychology. In fact, on 20 December 1924, Whitehead explicitly says to his students that the 'key idea to which [he is] working up is that of organism', and that 'the most concrete fact' is 'an enduring organism', to which he adds: 'This question of organisms as enduring functioning is immensely important now from biological and psychological conceptions. Also: it is key to [the] interpretation of the new ideas which . . . have entered into physics' (HL1, 153 – Whitehead already highlighted the notion of organism in 1919 in PNK, §1.4).

Whitehead's philosophical point of departure is the first and common presupposition of physics, biology and psychology, that the key to understanding the universe and all its constituents – electrons, cells, specious presents, etc. – is the notion of an organic whole of internally related parts. In other words, the key concept to solve the root question animating Whitehead's philosophy, the 'question of unifying into a coherent whole the presuppositions of science' (HL1, 3), is the concept of organism. No wonder Whitehead would later baptise his philosophy 'the philosophy of organism' (PR, 18). However, the omnipresence of the notion of process in HL1 equally justifies the current convention of calling Whitehead's philosophy 'process philosophy'.

Whitehead holds that without the first presupposition of science – the essential togetherness of things, the internal relatedness of events, the organic interdependence of processes of realisation, the inherent interconnectedness of processes of becoming – an 'inherent rationality of things' is inconceivable. In fact, according to him, 'science collapses if you assume an independent atomicity of facts' (HL1, 4). To make this clear, Whitehead – already in his first lecture – puts the organic character of his philosophy in opposition to some of the characteristics of the philosophies of Aristotle, Hume, Kant and their followers. His critique of these non-relational, non-organic characteristics will be a recurrent theme in HL1.

## Whitehead versus Aristotle

With respect to Aristotle, Whitehead states:

> [The] brilliant and deserved success of [the] Aristotelian system of classification obscured his followers' attention to this togetherness of things. Half of the difficulties of philosophy come from too exclusive attention on the isolated individual. The predicates belong to some part of [the] environment as well as to the thing. . . . Predication is a one-sided way of seeing the togetherness. This togetherness of things takes [the] form of a flowing process of becoming – of realization. This was so obvious that [it was] overlooked. (HL1, 5)

Whitehead's claim of the limited relevance of the subject-predicate relation already stems from his joint work with Bertrand Russell on the foundations of mathematics as well as from his work in the philosophy of science. The key notion of the mathematical logic of Whitehead and Russell was the notion of multi-term relation (or propositional function). This notion sets logic free from the classical shackles of the two-term relation of subject and predicate (or substance and quality), and philosophy from the devastating idea of the bifurcation of nature into the material world of primary qualities (such as size, mass, charge, etc.) and the mental world of secondary qualities (colours, sounds, smells, etc.). For Whitehead no subject-predicate relation holds between material substances and primary qualities, nor between mental substances and secondary qualities. The ingression of all qualities into a process of becoming or realisation (which is physical *and* mental) involves complex multi-term relations (cf. HL1, 427). In a sense, to adequately describe the ingression of a quality 'you'd have to take in [the] whole universe' (HL1, 382)!

As from HL1, Whitehead utilises 'value' as a synonym for 'quality' – values include (next to primary and secondary) tertiary qualities (such as beauty and truth). Hence he says:

> There is nothing but this process of becoming real ... – in varying degrees. .... A may be real for B. B for A. But it's nonsense to say that either A or B is absolutely real. B's becoming real for A = B's inherent, individual, qualitative character becoming significant for A. Thus realization is a matter of reactive significance – of valuation. (HL1, 5; for the notion of significance, cf. already PNK, §3.5)

Whitehead's notion of valuation is closely related to his notion of envisagement. Like the former notion, the latter is at play in HL1 right from the start. Moreover, 'envisagement', according to Whitehead, 'is the term corresponding to Bergson's intuition' (HL1, 525). Henri Bergson is prominently present in HL1, and his *Creative Evolution* is on the list of recommended literature that Whitehead gives to his students (HL1, 69). Hence, in the context of HL1, the above quote foreshadows Whitehead's later speculations with regard to freedom, creativity and God. However, at this point in the evolution of this thought, Whitehead 'finds Spinoza the most suggestive of modern philosophers' (HL1, 5; cf. also HL1, 413). Indeed, in HL1, like Spinoza, Whitehead does not distinguish his notion of God from the one substance or 'ether of events' (HL1, 415); in other words, he does not yet emancipate God from the creativity of which all processes of becoming are instances, and this prevents him from already arriving at the notion of fully-fledged freedom.

There is another reason not to read too much of Whitehead's later notion of freedom in this phrase of the very first lecture of HL1, 'realization is a matter of reactive significance – of valuation'. Prior to his introduction of the atomicity of becoming in the second semester lectures of HL1 (cf. §2), Whitehead leaves open the question of whether there is room for freedom (HL1, 126, 128), and even though he holds that everything 'in a sense is a cause of itself as it is', he speaks of this as a 'secret' (HL1, 458). Then in one of the lectures introducing the atomicity of becoming, he speaks of 'the envisagement' of the subject, 'not an independent one – but part of [the] general taking account of [the] order of reality', as follows:

> The subject holds out before it the conditions into which it is entering. It is how conditions are dealt with, which is . . . the permanent selective character – [the] permanent purpose of being . . . a definite achievement, and [the] underlying activity to be itself has to bring in the definite and exclusive atomism. That is where freedom comes in. (HL1, 323)

Here we see Whitehead's stoic notion of freedom arising: freedom is the envisagement of *what* conditions the subject's becoming, and the decision of *how* to deal with these conditions. And if becoming were continuous instead of atomic, there would be no room for freedom. In fact, Whitehead now holds that there is 'no alternative except to describe a universe in which there is room for freedom' (HL1, 351), and says: 'We have a certain atomic independence of immediate (simultaneous) occasions . . . That atomic independence of what is immediately present is absolutely necessary if you are to have any freedom or error. And these are in the universe' (HL1, 353). 'The atomic independence . . . is necessary if you are to have a breath of freedom or of error' (HL1, 355). From this point on, the question 'Does [. . . the] accumulation of conditions . . . completely determine what is to be' (HL1, 362) gets a firm and negative reply. Whitehead says: '[I] personally . . . believe that [. . . it is] natural to ascribe [self-perpetuation] to [the] very inmost character of the activity of realization and not to any casual conditions' (HL1, 362), and hence: 'If we are to make metaphysics agree with direct apprehension, we have got to describe [the] ontological occasion leaving room for freedom' (HL1, 363).

Returning to the subject-predicate relation, this relation only makes sense when abstracting from the internal relatedness of events. Our subject-predicate language only applies to the abstract notion of isolated individuals, hence obscuring the more concrete reality of internally related events. As from HL1, Whitehead calls the error of 'taking [abstract] things to be more concrete than they really are', the 'fallacy of misplaced concreteness' (HL1, 425). We commit this error when forgetting that 'in language we express very <u>high abstractions</u> of the real concrete fact' (HL1, 381), that 'the attribution of quality to object [is] a simple two-term relationship [that] carries us along pretty well', but only at a 'high level of abstraction', and that 'the more concrete you are the more complex . . . your relationships [are]' (HL1, 382). The subject-predicate instance of the fallacy of misplaced concreteness is a recurring theme in HL1.

## Whitehead versus Hume

Whitehead also opposes the non-relational, non-organic traits of 'Hume's philosophy and its modern derivatives', especially Ernst Mach's phenomenalism, which infected the thought and writings of Karl Pearson and Russell, who are both subject to Whitehead's critique in HL1. 'Whitehead accepts [the] basis that phenomenalism lays down: we must include nothing that's not observable' (HL1, 33), but he also holds that we need to broaden its narrow concept of observation – the 'over-simplification' that observation merely offers an 'immediate display of sense-data' and nothing 'besides this "immediate fact"' (HL1, 35).

Looking at Einstein's General Theory of Relativity (GTR) for example, Whitehead mocks the idea of phenomenalists that Einstein is one of them: 'It is an audacious statement to imply that Einstein's work represents a step towards the adoption of phenomenalism. Especially as it kicks out the idea of field of force which seems to be resolvable into sense-data & puts in its place the 16 tensor equation as a condition of space-time' (HL1, 423). 'Take Einstein's 16 equations and tell the poor experimental physicist that that's what he observes' (HL1, 23). Contrary to most phenomenalists and their descendants (the logical positivists), Whitehead has always been clearly aware of today's commonplace that Einstein's development of the theories of relativity had to push him from a Machian to a Kantian philosophical position.

In *The Principle of Relativity*, Whitehead endorsed John Henry Poynting's aphorism – 'I have no doubt whatever that our ultimate aim must be to describe the sensible in terms of the sensible' (R, 5). But Whitehead also held that the sensible is broader than the phenomenalist's observable, and that the notion of a field of force against the background of a uniform space-time had to be restored in order for GTR to be broadly observable, that is, to pass not only 'the narrow gauge' of empirical testing, but also 'the broad gauge which tests its consonance with the general character of our direct experience' (R, 4).

Exclusive attention to isolated sense-data leads Hume and his followers to deny that causal relations are observable and real, even though they assume that the habit of experiencing first A and then B really causes the impression and idea of a necessary relation of causation from A to B. Instead of broadening the notion of sense perception beyond the mere perception of a spatial display of sense-data in order to include our perception of causation and ground the idea of causation in the reality of causation, they tacitly assume the reality of a relation of causation from the recurrence of a non-causal association to the mere idea of a causation. In short: 'Hume assumes a causation of association to account for the assumption of causation' (HL1, 4).

Consequently, Hume and his followers cannot justify the use of 'Inductive Logic' in science (HL1, 4). Without real causation, the scientist's inductive generalisation from a particular regularity in the present to a general regularity valid for past, present and future is ungrounded. If there is no real causation, then the current idea of causation of B by A can well be refuted tomorrow. Indeed, if there is no inherent reason for the association of yesterday's A's and B's and today's A's and B's, then tomorrow's A's and B's might well be dissociated. Clearly, 'your belief in the rationality [of science] should be weakened by this analysis' (HL1, 4). In fact, Hume's analysis turns science into a 'sheer irrational practice [of] which you can't justify nor forecast [the] success' (HL1, 55).

Clearly, Hume's theoretical demolition of the internal relations that in practice ground Hume's external spatio-temporal relations between isolated sense-data is an instance of the fallacy of misplaced concreteness. The spatio-temporally related sense-data are taken as more concrete than they really are, for they are abstractions from the full process of sense perception, which also involves the vague perception of the causal relatedness of things – 'William James showed us that we do perceive relationships' (HL1, 504)! In HL1, Whitehead speaks about the observation of the field of display and the field of control, and not yet about perception in the mode of presentational immediacy and the mode of causal efficacy, but you can witness the genesis of these later concepts. Anyhow, the sense-data instance of the fallacy of misplaced concreteness is a recurrent theme in HL1.

Moreover, Hume, instead of recognising his fallacy, 'in practice acts on things which [his] philosophy does not justify' (HL1, 423). For example, as highlighted above, in practice Hume acts on real causation which in theory he denies. Nowadays, this is called a 'performative contradiction'. To avoid performative contradictions, Whitehead appeals to 'William James . . . fundamental line here – if you appeal to practice you must bring practice into [the] fundamental meaning of truth. In being tried, this point of view gave very valuable contributions to thought. William James did what Bertrand Russell and Hume ought to have done' (HL1, 42–3; cf. also HL1, 433). Like fallacies of misplaced concreteness, performative contradictions are a recurrent theme in HL1.

## Whitehead versus Kant

According to Whitehead, nature's inherent rationality and hence natural science are only possible if we presuppose an essential togetherness of things. Therefore, he does not agree with Kant's intellectual 'endeavor to restore some theory of relatedness to replace the one demolished by Hume's youthful skepticism' (R, 13). In fact, Kant's philosophy implies no restoration of the internal relatedness of things, but exclusively focuses on the cognitive relatedness of things.

Kant seems to hold that cognition transcendently imposes universal spatio-temporal and causal relations on the isolated sense-data. Kant views cognition as a kind of legislative power forcing isolated sense-data into the knowable format of spatio-temporally and causally related objects. Instead, Whitehead sees a cognitive experience (a thought event) as a high level aesthetic experience (a sense event), and its relations of cognition as outgrowths of its internal and pre-cognitive relations with all other events, including the events constituting the enduring organisms that are ultimately known as causal objects in space and time (cf. HL1, 30). Whitehead holds that the relation of 'cognition is just one of the group of relations between [all things in the] universe' (HL1, 4), and that 'Kant [is] guilty of [the] fallacy of misplaced concreteness' (HL1, 43) when abstracting from the concrete and non-cognitive relations that ground the cognitive relations with the objective world (a world to think about), and then taking abstract cognitive relations as the concrete ground for all the relations needed to construct the objective world (a world of thought). This instance of the fallacy of misplaced concreteness – which leaves Kant and his followers with a 'common world of thought, but no common world to think about' (HL1, 337) – is a recurrent theme in HL1.

According to Whitehead, the Kantian position of constructing a common world of thought, while forgetting about the common world of sense, is 'a position which Eddington and other extreme relativists are tending to take up' (HL1, 337). Indeed, as said before, Einstein's development of the theories of relativity pushed him away from a Machian and towards a

Kantian philosophical position. However, Einstein's Kantian position was no orthodox Kantianism, involving the construction of a common world of thought by means of *a priori* forms of spatial, temporal and causal relatedness, but a kind of pragmatic Kantianism, involving the construction of a common world of thought by means of freely invented mathematical forms – hence, ultimately, a world of mathematical formulae, which is agreed upon because of both its logical consistency and its empirical adequacy. Consequently, according to Einstein, the relation between the mathematical world of thought and the familiar world of sense is 'not analogous to that of soup to beef but rather of check number to overcoat'.[1] And as Whitehead says, all this definitely also holds for Eddington, who conceives of physics as mathematical world building. Indeed, according to Eddington:

> As a result of two great theories – the relativity theory and the quantum theory – the familiar world and the physical world have become entirely distinct. . . . A priori we have no more expectation of finding resemblances between objects in the familiar world and objects in the physical world than of finding resemblance between a clue and a criminal.[2]

According to Whitehead, the Kantian position involves performative contradictions. In theory Kantians only rely on the world of thought, but in practice they tacitly rely on the world of sense. Whitehead quips: 'Kant should have thought of his *Practical* before writing his *Theoretical* Critique' (HL1, 337). Especially if the world of thought is seen as the result of free invention instead of necessary legislation, the Kantian position is liable to solipsism, which even more clearly involves performative contradictions. Whitehead tells his students the funny story of 'Russell's experience with the solipsist surprised that there are so few of them' (HL1, 338) – in theory the solipsist, *in casu* 'Miss Ladd-Franklin' (HL1, 339), holds that there are no other solipsists, but in practice she does, as is clear from her utterance that there are so few of them. In *The Principle of Relativity*, to give a last example, Whitehead highlights the most devastating performative contradiction that is entailed by Einstein's Kantian interpretation of GTR: GTR holds that the space-time structure is contingently contorted, but its measurement practices tacitly rely on our recognition of congruence, and hence, on a necessarily uniform space-time structure (cf. R, 83). In general, we simply cannot resist believing in what the common world of sense prompts us to believe. Hence, Whitehead links common sense to a phrase attributed to William Kingdon Clifford: 'the still small voice that whispers "Fiddlesticks"', and he adds: 'Philosophy gets into trouble disregarding this' (HL1, 79).

## Conclusion

Aristotle's isolated substances and qualities, Hume's isolated sense-data, Kant's isolated cognition, and the accompanying 'oversimplified relations' (HL1, 381) of subject-predicate, association and legislation, are all instances of the fallacy of misplaced concreteness, and entail performative contradictions. Whitehead, aware of these and more fallacies and contradictions that can do no justice to the scientist's first presupposition of the complex internal relatedness of things, starts developing a philosophy that *can* do them justice, a philosophy that is more concrete and in line with the world of sense than Aristotle's, Hume's or Kant's.

Obviously, Whitehead's method of philosophy is 'to criticize . . . abstractions', and he highlights that the philosopher has four 'auxiliary methods' at his or her disposition:

1) [The] strict logical method . . .
2) Literary presentation
3) History of thought . . .
4) To have an active interest in immediate general thoughts . . . .
   (HL1, 226)

The twentieth-century philosophical movement of logical positivism, while also aiming at a scientific worldview, fell into the trap of an uncritical scientism. Whitehead, on the contrary, subjected all abstractions – scientific or theological, philosophical or ethical – 'to critical examination' (HL1, 80). And whereas logical positivism overemphasised the first auxiliary method at the detriment of the other three, Whitehead was committed to all four of them. In HL1, for example, Whitehead invokes the logic of relations to overcome the limitations of the subject-predicate relation, and does not fail to stress the 'importance of [this] mathematical logic' for his 'method of extensive abstraction' (HL1, 203; cf. §2). He is in permanent dialogue with main figures in the history of thought: Aristotle and Spinoza, Hume and Kant, James and Bergson, Russell and Einstein, etc. Also, Whitehead is deeply concerned to keep his thought in line with common sense and intuition because: 'There is no method in any science which will supersede common sense and real insight' (HL1, 226). Finally, the end of his first lecture also shows how important literary presentation is for Whitehead (notice that for Whitehead 'relatedness' and 'relativity' are synonyms): '[My] doctrine of [the] complete relativity of reality . . . is not the mere handmaiden of science' (HL1, 5). 'Metaphysical philosophy is critical appreciation of [the] whole intellectual background of man's life' (HL1, 413). '[It] stands as near to poetry as to science, and needs them both' (HL1, 5; cf. SMW, 87).

## §2 Continuity versus Atomicity of Becoming

On 12 July 1924, at University College, Reading, Whitehead chaired a symposium that was part of the fourteenth session of the Aristotelian Society and the Mind Society. Its title was: 'The Quantum Theory: How far does it modify the mathematical, the physical and the psychological concepts of continuity?'[3] The high level speakers at this symposium were: mathematician and astronomer John William Nicholson; mathematician and philosopher of science Dorothy Wrinch, who had studied mathematical logic with Russell and later contributed to theoretical biology; famous physicist (and friend of Einstein) Frederick Lindemann, who later became the influential scientific advisor of Winston Churchill; and idealist philosopher (and promoter of Bergson in England) Herbert Wildon Carr, who was a personal friend of Whitehead. In her talk, Wrinch referred a few times to the second edition of Jeans' *Report on Radiation and the Quantum Theory*. Jeans, like Eddington, had been a student of Whitehead, and is the only quantum physicist whose name is mentioned by Whitehead in the context of his speculations on the topic (cf. HL1, 309).

The exchange of ideas at the symposium in July 1924 in England was still reverberating when Whitehead, in September 1924, after giving his first lecture at Harvard – which was general and could serve as an introduction to his whole lecture course on the philosophical presuppositions of science – had to choose a specific subject for his next lectures. No wonder he decided to first talk about the concepts of continuity and atomicity in the context of quantum theory. On 27 September 1924, Whitehead starts his second lecture as follows:

> Process [is the] fundamental and underlying fact in every detail of experience. . . . Consideration of process throws light on two contrasting ideas: continuity [and atomicity]. Not [the] ordinary mathematical form of continuity (as in mathematical books) though closely allied with it. [The] true contrasted idea is atomicity. The continuous always has divisibility in it somewhere. Continuity and atomicity have maintained a very equal duel through [the] history of human thought. [. . . N]either can be missed. Through slight mishandling [we] can exhibit atomicity as discontinuity, [but] this won't do. Process exhibits atomic character imposed upon a continuous field. Science illustrates this. [Hence:] Now [follows a] highly speculative lecture on the structure of energy. (HL1, 6)

Whitehead holds that the notion of process can help us to think continuity and atomicity together, to harmonise the concepts not of mathematical continuity and discontinuity, but of divisibility and indivisibility. And he immediately points out how: 'Process exhibits atomic character imposed upon a continuous field.' With *Process and Reality* in the back of our minds, we might think that Whitehead is making a distinction here between the atomic character of the process of becoming and the continuous character of the extensive continuum, between the atomicity of becoming and the continuity of space and time. But then we are jumping ahead. In the first semester of the 1924–25 academic year Whitehead is not yet convinced that there is an atomicity of becoming. On the contrary, in early October 1924 he makes it clear: 'Reality is a flux, a process, a continuity of becoming. [. . . The] continuity of flux exhibits atomic structures as imbedded in itself' (HL1, 417).

To understand the September 1924 statement, 'Process exhibits atomic character imposed upon a continuous field', we should ignore *Process and Reality* and look at the notes Whitehead added in August 1924 to the second edition of *The Principles of Natural Knowledge*. There we can read: 'In §15.8 [of this book] it is pointed out that continuity is derived from events, and atomicity from objects. This . . . requires development. It must suffice for the moment to suggest that a scientific object is an atomic structure imposed upon the continuity of events' (PNK, 203). Whitehead's quantum theory (with its notion of 'primate') provides an 'especially neat example' of a scientific object that is an atomic structure (HL1, 17). And what Whitehead means by the continuity of events is especially clear in *The Concept of Nature*, where he writes: 'The continuity of nature arises from extension. Every event extends over other events, and every event is extended over by other events' (CN, 59).

In *The Concept of Nature* (as in OT, PNK, R and HL1, 199–298 and 473–502), Whitehead introduces his method of extensive abstraction to abstract from the passage of nature, which belongs to the world of *sense* ('Nature is that which we observe in perception through the senses' (CN, 3)), the points of space and instants of time that belong to the world of *thought* (and are never observed in perception through the senses). More specifically, with the method of extensive abstraction, Whitehead deduces the 'exact geometry' (HL1, 199) of multiple space-time systems by means of convergent series of a special type of events called durations. A 'duration' is not an instant of time without temporal thickness, but 'the whole simultaneous occurrence of nature which is now for sense-awareness' (CN, 53), and which has temporal thickness – a duration is a 'slab of reality presented for your knowledge' (HL1, 18). In fact, moments (instantaneous spaces without temporal thickness) are arrived at by convergence of durations, and this convergence is defined in terms of the relation of extension among durations. Whitehead writes:

> The continuity of nature arises from extension. Every event extends over other events, and every event is extended over by other events. Thus in the special case of durations which are now the only events under consideration, every duration is part of other durations; and every duration has other durations which are parts of it. Accordingly there are no maximum and no minimum durations. Thus there is no atomic structure of durations ... (CN, 59)

Simply saying that time is the passage of nature because time is abstracted from it can lead to confusion and needs qualification. The passage of nature is the perceived time of the world of sense; it is psychological time. The time of the physicist's abstraction is the mathematical time of the world of thought; it is measurable time. The whole point of Whitehead's philosophy of nature is to make sure that there is no bifurcation of nature into the world of sense and the world of thought. The whole point of Whitehead's method is to prevent too great a separation between psychological time and measurable time by abstracting the latter from the former. Here lies the philosophical difference between the two empirically equivalent theories – the theory of multiple space-time systems and Einstein's Special Theory of Relativity (STR). Here lies the philosophical difference between Whitehead on the one hand, and Einstein and Eddington on the other.

I was the first to research the 1921 discussions of Whitehead with Einstein concerning their philosophical differences. So it pleases me that HL confirms the discussion at the home of Lord Haldane, in 'Haldane's study' (HL1, 187) at 'Queen Anne's Gate' (HL1, 185). In that discussion Einstein said of Whitehead's approach: 'That concerns psychological time. I have nothing to do with psychological time' (HL1, 185, 187; cf. also HL1, 319). Einstein's 1921 dismissal of Whitehead's approach did not knock Whitehead out of his orbit, and in 1922 he wrote: 'It follows from my refusal to bifurcate nature ... that we must reject the distinction between psychological time which is personal and impersonal time' (R, 66). Also, in 1924–25, in HL1, Whitehead – referring to Einstein's notion of the proper time of an entity, the time that is measurable in a space-time frame fixed to this entity – offers the following comments:

> But of course it is the essence of everything I have been saying that if you once lock yourself up in a private world you can never get out of it. The proper time & the psychological time are the same thing. The psychological time is the proper time of an entity that has cognition (HL1, 187). [I] dislike that you divorce the psychological field – what is actually before

you – from . . . physics [because] <u>then</u> you get into difficulties. [Then it is] hard to know what you are talking of. The physical world becomes a mere scheme of thought. . . . But it is obviously a 'scheme' about your own psychological field. (HL1, 317)

Even Eddington etc. start by putting down <u>equations</u>. And equations must be <u>in something</u>. (HL1 143)

[Eddington is left with a] common world of thought [of equations of higher mathematics] but no common world to think about. (HL1, 337)

Eddington tends to take up [an] extreme subjectivism [following] Kant, [whereas I take up a common sense] objectivism – [the] elements perceived by the senses are the elements of a common world. . . . I do not see how a common world of thought can be established apart from a common world of sense. [You] can't remedy it by saying 'anyhow we have a common world of thought' – Any community must presuppose the immediate objective position of the world of immediate experience. (HL1, 339)

When Whitehead says that psychological time and measurable time are the same, he actually means that the latter can be abstracted from the former, and that you should avoid the fallacy of misplaced concreteness. This error is committed by disregarding the concrete passage of nature in our immediate experience, that is, by disregarding that from which the measurable time of mathematical physics can be abstracted, and by dealing with measurable time as if it is the most concrete thing to take into account.

It is worth noticing that Einstein's reaction in the famous 1922 discussion with Bergson was the same as his reaction in the less known 1921 discussion with Whitehead. According to Einstein in 1922, the philosopher wants a time that is 'psychological and physical at once', but in his theories of relativity 'the concept of simultaneity passed from perceptions to objects . . . There is therefore no philosopher's time; . . . psychological time . . . differs from the time of the physicist.'[4] Bergson shared Whitehead's critique of Einstein, and hence provoked the same reaction.

The Whitehead-Bergson commonality brings us back to our discussion of continuity and to *The Concept of Nature* with its 'concept of extension' that 'exhibits in thought one side of the ultimate passage of nature' (CN, 58):

The process of nature can also be termed the passage of nature. I definitely refrain at this stage from using the word 'time,' since the measurable time of science and of civilized life generally merely exhibits some aspects of the more fundamental fact of the passage of nature. I believe that in this doctrine I am in full accord with Bergson . . . (CN, 54)

Time is known to me as an abstraction from the passage of events. The fundamental fact which renders this abstraction possible is the passing of nature, its development, its creative advance, and combined with this fact is another characteristic of nature, namely the extensive relation between events. The two facts, namely the passage of events and the extension of events over each other, are in my opinion the qualities from which time and space originate as abstractions. (CN, 34)

In *The Concept of Nature*, Whitehead makes a distinction between the passage of nature and the time of the field of extension, but – as the passage of nature is the passage of events and the extensive relatedness of events accounts for continuity – he holds that both are continuous. The distinction made corresponds with the distinction between the process of becoming and the time of the field of extension in HL1. However, in HL1 there is a difference between the first and the second semester lectures with regard to continuity. In the former Whitehead holds that the distinction is one between the *continuous* process of becoming and the *continuous* time of the field of extension, whereas in the latter he holds that the distinction is one between the *atomic* process of becoming and the *continuous* time of the extensive continuum.

Indeed, in the second semester lectures of HL1, Whitehead drops the continuity of becoming. Late March, beginning April 1925, Whitehead makes it quite clear: on the one hand, the process of *becoming real* is not happening in the field of extension, it is not divisible ('what becomes real is not divisible') and cannot be a temporal transition of its parts (for then 'Zeno has you'); on the other hand, each process in *being real* has its region in the field of extension, it is divisible ('the real must be <u>there</u> to be divided') and it has temporal transition in its essence – what becomes real 'doesn't become real because of the transition, but what is real has in its essence transition' (HL1, 302, 317).

In summary: when we compare the September–October 1924 lectures with the March–April 1925 lectures, there is a clear shift from a continuous becoming to the atomic becoming of continuous time. And that Whitehead holds fast to this new idea is clear from the following quote from *Process and Reality*, 1929, in which he calls each 'atomic process of becoming real' an 'actual occasion', and is not merely speaking of temporal transition, but of spatio-temporal extension (and even of a more general notion of extension, but that need not bother us here):

There can be no continuity of becoming. There is a becoming of continuity, but no continuity of becoming. The actual occasions are the creatures which become, and they constitute a continuously extensive world. In other words, extensiveness becomes, but 'becoming' is not itself extensive. Thus the ultimate metaphysical truth is atomism. The creatures are atomic. (PR, 35)

Prior to *Process and Reality*, Whitehead's treatment of this topic at times obscures the distinction between the atomicity of becoming and the continuity of time. For example, in *Science and the Modern World*, in 1925, Whitehead holds that 'temporalisation is realisation', that 'realisation is the becoming of time in the field of extension', and that consequently 'temporalisation is not another continuous process' but 'an atomic succession' (SMW, 126) – so far, so good. However, Whitehead's next sentence reads: 'Thus time is atomic, (i.e. epochal)' (SMW, 126). This comes as a surprise and seems to lead to a *reductio ad absurdum*. If time is atomic, then time is an atomic succession (in fact, Whitehead writes: 'Time is sheer succession of epochal durations' (SMW, 125)). Hence there is no difference between time and temporalisation and, consequently, time is the becoming of time. The last phrase seems absurd indeed. However, if we are careful and observe the distinction between time$_1$ = the time of the becoming of time in the field of extension, and time$_2$ = time in the field of extension, then the seemingly absurd phrase still makes sense. It then means: the time of becoming is the atomic becoming of the continuous time of extension. And indeed, Whitehead warns the readers of *Science and the Modern World*: 'In this account "time" has been separated from "extension"' (SMW, 125). So when he says that time is atomic or epochal, he is actually saying that the time of becoming is epochal, without implying that the time of extension is.

Comparison of the September–October 1924 lectures with the March–April 1925 lectures leads to the identification of a change in Whitehead's thought from his idea of 'a continuity of becoming' (HL1, 417) to his idea that 'process must be atomic' (HL1, 309), that 'generation . . . is atomic' (HL1, 311), that an 'atomic theory of generation' is needed (HL1 506). The same identification can be made when comparing the 1920 conclusion of *The Concept of Nature*, 'Thus there is no atomic structure of durations' (CN, 59), with the 1925 conclusion of *Science and the Modern World*, 'Time is sheer succession of epochal durations' (SMW, 125).

This change cannot have been an easy one, for it is easier to argue that the continuous space-time of STR is an abstraction from the continuous passage of nature than that it can be seen as an abstraction from the atomic process of becoming. Whitehead's atomic theory of generation holds that each 'event in some way is given as [an] atom', and yet Whitehead also holds fast to 'space-time as infinitely divisible' (HL1, 506). In HL1, Whitehead introduces the

atomicity of the process of becoming *after* dealing with the extensive abstraction of continuous time from the process of becoming, and he does not per-
form this extensive abstraction all over again to show how it must be modified
in the light of this introduction. However, in line with what I wrote above –
each process in *being real* has its region in the field of extension – I can make
the following suggestion.

The ultimate result of Whitehead's reconceptualisation is an atomic
process of becoming of which each realised atom has its region in the eternal extensive continuum. In this sense, realisation is the atomisation of the
continuum of extensively connected potential regions into the universe of
internally related actual occasions (also called actual entities). It will be
clear that the reconceptualisation of becoming involves a reconceptualisation of the extensive continuum. 'The space-time continuum' can be conceived as 'eternal' and as the 'scene of generation' – 'in space-time qua eternal
you get the potentiality of generation' (HL1, 309) and in space-time qua
scene of generation you get the generation of 'an atomic version of itself'
(HL1, 311). This reconceptualisation involves taking a position in between
Francis Herbert Bradley's idealist and Bergson's evolutionist position because
'Bradley represents a revolt against generation [and] Bergson a revolt against
the eternal side' (HL1, 313).

My suggestion is supported by Part II, Chapter II of *Process and Reality*,
'The Extensive Continuum', in which we can read: 'The conclusion is that
in every act of becoming there is the becoming of something with temporal
extension; but that act itself is not extensive' (PR, 69). The 'extensive continuum is one relational complex in which all potential objectifications [all
possible standpoints] find their niche. It underlies the whole world, past, present, and future' (PR, 66). 'The actual entities atomize it, and thereby make
real what was antecedently merely potential. The atomization of the extensive
continuum is also its temporalization' (PR, 72). There is an 'atomized quantum of extension correlative to [each] actual entity' (PR, 73). My suggestion
is also supported by Part IV, Chapter II of *Process and Reality*, in which the
relation of 'Extensive Connection' between all potential *regions* replaces the
earlier relation of extension between all *events*.

I am not the first person to highlight Whitehead's change from continuous to atomic becoming – 'The Emergence of Temporal Atomicity' has been
a topic of discussion among Whitehead scholars since the 1984 publication
of Lewis Ford's *The Emergence of Whitehead's Metaphysics: 1925–1929*.[5] And
since then there have been a lot of speculations with respect to the reasons
for this change. Was Whitehead's motive that he wanted to offer a solution to Zeno's paradoxes ('Real difficulty is when Zeno comes on the scene'

(HL1, 301))? Or was it that he wanted to enrich his philosophy with the concepts of freedom and error (cf. §1)? I think neither of these two conjectures will do. In fact, HL1 leads me to suggest that these two, and all other conjectures on Whitehead's motive that I have encountered in the literature, were not the main reasons for Whitehead to introduce the atomicity of becoming, but the favourable consequences of this introduction.

Whitehead's main motive towards the atomicity of becoming was to account for a common sense feature of the process of becoming to which he had previously not given sufficient attention, and the absence of which was brought to his attention by some paradoxes of STR and his own theory of multiple space-time systems: the irreversibility of becoming (the direction of time). As Whitehead puts it to his students:

> You . . . get atomism by making temporality something more than mere extension and divisibility. . . . The difference between temporality and extensiveness . . . was brought in our logical investigation . . . as rather a second rate thing to help us out of a difficulty. [The] idea of extension doesn't tell you which way time's going. That has to be dragged in by [the] scruff of [the] neck. . . . In the extensive complex . . . the forward-moving feature of time finds no recognition. [It does find recognition, however, in the idea of] temporalization, [which] is just another way of talking of . . . realization. . . . The atomic view . . . looks on realization as realization . . . qua succession . . . Temporality is the succession and this brings in the direction of succession. (HL1, 315–17)

> [In short:] The question of the direction of time is fundamental. . . . The idea of extension doesn't include time-direction. Mere extension soon demands that you should go beyond it [. . . to] the atomic view of succession. (HL1, 318–19)

> According to the modern view of relativity . . . the sharp distinction between future & past does not hold. (HL1, 504; cf. also HL1, 300, 302, 503)

> The direction of time . . . is generally merely assumed. If we slip in the obvious, we ought to give it a <u>fundamental</u> character. This essential character of the 'forwardness' of time should be more emphasized than we've been doing. And . . . the directional character entirely comes from [the atomicity of] realization & is not in the [continuity of] extension. (HL1, 507)

The irreversibility of becoming points at an especially clear example of the fallacy of misplaced concreteness. The reversible time of classical as well as relativistic physics abstracts from the irreversible character of becoming, but because of the success of physics, physicists and philosophers started saying that all temporality simply *is* reversible, and that irreversibility is an illusion that needs explaining away in terms of a fundamentally reversible time. The whole order of concrete temporality (psychological time) and abstract temporality (measurable time) is reversed here. Some philosophers, such as Bergson, and some physicists, such as Ilya Prigogine, refuse to commit this fallacy. Whitehead is one of them. When he states that 'time-systems . . . simply manifest one aspect' of 'the general passage or development of things', and that 'we want [the] idea of getting ahead – of becomingness', of irreversibility, he exclaims: 'Bergson of course', and adds:

> Bergson [is] here on the whole right, but phrases it so that you never can be quite sure what he means. This is why Russell dislikes him so. Bergson has a merit greater than clearness even – philosophical originality – putting things in which he feels and sees, whether he can make them clear or not. (HL1, 299)

One might suggest that it is obvious that next to the irreversibility of becoming, the quantum phenomena physicists observed in the first quarter of the twentieth century prompted Whitehead to introduce the atomicity of becoming. But the matter is less obvious than it seems, and the suggestion is wrong.

Let's first look again at Whitehead's first semester statement that we should not exhibit atomicity as discontinuity, that atomicity does not imply discontinuity. The latter claim is closely related to the following series of claims Whitehead makes: there is 'no reason to be compelled by quantum theory to accept [the] discontinuity of space and time' (HL1, 7; cf. also HL1, 421) or even 'to assume any discontinuity whatsoever' (HL1, 17); such an assumption is sheer 'nonsense' (HL1, 10, 418); 'the theory of "primates" [is] a warning [that] quantum theory need not imply [the] discontinuity of space-time' (HL1, 526), nor that of the process or flux of becoming; 'Process must have [a] foundation of continuity [but] on process [we] must embroider some idea of atomic structure' (HL1, 422); the 'continuity of flux exhibits atomic structures as imbedded in itself', and 'these [structures] represent permanent character[s] impressed in that flux . . . – permanent & also rhythmic characters' (HL1, 417). Well, 'primates' are such structures representing rhythmic characters in the flux; in fact, each primate is 'an atomic structure of vibrations with a definite frequency' (HL1, 12). In conclusion, quantum phenomena are not the reason for Whitehead's introduction of temporal atomicity, and his own quantum theory is even especially motivated to show by example that a theory can describe quantum phenomena while holding fast to the continuity of *both* becoming and space-time – 'The "primate" shows that atomicity is not the negation of continuity' (HL1, 527).

Things shift in the second semester, without however changing the conclusion. While introducing the atomicity of becoming, Whitehead no longer firmly rejects Jeans' statement that 'you've got to take your time in chunks' (HL1, 309). He now holds that if the quantum physicist (*in casu* Jeans) asks for 'an atomic theory of time', the speculative philosopher (*in casu* Whitehead) must not tell him: 'You can't have it', and run the 'danger of [developing a] metaphysics clothing itself in [the] viewpoint of science of the past' instead of exploiting today's 'scientific results' and utilising the '<u>own</u> viewpoint to get a bit <u>ahead</u> in vision' (HL1, 315). Moreover, he now holds that he can give the quantum physicists what they are asking for, because in his metaphysics he introduced temporality as the atomic succession of becoming in order to bring in the direction of succession and, hence, to help him out of the difficulty that extension doesn't tell which way time is going (cf. HL1, 315–17). The succession of atomic processes of becoming – Whitehead's atomic theory of time – does not 'naturally grow out of the metaphysical point of view of [his Harvard lecture] course', but seems required by it because of the 'blur between past, present & future due to relativity' and, thus, because of the lack of 'direction of time' (HL1, 506–7). Clearly, despite the shift in the second semester, Whitehead does not say that he changed his metaphysics with respect to becoming from continuous to atomic because of quantum theory, but that he can give quantum theory an atomic theory of time because he thus changed his metaphysics.

I can add that, during the second semester, Whitehead can give more to quantum physicists than a metaphysical theory of atomic time. By combining his second semester theory of the atomicity of becoming with his first semester theory of primates, he can 'drop the continuity of path' (HL1, 173) and explain the discontinuous path of atomic structures representing rhythmic characters in the process of becoming (such as the path of a primate) in opposition to the continuous path of such structures representing permanent characters (such as the path of an electron as conceived *prior* to HL1 – in HL1 Whitehead conceives 'electrons as vibrant rather than passive charges' (HL1, 526)). This combination and conclusion are not explicit in HL1, but in *Science and the Modern World* they are:

> The discontinuities introduced by the quantum theory require revision of physical concepts in order to meet them. In particular, it has been pointed out that some theory of discontinuous existence is required.

What is asked from such a theory, is that an orbit of an electron can be regarded as a series of detached points, and not as a continuous line. The theory of a primate or vibrating pattern . . . *together* with the distinction between temporality and extensiveness . . . yields exactly this result. (SMW, 135; my italics)

In this sense, Whitehead contradicts in 1925 what was crucial for the development of his 1924 quantum theory, namely, that atomicity does not imply discontinuity. However, the discontinuity of the path of a primate or other atomic structure (the required discontinuous existence) does not imply the discontinuity of space and time. In fact, the atomic theory of time that Whitehead gives to Jeans is an atomic theory of the time of becoming (temporality) and not of the time of extension (transition). The field of space-time is still continuous, the extensive continuum still a continuum.

## Notes

1. Einstein, *Ideas and Opinions*, 294.
2. Eddington, 'Physics and Philosophy', 31.
3. Aristotelian Society, *Supplementary Volume IV*, 19–49.
4. Bergson, *Duration and Simultaneity*, 158–9.
5. Ford, *The Emergence of Whitehead's Metaphysics*, chapter 3. Notice that whereas I find proof in HL1 to agree with Ford on this change in Whitehead's thought, Paul A. Bogaard (in his Introduction to HL1) and Gary Herstein and George R. Lucas (in chapters 6 and 16 of the present book) claim that HL1 contradicts Ford's thesis of the emergence of temporal atomicity.

## Bibliography

Aristotelian Society, *Supplementary Volume IV: Concepts of Continuity* (New York: Johnson Reprint Corporation, 1964).

Bergson, Henri, *Duration and Simultaneity* (Manchester: Clinamen Press, 1999).

Bogaard, Paul and Jason Bell (eds), *The Harvard Lectures of Alfred North Whitehead, 1924–1925: Philosophical Presuppositions of Science* (Edinburgh: Edinburgh University Press, 2017).

Eddington, Arthur, 'Physics and Philosophy', *Philosophy*, 8 (1933), 31.

Einstein, Albert, *Ideas and Opinions* (New York: Wings Books, 1954).

Ford, Lewis, *The Emergence of Whitehead's Metaphysics: 1925–1929* (Albany: State University of New York Press, 1984).

Whitehead, Alfred North, *An Enquiry Concerning the Principles of Natural Knowledge* (New York: Dover Publications, [1919] 1982).

Whitehead, Alfred North, *The Concept of Nature* (Cambridge: Cambridge University Press, [1920] 1971).

Whitehead, Alfred North, *The Principle of Relativity: With Applications to Physical Science* (Cambridge: Cambridge University Press, [1922] 2011).

Whitehead, Alfred North, *Science and the Modern World* (New York: The Free Press, [1925] 1967).

Whitehead, Alfred North, *Process and Reality: An Essay in Cosmology* (New York: The Free Press, [1929] 1978).

# 8

# Whitehead's Highly Speculative Lectures on Quantum Theory

*Ronny Desmet*

The aim of this chapter is to try to make sense of Whitehead's 'highly specula-tive' lectures on quantum theory (cf. HL1, 6–22, 414–22). Prior to the pub-lishing of *The Harvard Lectures of Alfred North Whitehead, 1924–1925* (HL1), Whitehead scholars already knew from *The Principles of Natural Knowledge*, *The Concept of Nature* and *The Principle of Relativity* that Whitehead devel-oped a theory of multiple space-time systems and an alternative theory of gravitation – two theories of relativity that are empirically hard to distinguish, but philosophically quite different from Einstein's Special Theory of Relativ-ity (STR) and his General Theory of Relativity (GTR). They already knew that when in *Science and the Modern World*, in the chapter on 'Relativity', Whitehead criticises Einstein for taking the abstraction of space-time as more concrete than it really is, and for even interpreting gravitation in terms of con-tortions in space-time, Whitehead is referring to his own two alternative theo-ries of relativity. However, with the publication of HL1, Whitehead scholars have learned that Whitehead not only developed his alternative theories of relativity, but was also struggling to cope theoretically with the closely related quantum phenomena of black-body radiation (Planck), photo-electric effect (Einstein) and atomic emission spectra (Bohr), as in fact all mathematical physicists did at that period in time – de Broglie, Schrödinger, Heisenberg, etc. They now know that when in *Science and the Modern World*, in the chap-ter on 'The Quantum Theory', Whitehead loosely talks about the theory of 'primates' (read 'quanta', not 'apes'), there is a more detailed sketch of this theory to be found in HL1.

This chapter looks at the sketch of the theory of primates in HL1, and it will make clear that Whitehead's search for a quantum theory had a lot in common with his search for a relativistic theory of gravity. The undisputed starting point for Whitehead's speculations as a mathematical physicist was his interpretation of Maxwell's theory of electromagnetism, joined with his refusal to abandon the concept of a uniform and continuous space-time. And in both his gravity and his quantum research the mathematical vehicle guiding Whitehead was the wave equation. Hence, Whitehead's primates – the quanta constituting photons, electrons and protons, and explaining the Planck-Einstein-Bohr quantum phenomena – are atomic structures imposed upon the continuity of events. In essence, they are standing waves in the electromagnetic field.

Whitehead's professional background included the best publications at the time on the topics of relativity and quantum theory – for example Arthur Eddington's 1918 *Report on the Relativity Theory of Gravitation* and James Jeans' 1914 *Report on Radiation and the Quantum Theory*. In fact, one might say of Whitehead what he said of Einstein: his theory is not 'team work', but 'it's not [Whitehead] *in vacuo*' either; [Whitehead's] speculations were firmly embedded in the 'history of thought' (cf. HL1, 296, 298). The result is that in some respects, Whitehead's 1924 sketch of the theory of primates foreshadows the 1924 thesis on the theory of quanta by Louis de Broglie (published in 1925) as well as Erwin Schrödinger's later wave mechanics.

## §1 Whitehead's Failure to Popularise Mathematical Physics for his Philosophy Students

On 27 September 1924, Whitehead announces to his students a 'highly speculative lecture' (HL1, 6), which is 'not in any sense [a] philosophy lecture but an attempt to give the scientific outlook, of which we are to study the presuppositions' (HL1, 414). In order to do so, Whitehead says he will 'get science into [a] form in which one can expect philosophers to understand it' (HL1, 10). Whitehead is not one of those seeking the 'pleasure of making mathematics mysterious' (HL1, 289, 291). He genuinely aims at popularising the mathematical physics of electromagnetism, relativity and quantum theory, and sometimes refrains from using 'frightening' mathematics and physics (HL1, 183). For example, when his mathematical discussion of the considerations of symmetry to deduce multiple space-time systems gets complicated, he is 'leaving this for fear of confusing [the] issue' (HL1, 290). He is well aware that 'all 4-dimensional investigations are a strain on the imagination', and admits that he himself is at times 'struggling (unsuccessfully) with [the] mathematics of relativity' (HL1, 299). Yet, he was probably too optimistic when saying: 'The relativity hypothesis presents us with the notion of alternative progressions in time [which is] not obvious to myself, [and it is] only by a miracle that I have made it obvious to you' (HL1, 302).

On top of the difficulty of mathematical physics, there is the difficulty that Whitehead's lectures were not presentations of clear-cut theories, but instances of philosophy in the making. And a philosopher can be 'either clear-headed by leaving out half the facts [or . . .] adequate and muddled. Every-body steers [an] uneasy course between [the] desire to be clear and [the] desire to be adequate. So everyone is partly superficial and partly muddled', but as Whitehead is very cautious not to leave out facts, for him 'clearness [is . . .] now [and again] practically impossible' (HL1, 74), and as the 'result of discussion' with his students, Whitehead sometimes had to admit that his 'main point [was] not made clear' (HL1, 91). No wonder that his students, no matter how talented, were sometimes desperate. For example, on 16 October 1924, Bell laments: 'Whitehead here becomes incoherent for the $n^{th}$ time' (HL1, 38).

The lack of knowledge of mathematical physics joined with the difficulty of Whitehead's speculative method led to a multitude of mistakes with respect to mathematical physics in the notes of Bell, Hocking and Heath which I will not endeavour to set straight here. These mistakes, together with the fact that Whitehead left out a lot of details in order not to confuse his students, often obscure what Whitehead aimed at and, in particular, make a detailed recon-struction of his quantum theory impossible (at least for me). Nonetheless I try to give a first impression that can be improved upon by further research.

## §2 Maxwell's Theory of Electromagnetism

The starting point is Maxwell's theory of electromagnetism. It is a com-monplace that Whitehead's philosophy is rooted in relativity or quan-tum mechanics, but I hold, and HL1 confirms, that it is Maxwell's theory that influenced him most. Not only was it the basis on which his theories of relativity and quanta were built, it was also the starting point of his philosophical speculations. Whitehead says: 'All modern theory [is] just a modification of Maxwell' (HL1, 7). '[My] fundamental point of view of all physical science is that the electromagnetic phenomena on the whole give one the fundamental elements on which [the] universe is built [and the] whole theory is [based] upon [a] group of formulae discovered by . . . Clerk Maxwell' (HL1, 414). '[I] have strong reasons to believe that Clerk Maxwell's equations, if not true, are tending toward the truth. Therefore [they] will be our starting point' (HL1, 417).

Whitehead's 1924 popular account of Maxwell's equations in HL1 (cf. HL1, 7–8, 20, 414–15, 418) is not new. It corresponds with his 1917 popular account in *The Organisation of Thought* (OT, 183–6) and with his more technical 1919 account in *The Principles of Natural Knowledge* (PNK, §6, Appendix II to Chapter II). Whitehead indicates that one scalar and three vector quantities are involved, of which the components are all functions of place $r = (x, y, z)$ and time $t$: the scalar field of the distribution of electric charges expressed as electric charge density $\rho$; the vector field of electric force $\mathcal{E} = (f, g, h)$; the vector field of magnetic force $B = (\alpha, \beta, \gamma)$; and the electric current $j = (i_1, i_2, i_3)$, which is often conceived as the multiplication of charge density $\rho$ and velocity $v = (u, v, w)$ of the individual parts of the distribution of charge, hence, $j = \rho v$. Then he makes clear that Maxwell's equations are relations involving the temporal and the spatial rates of variation of the components of the vector fields of electric and magnetic force.

As Whitehead's popular account and the many mistakes by his students in their lecture notes obscure the mathematics underlying Whitehead's philosophical speculations, I will now give – for readers that have an undergraduate knowledge of mathematical physics – some recognisable details with respect to Maxwell's equations, the electromagnetic field of an electron in motion, and STR (but I will do so from the standpoint of one space-time system, without bothering about transformations from one to another such system). These details render Whitehead's Harvard lectures more intelligible. Readers without a background in mathematical physics, however, can skip the mathematical details in the rest of this chapter.

Determining the rates of variation Whitehead talks about corresponds with determining the partial derivatives with respect to time and space coordinates: $\dfrac{\partial}{\partial t}$ and $\dfrac{\partial}{\partial x}$ and $\dfrac{\partial}{\partial y}$ and $\dfrac{\partial}{\partial z}$. And taking inyto account that for a vector field $F = (X, Y, Z)$ one can define:

$$\frac{\partial F}{\partial t} = \left( \frac{\partial X}{\partial t}, \frac{\partial Y}{\partial t}, \frac{\partial Z}{\partial t} \right)$$

$$divF = \frac{\partial X}{\partial x} + \frac{\partial Y}{\partial y} + \frac{\partial Z}{\partial z}$$

$$curlF = \left( \frac{\partial Z}{\partial y} - \frac{\partial Y}{\partial z}, \frac{\partial X}{\partial z} - \frac{\partial Z}{\partial x}, \frac{\partial Y}{\partial x} - \frac{\partial X}{\partial y} \right)$$

Maxwell's equations, with $c$ the velocity of light *in vacuo*, read:

$$div\,\varepsilon = \rho$$

$$div\,B = 0$$

$$curl\,\varepsilon + \frac{1}{c}\frac{\partial B}{\partial t} = 0$$

$$curl\,B - \frac{1}{c}\frac{\partial \varepsilon}{\partial t} = \frac{1}{c}j$$

These correspond respectively with Maxwell's equations (1), (2), (4) and (3) as given in Appendix II to Chapter II of *The Principles of Natural Knowledge* (PNK, 30).

In lecture 34 of HL1 (HL1, 148–52, 463–4), Whitehead also introduces the electromagnetic potentials: the scalar potential $\phi$ and the vector potential $A = (a_1, a_2, a_3)$. Taking into account that for a function $\xi$ one can define:

$$grad\,\xi = \left(\frac{\partial \xi}{\partial x}, \frac{\partial \xi}{\partial y}, \frac{\partial \xi}{\partial z}\right)$$

the following relations hold between the vector fields of electric and magnetic force and the electromagnetic potentials:

$$\varepsilon = -\,grad\,\phi - \frac{1}{c}\frac{\partial A}{\partial t}$$

$$B = curl\,A$$

Clearly, by means of the electromagnetic potentials the vector fields of electric and magnetic force can be determined (and the other way around). If the potentials satisfy the Lorentz gauge condition:

$$div\,A = -\frac{1}{c}\frac{\partial \phi}{\partial t}$$

then the fact that the vector fields satisfy Maxwell's equation is equivalent to the fact that the potentials satisfy the inhomogeneous wave equations:

$$\frac{\partial^2 \phi}{\partial x^2} + \frac{\partial^2 \phi}{\partial y^2} + \frac{\partial^2 \phi}{\partial z^2} - \frac{1}{c^2}\frac{\partial^2 \phi}{\partial t^2} = -\rho$$

$$\frac{\partial^2 A}{\partial x^2} + \frac{\partial^2 A}{\partial y^2} + \frac{\partial^2 A}{\partial z^2} - \frac{1}{c^2}\frac{\partial^2 A}{\partial t^2} = -\frac{1}{c}j$$

Now consider the case of a moving electron with charge $e$. Picture the electron as a little charge-sphere. The potential influence this electron has *outside* the charge-sphere at place $r(t) = (x(t), y(t)), z(t))$ at time $t$ is given by the potentials $\phi$ and $A$ at this place at this time. In order to find the relevant potentials at place $r(t)$ at time $t$, you must not consider what is going on at other places at the same time $t$. You must consider what was going on at any place at such an earlier time $t'$ in the past that its influence would reach the given place $r(t)$ at time $t$. More specifically, the relevant potentials $\phi$ and $A$ are not determined by the electron at time $t$, but by the electron at such an earlier time $t'$ in the past that its influence would reach the given place $r(t)$ at time $t$. In other words $\phi$ and $A$ are not determined by the electron's place $r_e(t) = (x_e(t), y_e(t), z_e(t))$ and velocity $v_e(t) = (u(t), v(t), w(t))$ at time $t$, but by the electron's place $r_e(t') = (x_e(t'), y_e(t'), z_e(t'))$ and velocity $v_e(t') = (u(t'), v(t'), w(t'))$ at an earlier time $t'$, which is why they are called retarded potentials. As the potentials $\phi$ and $A$ are solutions of the wave equation, they are wave-potentials propagating with velocity $c$, and the time that was needed for these wave-potentials to propagate from $r_e(t')$ to $r(t)$ with velocity $c$ is equal to the distance $d(r_e(t'), r(t))$ between the two places $r_e(t')$ and $r(t)$ divided by velocity $c$. Consequently the earlier time is:

$$t' = t - \frac{d\big(r_e(t'), r(t)\big)}{c}$$

In this case the retarded potentials – the solutions of the above wave equations – are given by the formulae of Liénard-Wiechert:

$$\phi\big(r(t)\big) = \frac{e}{d\big(r_e(t'), r(t)\big) - \frac{1}{c}v_e(t') \cdot [r_e(t') - r(t)]}$$

$$A\big(r(t)\big) = \frac{\phi\big(r(t)\big) v_e(t')}{c}$$

By means of these retarded potentials, we can determine the vector field of electric force $\varepsilon = (f, g, h)$ and the vector field of magnetic force $B = (\alpha, \beta, \gamma)$ due to a moving electron with charge $e$, but *outside* its charge-sphere, in other words, we can determine its electromagnetic field outside its charge-sphere. In HL1, Whitehead speaks not only of the vector fields of electric and magnetic force, and of the retarded potentials, but also of 'Poynting's Formula for [the] transference of Energy' (HL1, 20). In fact: 'The discussion of the Poynting Flux of Energy', Whitehead later wrote in *Adventures of Ideas*, 'is one of the most fascinating chapters of Electrodynamics' (AI, Chapter XI, §16). According to Poynting, the flux of energy S of the electromagnetic field due to a moving electron with charge e is determined at place $r = (x, y, z)$ and time $t$, but *outside* the electron-sphere, by light-velocity $c$ multiplied with the vector-product of $\varepsilon = (f, g, h)$ and $B = (\alpha, \beta, \gamma)$. Thus:

$$S = c\varepsilon \times B = c(g\gamma - h\beta, h\alpha - f\gamma, f\beta - g\alpha)$$

Can't we say anything about what happens *inside* the charge-sphere of the electron itself? Well, if we consider the electron as not-moving, as static, and hold that the charge $e$ of this static electron is uniformly distributed over the *surface* of a charge-sphere with radius R, then the charge density is the surface charge density $\rho s = \dfrac{e}{4\pi R^2}$ and the electrostatic self-energy of the electron is proportional to $\dfrac{e^2}{R}$ (with proportionality factor $\dfrac{1}{2}$). If we hold that the charge $e$ of this static electron is uniformly distributed over the *volume* of a charge-sphere with radius R, then the charge density is the volume charge density $\rho v = \dfrac{e}{\frac{4}{3}\pi R^3}$ but the electrostatic self-energy of the electron is again proportional to $\dfrac{e^2}{R}$ (even though, of course, with a different proportionality factor). Apparently the self-energy of the electron is always proportional to $\dfrac{e^2}{R}$ with a proportionality factor depending on the charge density on or in the electron's charge-sphere.

We can reformulate the above in the four-dimensional space-time of STR, also called the Minkowski space-time. We can go from the scalar potential and the three-component vector potential to the four-potential $\varphi^\mu$ by putting $\varphi^1 = \phi$, $\varphi^2 = \alpha_1$, $\varphi^3 = \alpha_2$, $\varphi^4 = \alpha_3$ and from the scalar charge density and the three-component current vector to the four-current $j^\mu$ by putting $j^1 = \rho c$, $j^2 = i_1$, $j^3 = i_2$, $j^4 = i_3$. And we can then write the above inhomogeneous wave equations as one equation:

$$\frac{\partial^2 \varphi^\mu}{\partial x^2} + \frac{\partial^2 \varphi^\mu}{\partial y^2} + \frac{\partial^2 \varphi^\mu}{\partial z^2} - \frac{1}{c^2}\frac{\partial^2 \varphi^\mu}{\partial t^2} = -j^\mu$$

This equation (actually four equations as $\mu$ takes the values 1, 2, 3 and 4) is the wave equation as encountered in STR. It is equivalent to the four

Maxwell equations given above because if, by solving it, we find the four-potential $\varphi^\mu$, then we have the scalar potential $\phi$ and the vector potential A too and, hence, can calculate the vector field of electric force $\varepsilon$ and the vector field of magnetic force B. That is why, in this context, the wave equation is sometimes called the Maxwell-Minkowski equation. In STR, the three components of the vector field of electric force and the three components of the vector field of magnetic force are used (I leave out how) to define the 16 components of the tensor field of electromagnetism $F_{\mu\nu}$ (both $\mu$ and $\nu$ take the values 1, 2, 3 and 4). So when the four-potential is found as a solution of the Maxwell-Minkowski wave equation, we can determine the tensor field of electromagnetism; with this tensor field we can (for example) determine the electromagnetic action on a charged particle; and by means of the principle of least action we can determine the motion of this particle.

In STR the above Liénard-Wiechert formulae for the retarded potentials describing the potential influence of a moving electron outside of its sphere can also be reformulated. To do so, we need the four-velocity $v_e^\mu$ of the electron of which the components are $v_e^1 = \Omega_e c$, $v_e^2 = \Omega_e u$, $v_e^3 = \Omega_e v$, $v_e^4 = \Omega_e w$, with:

$$\Omega_e = \left(1 - \frac{u^2 + v^2 + w^2}{c^2}\right)^{-\frac{1}{2}}$$

It is easy to see that the above Liénard-Wiechert formulae are equivalent to the following formula for the retarded four-potential:

$$\varphi^\mu = \frac{\varphi_e(r(t)) v_e^\mu}{c}$$

with

$$\varphi_e(r(t)) = \frac{e}{\Omega_e\left\{d(r_e(t')\, r(t)) - \frac{1}{c} v_e(t') . [r_e(t') - r(t)]\right\}}$$

By means of this retarded four-potential, we can determine the electron's tensor field of electromagnetism; with this tensor field we can determine the electron's electromagnetic action on another charged particle; and by means of the principle of least action we can determine the motion of this other particle.

## §3 Whitehead's Alternative Theory of Gravitation

The reason for bringing in this particular special relativistic formulation is that it is at the core of Whitehead's alternative theory of gravitation.

Whitehead rejects GTR because it replaces the uniform space-time of STR (which coheres with the uniform spatio-temporal texture of the world of sense) with a contingently curved space-time (belonging to a world of thought completely detached from the world of sense). Whitehead's relativistic theory of the gravitational field due to (but outside of) a non-rotating spherical object with mass $m$ is completely analogous to the special relativistic formulation of the electromagnetic field due to (but outside of) a spherical electron with charge $e$.

Instead of Einstein's field equation, Whitehead utilises the wave equation. The solution of Einstein's field equation for mass-sphere $m$ is the Einstein-Schwarzschild tensor field of gravitation (which is equal in Einstein's theory to the fundamental tensor field of the contingently curved space-time). The solution of Whitehead's wave equation (cf. equation 16 in R, 82) for mass-sphere $m$ is a retarded scalar potential that is completely analogous to $\varphi_e\left(r(t)\right)$ above, but instead of charge $e$ it deals with mass $m$, and it involves the gravitational constant $\gamma$:

$$\varphi_m\left(r(t)\right) = \frac{\gamma m}{\Omega_m\left\{d\left(r_m(t^{'}),\ r(t)\right) - \dfrac{1}{c}v_m(t^{'}) . [r_m(t^{'}) - r(t)]\right\}}$$

By means of this scalar potential (given in equation 15 in R, 82 for multiple masses), Whitehead defines (cf. equation 17 in R, 83) the potential impetus tensor field of gravitation (which is not equal to, and does not contingently curve the Minkowski tensor field of the uniform space-time of STR).

With the Einstein-Schwarzschild tensor field of gravitation we can determine the spherical object's (e.g. the sun's) gravitational action on another mass-object (e.g. the earth); and by means of the principle of least action we can determine the motion of this other object. With Whitehead's potential impetus tensor field of gravitation we can determine the spherical object's gravitational impetus on another mass-object; and by means of the principle of least impetus we can determine the motion of this other object. In 1924, Eddington expressed both the Einstein-Schwarzschild tensor and Whitehead's potential impetus tensor in spherical coordinates (we've tacitly been using Cartesian coordinates), and then showed by means of a clever transformation of the time-coordinate that both tensors are actually identical. In other words, Eddington showed that Einstein's and Whitehead's theories give identical results for non-rotating spherically symmetric objects. And in 1986, Robert John Russell and Christoph Wasserman showed that both theories also give identical results for rotating, axially symmetric and stationary objects. In this case, the solution of Einstein's field equation is the Einstein-Kerr tensor field of gravitation, and the solution of Whitehead's wave equation is a scalar potential that gives rise to a potential impetus tensor field of gravitation that can be shown to be identical to the Einstein-Kerr one.

However, Whitehead mainly proposed his alternative theory of gravitation as *an example* that a theory of gravity need not bifurcate nature into, on the one hand, the uniform world of sense and of practical measurement, and on the other, a contingently curved world of thought and theoretical mathematics. And that is exactly why he proposed his quantum theory as well, namely, as *an example* that a quantum theory need not bifurcate nature into the continuous world of sense and a discontinuous world of mathematical thought. Notice that Whitehead developed his quantum theory when still holding that becoming (the passage of nature that we observe in perception through the senses) is continuous. He developed his theory of primates as an 'especially neat example' to prove 'that there's nothing in the quantum theory that makes it necessary . . . to assume any discontinuity whatsoever' (HL1, 17).

## §4 Whitehead's Paradigm of the Electron as a Complex Organism

Instead of immediately presenting Whitehead's theory of primates, let us first present the return of insight on our investment in mathematical physics. Let's first look again at the 'theory of the retarded potential' (HL1, 28), which shows how past entities (such as electrons) condition the present or, in other words, how present 'entities condition the future' (HL1, 28). As said, Whitehead deals with the 'theory of the retarded potential' in lecture 34 of HL1 (HL1, 148–52, 463–4), and it is interesting to see that in this lecture he stresses that even though this 'theory looks like action at a distance', it is really a field theory of 'transmission of influence . . . travelling with a definite velocity – that of light *in vacuo*' (HL1, 149–50) – in fact, the theory of retarded potentials is often mistaken as an action at a distance theory! It is also interesting to see that he pictures the transmission of influence of an electron, expressed by 'the scalar potential $\phi$ and the vector potential $(a_1, a_2, a_3)$', as a spherical wave 'travelling outward' (HL1, 150) – this is the best way of picturing these potentials as solutions of the wave equation. Also, it is funny to see that Whitehead says that if the electron is thought of as static, 'time drops out and you get Newton's law of gravitation' (HL1, 150) – if the electron is not moving, there is no retardation effect anymore, and you get *Coulomb's law of electricity*. This proves that Whitehead, especially after developing his alternative theory of gravitation, was always thinking of gravitation and electromagnetism as completely analogous.

Less funny, even unfortunate, is that Whitehead brought in the retarded potentials of moving electrons to illustrate 'the idea of electron as complex organism' (HL1, 149) – the idea at the basis of his physics and his philosophy – and that the notes of Bell, Hocking and Heath of lecture 34 convey this point very poorly. To compensate for this, I give a rather long, but superior quote from *The Organisation of Thought*. It highlights exactly what Whitehead's students should have noted down:

> For example, consider an electron. There is a scalar distribution of electricity, which is what is ordinarily called the electron. . . . It follows from [the electromagnetic] laws that the electron . . . is to be conceived as at each instant propagating from itself an emanation [$\phi$ & A] which travels outwards with the velocity of light *in vacuo* and from which $\varepsilon$ and B can be calculated, so far as they are due to that electron. Thus the field, at any time, due to the electron as a whole depends on the previous history of the electron, the nearer the electron the more recent being the relevant history. The whole scheme of such a field is one single thought-object of science: the electron and its emanations form one essential whole, namely one thought-object of science, essentially complex and essentially filling all space. The electron proper, namely, the scalar distribution of [electricity], is the proper focus of the whole, the essential focal property being that the field at any instant is completely determined by the previous history of the focus and of its space relations through all previous time. But the field and the focus are not independent concepts, they are essentially correlated in one organised unity, namely, they are essentially correlated terms in the field of one relation in virtue of which the entities enter into our thoughts. (OT, 184–5)

Clearly the electron is not just a momentary thing, and it is not just its charge, nor the potentials it transmits. It is the 'historical route' (HL1, 175) of its focal centre and its emanations. The 'physicist considers . . . how the electrons interfere with one another's life history in the field of force' (HL1, 196), and you cannot simply say that the electron *is* a 'little spot of mist' there and then (HL1, 26), nor that the 'electron is merely a way in which other electrons in the future are going to be influenced' (HL1, 27). In both cases, you are making the 'poisonous' error (HL1, 26) that Whitehead calls the 'fallacy of misplaced concreteness' (HL1, 26).

If you take the isolated charge as the most concrete thing, you abstract from the relatedness. Whitehead calls this instance of the fallacy of misplaced concreteness, the fallacy of 'simple location', and according to him 'simple location' is the 'wrong concept to apply' (HL1, 167) because 'with simple location, we get back to stuff' (HL1, 160); it is 'the wrong basis', which 'leads to [the] bifurcation of nature' into a world of isolated bits of matter and a world of legislative minds (HL1, 170). Whitehead suggests 'that we discard [the] idea of material (simple location) at once' and consider instead the 'idea of organism' (HL1, 161). He reminds his students that 'Faraday and J. J. Thomson' already said that the electron is 'something spreading throughout all space', something far removed 'from Descartes' idea of "lump of matter"', and Whitehead welcomes this holistic idea of one of the physicists he admired most (Faraday, Maxwell's main source of inspiration) and one of his own former teachers (J. J. Thomson, the discoverer of the electron), for he sees the idea of matter as 'inconvenient for physics as well as for biology and psychology' (HL1, 343).

Saying that the electron '<u>is</u> "<u>there</u>"', isn't really stating [the] facts of the case. It's assuming that there is a meaning of "being <u>there</u>" *simpliciter* [whereas] there are senses in which the object is <u>everywhere</u>' (HL1, 102). Forget the 'billiard-ball view' of electrons because an electron 'is really <u>everywhere</u>' and so the '<u>location</u> of [an] electron rather loses its sense – you can't disjoin it from its field' (HL1, 108). The electron is 'a structure . . . which has reverberations to all points, <u>extends</u> to all space, and yet [has] a <u>home</u>', so stop saying: '<u>There</u> it is', for it is 'a centre of <u>activity</u>' (HL, 75) that 'imposes itself on the environment' (HL1, 156). 'The electron doesn't simply passively accept its environment . . . Therefore (important as showing [the] essentially <u>organic</u> character of nature) you cannot determine [an] electron apart from the total to which it belongs – and <u>vice versa</u>' (HL1, 154).

> You cannot consider the nature of an electron without considering the whole, nor the whole without considering the electron. Contrast [electrons with] Lucretius' atoms, each perfectly happy and on its own, [only] influencing each other's mode of motion – [you] can't get an organism out of that. [You] have to get something extra when you want a totality to enter into the nature of the parts. [However,] the organic principle must not be brought in on top of [a] mechanistic principle. (HL1, 156)

> The billiard ball idea of an atom [renders the idea of] <u>organism</u> unintelligible . . . The atoms affect one another's <u>motion</u>, but that's all. As soon as you want an organism (a totality to enter into very nature of parts) you can only lug in by [the] scruff of [the] neck some 'vital principle' to put <u>on top of</u> your atoms. But this is most unsatisfying. (HL1, 154)

Clearly, the electromagnetic theory of electrons leads Whitehead to his 'key idea', the idea 'of organism and not that of matter [as] something [simply] there' (HL1, 153). And Whitehead takes the idea of the electron as an organism as far as he can when he says to his students: 'The electron . . . we are studying doesn't remain what it would be in the absence of [its] environment. . . . Its pattern of functioning is itself dependent on the particular environment in which it finds itself' (HL1, 154). For example, Hendrik Lorentz pictured each electron as a 'rigid electron', which 'is always a spherical distribution of electricity, i.e. always the same under different circumstances', but Max Abraham pictured each electron as a 'plastic electron', which 'modifies itself', and 'becomes a spheroid under [some] field of force' (HL1, 469). Because 'the electron adapted itself to the field of force' (HL1, 175), one might say that an 'electron will adapt itself to its environment' (HL1, 173). So when Whitehead asks himself, 'What is the electron in the whole body?', his answer reads that it 'will exhibit properties it would never exhibit elsewhere' (HL1, 174). The electron in the body 'is what it is . . . by virtue of being within the whole living body', and hence, electrons in the body 'follow the laws of nature, but it would not be surprising if they behaved in ways that had no exemplification outside the body' (HL1, 175–6).

Whitehead is well aware of the scepticism of most scientists when confronted with his idea that the electron is an organism, but that does not impress him because 'scientists' always 'regard you as talking metaphysical nonsense when you are just phrasing what is implicit in all their own statements' (HL1, 343). Whereas most physicists are unaware of the implicit presuppositions of the electromagnetic theory of electrons, Whitehead's philosophical aim in HL1 is precisely to raise awareness of these presuppositions, and to harmonise them. It is Whitehead's study of the electromagnetic theory of electrons which prompts him to interpret an electron as 'an enduring organism', where 'enduring' refers to 'an identity of pattern throughout an historic route' (HL1, 137). His philosophical statement that 'ultimate fact is an enduring <u>organism</u>' (HL1, 153) is no creation out of nothing. 'When you go to the abstractions of physical science', he says, and study 'electrons – these are simply enduring objects looked on from the point of view of the interrelations of their life histories', then 'you find the psychological field reproducing itself', for in both cases, there is the 'same idea of aspects prehended into a unity' (HL1, 473). Indeed: 'you have prehension of all the electrons – prehended together into [one] field of force. [. . . The] fundamental fact or concrete unit is an event looked on as

a grasping together of a number of limited aspects of [the] totality. It isn't
mere multiplicity . . .: events can't be looked on as . . . disjoined from one
another' (HL1, 196). Again, and in conclusion, Whitehead's study of the
electromagnetic theory of electrons is the starting point of his philosophy of
the essential togetherness of things.

## §5 Whitehead's Notion of Primate

Let's now deal with Whitehead's quantum theory, that is, his theory of primates. One might think, given the paradigmatic role of electrons for Whitehead, that his primates will be enduring organisms in exactly the same way as
his electrons. A primate – 'the fundamental structure out of which all other
structures [are] built' (HL1, 14) – indeed 'can be in all parts of time & space
& yet be somewhere' (HL1, 77), but this 'structure in space-time' (HL1,
430) also has something that the electrons in the electromagnetic theory
did not have. When Whitehead says that a primate is a 'structure of vibrations throughout all space and time but focused somewhere' (HL1, 34), he
repeats the old message, but also makes clear that, contrary to the electron
in the electromagnetic theory, the primate is 'an atomic structure of *vibrations*' (HL1, 12, my italics). So we should be aware that Whitehead distinguishes two types of 'atomic structures' in the continuous flux of becoming,
those that impress 'permanent character' in that flux, and those that impress
'rhythmic character' in it (HL1, 417).

The notion of an electron – or: the general notion of a charge-particle –
as an enduring organism in Whitehead's interpretation of the theory of
electromagnetism has an aspect of permanence derived from the identity or
sameness of the electron's charge-character throughout an historic route,
whereas his notion of a primate as an enduring organism in his theory of
primates involves 'recurrence – a structure of "vibrations"' (HL1, 6). Also,
Whitehead's notion of a mass-particle as 'an enduring existence' in *The Principle of Relativity* involves 'a historical route amid the structure of events' and
'a pervasive adjective of that route', the particle's mass-character, 'qualifying
in the same sense every stretch of that route' (R, 32) – in fact, Whitehead's
notion of historical route is close to Minkowski's four-dimensional world-
line, which Whitehead in HL1 refers to as Minkowski's '"worm" of space-
time' (HL1, 20). However, by assuming endurance to mean undifferentiated
sameness of charge- and mass-character throughout the life-history of particles, Whitehead's earlier notion of endurance may still have been tainted
too much by the materialistic theory he wants to replace with an organic

theory. So when launching his theory of primates, he holds that endurance or 'retention amid "change" necessitates either "identity" or "recurrence"' (HL1, 416). Hence, a particle need not endure because of undifferentiated sameness of charge- and mass-character through time. The recurrence or reiteration of certain charge- or mass-patterns can also imply endurance. And this is not all – Whitehead also makes the 'prophecy' that the 'intimate structure of matter is essentially rhythmic', and that despite what he said in earlier lectures (he mentions those published in CN, but we can add those of R), his 'most fundamental point of view is that of something rhythmic, something recurrent, [with] a focal region . . . & . . . tentacles stretching out throughout all space & all time' (HL1, 416).

Whitehead does draw the attention of his students to the fact that he already had a 'doctrine of rhythms with regard to living organisms, stated in [the] last chapter of *Principles of Natural Knowledge*', but that this doctrine was indeed formulated with 'respect to life' (HL1, 417). It's quite interesting to give a small quote from that chapter:

> A life-bearing object is not an 'uniform' object. Life (as known to us) involves the completion of rhythmic parts within the life-bearing event which exhibits that object. We can diminish the time-parts, and, if the rhythms be unbroken, still discover the same object of life in the cur-tailed event. But if the diminution of the duration be carried to the extent of breaking the rhythm, the life-bearing object is no longer to be found as a quality in the slice of the original event cut off within that duration. This is no special peculiarity of life. It is equally true of a mol-ecule of iron or of a musical phrase. Thus there is no such thing as life 'at one instant'; life is too obstinately concrete to be located in an extensive element of an instantaneous space. (PNK, 196; for non-uniform objects, cf. also CN, 162)

In 1919, Whitehead holds fast to the fact that 'the diminution of the dura-tion' can be carried on as far as one wants, that there is no atomic but a continuous structure of durations. And this is still the case when he presents his theory of primates to his Harvard students in 1924. The epochal structure of durations is not introduced prior to 1925. So the quote also gives us a fair idea of how Whitehead in 1924 reconciles the continuity of events and dura-tions with the atomicity of his rhythmic primates. As he sees a primate as a 'structure of vibrations with a definite frequency' (HL1, 12), and hence as the periodic recurrence or reiteration of a pattern, he can define one com-plete period as the duration required for the complete pattern, and thus even hold that the primate can be conceived as a succession of durations, without holding that these period-durations cannot be further divided into smaller durations, in which the complete pattern is no longer to be found. In other words: 'There may be a temporal minimum for the physical field [the period-duration, but] not for space-time', which is infinitely divisible (HL1, 527; for Whitehead's view shortly *after* introducing the notion of becoming as a succession of epochal durations, I refer to SMW, 135–6).

Let's finally turn to a provisional account of Whitehead's more technical sketch of his quantum theory. I first list some facts of which Whitehead was well aware in 1924.

## §6 The Planck-Einstein-Bohr Quantum Phenomena

In an attempt to explain the radiance of a body as it changes temperature, Planck had launched the hypothesis that the exchange of energy $E$ between electromagnetic radiation and matter did not occur continuously, but that this exchange could only happen in discrete quanta – quantities that would be whole number multiples of the product of Planck's constant $h$ with the frequency $v$ of the electromagnetic radiation. Whitehead writes $E = Shv$ with $S$ a whole number or integer, and as the period $T$ of electromagnetic radiation is the inverse of its frequency $\left( T = \dfrac{1}{v} \right)$, the action associated with the energy $(ET)$ equals $Sh$ (HL1, 10, 415). Consequently, the action is always (regardless of the frequency) an integer multiple of Planck's constant. As this constant is the smallest possible action, it is also called the quantum of action.

In an attempt to explain a physical effect that need not occupy us here – the photoelectric effect – Einstein used Planck's discovery to launch his hypothesis that light consists of photons, and that if $v$ is the frequency of the light under consideration, each photon carries an energy equal to $hv$. The revival of a 'corpuscular theory of light' – even though Newton's 'looked utterly dead and buried' – is 'wanted for some things', such as the photoelectric effect, 'and won't work for others', which require the light-wave hypothesis (HL1, 12). This situation prompted William Henry Bragg to say: 'On Mondays, Wednesdays, and Fridays we use the wave theory; on Tuesdays, Thursdays, and Saturdays we think in streams of flying energy quanta or corpuscles.' Whitehead says: 'There's a set of scientific Bolshevists that is inclined to acquiesce in that view, [but I am] too much of a rationalist to acquiesce in that' (HL1, 12, notice that in the 1920s tough-minded bolshevists opposed the weak-mindedness of the bourgeois intelligentsia).

In an attempt to explain the atomic emission spectra, that is, why atoms can only emit and absorb radiation at very precise frequencies, Bohr used Einstein's discovery and launched the hypothesis that an atom can only stand in one of a series of states of precise energy, and that it will only be able to emit or absorb electromagnetic radiation by passing from one energy state to another. Suppose an atom passes from an energy state $E_2$ to a lower energy state $E_1$ by emitting a light quantum, then the energy loss of the atom must be equal to the energy carried by the photon: $E_2 - E_1 = h\nu$. If only precise energy states are permitted, only precise frequencies of light (colours) are possible (in the colour spectrum).

To explain the change of energy state of an atom, Bohr (following Rutherford) conceived of an atom as made up of a nucleus of protons with positive charge and electrons with negative charge orbiting around it (cf. HL1, 415); for example, the hydrogen atom as a one-proton nucleus with one electron orbiting around it, where proton and electron have different masses but equal though opposite charges (hence making the atom charge-neutral). Then Bohr launched the hypotheses that the electrons in an atom cannot orbit around the nucleus in arbitrary orbits, but only in permitted orbits corresponding with precise values of energy $E_1$, $E_2$, $E_3$, etc. Bohr further held that when an atom emitted (or absorbed) energy, this could only be because electrons made a quantum jump from one permitted orbit to another, hence decreasing (or increasing) the total amount of energy of the atom with the corresponding energy difference.

## §7 Whitehead's Reaction to Bohr's Model of the Atom

Not only do Bohr's selection of permitted orbits and the associated electron quantum jumps violate the deeply rooted idea that 'nature does not make leaps' (*natura non facit saltus*), his explanation also implies that Maxwell's equations do not hold inside the atom, for else the electrons, by orbiting and thus possessing acceleration, would radiate and hence would not be able to stay in one of the permitted orbits. To restore the continuity of nature and to make Maxwell's equations also valid inside the atom instead of only outside atoms – these are two of the three main reasons for Whitehead to launch his hypothesis of primates. Whitehead's theory of primates intends to show 'that atomicity is not the negation of continuity' (HL1, 527). But Whitehead also says to his students that it is 'held today that Maxwell's equations will not apply inside' atoms, and that he thinks 'this is an inadequacy' (HL1, 422). If 'Maxwell's equations work everywhere except inside' atoms, then – since 'it's only inside these that there's any charge' – one must conclude that 'the equations hold everywhere except where they apply' (HL1, 8). Also, as 'Maxwell's equations presuppose a general continuity', being able to apply them everywhere could restore continuity (HL1, 8). Whitehead wants Maxwell's equations to 'hold inside as well as outside' electrons, protons, atoms and molecules (HL1, 21), and he thinks it is an 'advantage' of his theory that it is 'supposing that Clerk Maxwell's equations hold within the nuclei, providing an odd field with ridges within the nuclei' (HL1, 527).

Outside atoms 'the electromagnetic field (fundamental fact in all physics today) manifests itself as electromagnetic waves', such as 'light waves' and 'radio waves (those on which we do our "listening in")', which are all to be conceived as 'vibrations of electric force and magnetic force', vibrations that 'may have various frequencies', and 'forces [that are] tangential to [the] wave front' – and these waves 'involve no current whatever and no density of charge at any point' (HL1, 12). Inside atoms, the imagination of most physicists is captured by Bohr's planetary model of protons and electrons. Not Whitehead, however, for the reasons just given, but also – and this is the third main reason – because he wants a radical break with the mechanistic worldview of externally related isolated bits of matter to make way for the organic worldview of internally related events.

## §8 Technical Sketch of Whitehead's Quantum Theory

'Let us suppose', Whitehead starts his quantum theory, that the 'physical field consists ultimately not only of "waves" but also "primates" – an atomic structure of vibrations with a definite frequency' (HL1, 12). Of course, waves are also vibrations, and what Whitehead means here is that we have to distinguish two types of vibration. There is the vibratory locomotion of the travelling or non-stationary electromagnetic waves outside the sphere of primates, but there is also the radically different vibratory organisation of standing or stationary waves inside the sphere of primates – in fact, primates *are* vibratory organisms in which no locomotion such as the orbiting of an electron around a proton is at play. Whitehead resists 'the tendency [of] mechanics to bring everything under [the] head of motion', because if you try to bring the quantum nature of radiation 'under the head of locomotion it gets so complicated that there must be something wrong' (HL1, 180). In this sense, Whitehead's theory 'prevents [quantum phenomena] from being brought under head of locomotion' (HL1, 182).

Light has been mentioned as an example of vibration of the first type. Light can indeed be conceived as a travelling electromagnetic wave. But light can also be conceived as made up of photons. And a photon can be taken as an example of a vibration of the second type, in other words, as one of White-head's primates: 'these primates ([with the] same amount of energy in each and with [the] same frequency) are the "corpuscles" of light, etc.' (HL1, 12). According to Whitehead, the quantum and the wave theory of light are 'on [the] <u>face</u> of them quite contradictory, but each [is] explaining so much that you can't believe either quite wrong' (HL1, 21). However, his theory of pri-mates is all about the 'idea of a[n atomic] structure of vibrations superimposed upon [the continuous] waves of [the] electro-magnetic field' (HL1, 12). That is, it does not only aim at conciliating atomicity and continuity, but at the same time at harmonising the corpuscular and the wave theory of light.

Notice that next to a corpuscle of light (a photon), Whitehead also looks at electrons and protons as potential primates. Now and again, he leaves open the possibility that the electron might be a primate, but most of the time he treats both electrons and protons as associations of primates. He says:

> <u>Now</u> [we] will run the theory that both electrons & protons are built up of ultimate corpuscles which [we] will call primates. [. . . It would be] a great thing if [we] can find two sets of primates, one [making] up electrons & [the] other protons. Although [the] electron has never been knocked to pieces, it may be made up of several primates. Protons have been knocked to pieces & then [we get] $Shv$. Therefore we must find something we can identify with $h$. If we could do this we would show that knocking energy in <u>bundles</u> out of [the] proton does not spell <u>discontinuity</u> although it spells atomicity. (HL1, 419)

It feels strange for us today that Whitehead is linking the quantum phe-nomena of whole number multiples of $hv$, in other words, of bundles of $hv$'s, to the proton instead of the atom. We are likely to picture the atom as a plan-etary system of a proton-sun and electron-planets, and to correlate energy with electron-orbits. Whitehead, however, does not link the energy emission of atoms with changes of electron-movements, but with changes in the pri-mate-constitution of the proton. He thinks electrons may be primates, since they have never been knocked to pieces. But he also thinks that protons are not primates, since nuclei have been knocked to pieces. This implies that Whitehead will have to deal with the stability or instability of the proton as made up of primates, an issue not addressed in HL1 (but touched upon in SMW, 132–4).

Even though Whitehead does not go for the circular orbits of Bohr, he does go for spherical primates – for reasons of 'simplicity, a dangerous guide, but always one' (HL1, 15) – and he asks what sort of conditions he will impose on Maxwell's equations in order for them to hold within the primate-sphere. The first condition he imposes is that the vector field of magnetic force needs to be zero. He writes:

> When you have an electron at rest, [it] gives you nothing magnetic whatever; [it is] merely electric. When a primate [is] at rest in space then $(\alpha, \beta, \gamma)$ simply doesn't exist. So there's to be vibration without any magnetic effect. [This] knocks out at once those waves in which electric and magnetic effects are combined [that is, the travelling electromagnetic waves that rule outside of the primate-sphere]. Now this sort of possibility hasn't been considered yet. So the next thing to do would be to go to Maxwell's equations and put the magnetic force = 0. (HL1, 13)

If we follow Whitehead's last suggestion, the second of Maxwell's equations becomes $0 = 0$, and the other three become:

$$div\mathcal{E} = \rho$$
$$curl\mathcal{E} = 0$$
$$\frac{\partial \mathcal{E}}{\partial t} = -j$$

Using the definitions given earlier for $\dfrac{\partial F}{\partial t}$ and $divF$ and $curlF$ and $grad\xi$, it is easy to see that if we apply $grad$ to the first equation, $curl$ to the second, and $\dfrac{\partial}{\partial t}$ to the last, and then take the new first equation minus the new second minus $\dfrac{1}{c^2}$ times the new third, we get:

$$\frac{\partial^2 \mathcal{E}}{\partial x^2} + \frac{\partial^2 \mathcal{E}}{\partial y^2} + \frac{\partial^2 \mathcal{E}}{\partial z^2} - \frac{1}{c^2}\frac{\partial^2 \mathcal{E}}{\partial t^2} = grad\rho - \frac{1}{c^2}\frac{\partial j}{\partial t}$$

Clearly, inside the sphere of the primate, the vector field of electric force satisfies an inhomogeneous wave equation, and the term that renders it inhomogeneous depends on the charge density and the current. But unfortunately, the solution of this inhomogeneous wave equation is not to be found in HL1. We can only find Whitehead's remarks that the 'electrical force <u>outside</u> [the sphere of the primate is] <u>varying</u> [proportional to] $\dfrac{1}{r^2}$ but <u>inside</u> much more complicated formulae [hold]' (HL1, 15). Of course, outside a static charge-sphere Coulomb's law holds and the electric force is proportional to $\frac{1}{r^2}$, but we are not interested in this here.

It might surprise you that Whitehead does not put the current $j = (i_1, i_2, i_3)$ equal to zero. It is often conceived as the multiplication of charge density $\rho$ and velocity $v$ of the individual parts of the distribution of charge, and White-head should take the velocity $v$ everywhere equal to zero since he takes the primate-sphere as in rest and also holds that locomotion is not to be the key notion inside the primate-sphere. However, whereas 'ordinarily' people 'think of $(i_1, i_2, i_3)$ [as] electrons coming thru wires', Whitehead holds 'that there is a current at every point whatever [the] motion of electrons' (HL1, 418), and he stresses:

> Maxwell [is] very vague as to what he <u>means</u> by a 'current.' When electrons and protons came along people said current is when your electron (little charge of electricity) moves – [I do not] believe in this view [because] this motion of electrons simply dims a more fundamental view of current, [and despite the fact that according to] Lorentz, current [is] zero everywhere where there's not an electric charge. [. . . I am] searching for an interpre-tation of $(i_1, i_2, i_3)$ which would allow [the] Maxwell equations to hold everywhere. (HL1, 8)

So according to Whitehead, 'he can't get rid of his current anywhere, and he must get a physical interpretation for this' (HL1, 12). But unfortunately, such interpretation is not to be found in HL1.

Whitehead does remark that he expects current 'to be associated with [the] <u>flow</u> of <u>energy</u>' (HL1, 418), but he is not quite clear whether he means outside or inside the primate-sphere. Remember that outside and in the dynamic instead of the static case, when there is both an electric and a mag-netic field, the Poynting flow of energy is given by $S = c\varepsilon \times B$. Whitehead, after referring to 'Poynting's formulae', remarks that 'you find that $(i_1, i_2, i_3)$ defines as [a] leading factor [the] direction and flow of energy', but he also adds: 'You find that <u>outside</u> [the] flow of energy accounts for all that happens, [but] <u>inside</u> not so' (HL1, 20). Thus I take it that Whitehead holds that a kind of Poynting flow of energy is also at play inside the primate sphere, but that there is another energy effect relevant in there as well (I will return to this other energy effect later on, because it is key to understanding the quantum phenomena). I do not know how Whitehead linked flow of energy with cur-rent inside the static primate-sphere. Unfortunately, all details are lacking in

HL1. On the other hand, I do know how to link the temporal rate of variation of energy density $\frac{1}{2}\varepsilon^2$ with the current $j$, namely, by taking the scalar product of both sides of the third remaining Maxwell equation with the vector of electric force. Indeed, this gives:

$$\frac{\partial \frac{1}{2}\varepsilon^2}{\partial t} = -j \cdot \varepsilon$$

Again, I do not know whether this is the flow Whitehead had in mind, but it is a special case of what is called Poynting's theorem, and this is as far as I can go.

Then Whitehead is confronted with the question of the distribution of the charge density inside the primate-sphere. Clearly, in there, '$\rho$ is <u>not</u> = zero', but: '[The] mathematical physicist ... will see when he looks at his [remaining Maxwell] equations, that [they have] absolutely nothing to tell him [about] <u>how</u> the $\rho$ rises and falls. He's one equation short. Then he'll bethink him: What's the right equation to bring in? The natural one would be to try whether $\rho$ doesn't obey there the wave equation' (HL1, 13). In other words, 'you have to bring in further conditions to show how $\rho$ comports itself inside spheres where it isn't zero', and 'Whitehead chooses for this the "wave-equation"' (HL1, 14–15). He thinks that the assumption 'that $\rho$ satisfies the wave condition in [the] focal field' is the 'simplest [of] conditions' (HL1, 420). He does not give the wave equation, but he does give an expression for $\rho$, namely

$$\rho = \tilde{\rho}\, e^{i2\pi vt}$$

Notice that Whitehead's student, Louise Heath, did not get this expression right (HL1, 419) but it is clear that she mistakenly wrote 1 instead of the imaginary unit $i$, and $\gamma$ instead of the frequency $v$, because the above expression is the complex expression for a standing wave undergoing an harmonic oscillation; in other words, it is the expression for a solution of the homogeneous wave equation varying sinusoidally with a constant angular frequency $\omega = 2\pi v$. This means – I think – that Whitehead brings in the homogeneous wave equation

$$\frac{\partial^2 \rho}{\partial x^2} + \frac{\partial^2 \rho}{\partial y^2} + \frac{\partial^2 \rho}{\partial z^2} - \frac{1}{c^2}\frac{\partial^2 \rho}{\partial t^2} = 0$$

as a further condition that $\rho$ has to obey. This expression has two factors of which Whitehead says: '$e^{i2\pi vt}$ defines vibration & [the] other factor is [the] amplitude' (HL1, 419). This makes clear that indeed a primate is a 'structure of vibrations with a definite frequency' (HL1, 12). It is a standing or stationary spherical wave that at each place within its outer sphere performs a harmonic oscillation with (place-dependent) amplitude $\rho$ and with (definite) frequency $v$. It is clear that 'he's got here <u>not</u> waves which move away, but "stationary vibration"' (HL1, 13).

Without further explanation, Whitehead holds that the electric force and the current are also harmonically oscillating by putting (if Heath got it more or less right):

$$\varepsilon = (f, g, h) = \left(\tilde{f}, \tilde{g}, \tilde{h}\right)e^{i2\pi vt}$$

$$j = (i_1, i_2, i_3) = \left(\tilde{i_1}, \tilde{i_2}, \tilde{i_3}\right)e^{i2\pi vt}$$

These last two expressions do make clear, however, why Whitehead is saying that primates are 'spheres [in which] everything [is always] at [the] same stage of vibration' (HL1, 419), 'everything' meaning: charge density, electric field, current, and hence energy as well. This is why Whitehead can hold that when you (do not look at the total average energy of the primate, but) look at the energy at any place ('at any point') inside the primate-sphere, there is 'a reciprocal production and disappearance, creation and destruction of energy', so that 'the focal region' of the primate is the scene of 'production' and 'destruction of energy' (HL1, 16). Whitehead also adds that the vector of 'electric force instead of tangent is <u>normal</u> to the wave-face' of the standing wave of charge density (HL1, 13; cf. also HL1, 419), and that there is also 'a form which is not being considered & depends on taking $(i_1, i_2, i_3)$ as all through [the] field' (HL1, 419). The last remark suggests that the above two expressions are arrived at by simplifying things, but unfortunately it does not shed any extra light on Whitehead's new interpretation of the current.

Whitehead compares the standing wave of charge density with a standing sound wave, which has nodes (of zero amplitude) and loops (or anti-nodes, where the amplitude reaches its maximum). The 'wave vibrations' of the charge density inside the primate-sphere are 'in three dimensions', so that one deals with 'nodal surfaces' and loop surfaces (HL1, 15). Of course Whitehead cannot draw such a three-dimensional vibration, hence he makes a two-dimensional drawing with circular nodal and loop lines instead of spherical nodal and loop surfaces (cf. the drawings in HL1, 15, 420). Then he asks

himself whether the outer surface of the primate-sphere, that is, of the standing wave of charge density, is a nodal or loop surface, and he chooses for 'a
loop-surface where you get <u>maximum</u> energy', because when you 'suppose it
[is] a nodal surface, [then there is] no [electric] force there', and this is not
continuous with the fact that beyond the primate-sphere there is non-zero
electric force, and 'so this won't do' (HL1, 15). The 'only respectable place'
for the 'vibratory field' to end is a nodal or loop surface, but as the 'essence
of a nodal surface is that nothing is happening there', the 'natural primate to
think about is one that ends at [a] loop & communicates itself to [the] external region' without 'sudden transformation' (HL1, 420). Whitehead also adds
that the 'centre must be a node', and that you 'must have a certain continuity
of transition in force from centre to circumference' (HL1, 15).

   Notice that Whitehead says that 'a loop surface' is one 'where you get
<u>maximum</u> energy' (HL1, 15). Now we know that a loop surface is one where
you get maximum amplitudes of charge density, electric force and current,
and so the question pops up: 'What is the link between all these quantities?'
I think that the non-homogeneous wave equation I gave above links elec-
tric force to charge density and current, and that the expression $\frac{1}{2}\varepsilon^2$ that I
gave for the energy density links energy to electric force. So when Whitehead
comes to the question of finding the energy $E$ associated with a primate, a
detailed calculation is due, which determines (for a given charge density and
current) the electric force by means of the non-homogeneous wave equation,
and then the energy $E$ of the primate (at some time $t$) by means of the integration of the energy density $\frac{1}{2}\varepsilon^2$ over the primate-sphere. However, Whitehead
makes a distinction between '[the] flow of energy caused by [the] current',
and '[the] remainder of energy [that] is proportional to the rate of change of
$\rho$', and he focuses on the latter (HL1, 420; cf. also HL1, 16). But if we can
leave out the current to isolate the $\rho$-effect, then we can use the first Maxwell
equation, $div\varepsilon = \rho$, to determine $\varepsilon$ (given $\rho$) and then the energy (given $\frac{1}{2}\varepsilon^2$)
by means of $E = \frac{1}{2}\int_{primate-sphere} \varepsilon^2 dv$ (where $dv$, of course, is just a differential
volume element).

   Finally, Whitehead considers two types of primates, electronic and protonic
primates, and he calls the latter 'corpuscular' primates (HL1, 16, 420). Then
he takes an electronic primate with radius $Sa$, and a corpuscular primate with
radius $Ga$, where $S$ and $G$ are whole numbers, and $a$ is the distance between
two nodal surfaces (cf. HL1, 15, 420). Indeed, when going from the centre of

the standing spherical wave of charge density to the outer surface, the total distance, and hence the radius $R$ of the electronic (respectively protonic) primate, is equal to $S$ (respectively $G$) times the distance $a$ from nodal surface to nodal surface. Because Whitehead said earlier that the outer surface must be a loop surface instead of a nodal surface, there is a problem here – after passing the largest nodal surface, you still need to go a distance $\frac{1}{2}a$ further to reach the outer surface – but Whitehead doesn't pay any attention to this problem, and so I will skip it here as well.

Then, without giving any calculation, Whitehead is giving the total average energy $E$ of the electronic primate with radius $Sa$,

$$E = \frac{3}{4}\frac{E^2 v}{Sc}$$

and the total average energy of the corpuscular primate with radius $Ga$:

$$E = G\frac{\pi^2}{16}\frac{E^2}{c}v = G\frac{3}{5}\frac{E^2}{c}v$$

In these expressions $v$ is the frequency of the primate, $c$ is the velocity of light *in vacuo*, and $\frac{\pi^2}{16}$ is approximately $\frac{3}{5}$, but what is the $E$ on the right hand side? It cannot be the energy of the primate, of course, because that is the $E$ on the left hand side, for which we were searching. And Whitehead gives no details, apart from the remark (if Heath understood it correctly) that 'E is intensity of vibration, a constant' (HL1, 421).

However, when we look at the total average energy of the static electronic primate with radius $Sa$, and suppose for the sake of the argument that this primate simply is a static electron of radius $R$ with total charge $e$, then $E = \frac{1}{2}\int_{electron-sphere} \mathcal{E}^2 dv$ is the electrostatic self-energy of this electron-sphere, and we have seen that both in the case of a uniform surface charge density $\rho s = \frac{e}{4\pi R^2}$ and a uniform volume charge density $\rho v = \frac{e}{\frac{4}{3}\pi R^3}$ this electrostatic self-energy is proportional to $\frac{e^2}{R}$. So it is reasonable to *assume* that with charge density $\rho = \tilde{\rho}e^{i2\pi vt}$ the average electrostatic self-energy of this electron is also proportional to $\frac{e^2}{R}$. But as $R = Sa$ and as the wavelength of the standing spherical wave $\lambda = 2a$ and hence the velocity of this wave $c = \dfrac{\lambda}{P} = \lambda v = 2av$ (cf. HL1, 16, 421) and hence $a = \dfrac{c}{2v}$, the average energy of the electron as an electronic primate is proportional to $2\dfrac{e^2 v}{Sc}$. Compare this with Whitehead's expression for the average energy $E$ of the electron as an electronic primate with radius $Sa$, $\dfrac{3}{4}\dfrac{E^2 v}{Sc}$, then you can see that the constant $E$ on the right hand side, which (according to Heath) Whitehead calls the intensity of vibration, must in the case of the electron as an electronic primate be proportional to the total charge $e$ of the electron. In general, the intensity of vibration of an electronic primate must – if our *assumption* is correct – be proportional to the total charge $q$ of this primate.

The reason I cannot calculate the total average energy of the static electronic primate and hence the proportionality factor linking the intensity of vibration and the total charge of the primate is that Whitehead does not give his expression for amplitude $\tilde{\rho}$. This factor may even be 1, since Whitehead uses the symbol $E$ in *The Principle of Relativity* for the 'electric charge' (cf. R, 79). If this were the case, then we would best replace intensity of vibration $E$ with charge $q$ in Whitehead's expressions for the total average energy of the electronic and the corpuscular primate. Notice that the total average energy of the static corpuscular primate is an even greater mystery to me than the total average energy of the static electronic primate, for they differ significantly, and whereas I could link the latter to the electrostatic self-energy of the electron, I have no clue to what expression I can link the former.

Anyway, and most important (cf. HL1, 17, 421), if one compares the total average energy of the corpuscular primate with radius $Ga$, that is: $G\dfrac{3}{5}\dfrac{E^2}{c}v$, with the findings of the quantum physicist about the absorption and emission of energy in whole number multiples of $hv$, then you can hold that if you put $h = \dfrac{3}{5}\dfrac{E^2}{c}$ or, in other words, the intensity of vibration (which then has to be the 'same for all primates whatever their frequency' (HL1, 421)) equal to $\sqrt{\dfrac{5}{3}hc}$, then you have an explanation for this quantum phenomenon. Indeed, if then the proton – made up of corpuscular primates, that is, being a structure of such atomic vibratory structures – absorbs energy some such atomic vibratory structures are created, and if it emits energy some such atomic vibratory structures decay and turn into radiation. In other words, Whitehead's explanation of the quantum phenomena involves two sorts of vibration, atomic stationary vibration and continuous travelling vibration, but the two co-exist in a continuous space and time, and can be turned into each other without requiring quantum jumps such as those of Bohr's electrons. Whitehead says:

> If you look on [a] proton as [a] mash up of [corpuscular] primates, you either have to shake out 1 [or] 2 [or] 3 etc. $\dfrac{3}{5}\dfrac{E^2}{c}\,v$ [in order to] account for quantum theory without any worry about [the] alleged discontinuity of time & space. [Of course, one] must suppose some conditions of permanence [that is, of stability] and [I have] not worked this out. [My view is] not [the] ordinary view, but [it] satisfies quantum theory & proves that quantum theory does not necessitate discontinuity of time & space. [It is] illustrative of [a] way of scientific thinking. (HL1, 421)

## Conclusion

Our account of Whitehead's quantum theory can serve both as a guide to better understand what Whitehead's students have noted down on this theory during Whitehead's Harvard lectures, and as offering a sketch to fill in some of the details of what Whitehead wrote on this topic afterwards (in SMW, 35–6, 129–37, and in PR, 78–9). Moreover, it can serve to compare Whitehead's approach with the approaches of Louis de Broglie and Erwin Schrödinger. This is not the place for a detailed comparison, but the similarity clearly resides in the use of stationary waves to shed light on the quantum phenomena as well as in the idea that all elementary particles have a wave-character. There are, of course, also important differences. Louis de Broglie's and later Erwin Schrödinger's standing waves offer a picture of the atom as consisting of a protonic nucleus and electronic standing waves. Whitehead's sketch of a quantum theory is more radical. He wants a complete reconceptualisation of the atom in terms of atomic structures of vibrations, and intends to leave behind all remnants of the materialistic theory in favour of an organic theory. On the other hand, of course, Whitehead's proposal is just a sketch to his students with a mainly philosophical aim, and not a detailed theory like Schrödinger's wave mechanics, which has been peer reviewed and published, and became one of the cornerstones to further evolutions in the field of quantum physics.

# Bibliography

Bogaard, Paul and Jason Bell (eds), *The Harvard Lectures of Alfred North Whitehead, 1924–1925: Philosophical Presuppositions of Science* (Edinburgh: Edinburgh University Press, 2017).

Eddington, Arthur, *Report on the Relativity Theory of Gravitation* (New York: Dover Publications, 2006).

Jeans, James, *Report on Radiation and the Quantum Theory* (London: 'The Electrician' Printing & Publishing Co., 1914).

Whitehead, Alfred North, *The Organisation of Thought, Educational and Scientific* (London: Williams & Norgate, 1917).

Whitehead, Alfred North, *An Enquiry Concerning the Principles of Natural Knowledge* (New York: Dover Publications, [1919] 1982).

Whitehead, Alfred North, *The Principle of Relativity: With Applications to Physical Science* (Cambridge: Cambridge University Press, [1922] 2011).

Whitehead, Alfred North, *Science and the Modern World* (New York: The Free Press, [1925] 1967).

Whitehead, Alfred North, *Process and Reality: An Essay in Cosmology* (New York: The Free Press, [1929] 1978).

Whitehead, Alfred North, *Adventures of Ideas* (New York: The Free Press, [1933] 1967).

# 9

# On Herstein's 'Quanta and Corpuscles'

*Ronny Desmet*

In the introduction to his chapter of this book, Gary Herstein correctly claims that the detailed materials of HL1 support his view that Whitehead's process metaphysics was not determined by the emerging science of quantum mechanics. Indeed, HL1 clearly shows that Whitehead's main source of inspiration in the domain of physics was Maxwell's theory of electromagnetism. Maxwell's theory inspired Whitehead to develop not only his alternative theories of relativity and his sketch for a theory of quanta (which he called 'primates'), but also his emerging process metaphysics. As Herstein points out, this does not imply that Whitehead's process metaphysics cannot serve as a basis to provide an interpretation of quantum mechanics, for it can.

Given this point of departure, it is surprising that Herstein's first step is a brief visit to the state of quantum mechanics two years *after* HL1, when the fifth Solvay conference was held in Brussels. However Herstein's excursion serves two purposes. One is to highlight that, even in 1927, physicists were at a complete loss as to how to deal with quantum phenomena. The other is to advance the idea that Niels Bohr and his followers, thanks to the high level of confusion, succeeded in dogmatically imposing the Copenhagen interpretation by means of 'ham-fisted methods', hence giving rise to a 'shut up and calculate' mentality,[1] leading to the unfair rejection of alternative interpretations, including interpretations that show affinity with or are inspired by Whitehead's process metaphysics.

I disagree with Herstein's reduction of Bohr's Copenhagen interpretation to the 'shut up and calculate' dictum, a phrase Herstein says 'is such a commonplace in physics that offering a citation would be meaningless'.[2] But it is instructive to observe that the phrase is used, for example, by David Kaiser in his book, *How the Hippies Saved Physics*. Kaiser describes how, in the 1970s, an eccentric group of physicists in Berkeley, California, reacted against the 'shut up and calculate' mentality of professional physicists in the United States, which emerged after the Second World War and especially during the Cold War, and shunted aside 'philosophical inquiry or open-ended speculation of the kind that Bohr, Einstein, Heisenberg, and Schrödinger had considered a prerequisite for serious work on quantum theory'.[3] These eccentric quantum physicists did not shy away from philosophical speculation, and in this context, to give just two examples, David Bohm's interpretative efforts[4] and Henry Stapp's Whiteheadian account of quantum mechanics[5] were revitalised. But the 1970s are half a century later than 1927, and to attribute the then reigning, strictly empirical and mathematical mentality of professional physicists to Bohr is not only an anachronism, but does no justice to Bohr's philosophical struggle to come to terms with the mind-blowing consequences of the various quantum phenomena.

Herstein is incorrect to claim that the Henry Bragg quote in HL1 (that on Monday, Wednesday and Friday one has to use the wave theory of light, and on Tuesday, Thursday and Saturday the corpuscular theory; cf. HL1, 12) 'essentially summed up the Copenhagen interpretation', that this interpretation of Bohr is a 'hand-waving abandonment of fundamental questions', and that Bohr's followers are 'conceptual cowards'.[6] Bohr was a first rank physicist-philosopher, as were Whitehead and Einstein, and his current of thought cannot be reduced to a cowardly retreat from the conceptual challenges posed by various quantum phenomena into a shelter of mathematical cleverness.

The young Bohr, thanks to Harald Høffding, got acquainted with the thought of Immanuel Kant, Søren Kierkegaard and William James, and this philosophical background was instrumental when he tried to make sense of the quantum phenomena in terms of 'complementarity' (Bohr's epistemology) and 'the coupling between phenomena and their observation' (Bohr's holism). In the Introductory Survey to Volume I of *The Philosophical Writings of Niels Bohr*, Bohr writes:

> In the years near the beginning of this century . . . the application [of mechanics and of the electromagnetic theory] to atomic problems was destined to reveal a hitherto unnoticed limitation that found its expression in Planck's discovery of the so-called quantum of action . . . The indivisibility of the quantum of action is itself, from the classical point of view, an irrational element which inevitably requires us to forego a causal mode of description and which, because of the coupling between phenomena and their observation, forces us to adopt a new mode of description designated as *complementary* in the sense that any given application of classical concepts precludes the simultaneous use of other classical concepts which in a different connection are equally necessary for the elucidation of the phenomena.[7]

Sure, like Einstein, Whitehead would never have agreed to Bohr's Kierkegaard-inspired idea that Planck's quantum of action is the irrational element preventing a rational synthesis in the domain of quantum mechanics. And whereas Bohr held that the concepts of classical physics (such as wave and particle, or position and momentum, or time and energy) are quasi-Kantian *a priori* concepts, and hence, due to the impossibility of a classical synthesis, *have* to be used in a complementary way, Einstein and Whitehead both hoped that a rational synthesis would emerge by means of an elaboration of electromagnetism (Whitehead in HL1) or by means of radically new, yet-to-be-discovered concepts (Einstein). But whereas Einstein's local realism conflicts with the holism that gradually came to dominate Bohr's view, Bohr's relational interpretation of the emergence of quantum properties has a lot in common with Whitehead's relational realism, which owes as much to James as to Maxwell. A more nuanced discussion of Bohr's views might have led Herstein to avoid a simplistic good guy versus bad guy story.

After claiming that Whitehead's HL1 is an antidote to Bohr's (alleged) lack of conceptual thinking, Herstein highlights the centrality of spatio-temporal continuity in Whitehead's thought. Herstein is absolutely right to emphasise that Whitehead insisted that any notion of discontinuity of space-time is 'nonsense' (HL1, 10, 418) and that the quantum phenomena that trouble physicists need not imply the abandonment of a continuous space-time (cf. HL1, 7, 421, 526). He is also absolutely right that Whitehead insisted that the true contrast to continuity is atomicity, while at the same time distancing his concept of continuity from the related one employed in mathematics (cf. HL1, 6).

It is, however, surprising that Herstein does not explicitly state what Whitehead's concept of continuity is, and how it differs from the mathematical one. The required statement is certainly not too complex for the readers of this book. Whitehead's continuity-atomicity contrast is the divisibility-indivisibility contrast (cf. HL1, 6), and it is easy to explain that divisibility is not sufficient to speak of mathematical continuity. For example, both real numbers and rational numbers are infinitely divisible, but only the real numbers can be said to form a mathematical continuum, because in between any two real numbers one can find real numbers and only real numbers, whereas in between any two rational numbers one can find not only rational numbers, but also non-rational numbers – irrational numbers to be more specific. (Topologically speaking, the real number set is both dense and connected, but the rational number set is only dense, not connected; and the latter implies, for example, that the real number function mapping all rational numbers to 0 and all irrational ones to 1 does not satisfy the epsilon-delta criterion of continuity that Herstein refers to.)

Herstein urges Whitehead scholars to learn a bit of mathematics when it comes to Whitehead's work, and he writes: 'How can one hope to understand the concept of continuity that Whitehead is pressing if one does not also know the mathematical concept he means to differentiate it from?'[8] But – again – why then does he not give an account of the mathematical concept of continuity in order to show that it is more comprehensive than the divisibility to which Whitehead restricts his concept of continuity? Maybe if Herstein had made clear that Whitehead's continuity-atomicity contrast is not mathematical, but the more familiar contrast of divisibility versus indivisibility, this would have prevented him from turning his correct claim of the centrality of spatio-temporal continuity in Whitehead's thought into the overstatement that the real issue is not between waves and particles, but between continuity and atomicity. Contrary to what Herstein implies, Whitehead held the wave-particle duality to be an instance of the continuity-atomicity contrast, and he tried to overcome this duality with his theory of primates (of which I gave a detailed account in my chapter, 'Whitehead's Highly Speculative Lectures on Quantum Theory'). In his sketch of this theory, Whitehead shows that particles are constituted by primates, and primates are in essence standing waves in the electromagnetic field, which is defined against the background of the space-time continuum – in other words, primates are processes that 'exhibit an atomic character imposed upon a continuous field' (HL1, 6). I cannot resist echoing Herstein here, and urge Whitehead scholars to learn a bit of mathematical physics when it comes to Whitehead's HL1, and to write: 'How can one hope to understand Whitehead's theory of primates if one does not also know the concept of standing, electromagnetic waves, which is the key to Whitehead's attempt to arrive – contrary to what Bohr deemed possible – at a rational synthesis of the seemingly contradictory classical concepts of wave and particle, and at an explanation of quantum phenomena that does not require one to abandon spatio-temporal continuity?'

Herstein highlights that Whitehead never gave up the idea that time is continuous, not even in view of the emerging quantum mechanics, but he does not highlight that Whitehead in his London triptych (PNK, CN, R) distinguished this continuous time, which is the measurable time of mathematical physics, from the passage of nature, the awareness of which is our psychological time, and from which the measurable time of mathematical physics is abstracted. In HL1-terminology, Whitehead distinguished the time of extension from the process of becoming. Moreover, in his London triptych, Whitehead held the passage of nature to be continuous. Likewise, in the first semester of HL1, he held the process of becoming to be continuous. But in the second semester of HL1, he changed his mind. While still holding that the time of extension is continuous, he then held that the process of becoming is not continuous, but atomic. This change (of which I gave a detailed account in the second part of my chapter, 'From Physics to Philosophy, and from Continuity to Atomicity') is not prompted by the development of quantum mechanics, but by the fact that Whitehead realised that whereas the measurable time of mathematical physics makes abstraction from the irreversibility of our psychological time, one can only do justice to our experience of the irreversibility of becoming by conceiving becoming as atomic instead of continuous. So, and again, I agree with Herstein that Whitehead held fast to the continuity of time, despite the rise of quantum mechanics, but I think Herstein should have highlighted the vital distinctions between time and becoming, and between the first and the second semester of HL1.

Awareness of Whitehead's second semester difference between 'extensiveness' (which 'doesn't tell you which way time's going' (HL1, 315)) and 'atomic temporality' (which is 'succession' and 'brings in the direction of successions' (HL1, 317)), or, again, his distinction between time (the continuous time in the field of extension) and temporalisation (the atomic becoming of the continuous time – conforming to the PR aphorism, 'There is a becoming of continuity, but no continuity of becoming' (PR, 35)), might have prevented Herstein from formulating his third and final – and according to me, invalid – claim, namely, that HL1 allows Whitehead scholars to put a stake through the heart of Lewis Ford's temporal atomism thesis.[9] Herstein writes:

> Ford argues that time, for Whitehead, comes 'chunky style', in discrete, 'atomic' bits, where Ford does not even follow Whitehead's own meaning of the word 'atomic'. Ford read into Whitehead's text this idea of 'temporal atomism,' a term that appears nowhere in any of Whitehead's texts, by applying . . . a profoundly questionable method . . . It is certainly the case that there is no trace of such a notion to be found anywhere in the Harvard lectures.[10]

I will not defend Ford's sometimes very speculative exegesis of Whitehead's writings, let alone Isabelle Stengers' dramatisation of Whitehead's (alleged and atypical) *sudden* change of heart *while lecturing* on the issue of the continuity or atomicity of the process of becoming,[11] and I agree with Herstein that we should stick to the primary texts. However, Ford's temporal atomism thesis is a thesis about 'the atomicity of temporalization',[12] about 'the epochal theory of becoming',[13] and not about the atomicity of the measurable time of mathematical physics, of time in the field of extension. True, when Ford quotes Hocking's notes and speaks of 'an atomic theory of time'[14] as well as when Whitehead writes in SMW that 'time is atomic' (SMW, 126), the 'time' terminology is confusing, but 'in this account "time" has been separated from "extension"' (SMW, 125), and 'by "time" here [Whitehead] means to restrict himself to temporal realization as processive and atomic'.[15] So, even though in the text of HL1, to which I stick as requested by Herstein, I cannot find Ford's terminology, I *did* find Ford's notion of temporal atomism – that is, the notion of the atomicity of becoming. As I already stated, even though Whitehead never changed his mind about the continuity of extensive time, and held fast to the notion of extensive *continuum*, he did change his mind from the idea of continuous becoming to the idea of atomic becoming, and that is the change Ford wanted to highlight.

Moreover, speaking of terminology, Ford *did* follow Whitehead's meaning of the word 'atomic', for Whitehead's meaning of 'atomic' is 'indivisible' and, according to Whitehead, each instance of the process of becoming is in fact indivisible, even though *ad hoc* it can be analysed spatio-temporally. And even though I did not find in Whitehead's writings Ford's terminology – 'temporal atomism' – I think that Ford's terminology can be justified. Indeed, in HL1, Whitehead speaks of 'becoming real' as 'temporalization', of 'temporalization . . . via realization of the potential', and of 'realization' as requiring 'a minimum duration', which is 'an atomic quantity' (HL1, 318–9).[16] Likewise, in SMW, Whitehead holds that 'temporalization is realization', that 'realization is the becoming of time in the field of extension', and that consequently 'temporalization is not another continuous process' but 'an atomic succession' (SMW, 126). So I do not follow Herstein, and think it is the other way around: because according to Whitehead temporalisation is atomic, and because he speaks of 'atomic temporality' (HL1, 317), Herstein is not justified to simply reject Ford's terminology – 'temporal atomism' – nor the corresponding thesis.

## Notes

1. See above p. 121.
2. See above p. 130n14.
3. Kaiser, *How the Hippies Saved Physics*, 3.
4. Kaiser, *How the Hippies Saved Physics*, 26–8.
5. Kaiser, *How the Hippies Saved Physics*, 55–6.
6. See above, p. 126.
7. Bohr, *Philosophical Writings of Niels Bohr, Volume I*, 4 and 10.
8. See above, p. 129.
9. Cf. Ford, *The Emergence of Whitehead's Metaphysics*, chapter 3.
10. See above pp. 127–8.
11. In her *Thinking with Whitehead*.
12. Ford, *The Emergence of Whitehead's Metaphysics*, 52.

13. Ford, *The Emergence of Whitehead's Metaphysics*, 53.
14. Ford, *The Emergence of Whitehead's Metaphysics*, 53, and also HL1, 318.
15. Ford, *The Emergence of Whitehead's Metaphysics*, 58.
16. Also in Ford, *The Emergence of Whitehead's Metaphysics*, 54.

## Bibliography

Bogaard, Paul and Jason Bell (eds), *The Harvard Lectures of Alfred North Whitehead, 1924–1925: Philosophical Presuppositions of Science* (Edinburgh: Edinburgh University Press, 2017).

Bohr, Niels, *The Philosophical Writings of Niels Bohr, Volume I: Atomic Theory and the Description of Nature* (Woodbridge, CT: Ox Bow Press, 1987).

Ford, Lewis, *The Emergence of Whitehead's Metaphysics: 1925–1929* (Albany: State University of New York Press, 1984).

Kaiser, David, *How the Hippies Saved Physics* (New York: Norton, 2011).

Stengers, Isabelle, *Thinking with Whitehead* (Cambridge, MA: Harvard University Press, 2011).

Whitehead, Alfred North, *Science and the Modern World* (New York: The Free Press, [1925] 1967).

Whitehead, Alfred North, *Process and Reality: An Essay in Cosmology* (New York: The Free Press, [1929] 1978).

# 10

# Reply to Desmet

*Gary L. Herstein*

Some brief responses to the first few generic points Desmet makes in his comment. Desmet is puzzled at my bringing the fifth Solvay conference into the discussion. I confess, I thought I was rather clear on this point, but evidently I was mistaken. The Solvay conference, as noted, took place after the lectures in HL1 occurred, and as such provides a good benchmark for the state of confusion, even chaos, that was rife in the physical theory of the quantum. This degree of chaos strikes me as being underestimated or entirely overlooked in much of the secondary literature on Whitehead. Consequently, understanding how thoroughly unsettled the field was at the time is important to understanding Whitehead's efforts to create a unified view of the field.

But that attempt was occurring in a maelstrom. I would argue that a significant number of Whitehead commentators underestimate the scale of that maelstrom, but that is only an impression I entertain. Yet in the absence of detailed statistical analyses which no one has yet even proposed, much less undertaken, such impressions are all we have to work from. So I was operating – and will continue to operate – from the impression that understanding the scale and scope of this chaos is essential to understanding the context in which Whitehead was writing.

With regard to the nature and result of Niels Bohr's 'Copenhagen interpretation' upon the conceptual (such as it is) basis of quantum physics, Desmet and I will have to remain fully at loggerheads. Fully exploring the history of a topic that would require entire books within the limitations of a 5,000 word essay is simply not possible. In no small part, this is because that history has been choked by an undergrowth of mythology that claims that Einstein was roundly defeated by Bohr in their debates at the fifth Solvay conference, which eventuated in Bohr's interpretation. But this mythology is, at the very least, open to dispute. It is far from clear that Bohr even understood, much less adequately replied to, Einstein's arguments. (And for those who don't know, I am not an Einstein enthusiast.)

Bohr's philosophical sophistication to the contrary notwithstanding, it remains the case that the Copenhagen interpretation is predicated upon the wilful, sanguine acceptance of a fundamental incoherence at the base of physical reality. Throw what nuanced dust one may in the air, it remains a matter of particles on Monday, Wednesday and Friday, but waves on Tuesday, Thursday and Saturday. (While on Sundays, we're just not sure.) The answers Einstein was looking for were almost certainly misplaced, but his questions were not. And regardless of what Bohr may have ideally intended, the reality is and remains the 'shut up and calculate' standard of orthodox micro-physics.

Next, I want to address Desmet's rather puzzling suggestion that I might easily have said more about the differences between contemporary mathematical/physical notions of continuity and Whitehead's radically different approach. Desmet is absolutely correct that I did nothing more than mention this difference, while wishing that Whitehead scholars would take the necessary steps to acquire some measure of mathematical facility so as to appreciate this difference. What utterly beggars the imagination is his evident suggestion that I could have filled in this gap with a few sentences, or even paragraphs, of exposition. My astonishment in this regard is made manifest by an example that Desmet himself offers.

Desmet points out the well-known example of an absolutely discontinuous function of the unit interval, where the rational numbers are all mapped to zero or one, while the irrational numbers are conversely mapped to one or zero. Desmet says nothing false here. But he presents this in the context of criticising me for not providing a comprehensive discussion of the 'punctiform' (my term, from other works) standard of continuity that is the basis of orthodox mathematical/physical approaches, and Whitehead's mereological (and later, mereotopological) approach.

Anyone with a background, even a single course, in real analysis, will be familiar with Desmet's example. The problem is that the only way one achieves that single course in real analysis is by first passing through two *years* of calculus. This is part of my amazement at Desmet's criticism: it appears to me that he thinks I should compress *years* – and I do not exaggerate: *years* – of mathematical study into a few sentences or paragraphs. Certainly he is correct, that anyone who is already facile with real analysis, set theory – most especially well- and non-well-founded versions – to say nothing of what (in contemporary terms) falls under the heading of 'atomless gunk' (which includes Whitehead's earlier mero- and later mereotopological, theories of

extension) would easily understand the differences between orthodox mathematical and Whiteheadian versions of continuity with only a few sentences,
or at most a paragraph or two, of explanation. Perhaps I am entirely mis-
reading the general Whitehead community, in which case I would appreciate
some educative evidence to the contrary. But my impression – and, at this
point, all we have are impressions – is that such advanced mathematical
facility is not widespread among Whitehead scholars. So I stand by my decision to do *no more than point out* the needed direction of study, particularly
since the actual span of such study comprehends some hundreds, if not thousands, of pages of detailed text.

Lastly, regarding Ford, whom Desmet discusses at the end of his comment,
I wish to focus on a single statement of Desmet's, from Chapter 7:

> I am not the first person to highlight Whitehead's change from continuous
> to atomic becoming – 'The Emergence of Temporal Atomicity' has been a
> topic of discussion among Whitehead scholars since the 1984 publication
> of Lewis Ford's *The Emergence of Whitehead's Metaphysics: 1925–1929*. And
> since then there have been a lot of speculations with respect to the reasons
> for this change.

I am not the first person to highlight the extreme dubiousness of Ford's
hypothesis, nor even the only person in this volume to do so.[1] There are
several problems with this statement, not least of which is the presupposition that its premises are true. It takes for granted that Whitehead actually
embraced what Ford described as 'temporal atomicity', even though there
is nothing in Whitehead's texts that correspond to this structure. It ignores
other changes in Whitehead's texts that were demonstrably occurring (the
shift from natural philosophy to metaphysics or, perhaps more appropriately,
speculative philosophy). It ignores the methodology Ford employed in constructing his hypothesis, and the radically dubious appropriateness of that
methodology as applied to Whitehead. And, taking the foregoing collectively, it treats Ford's hypothesis as a given fact rather than a highly chal-
lengeable hypothesis that does not stand up well when confronted by the full
range of evidence.

Per Ford's methodology, he applied the techniques of 'compositional analysis', such as he learned when studying theology, which were originally developed to fill in the gaps in fragmentary texts that were thousands of years old.
Ford's application of such a technique to Whitehead's texts could scarcely
be more out of place. Despite the evident (at the time) lack of any notes or
background materials, Whitehead's texts were hardly fragments lacking any

evident context. At the same time, Ford had no background in, nor demonstrated facility for, mathematical thinking. As such, he was poorly situated to
'read into' Whitehead's thought because he didn't have a substantial notion of
how Whitehead's mathematical habits of thought governed his (Whitehead's)
development and argument; as such, Ford makes the highly questionable
assumption that Whitehead's thought requires a radical reading-into such as
compositional analysis imposes.

Per Whitehead's methodology, those mathematical habits meant that
when he tackled a problem, he would set out his premises and terms as best
he was able to, and then build his argument from there. So as his problems
changed, so too did his language and areas of focus. And certainly it is the
case that his problems changed as he shifted from natural to speculative philosophy.[2] This change is becoming evident in HL1, especially with the introduction of terms like 'primate', which Desmet does such an outstanding job
of examining. But at this same time, according to Ford, Whitehead is supposed to be 'discovering' the vitally important concept of temporal atomism.
So why, then, isn't it in Whitehead's text, either the *Harvard Lectures* or his
published works? It doesn't matter that Whitehead does not use the exact
term 'temporal atomism' anywhere (which, indeed, he never does); but neither does he use any cognate or equivalent term. This concept is supposed to
be *vital* to Whitehead's philosophy, yet he never thinks to bring it up? This
is why Ford had to use compositional analysis to read the notion *into* Whitehead's philosophy.

Looking ahead of HL1, our question becomes, where did temporal
atomism go? This was supposed to be a fundamental reconstruction of the
natural philosophy found in the triptych, yet when we get to PR in 1929,
no such rejection of those earlier works is anywhere to be found. When
the subject comes up in PR, Whitehead's response, often enough, is to
tell his readers to simply read one or several of those earlier books in their
entirety. Whitehead's only criticisms of those earlier works come in Part IV
of PR, where he embraces Theodore de Laguna's argument to switch from a
mereological to a mereotopological theory of extension, and the introduction of strains and flat loci. (These latter two have never, in this author's
considered evaluation, received the measure or thoroughness of examination and analysis that they genuinely deserve.)

Putting matters mildly, Ford seldom showed any nuanced appreciation for
the order of analysis versus the order of reality, nor for the differing functions of natural and speculative philosophy. Instead, he treated Whitehead's
complete texts as though they were fragments that required a theologian's
interpolations. Meanwhile, Desmet's discussion quite frankly gains nothing by

the introduction of Ford's notions. The attempt to shoehorn HL1 into those concepts is surprising, at best. The aggressive reading-into that Ford insists we must do is neither necessary nor desirable.

## Notes

1. See George Lucas's chapter 'Uncovering a "New" Whitehead' in this volume.
2. I would argue that Whitehead's earlier philosophy, especially that triptych of volumes from 1919–22 (PNK, 1919; CN, 1920; R, 1922), is properly characterised as 'philosophy of nature', rather than 'philosophy of science'.

# Part IV

# Whitehead's Philosophical Context

# 11

# Whitehead and Kant at Copenhagen

*Jason Bell and Seshu Iyengar*

The relationship between what we would call philosophy and science is complex: despite the indubitable links between disciplines undertaken through those fields, there is always a discussion of what the nature of that investigative relationship is. At times, this discussion aims to explain a vision of one field or the other as somehow independent. A common 'refutation' of philosophy offers begrudging respect to it as the progenitor of scientific inquiry, but one that ultimately fails to come to meaningful terms with the knowledge accorded by modern science. This is not a new discussion: indeed, understanding the link between these fields in Western thought is a longstanding preoccupation of thinkers from both disciplines.

Recognising the deep links between philosophy and science, while also recognising they have disparate elements as well, is very important when tackling a philosophy such as Alfred North Whitehead's: along with figures like Bertrand Russell and Sir Arthur Eddington, he was part of a group of Anglo-American philosophers who were also mathematicians and physicists whose contributions mean their names are often mentioned in a variety of contexts. They also came at a time of radical change in science and philosophy. In science, relativity and the development of quantum theory were undermining the fundamentals of physics, while in philosophy the idealist-realist debate was in full swing, and the divides between 'analytic' and 'continental' thought were emerging in the post-Lotzean period.

It is not surprising then that works like Michael Epperson's *Quantum Mechanics and the Philosophy of Alfred North Whitehead* have seen Whitehead's philosophy through that lens. Furthermore, it has been a longstanding question whether Whitehead knew of the radical new science that was just being formulated by Heisenberg and Schrödinger at the time – quantum mechanics being a mathematical system that aimed to cohere the body of quantum theory that Whitehead himself played a part in exploring.[1] Indeed, the connections between Whitehead and quantum mechanical philosophy have been explored since the 1960s.[2]

But there is a tension between Copenhagen-style quantum mechanics and Whitehead's philosophy: the Copenhagen interpretation is connected more strongly to a Kantian tradition.[3] In contrast, Whitehead is not associated with this interpretation, favouring his own theory more reminiscent of interpretations credited to de Broglie and Schrödinger.[4] Furthermore, Whitehead is explicitly critical of Kant both inside and outside of the Harvard/Radcliffe lectures: 'performative self-contradictions' in the Kantian interpretation of relativity are discussed in his *Principle of Relativity*, and he generally rejects what he views as the Kantian fixation on the cognitive relationship of things.[5] Yet he explicitly praises Kant as well. Indeed, these lectures show Whitehead's deep and nuanced engagement with Kant's thought: he praises Kant, criticises Kant, and seeks to revise, or to 'throw' Kant in a processive direction. We should not let his harsh critique of 'Kantianism' distract us from his devoted engagement with Kant himself.

This appreciative critique of Kant, as we might term it, may help to point us towards enduring and mutually enlightening points of connection between philosophy and the natural sciences. In this interpretative process, one uniting quantum mechanics and Whitehead, as well as classical mechanics and Kant, we can find a way to put parts and wholes on an interpretive 'equality', rather, we might say, than following the tendency of realism and empiricism to reduce to sense-data and atomistic parts, and the tendency of post-Kantian idealism to reduce to subjectively constructed, *a priori* wholes. In essence, we can use the connections between their respective systems of philosophy and the scientific contexts in which they emerged in order to draw connections between their systems of philosophy as well.

The nature of this intersection between Kant, Whitehead and quantum mechanics has not been explored in depth, but the 1924–25 Harvard lecture notes from Whitehead's course taken by Bell, Hocking and Heath offer insight into the question. They show a picture of Whitehead taking on a Kantian project in the face of philosophical uncertainty over a new science, and in the process of synthesising the knowledge of physics and philosophy to build what would become *Process and Reality*. As a result, Whitehead draws on Kantian influences but avoids removing metaphysics, instead going back to Aristotle to observe how metaphysics and physics can be explored simultaneously with a recognition that Kant and Aristotle's philosophies needed radical changes. But perhaps it is the case that contemporaneous developments in philosophy, mathematics and physics meant that metaphysics could again, finally, be done without recourse to the 'dogmatism' that Kant rejected, with

Whitehead himself playing a key role in this interpretation[6] – and contributing to the Kantian hope that metaphysics might again be rediscovered on a non-dogmatic basis (in place of an incorrect notion that Kant dogmatically rejected the possibility of any such future metaphysics).

This chapter will outline the similar nature of Kant's project in the *Critique of Pure Reason* and the themes Whitehead aims to capture in his Harvard lectures: namely, their aims to explore the philosophical presuppositions required for science in light of radical scientific discovery. Then it will discuss the Kantian ground for the Copenhagen interpretation, and Heisenberg's challenges to Kant's philosophy. Finally, it will examine the anti-Kantian role Whitehead takes on in the Harvard lectures as his contribution to the development of quantum mechanics by offering a better set of foundational principles to adapt to the Copenhagen interpretation. This not only strengthens the recent literature on process philosophy and quantum mechanics, but also offers a point in the debate over the influences between the European physicists and Whitehead's metaphysics.

## Kant's Philosophical Presuppositions of Science

The project of grounding science in philosophical presuppositions is far from a new one, and certainly goes back at least as far as the Greeks. However, prior to Whitehead the explicit need to ground new science philosophically within modern philosophy is most clearly seen in Immanuel Kant. It is instructive to understand the type of philosophical inquiry Whitehead is undertaking in the period of the Harvard lectures, culminating in *Process and Reality*, by understanding Kant's own project.

The modernist movement, often considered to be heralded by Descartes and the statement *cogito ergo sum*, created a philosophical ground for science based on Descartes' hope that his indubitable discovery of the I led from here to indubitable certainty regarding the world. *Doubting*, rather than being the permanent work of philosophy, would instead be rigorously undertaken once, and lead thenceforth to the end of doubt. This methodology's failure, per Kant, is the origin of Humean scepticism.[7] Hume not only denounces the apodictic certainty of empirical investigations, but also denounces the frameworks within which these investigations are made. Famously, he rejects the metaphysical idea of causation;[8] he also in the same piece rejects the idea of a classical 'physics', involving ideas like Force, Power and Energy, as equally and falsely dogmatic.[9] Hume's radical scepticism denounces any work which requires an inference of pure reason, essentially renouncing all knowledge that claims certainty to any extent. This marks the problem facing natural science as a field of certain knowledge, as a Humean would insist that any natural scientific theory which aims to make predictions and develop any absolute schema of causes and effects must be rejected and replaced with purely 'experimental reasoning concerning matter of fact and existence'.[10]

Kant's project is one of rediscovering the appropriate realm of certainty in face of Hume's radical empiricist project; he hopes to find out how reason can maintain its 'purposive activity'.[11] Specifically, Kant hopes to recover the ability of natural science – or *Physica* – to formulate principles and 'laws'. Kant seeks to find a remainder of certainty among that which Hume categorically rejects: necessary knowledge that goes beyond tautologies derived from deconstructing concepts. Kant's solution to avoid this radical scepticism regarding pure reason is his insistence that two distinct sciences are required for human understanding. Recognising the failure of pure reason to quantify real existence, he restricts it to questions of validity instead (a thought which continued to be worked by the neo-Kantian Lotze in his *Logic*). The transcendental philosophy does not declare that all experience is the result of synthetic *a priori*; rather, the synthetic principles merely capture the totality of the possibility of experience.[12]

The first book of the *Critique* explains this for the case of logic. Logic can be divided into two domains: the pure or general logic which is concerned with the validity of logical statements and inferences, and applied logic which is concerned with speculative inferences considering earlier information. The former can point out whether an argument or judgement is valid, something which applied logic cannot do with certainty. Yet when it comes to the soundness of such a judgement – whether it actually holds as true in relation to the real things-in-themselves – the general logic has no tools.[13] In analogy, Kant posits that two fields of inquiry are needed, related to the conditions of experience and to reflections on experience – a distinction that does not however reduce the matter to the metaphysics of 'essential versus accidental', wherein the former is supposed to represent a higher, eternal kind of metaphysical reality, while the latter is given contingently and temporally.

The first science is the theoretical philosophy, which seeks only to understand what the limits of pure reason are and by what rules cognition can accord with itself.[14] Then, once the limits of reason and its functioning have been understood, the *a priori* principles function as the logical rules under which experience occurs and investigations of natural science and metaphysics may occur, but without predicting what experience will occur. In this realm of science, apodictic certainty relates to conditional possibilities of experience, not actualities of experience. The second science is the empirical science, which relates to actualities of experience. Kant discusses these two distinctions as two types of deduction. First is the transcendental deduction which asks how objects may be related to concepts, and second is the empirical deduction which shows the possibility of a concept being acquired through reflections on experience.[15] These two distinct deductions are the tools needed to rescue the natural sciences from a Humean approach which has no room for any certain theory: ideas like space, time and causality that cannot be derived from experience, but that are the conditions of experience, can be found through what may be termed epistemological investigations of pure reason. Meanwhile, the empirical philosophy – within which both a future metaphysics (a metaphysics not to be based on dogmatism) and natural science are contained – deals wholly with using reason within its limits and functions to interpret the experiences and information that are actually seen, allowing theory in natural science to exist. Nowadays we would point to the distinction between deductive and inductive logic, which preserves the Kantian insight: there is then less certainty than in Descartes' approach, where self-certainty leads to certainty about the real, and more certainty than in Hume, where there is no certainty anywhere.

Limiting reason implies the possibility, albeit unknowable, of something outside of its realm; this leads to Kant's infamous distinction between the noumenal and the phenomenal, but without making a metaphysics thereby – as of a noumenal realm, for instance – a higher kind of reality. Kant uses the metaphor of an island: without a boat one is restricted to the island but can explore it fully; however, no meaningful inference can be made about what lies in the fog and ocean beyond the island, other than the fact that the outside is given in problematic relation to the self.[16] This is neither solipsism and sceptical denial nor infallibilist certainty: I can know quite a bit about the island (even if perhaps less than the *complete* mapping that Kant hoped for). That is, I can know about the conditions of my experience, and I know that the outside is given problematically. That is not to say that it is impossible to know facts about the noumenal 'outside', just that knowledge about the noumenal is limited in contrast to the apodictic certainty about the conditions of experience, and the thing cannot be given to my thinking except through my ideas. For Kant, the noumenal objects beyond this are thinkable as limits – the negative, but not positive, conception of noumena which are not given in space and time and which knowledge-of can be approached, but not absolutely gained. This is because to him the noumena exist as a boundary concept, defined largely by their inability to be drawn in intuition.[17]

In contrast to noumena, there exist phenomena, or objects given within space and time. Appearance has its own being, and can be studied in itself, as the matter was formulated by latter-day phenomenologists like Lotze and

Husserl: even as these new-Kantianisms continued to resist on the one side a dualism – by which indubitable self-certainty would lead to indubitable certainty about the mirrored things of the world – and on the other side, a scepticism – which urged the impossibility of any knowledge. Philosophers like these could advance Kant as a pragmatic thinker, both idealistic and realistic, whose ideas really do indicate a meeting-point with a reality not reducible to itself. The island analogy indicates that yes – a problem of genuine relation between inner and outer *does* exist, but since the inner had not yet been sufficiently mapped, he would map the inner. Whitehead is indeed critical of Kant for taking this internal territory to be fully mapped, when the task was not in fact finished (HL1, 387). But there is nothing to forbid those who follow in his wake to seek to still better map the inner territory, and to begin making some advances in mapping the problematically given outer sea. (An example of pushing Kant in the pragmatic direction of interpretive engagement between thought and reality is given by Whitehead at HL1, 337.)

These external objects which are given problematically are what would be considered existentially (but not indubitably) real: namely they are cognised and objectified within the intuition and put into the organising manifolds of space and time. Objects are derived from appearances by sensibility and the understanding working in combination.[18] But again, as a logical description this is not a metaphysics, but a setting forth of two domains of science. The first science is the one that develops the certainty appropriate to understanding the necessary conditions of experience. The second science then seeks to discover the experiences under these conditions, but is unable to guarantee a full knowledge of 'what experience is'. Neither is it a declaration of existence preceding essence, as for Sartre, nor its opposite, as Sartre takes his opponents to hold; rather, it is a distinction between the form and contents of our experience. This definition of phenomena extends beyond the common-sense notion of the object as merely given to a passively mirroring subject: the process of ideally 'creating' an object includes inferences based on phenomena. In other words, the phenomena do not have to be – and in fact are not – the object-in-itself.

A key difference between these two classes of scientific entities, which we may term indubitable validities and fallible inductions, is the role of intuition in forming knowledge about them. Intuition is a common term in both realms, but is expressed in different ways. Kant refers to intuition as the faculty by which appearances are intuited or 'seen'. Intuition is effectively a medium between a sensation and judgement: when concerning physical sensations, it is termed the 'sensible intuition'; but one can also draw symbols through the imagination without recourse to experience in one's 'pure intuition'. For an instance of the latter, Kant uses the example of geometry, where geometrical facts are deductive and universal but derived only by drawing a figure in the intuition.[19] The mental interpretation of a sensory experience – what is contemporarily called qualia and Kant terms an 'appearance' – is an example of the former.[20] Kant notes that intuition requires cognitive faculties to represent things in the intuition in the forms of space and time. Drawing even a generalised shape requires an *a priori* concept of spatial relation, and all appearances are given a temporal sequencing from the primal, pre-organisational before and after.[21]

That space and time are forms of pure intuition leads to the implication that the noumenal object-in-and-of-itself *may* not be located in space or time: as far as reason is concerned, space and time are effectively traits of the appearances of objects. Of course Kant would be violating his own dictum about the limits of metaphysical description to say that such objects *are* not located in space or time – although it is not uncommon for post-Kantians to think that Kant made this negative claim. But it is better to understand his idea that space and time are merely the limits of our own experience as a limit-warning about the nature of our experience. The colour of the grass on our own side of the fence does not predetermine the colour of the grass on the opposite side of the fence – not even negatively. That is, that our form of space and time is our form does not confirm or deny its similar or dissimilar formation (or lack of formation) outside these limits. Our grass is its colour, our spatio-temporal organisation is our own – but Kant warns: do not proceed from this to a false apodictic certainty or a sceptical denial about that which is beyond our own.

Phenomena can be organised into both manifolds, but noumena like the *Ding an sich* are completely outside of this organisational activity, as by definition positive knowledge of them would require an intellectual intuition beyond human cognition.[22] To say that these are just like what we think, or nothing like what we think, would each alike be absurdities. One cannot leap over one's own transcendental shadow, but this impossibility of leaping simply means that we cannot know what is outside with the same apodictic certainty as we can know the limits of our own experience – we can indeed know in a different way, in the way of empirical reflection of experiences, in relation to existential objectivities sought through experiences. The manifolds of formal conditions are also part of the preconditions for empirical judgements; without this organising capacity, judgement cannot link concepts together. This also highlights that judgements made on empirically derived concepts are not pure or basic in the way Hume's project envisions. Instead, the empirical concept is the by-product of a large amount of cognitive work: the raw sensation must be adjusted into the forms of space and time, being placed in relation to other raw senses, before being intuited as the experiential qualia. It is from this position that *a posteriori* judgements which are the backbone of natural science can occur.

## A Kantian Picture of the Copenhagen Interpretation

It is helpful to highlight how the Copenhagen interpretation is in line with a Kantian empirical-scientific theory. Quantum mechanics is a mathematical system which aims to provide the ability to make predictions about actual phenomena outside of its scope.[23] That mathematical 'substratum' is dependent on the wavefunction, the relation of that wavefunction to mathematical operators, and the evolution of that wavefunction via a mathematical equation of motion – the Schrödinger equation. To link mathematical frameworks to a coherent 'physics' requires interpretation of the symbols into meanings about physical objects. Interpretations of quantum mechanics have to explain: how the wavefunction – abstractly a mathematical vector or function – relates to an actual physical state; how the operator – abstractly a matrix or map between spaces of functions – relates to observable quantities; and why predictions of experiments produce many possible outcomes, all of which are possible, but only one of which will be observed.

The Copenhagen interpretation is certainly a dominant 'interpretation' of quantum mechanics, although the degree of its prevalence is debatable.[24] This interpretation is a traditional interpretation and is not necessarily always well defined; it was re-evaluated by its progenitors repeatedly throughout their own investigations.[25] The Copenhagen interpretation is founded on a few simple principles, but is largely based on the idea that quantum mechanics must be in accordance with actuality. This is in contrast with the initial hopes of individuals like Schrödinger, who hoped that the new mathematics would lead to a completely new picture of reality.[26]

Its founder, Niels Bohr, took a view very similar to Kant's: knowledge of a physical nature could only be accrued if subjective experiences and objective system were correctly separated.[27] The fundamental principle behind the interpretation of quantum mechanics is the 'correspondence principle'; this can non-technically be described as the idea that quantum mechanics must agree with classical predictions of physical behaviour on the scales akin to everyday life – or those corresponding to 'large' quantisation numbers.[28] In elucidating this principle Kantian perspectives on science abound; for instance, the very notion of 'scale' being a feature of scientific predictions is one that Kant endorses explicitly in the *Critique*. Another important feature is Bohr's commitment – through this principle – to preserving the phenomenal experience of the subject. Through this principle Bohr acknowledges that the realm of the small is fundamentally inaccessible to ordinary human experience – therefore its rules need not match the physics of ordinary human experience. However, when those rules make predictions about human experience, those predictions must conform to experience: the principle of complementarity which is fundamental to the Copenhagen interpretation.[29]

In a lecture presented at the University of St Andrews in 1955, Werner Heisenberg elucidated what this interpretation meant to him. This interpretation declares that any physical object – or state – may be represented by a wavefunction which can be used to represent a probability density for the possible outcomes of any given experiment. Quantum theory then predicts the evolution of these functions, a fact that can be measured at a later time. After observation, the probability function is said to 'collapse': the new physical state of the system is the one that ensures a complete certainty that the observation would occur. Heisenberg notes that the most common conceptual difficulty with the Copenhagen interpretation comes here: what happens in such an event?

Quite simply put, Heisenberg notes, the word 'happens' is problematic here. To dictate in an event – the infamous example being a photon traversing a double-slit to hit a screen – that one of the possible situations 'happened' leads to logical contradictions. Instead, 'happens' is a verb which can only be applied to something a human observes. In the Kantian language, we can only call something real through our ideas, even as this ideal condition does not predetermine what the real is or is not – simply that if the real happens in our experience, it must be conditioned by our ideal structuring of experience and reflections upon this experience.

This opens another 'Kantian' point in the Copenhagen interpretation: wavefunction collapse, as it is often called, is not a physical process, but rather a mathematical tool to explain the phenomena observed in physical experience. To suggest that the state itself must be doing something outside of observation is to seek positive knowledge of the noumenon – something inaccessible to human perspective or reason. This is neither noumenalism nor anoumenalism about the existential state outside of observation, so to speak, but agnosticism. Heisenberg in many ways takes a phenomenological perspective, complete with its limits and access (but not in all ways, given the lack of the explicit acknowledgment of the first-person perspective), pointing out that:

We are not interested in the universe as a whole, including ourselves, but we direct our attention to some part of the universe and make that the object of our studies. In atomic physics this part is usually a very small object, an atomic particle or a group of such particles, sometimes much larger – the size does not matter; but it is important that a large part of the universe, including ourselves, does not belong to the object.[30]

In observation, the Copenhagen interpretation holds that a transition between the logically 'possible' outcomes of an experiment become 'actual' in experiential observation: a major difference between it and other interpretations which aim to explain how mathematical objects describe *actual* states of affairs before and after observation. In effect, the Copenhagen interpretation 'resigns' the scientist from understanding with certainty the full nature of experience. Instead, it indicates merely that the actual experience of phenomena must belong to the logically possible experience of phenomena. This resignation of the quest for certainty that Bohr and Heisenberg have to allowing the pre-observed state to remain probabilistic and 'subjective' indicates the Kantian transcendental philosophy's influence on their interpretations; they are in opposition to naive realism about the experience but are also in opposition to mere empiricism which would only study the actual experience itself. Here, the logical possibilities of experience are treated as a set of valid outcomes, and the actual experience that is empirically observed occurs under the constraint that its form is a member of the set. The real can only be approached through the ideal act of attention. It acknowledges that phenomena are not objects in themselves even as the phenomena are investigable *as* phenomena: the objects of quantum physics are constructs derived from the attention of scientists, even if they are constructs oriented towards aspects of received phenomenal experience. The *logos* constructs the phenomena as *objects* in systems, even if the phenomena that comprise objects may be said to arrive without logical construction. As a result, it is not sound to dictate what the actual nature of the object is prior to it being 'actualised' in observation: drawn in human intuition. From here Kantian rules on causation, space, time and science take over, and notably this is where theorising on quantum mechanics takes place.

## Whitehead's Philosophical Presuppositions of Science

When Kant approaches the question of the philosophy of science, he suggests that philosophy plays an important role in determining the conditions under which reason can determine proper laws of nature. Whitehead takes on a similar project in the 1924–25 lectures presented at Harvard: he examines what presuppositions must be made for science to do its work. The parallels between their projects go further: Kant is reacting to save the

successes of the Newtonian theory laid out in the *Principia* from a philosophical attack by sceptical empiricists; Whitehead is reacting to save the
successful modern physics paradigm from a philosophical scepticism about
its implications.

This connection offers an insight into how to interpret Whitehead's
Harvard lectures. The context of modern physics is not ignored: in fact,
Whitehead's earliest lectures are filled with reviews of electromagnetism and
early quantum theory to make the science accessible to the philosophical
community (HL1, 10). Like Kant, Whitehead examines the preconditions of
the science after the science has started: his work is contemporaneous with
the formalisation of quantum mechanics, after many of Bohr's major experimental and theoretical breakthroughs, and a decade after the elucidation of
Einstein's relativity.

The major difference between Kant and Whitehead is Whitehead's refusal
to reject metaphysics as dogmatic, as Kant does – although Kant's protest was
against contemporary metaphysics and not against the possibility of metaphysics as such. Instead, Whitehead takes cues from Aristotle on how one can
make limited assertions about the 'beyond' from experience. As Bell writes
in his record of Whitehead's lecture, 'Whitehead's own account of what he's
endeavoring to do is to rewrite Aristotelian line of thought' (HL1, 42). This
small piece of beyond which Whitehead sees is the idea of organism and process as the substratum on which scientific endeavours are founded, or what
Heath interprets as the 'process of becoming' (HL1, 413). The cleaving of
science and metaphysics was the result of the mistaken belief in modernist
philosophy that there was some form of static reality: in contrast, Whitehead
holds that reality itself is merely the realisation of change over stretches of
time (HL1, 11). This view does not relegate metaphysics as a handmaid of
science, but instead regards metaphysics as the 'critical appreciation of [the]
whole background of man's life' (HL1, 413).

The lectures show that Whitehead's position on process as the fundamental unit was quite firmly entrenched, not only for physics and the analysis of
physical systems, but for the analysis of biological systems like evolution as well
(HL1, 416). Whitehead notes that while it is common to talk of spatial points
as abstract, it is similarly true but less acknowledged that temporal points are
equally abstract: only things with duration and extent can claim to exist (HL1,
508).[31] Objects do not exist as instantaneous monads: rather everything has to
be understood as a mereological summation of complicated interactions, chief
of which is the process of becoming real to the observer (HL1, 27). This can
be seen in how Whitehead talks about electrons: he opens by taking the scientific definition of them as 'excitations of a field' (HL1, 12), and slowly over

the course of the lectures asks students to examine the nature of 'system' and interaction as the substratum on which 'electron' can come to be defined and exist, alongside their future and past interactions (HL1, 27, 108, 173). The very problem of the philosophy of science revolves around using metaphysics to find meaningful interpretations of these objects without circular reasoning (HL1, 27). These discussions showcase the uncertainty underlying the time in placing philosophy and science together, and Whitehead's belief in process as the interpretative force behind science.

The Harvard lectures show Whitehead is in deep thought about Kant during the 1920s, and in particular the challenge posed by Hume. Many of the first lectures presented in this series are focused on exactly this: how can one interpret scientific knowledge in light of Hume's challenge and Kant's response? It would make sense for this to be important in a course on philosophy of science: Whitehead and his students are standing in the midst of a revolution in science where discussions on what science was investigating were incredibly pertinent. This is the exemplification of his pursuit of a synthesis between science and experience which he sees as necessary for successful philosophy.[32]

## Heisenberg's Challenge to Kant

Kantian philosophy and the later neo-Kantian movements were a dominant force in German universities throughout the nineteenth century and leading into the twentieth. It was in this academic context that many of the early German and European physicists who developed quantum theory were working. Strong connections have recently been revealed between the early philosophical groundings of quantum theory and Kantian philosophy, primarily focusing on Niels Bohr's Kantian leanings.[33] However, there is also a large focus placed on apparent contradictions between Kant's philosophy and the implications of modern physics. Werner Heisenberg himself writes about two conflicts: the first, he argues, is the physical picture of space and time in modern physics; the second is the inconsistency between quantum mechanical theories and Kant's law of causality.[34] These conflicts offer an example of why Whitehead sees the need for a new Kant-style reinterpretation of philosophy in light of changes that are seen.

Kristian Camilleri notes in his 2006 paper 'Heisenberg and the Transformation of Kantian Philosophy' that Heisenberg's solution to Kantian problems is to modify the meaning of *a priori*. Instead of seeing it as having apodictic certainty, he views it as the result of historical linguistic development. Camilleri finds two distinct transformations:

First, the a priori status of space, time, and causality is retained by Heisenberg in the sense that they remain the presuppositions of experience, but the a priori is deprived of its necessity in Kant's sense. The indispensability of classical concepts originates from the historical fact that we have no other language through which we describe what is given to us in experience. Second, the concepts of classical physics are no longer understood to have universal applicability as they do for Kant. Beyond certain limits, the concept of the electron's location in space ceases to have applicability in quantum mechanics. At this point, 'the contours of this "objectively real" world dissolve – not in the mist of a new and yet unclear idea of reality, but into the transparent clarity of a mathematics whose laws govern the possible and not the actual.'[35]

Heisenberg's critique of Kant is that his apparent insistence on bringing Newtonian laws into a 'necessary' paradigm through ideas like the law of causality and his specific vision of space and time have left him unable to adapt to the world of quantum objects, with probabilistic, non-sensible outcomes. Instead, Heisenberg seems to develop quantum ontology by building on a philosophy that is 'practically' Kantian, but seeks to discuss the 'potential' for classical outcomes instead.[36]

## A Kantian Rejoinder

While Heisenberg claims to see a simultaneous departure from Kantian perspectives, this is in fact the result of misinterpreting Kantian idealism to be like Berkeley's in nature: focused on describing the totality of existence through the transcendental philosophy, and not attending to Kant's refusal to propose a metaphysics within his own philosophical programme (while not forbidding others the possibility of metaphysics on improved grounds). There are Kantian solutions to the problems noted by Heisenberg in his Gifford lectures.

This is clearest in Heisenberg's assertion that the theory of relativity reveals 'entirely new features of space and time' not found in Kant's description of the forms of pure intuition, or essentially that Kant's space and time have been 'rejected' by science.[37] A simple refutation is offered by Edmund Husserl in his Vienna lecture. Husserl notes that while Einstein's revolutionary physics does change how science objectifies appearances, 'Einstein does not reform the space and time in which our vital life runs its course.'[38] In other words, modern physics as an empirical science cannot after the fact alter its *a priori* conditions in the form of intuitions; it is merely a descriptor of how one should make judgements about intuited objects. Suggestions that

Kant is incorrect because of his commitment to Euclidean space ignores the fundamental point that the transcendental philosophic descriptions of space and time are not concerned with what theoretical manifold best predicts future appearances, but about the conditions of appearances to us. The forms of pure intuition are concerned only with how space and time actually are to the human reason.[39]

A similar deconstruction of Heisenberg's counter-argument to Kantian transcendental philosophy based on causality can be explored. Heisenberg cites Kant's law of causality as the assumption that 'there is a foregoing event from which the other event must follow according to some rule' and that scientific investigation is the process of finding these foregoing events.[40] Since atomic physics provides only the ability to declare an average time for an emission to occur, it is an error to look for the foregoing event from which the emission must follow. Instead, quantum theory leaves this and many other measurements as indeterminate – the same initial physical state upon measurement can have many possible outcomes without any mechanism to indicate which one will actually follow through rules.[41] This creates an apparent conflict with the Kantian *a priori* form of causality.

That contradiction is resolved again by recognising that the law of causality does not require a determinate result from any given prior instance. Instead, the law of causality is merely the *a priori* condition for reason to make judgements of the form 'if A, then B' and objectify them.[42] This law does not require that A and B *are* uniquely joined, but does not preclude it either. Kant's law of causality fails only if one mistakenly asserts that it demands as a matter of apodictic certainty a certain existential outcome from an existential precondition. This is the mistake of confusing 'validity as the condition for soundness' with actual soundness, when pure idealism can indeed only speak of the conditions of truth. Pure idealism investigates the conditions of valid experience, but it must leave the investigation of truth as *soundness* to the validity-seeking-truth combination of formal logic *and* sensuous or empirical investigation. But to investigate the latter (the empirical or sensuous) does not exhaust the home domain of the former (the pure logic). For Kant,

> The understanding, by means of the unity of apperception, is the *a priori* condition of the possibility of a continuous determination of all positions for the appearances in this time, through the series of causes and effects, the former of which inevitably draw the existence of the latter after them and thereby make the empirical cognition of temporal relations (universally) valid for all time, thus objectively valid.[43]

Such validities can permit the possibility of a sound observation. In Heisenberg's example of the decaying atom, A might be the physical state of an atom. While Heisenberg believes that the consequent B or not-B precludes Kantian causality, all the law of causality does is make it possible for Heisenberg to say that 'if a radioactive atom is observed, then its decay will be observed or not'. After repeated investigations, one can then make the judgement 'if a radioactive atom is observed, on average a decay will be observed after observing it for $n$ seconds'. Without an *a priori* form of causality the objectification into a rule – probabilistic or otherwise – would be impossible, something Heisenberg himself admits.[44] All that is relevant is that one can order appearances determinately, which still occurs when observing the atom as its decay or failure to decay precedes the appearance of the atom as an object in intuition.

These rebuttals to modern physics-based critiques of Kantianism are fundamentally attributable to one force, which Heisenberg himself unknowingly elucidated. He writes that 'what Kant had not foreseen was that these *a priori* concepts can be the conditions for science and at the same time have only a limited range of applicability'.[45] In fact, this is exactly what Kant asserts from the beginning, and why the philosophy is well-harmonised to a modern physicist's paradigm. The project of the transcendental philosophy, and the synthetic *a priori* judgements it makes, is to limit its domain until the necessity required for *a priori* knowledge can be met.[46] Concepts like space, time and the law of causality are not able to discuss how appearances will be present in the sensible intuition; they are merely descriptions of the conditions for human reason to be able to make past, present and future judgements and speculations. Yet they also represent a certainty: the subject's reason is dependent on them as forms of intuition and concepts of the understanding. Quantum mechanics from an experimental and theoretical framework respects the power of the transcendental as a conditional rather than predicative force, without abusing it by conflating the conditional and predicative realms, nor by asserting one and denying the other. Instead we can say that the respect is precisely along the lines of recognising the limits, and relation, of apodictic and empirical knowledge.

Heisenberg points out that adherents to the Copenhagen interpretation do in fact appear to develop modern physics per a Kantian framework. Causal chains are assumed, and events are framed into the manifold of Euclidean space and that formation does occur *a priori* to the observational work.[47] Yet, Heisenberg mistakenly asserts that these *a priori* synthetic judgements are transformed by modern physics from a 'metaphysical' possibility to a 'practical' one; they are relative truths that appear in empirical investigations.[48] This is sorely mistaken. In fact, what has occurred is that modern physics has disposed of metaphysical notions of causality, space and time, which a classical physics required, and what Heisenberg sees as 'practical' ascriptions to Kantian formulations are merely empirical manifestations of what Kant identifies in the transcendental philosophy as the conditions of pure understanding.

Uniting the theoretical and mathematical framework of quantum mechanics with Kantian philosophy does not require taking Heisenberg's position that Kant has merely elucidated a 'practical' picture. Instead, it is more reasonable to assert that quantum mechanics has moved natural science into a truly Kantian paradigm. For example, Newtonian and classical physics ascribe definite objects' locations within a space-time that exists independently and absolutely outside them. In contrast, quantum mechanics discards that view: physical state parameters like location, momentum and even particle numbers are regarded as beyond the possibility of drawing in intuition.[49] Instead of the definite conclusions about objects themselves moving in a certainly existing space-time which is required in the classical picture, the modern picture regards the object, the space and the times as indeterminate; this new picture focuses solely on what empirical probabilities follow from a starting condition.[50] This indeterminacy seems more akin to Kantian distinctions between the appearance and the object itself than the Newtonian picture.

Theory in modern physics no longer attempts to comment on things Kant explicitly sees as noumenal, and is agnostic to the *Ding an sich*. The classical picture contains no such ambiguity: when one makes a prediction about an object, one asserts to know it completely from sufficient initial conditions – characterised by Laplace's demon thought experiment.[51] The modern picture removes such determinate notions about an object, instead referring only vaguely to the wavefunction for a system: a complicated mathematical object which mixes many different entities, and which has the sole purpose of being used in a mathematical way to accord with past experiments and predict probabilistically future experiments.[52]

The addition of the complementary principle to quantum theory reinforces the Kantian nature of the field. Effectively, the complementary principle asserts that all mathematical predictions of quantum mechanics must be interpreted as if they abide by common-sense notions of causality and certainty at the macroscopic limit. Instead of quantum physics claiming to provide a mirrored picture of the whole of reality, it merely seeks to understand and predict all possible objective knowledge of the system without ascribing to that set of knowledge ultimate reality.[53] In other words, the complementary principle repeats what Kant says at the beginning of the *Critique*, namely 'Natural Science (*Physica*) contains within itself the synthetic a priori as principles.'[54] Modern physics does not overturn Kant's synthetic *a priori*, but rather recognises this as the principles by which physics must be done and accepts the limitations that are subsequently imposed on speculative reason by these principles – as a respect for the power and the limits of our experiential observation.

## Whitehead's Copenhagen Interpretation

So far two possible ways to ground the Copenhagen interpretation have been discussed: the first is as a Kantian theory of science itself, similar to how Bohr likely envisioned it; the second is Heisenberg's 'practical' Kantianism which eschews the necessity of Kantian concepts in favour of a more Wittgensteinian approach. However, another approach can be seen, and that is through Whitehead's philosophy. Whitehead in the Harvard lectures, as mentioned before, is very preoccupied with Kant and Hume and the role they played in grounding science.

Although immediately preceding the Copenhagen theory's 'development' after Heisenberg's publication of a formalised system of quantum mechanics in 1925, Whitehead's 1924–25 discussions of science demonstrate the philosophical soundness of the Copenhagen interpretation of quantum theory and show how the philosophical moment may have yielded this interpretation. Of course it is even plausible that Whitehead's own interpretations helped to ground or frame the Copenhagen interpretation, given his transatlantic renown. Lecture 6 shows the intimate link between Whitehead's thought and the soon-to-be-developed Copenhagen interpretation: Whitehead sees the 'observable' and the observer as fundamentally linked entities – linked through process. Science being empirical does not imply only allowing for 'concrete' entities – rather the empirical requires that science also take into account the observations and the positing of a subject (HL1, 24).

Whitehead and the Copenhagen interpretation agree on the importance of process and its link to time. It is interesting how intimately both Whitehead's philosophy and quantum theory link process and time to the fundamental nature of reality: Whitehead's metaphysics is largely based on a notion of loose energy conglomerations changing through time, while quantum theory holds that every physical state evolves based on its Hamiltonian, a mathematical object designed to represent its energy. Whitehead notes that science cannot talk about instants because observers must observe through durations – one witnesses entire processes and not mere spatio-temporal slices (HL1, 34). This is particularly useful as it gives a Whiteheadian defence of the anomaly of wavefunction 'collapse': the question of how a physical state 'changes' from the many-possibility state to the singular possibility state is nonsensical, as it is asking a question about an instant, which per Whitehead does not exist other than as an abstraction (HL1, 35). Instead, one must examine the process of a state being observed by an observer.

Process-based philosophy seems well equipped to deal with the challenges that the philosophy of science presents in the context of modern physics. Scientific realism is difficult to defend, as 'ultimate entities become abstract and empirically impure' (HL1, 23). Yet, the alternative constructivist approaches want to completely turn these entities into fictions, an action Whitehead notes robs science of meaningful explanatory power (HL1, 25). What is needed is a middle way between discrete realism and subjectivistic idealism, with their tendency to reduce to material or to form respectively. By engaging with process, modern physics' abstract yet useful sense can be explored: no physical state exists instantaneously and fully. Rather, all physical states are 'realised' by the observer over some time interval (HL1, 301). To ask – as many non-Copenhagen interpretations seek to – what existed 'just prior' to the observation is a nonsensical question for science, except insofar as the existent can be brought into view of an observation. But it is useless and contradictory to demand the observation of the existent that is not given through an observation. In other words, while a 'history' of a physical state is possibly knowable it cannot be known through an unobservable 'other' process.

Michael Epperson's 2004 work *Quantum Mechanics and the Philosophy of Alfred North Whitehead* gives a detailed description of how *Process and Reality* reacted to the modern physics developments of its era. Epperson concludes that Whitehead took great effort to make his philosophy 'empirically applicable', its great success being its ability to bridge classical and quantum through the realms of experience.[55] Whitehead is dedicated in his cosmology to two principles related to the Copenhagen interpretation: first is the shift from focus on the attributes of physical bodies, a thought Whitehead associates with Descartes, to a focus on 'relationships between occasions'; second is the commitment to Heisenberg's statement that the potential becomes actual upon the interaction of a system with an observer, which Whitehead views as the limit of apodictic scientific knowledge.[56] In other words, Epperson shows that Whitehead fully incorporates modern physics into his cosmology. Epperson suggests that Whitehead's affinity to the Copenhagen interpretation is not merely coincidental or reactive: rather he indicates that process philosophy has been designed with the theoretical physics of the early twentieth century in mind.[57] This claim is furthered by reading the lecture notes: they show that Whitehead's ideas on the presuppositions of science bind him to the Copenhagen interpretation even prior to its creation.

Since Whitehead is discussing the presuppositions of science, he is embarking on a similar project to Kant's own, even though, as we have seen, he suggests that Kant needs a shove away from subjectivism in the direction of an understanding of subject and object as related in a larger whole. This shows the fundamental similarities in Whitehead and Kant's approach to the philosophical presuppositions of science, and as a result their philosophies both contain guiding principles to determine how one should deal with the challenge of indeterminacy in modern physics. Both Whitehead and Kant acknowledge the importance of preserving physical mechanics: Kant starts the *Critique* by discussing how natural science may produce 'laws', while Whitehead starts his lecture by laying out the 'facts' discovered by theoretical physics. Furthermore, both philosophers see the need to reject Humean scepticism as a possible philosophical escape, or as Whitehead terms it, 'phenomenalism' (HL1, 24). They both also recognise the need for any mechanics to have a limit to their applicability: Kant suggests that there is the idea of the noumenal, something outside the realm of speculative reason; Whitehead in turn firmly notes in his first lecture that there is a limit to scientific knowledge: it can gain no access to a 'reality' that is 'behind' becoming, instead, it must be content with the realisation 'There is nothing but this process of becoming real' (HL1, 5). A 'behind' in this sense is comparable to Kant's 'noumenal' – an absurdity. This of course involves a reading of Kant's 'noumenal' as a negative limit, rather than as positive claim: it is absurd to knowingly speak of the noumenal or the 'behind' to which we have no possible knowledgeable relation. If, for Kant, the non-access to the noumenal is a mere observation about the absurdity of any attempt to describe an exterior object to which we have no internal relation (making the noumenal a 'nothing' as a limit, a limit that renders absurd any positive attempt to describe it), then we indeed see a relation between Kant and Whitehead's real 'becoming' behind which there is nothing. This shared view of limits should not be read as Whitehead's endorsement of the noumenal of an unknowable existent: rather Whitehead seeks to reject the sharp contrast many Kantians draw between the noumena and phenomena to escape Kant's epistemic 'prison'.[58] These similarities are ones that draw the philosophies to a Copenhagen interpretation of physics.

The Copenhagen interpretation gives a mathematical framework the predictive power to distinguish possible events which can become, which is more than Hume's vision of a constant conjunction, but which nevertheless has no interest in dogmatically ascribing additional knowledge of other universes or pilot waves. This accords with Whitehead's own goals for science, which argue that the more abstract a theory is the more useful it is (HL1, 393) and that physics must take a 'daringly' abstract form through mathematics. This becomes interesting as within two years both Heisenberg and Schrödinger did exactly that, completely mathematising quantum theory and abstracting quantum objects into the general concept of wavefunction state, a supposed description of the entire physical system.

## Whitehead's Critique of Kant: The Object of Deep Empiricism

While there are similarities in the affinity between Whitehead and Kant's philosophies and the Copenhagen interpretation, it is important to remember that they may have different foundations within the history of philosophy, at least according to their authors. In fact, Whitehead describes himself as anti-Kantian (HL1, 39), a view which is corroborated by his rejection of neo-Kantian, analytic tendencies.[59] This is largely due to how they each treat metaphysics. Kant is seeking to reject dogmatic metaphysics entirely: as a result the Copenhagen interpretation works well due to its rejection of making claims that would be positive descriptions of the noumenal. In contrast, Whitehead implores scientists to think metaphysically in order to engage creative faculties to better do their task (HL1, 19). But in both cases, the 'noumenal' is unknowable as *merely* external. Here we might note again that Kant did not himself forbid the possibility of metaphysics, ever, but merely rejected the dogmatic metaphysics – the kind of metaphysics that could hypostatise the real on the one side or the ideal on the other, without accounting for their processive relation.

Whitehead sees the divergence between himself and Kant in this understanding of metaphysics based on processive relation. In response to Hume's dilemma, Kant denies that we have 'no idea not from an impression' (HL1, 434), and indicates that universal assertions like those of science are not based on the object, but rather the intuition of the sensing subject. This is something Whitehead agrees with to a point: there is no privileged access to a localised object, but it would be incorrect to exclude the object in its entirety. There is an access point to what Kant terms the *Ding an sich* per Whitehead: their existence can be viewed as their relevance to realisation of process and change.

It has been written that Kant's 'scandal' in philosophy has been turned into Whitehead's 'scandal': namely the problem of idealism being unrefuted has become a problem with induction being unrefuted.[60] The lectures suggest Whitehead himself was very conscious of this, first evidenced by his clear elucidation of the problem of induction presented by Hume and his thoughts on Kant's response; but he also directly indicates this by suggesting he wishes to 'stand Kant on his head' by giving objects a metaphysical role through process into the realisation of the subject (HL1, 113). In other words, Whitehead seeks to focus the attention of scientists on understanding the world where their realisations and the environment exist reciprocally, a theme which is made salient by Heisenberg's thoughts on the observer being an active participant in wavefunction collapse.

'Kant', we notice, gains a fair bit more credit in Whitehead's description than do Kantians. For Whitehead, Kant's view was 'luminous . . . because Kant was last great philosopher who was a Mathematician'. It was indeed a 'Calamity that Kant's followers hadn't Kant's intellectual equipment' (HL1, 304). With his Newtonian background, Kant was able to show a relation between parts and wholes that is fundamental to Whitehead's thought as well (and, we may note, to Husserl's *Logical Investigations*). Bell's recording continues: 'Spatio-Temporal relations taken as a whole (for Whitehead) "internal", whereas general view is that these are the very examples of External relations. Whitehead suggests this as root of whole difficulty. Kant's doctrine has sense only in taking Part-Whole relation as "internal" for the whole' (HL1, 304). If Kant slips, and Whitehead suggests that at times he does, still his fundamental insight was that (now citing from Hocking): 'The whole is of the essence of the part, just as the part is of the essence of the whole', and by this, Kant shows the way out of the infinite regress problem (HL1, 307).

Kant's influence on Whitehead was enduring. For instance, Whitehead speaks, in Winthrop Bell's notes on the Harvard seminar, of his own early delight in Kant (HL1, 305), and Hocking records Whitehead as crediting Kant as a main reason he turned to philosophy (HL1, 307). Kant put 'in more general terms what Whitehead was getting in his science (classical mechanics)'. Whitehead indeed criticises Caird for ignoring this fundamental scientific aspect of Kant's thought. It is not just the 'early' Whitehead who appreciates Kant, and he continues to remark in these lectures on points of fundamental agreement. For Whitehead, at the time of these lectures, Kant's 'conceptual machinery' remains particularly valuable, for instance, in showing how 'Objects are outcome of conceptual activity'. And at this point, Bell's notes continue, 'all philosophical world has got to go to Kant' (HL1, 30). Again, the relation of subject to object is an internal one, although the 'object' is irreducible to the subject – a distinction that Kant sometimes misses, in what Whitehead labels as Kant's turns to subjectivism. Yet, despite these missteps, Kant directs our attention to the right place, as Bell records:

Activity . . . is, then, what makes Knowledge possible, but Whitehead holds it only makes Knowledge possible because it's what makes process of realisation possible. Process of knowing is only an exceptional example

embedded in total process of realisation . . . Entities [are] discerned as setting the conditions satisfied by concrete procession of reality itself. Whitehead discover these where Kant does:–in perceptual objects. Strains of
self-conditioning process. (HL1, 31)

The object is neither merely separated from the subject, nor is it monistically
unified, but it is given in a process of discovery.

Both Bell and Hocking record Whitehead's use of Kant's 'given', renamed by
Whitehead the 'Actual potentiality' of the past: 'that is outcome of the Past in the
present' (HL1, 130). And later, for Whitehead, 'Kant has said what Whitehead
has been trying to say' – that 'Points and moments are mere places of limitation
. . . you've got to have some point of view like Kant's about Time and Space –
Parts and Wholes' (HL1, 301). At Radcliffe, as well, Whitehead points to an
agreement of Plato, Kant and Whitehead on the 'nature of point & moment as
limit', and their disagreement with Aristotle on this point (HL1, 502).

Yet Whitehead is critical of Kant as well, particularly his subjectivism. For
Whitehead, Kant's *transcendental* conditions of the possibility of subjective
experience missed the *transcendent* possibility of experience to give knowledge
of 'beyondness' (HL1, 433). (Here, Kant might have objected: that beyondness is a task for other modes of science – my task is simply to provide a
science of the transcendental conditions of experience.) But we should be
careful not to conflate Whitehead's nuanced appreciation and criticism of
Kant with his brusque rejection of the 'Kantian' and 'Kantianism'. Whitehead
is dismissively critical of certain 'Kantian' interpretations – particularly those
uninformed by mathematics and science – whereas Kant himself is to be critically revised (cf. the critique of Kantianism, not Kant (HL1, 66, 213, 241) and
his critique of 'Caird-Kant' (HL1, 43)). It is this Kant-but-not-Kantian distinction that is fundamental to Whitehead's rejoinder to Hume, which is 'In
exactly same spirit as Kant (but anti-Kantian himself . . .)' – wherein Whitehead, like Kant, understands that 'It's not a question of first observing a fully
determinate fact and then plastering it over with assumptions from without.
The process of Reality carries with it all that you can infer about it' (HL1, 39).
The subject has an access point to Reality, even as there is no access to Reality, for us, save through this subjective approach – a reciprocal subject-object
relation that is no single-poled 'subjectivism'. As Lotze sided with Plato versus
the 'Platonists', so too Whitehead makes it possible to agree with Kant while
disagreeing with Kantians.

Comparisons between Whitehead and Kant thus show agreement and
disagreement, but both showcase the reintroduction of subjectivity into the
framework of the causal structures hypothesised by physics: a 'subjectivity'

that will avoid succumbing to 'subjectivism' and its 'epistemic prison'. Paul Stenner (2008) suggests that for Whitehead this reaction stems from the scientific materialism threatening to undermine the project of physics in 'that subjectivity is ignored, but that it is actively excluded from consideration (or "negatively prehended")'.[61] He indicates Whitehead aimed to replace 'shallow empiricism' with 'deep empiricism', a philosophical project that aimed to examine atoms of experience and how they endure and change in a manner consistent with the development of modern physics. The goal is a cosmology that not only is faithful to scientific development but can also give subjectivity its proper role and examine 'all types of reality'.[62] This view is certainly corroborated by the evidence presented in his Harvard lectures on the philosophy of science.

It is not so much Whitehead's praise or criticisms of Kant, but his efforts at critical improvement, that help us see the foundation and direction of Whitehead's turn to process philosophy. The subject and object stand in processive relation, versus the externalism of Realism and the subjectivism of Kant. This revision can be found for instance in Whitehead's work to rescue Kant from his 'wavering between an external and internal view' at the point of generation (HL1, 305) – Kant needs a push, so to speak, in the internalist but not subjectivist direction, in which the subject is indeed related, in knowledge, to meant objectivities – replacing the duality of 'inner' and 'outer' with the three-part interpretive or becoming *relation* of subject and object. Here, Whitehead continues, 'What is wanted in Philosophy is to attempt to do same sort of thing Kant does, getting rid of Subjectivist basis of it' (HL1, 311). So too, Whitehead removes one of Kant's incorrect dictums on Extensive Quantity, to preserve Kant's correct insight on Intensive Quantity, thus showing that reality precedes divisibility, rather than divisibility preceding reality (HL1, 317). Kant is not, in Whitehead's telling, *quite* there, but he shows the way to resolving the dilemma of how to provide a shared home for Entity S and Environment O, rather than falling into the regress problem of priority and derivation of these two abstract moments. For Whitehead, the Kantian (again, not 'Kant') prioritises the S, and Realism looks upon an unaffected 'O'. Kant himself is a kind of halfway house (to borrow Hocking's phraseology) showing the way to the true solution, which is not priority and derivation, but a 'larger togetherness' (HL1, 66), And in turn we may see that this together-relation of subjective observer and objectively observed, rather than a mere dualism of S and O, is key to understanding the philosophical importance of quantum mechanics as an interpretive science.

Stenner developed the term deep empiricism independently but shortly after Derek Malone-France, who uses the idea in a different – but per Stenner, complementary – manner.[63] Malone-France views the context of Whitehead and Kant in a similar vein: both are mathematical physicists turned philosophers prompted by 'the perceived failure of theoretical frameworks' to build new philosophical systems.[64] They are linked by an examination of deep empiricism: namely 'the attempt to "sound the depths" of reality, in search of explanatory principles related to the very "nature of things"'.[65] This framework links, per Malone-France, the *Critique* and *Process and Reality* – which can be seen as the formalisation of the themes in Whitehead's lectures – and offers a mechanism for comparing transcendental idealism and organic realism. Malone-France argues that the '*promise* of the *Critique* – to justify the "synthetic" propositions and inductive generalizations of science and the idea of "objective truth" – is better, more coherently realized in the ontology and epistemology that are presented in Whitehead's *Process and Reality*'.[66] Without commenting on which realises the project better, it is clear that for Malone-France, *Process and Reality* does achieve what Whitehead sets out to do in his lectures a few years earlier in his Harvard lectures: namely realise the subjective conditions under which science occurs.

This lends the project an affinity to the Copenhagen interpretation, which places the subject at the centre of a quantum process-wavefunction collapse. While a Kantian may be tempted to suggest that inquiring into the nature of that process is *verboten*, it is clear it is consistent with a Whiteheadian deep empiricism to use the access point of process and change to gain insight into 'stubborn facts' or the 'nature of things': a move beyond noumenal agnosticism into 'reality'. And of course there is another kind of Kantian, who will be quite comfortable in suggesting a processive relation of knower and known: an idealistic-empirical approach that hypostatises neither in the direction of 'idealism', nor of 'realism', but finds in science their reciprocal relation: a 'deep empiricism', or an 'idealistic empiricism' that makes space for metaphysical knowledge through pure and applied logic. Indeed, Whitehead (like mathematically and scientifically informed 'neo-Kantian' thinkers such as Lotze, Royce and Husserl) may be seen as contributing to this second tradition, and we may see him not so much as an anti-Kantian overall, but rather as anti-Kantian in the first of these two Kantian traditions.

## The Harvard Lectures: Bridging the Atlantic, Bridging Science and Philosophy

As mentioned, Whitehead's process philosophy has long been recognised for its historical and intellectual links to quantum mechanics and its interpretations. The Harvard lectures present an exciting opportunity to explore

Whitehead's thoughts on the matter, from a perspective that would not be delivered by a published book like *Process and Reality*. The lectures are contemporaneous with Heisenberg and Schrödinger's work that would turn quantum theory into a coherent system of mechanics, and Bohr's discussions of complementarity which formed the basis of the Copenhagen interpretation. It would be difficult to parse 'which came first', but per Whitehead's concept of organic synthesis, that may be a poor question to ask at all. The lectures do clearly demonstrate, however, that Whitehead was taking on a Kantian project on evaluating philosophy in light of rapid scientific change.

This is particularly important as a bridging point between Whitehead and thinkers such as Husserl, a mathematician-physicist who in the 'continental' tradition aimed to do a similar task through phenomenology. The philosophical connections between Husserl and Whitehead are fruitful: reading the *Logical Investigations* we can see Husserl add similar modifications to German idealism, introducing the processive relation between the consciousness which objectifies and the object itself to move 'towards' the object itself.[67] This is achieved by rejecting the idea that there is an absolute hierarchy to the 'givenness' and 'interpretative nature' of an object: rather, the object for both philosophers becomes interpreted and given. (And here it is interesting to note that Husserl, like Whitehead, has significant praise for Kant, and significant criticism of 'Kantian' thought.) Through the mediation of Winthrop Bell, who was close to both Husserl and Whitehead, the historical connections between them are made clearer, and analysing the Harvard lectures – including the notes of Bell, who was Husserl's doctoral student and later Harvard professor – offers a chance for an exchange between continental and Anglo-American philosophical traditions. Furthermore, it links Whitehead's personal thought to Kant. Since the Copenhagen interpretation can appear to be understood through both Whitehead's philosophy and neo-Kantian/continental approaches, it provides a very powerful philosophical connection between seemingly disparate philosophical schools. These links prove very important in a world where philosophy of science is moving to a phase where integrating different systems of philosophy is the best way forward to find meaningful answers.

Whitehead's views on science and its philosophical basis represent a harsh rejection of anti-scientific 'Kantianism', but a more careful editorial revision of the scientifically minded Kant, with the addition of new discoveries in science to which Kant did not have access (along with a fundamental reliance on Aristotle's organicist thought, and an evident appreciation of the pragmatism that had flourished at Harvard, to permit more pragmatic, processive thought than Kant's primarily delimiting work alone would permit). We might even consider that Kant himself would have been delighted by the direction of Whitehead's critique, informed by a quantum mechanics to which Kant did not, of course, have access. Indeed Kant might protest against his latter-day friends, the Kantians, that he never intended to develop an 'epistemic prison', or to promote subjectivism. Rather, he merely wished to develop a pure science of the subject that could exist *alongside* other sciences, like mechanics, with distinctive and non-contradictory domains – just as Kant's 'pure morality' does not forbid a moral subject from being happy, but rather simply insists that pure morality is one science, while happiness-seeking belongs to another science. In both cases, the distinction between realms of science is not intended to obviate distinctions in the reality of which science is 'of'.

Like Heisenberg, Whitehead raises serious questions about the viability of Kantian frameworks when considering the changing landscape of science. Kant's philosophy was well-equipped for deterministic classical physics, but failed to explicitly account for the probabilities imposed by modern physics, or even the relativity imposed by Einstein. These concerns have Kantian rejoinders and may be criticisms more related to the state of neo-Kantian philosophy, but Heisenberg and Whitehead each offer alternative metaphysics to ground science in which share common themes with Kant. These themes include the limits of both empirical and cognitive investigations, and the role of the subject in generating mechanics. These themes thus demonstrate how multiple philosophical approaches could generate the Copenhagen interpretation. The Copenhagen interpretation is itself diffuse, occasionally even considered a 'myth'.[68] To acknowledge it as a 'myth' is not, of course, to imply that it is false – but rather to observe that it is very much in a process of becoming. Acknowledging these related philosophic influences founded on grounding science in proper philosophy offers a great chance to understand it, and philosophy, better.

## Notes

1. Folse, 'The Copenhagen Interpretation', 32.
2. Malin, 'Quantum Physics and Whitehead's Philosophy' (video, pirsa.org).
3. Cuffaro, 'The Kantian Framework', 309.
4. Desmet, 'Whitehead's Highly Speculative Lectures on Quantum Theory', above pp. 155, 180.
5. Desmet, 'From Physics to Philosophy, and From Continuity to Atomicity', above p. 140.
6. Desmet, 'Whitehead's Highly Speculative Lectures on Quantum Theory', above pp. 170–1.
7. Kant, *Critique of Pure Reason*, 148, B23.

8. Hume, 'An Enquiry', 843.
9. Hume, 'An Enquiry', 856.
10. Hume, 'An Enquiry', 899.
11. Kant, *Critique of Pure Reason*, 226, B128.
12. Kant, *Critique of Pure Reason*, 282, B195.
13. Kant, *Critique of Pure Reason*, 195, B74–75.
14. Kant, *Critique of Pure Reason*, 218, B116.
15. Kant, *Critique of Pure Reason*, 220, B117.
16. Kant, *Critique of Pure Reason*, 354, B295.
17. Kant, *Critique of Pure Reason*, 363, B312.
18. Kant, *Critique of Pure Reason*, 364, B314.
19. Kant, *Critique of Pure Reason*, 170, B24.
20. Kant, *Critique of Pure Reason*, 172, B34.
21. Kant, *Critique of Pure Reason*, 185, B59, and 272, B178.
22. Kant, *Critique of Pure Reason*, 363, B312.
23. Epperson, *Quantum Mechanics*, 69.
24. Schlosshauer et al., 'A Snapshot of Foundational Attitudes Toward Quantum Mechanics'.
25. Joos, *Decoherence and the Appearance of a Classical World in Quantum Theory*.
26. Faye, 'Copenhagen Interpretation', 4.
27. Faye, 'Copenhagen Interpretation', 2.
28. Faye, 'Copenhagen Interpretation', 4.
29. Bitbol and Osnaghi, 'Bohr's Complementarity', 156.
30. Heisenberg, *Physics and Philosophy*, 20.
31. Irvine, 'Alfred North Whitehead', 3.
32. Epperson, *Quantum Mechanics*, 71; Irvine, 'Alfred North Whitehead', 3.
33. Faye, 'Copenhagen Interpretation', 4.
34. Heisenberg, *Physics and Philosophy*, 62.
35. Camilleri, 'Heisenberg and the Transformation', 287.
36. Camilleri, 'Heisenberg and the Transformation', 285.
37. Heisenberg, *Physics and Philosophy*, 62–4.
38. Husserl, *The Crisis of European Sciences and Transcendental Phenomenology*, 295.
39. Kant, *Critique of Pure Reason*, 186, B61.
40. Heisenberg, *Physics and Philosophy*, 62.
41. Heisenberg, *Physics and Philosophy*, 63.
42. Kant, *Critique of Pure Reason*, 312, B248.
43. Kant, *Critique of Pure Reason*, 316, B256.
44. Heisenberg, *Physics and Philosophy*, 63.
45. Heisenberg, *Physics and Philosophy*, 64.
46. Kant, *Critique of Pure Reason*, 151, B29.
47. Heisenberg, *Physics and Philosophy*, 64.
48. Heisenberg, *Physics and Philosophy*, 65.
49. Griffiths, *Introduction to Quantum Mechanics*, 433.
50. Griffiths, *Introduction to Quantum Mechanics*, 3.

51. Hoefer, 'Causal Determinism', 1.
52. Griffiths, *Introduction to Quantum Mechanics*, 433.
53. Faye, 'Copenhagen Interpretation', 4.
54. Kant, *Critique of Pure Reason*, 145, B18.
55. Epperson, *Quantum Mechanics*, 223.
56. Epperson, *Quantum Mechanics*, 125.
57. Epperson, *Quantum Mechanics*, 128.
58. See George Shields' 'Whitehead's Early Harvard Period', in this volume, p. 248.
59. Malone-France, *Deep Empiricism*, 90.
60. Agassi, 'Positive Evidence', 262.
61. Stenner, 'A. N. Whitehead and Subjectivity', 96.
62. Stenner, 'A. N. Whitehead and Subjectivity', 97.
63. Stenner, 'A. N. Whitehead and Subjectivity', 107.
64. Malone-France, *Deep Empiricism*, ix.
65. Malone-France, *Deep Empiricism*, x.
66. Malone-France, *Deep Empiricism*, xiii.
67. Husserl, *Logical Investigations*, Investigation V, Section 27.
68. Howard, 'Who Invented the "Copenhagen Interpretation?"', 675.

## Bibliography

Agassi, Joseph, 'Positive Evidence in Science and Technology', *Philosophy of Science*, 37:2 (1970), 261–70.

Bitbol, Michel, and Stefano Osnaghi, 'Bohr's Complementarity and Kant's Epistemology', *Niels Bohr, 1913–2013* (Basel: Springer, 2016), 199–221.

Bogaard, Paul and Jason Bell (eds), *The Harvard Lectures of Alfred North Whitehead, 1924–1925: Philosophical Presuppositions of Science* (Edinburgh: Edinburgh University Press, 2017).

Camilleri, Kristian, 'Heisenberg and the Transformation of Kantian Philosophy', *International Studies in the Philosophy of Science*, 19:3 (2005), 271–87.

Cuffaro, Michael, 'The Kantian Framework of Complementarity', *Studies in History and Philosophy of Science Part B: Studies in History and Philosophy of Modern Physics*, 41:4 (2010), 309–17.

Epperson, Michael, *Quantum Mechanics and the Philosophy of Alfred North Whitehead* (New York: Fordham University Press, 2004).

Faye, Jan, 'Copenhagen Interpretation of Quantum Mechanics', *Stanford Encyclopedia of Philosophy* (Fall 2014 Edition), ed. Edward N. Zalta <https://plato.stanford.edu/archives/fall2014/entries/qm-copenhagen>

Folse H. J., 'The Copenhagen Interpretation of Quantum Theory and Whitehead's Philosophy of Organism', in R. C. Whittemore (ed.), *Studies in Process Philosophy I. Tulane Studies in Philosophy*, 23 (Dordrecht: Springer, 1974).

Griffiths, David J., *Introduction to Quantum Mechanics* (London: Pearson Education, 2005).

Heisenberg, Werner, *Physics and Philosophy: The Revolution in Modern Science* (New York: Harper, 2007).

Hoefer, Carl, 'Causal Determinism', *Stanford Encyclopedia of Philosophy* (Spring 2016 Edition), ed. Edward N. Zalta <https://plato.stanford.edu/archives/spr2016/entries/determinism-causal>

Howard, Don, 'Who Invented the "Copenhagen Interpretation?" A Study in Mythology', *Philosophy of Science*, 71:5 (2004), 669–82.

Hume, David, 'An Enquiry Concerning Human Understanding', in Steven M. Cahn (ed.), *Classics of Western Philosophy* (Indianapolis: Hackett Publishing Company, 2012), 834–99.

Husserl, Edmund, *The Crisis of European Sciences and Transcendental Phenomenology*, trans. David Carr (Evanston: Northwestern University Press, 1970).

Husserl, Edmund, *Logical Investigations, Volume II*, trans. J. M. Findlay (Abingdon: Routledge, 2001).

Irvine, Andrew David, 'Alfred North Whitehead', *Stanford Encyclopedia of Philosophy* (Winter 2015 Edition), ed. Edward N. Zalta <https://plato.stanford.edu/archives/win2015/entries/whitehead>

Joos, Erich et al., *Decoherence and the Appearance of a Classical World in Quantum Theory* (New York: Springer Science & Business Media, 2013).

Kaiser, David, 'More Roots of Complementarity: Kantian Aspects and Influences', *Studies in History and Philosophy of Science Part A*, 23:2 (1992), 213–39.

Kant, Immanuel, *Critique of Pure Reason*, ed. Allen W. Wood and Paul Guyer (Cambridge: Cambridge University Press, 2009).

Lotze, Hermann, *Logic*, trans. Bernard Bosanquet (London: Clarendon Press, 1884).

Malin, Shimon, 'Quantum Physics and Whitehead's Philosophy: A Tribute to Abner Shimony', Perimeter Institute Recorded Seminar Archive, Perimeter Institute, 7 July 2006 <http://pirsa.org/06070041>

Malone-France, Derek, *Deep Empiricism: Kant, Whitehead, and the Necessity of Philosophical Theism* (Lanham: Lexington Books, 2007).

Sartre, Jean-Paul, *Existentialism is a Humanism* (New Haven: Yale University Press, 2007).

Schlosshauer, Maximilian, Johannes Kofler and Anton Zeilinger, 'A Snapshot of Foundational Attitudes Toward Quantum Mechanics', *Studies in History and Philosophy of Science Part B: Studies in History and Philosophy of Modern Physics*, 44:3 (2013), 222–30.

Stenner, Paul, 'A. N. Whitehead and Subjectivity', *Subjectivity*, 22:1 (2008), 90–109.

# 12

# Whitehead's Early Harvard Period, Hartshorne and the Transcendental Project

*George W. Shields*

## Introductory Remarks

When Whitehead arrived at Harvard in Fall 1924 and delivered his first Lowell lecture, 'Philosophical Presuppositions of Science', most of the assembled audience of philosophy majors, graduate students and faculty were not receptive to his apparent interest in the grand questions of cosmology and metaphysics. In fact, most were quite perplexed, as they had expected a display of the technical scientific mind behind the *Enquiry Concerning the Principles of Natural Knowledge* and his (at the time) much-read *The Concept of Nature*. The mood of the majority was well described by R. W. Miller's remembrance:

> The opening lecture plunged us into a morass of absolutely unintelligible metaphysics ... [Whitehead's] longest and most difficult sentences all ended ... with the gleaming words, ". . . you know." We, of course, didn't know *anything*, so far as that lecture was concerned. When the hour ended we were completely baffled and in despair about the course, but we were also all in love with Whitehead as a person, for somehow the overwhelming magic of his being had shown through.[1]

Miller was typical of the students assembled: concern with questions of epistemology and a focus on the perspectives of Hume and Russell accompanied by little interest in grand-scale metaphysics was the prevailing orientation of the day. In Victor Lowe's pithy expression, 'profundity was out, cool analysis was in'.[2] However, a minority of the audience members were quite sympathetic to the direction of Whitehead's thought, including the unflappable metaphysician William Ernest Hocking and Department of Philosophy Chair James Haughton Woods, the specialist in Sanskrit and Indian philosophy.

Had Charles Hartshorne, often regarded as Whitehead's greatest 'intellectual descendant', been present, he surely would have sided with his former professor, Hocking, and former chief advisor, Woods. For, one year and some months earlier, Hartshorne had produced an ambitious 306-page PhD dissertation in the tradition of grand systematic metaphysical philosophy entitled 'An Outline and Defense of the Argument for the Unity of Being in the Absolute or Divine Good'. Hartshorne returned to Harvard in Fall 1925, after completion of his Traveling Sheldon Fellowship in Europe. He was then made Instructor in Philosophy and Research Assistant, assigned to Whitehead. This assignment initiated a personal relationship with Whitehead in the early Harvard period (lasting from 1925 to 1928) that would affect Hartshorne's entire subsequent career and consequently would profoundly shape the direction of Whitehead studies throughout the twentieth century and beyond.

The exact nature of this relationship, however, has been the subject of considerable scholarly discussion. Hartshorne himself has declared that, contrary to the frequent descriptions of him as a 'disciple of Whitehead', and the common practice of mentioning 'Whitehead and Hartshorne' together in the same breath, in fact he has been an original philosopher in his own right, and his encounter with Whitehead (as well as Peirce) could be characterised, not as one of discipleship, but rather as one of 'pre-established harmony'. He says that, in his doctoral thesis, he had already 'reached the main outlines of the philosophy to which I still adhere . . . [but his encounter with Whitehead showed him] a coherent system containing most of the significant ideas which I had detected as scattered fragments in various twentieth century philosophers' (WP, 112).

In a now deservedly famous essay on 'Hartshorne's Early Philosophy', William Ladd Sessions expounds upon this theme at some length and shows that a close study of Hartshorne's thesis on 'The Unity of Being' asserts major philosophical tenets that Hartshorne would hold in his mature philosophy: for example, the basic doctrines that experience is socially structured, that experience and value are coeval, that temporal process is objectively real, that the future is open to determination, that not even God can absolutely determine other entities who have some autonomy of decision, etc.[3] Consequently, Whitehead provided primarily the means for clarification and deeper elucidation of such tenets but was not the source of such tenets. However, Sessions does not touch upon a number of issues that lie underneath the concerns with specific material doctrines that preoccupy his discussion. In particular, and what will be the focus of this essay, is the deep and mutual commitment to the very possibility of metaphysics, or to use the contemporary parlance favoured by Karl Otto-Apel and Franklin Gamwell,[4] the possibility of the

'Transcendental Project' – that is to say, the limning of the presuppositions or preconditions of all coherent discursive thought. In this essay, I shall argue that what Sessions and David Griffin have intimated – namely, that there is a sharp divergence between Whitehead and Hartshorne on the topic of the Ontological Argument – requires important, perhaps even severe, qualification. My contention is rather that, while Whitehead was certainly not a proponent of any detailed historical version of the Argument as found in Anselm or Descartes or Leibniz, etc., he nonetheless was a proponent – from the *Principia* through the *Harvard Lectures*, *Process and Reality* and *Modes of Thought* – of what Hartshorne calls the 'essential argumentative kernel' of the Ontological Argument, that is to say, Hartshorne's ground-level Principle Zero (or 'P-Zero'), the proposition that 'something exists is a necessary truth' (PCH, 571). Indeed, in *Process and Reality*, Whitehead will quite explicitly connect the necessity of this proposition with 'the primordial power' of the universe or with an eternal 'aboriginal actuality' – in effect, God – via the Ontological Principle and the Principle of Process that God aboriginally exemplifies (PR, 21–4, cross-indexed with 345 for God's consequent nature as 'everlasting' and primordial nature as 'infinite'). Importantly, the probity of the Ontological Argument's essential kernel and the possibility of the Transcendental Project are intimately connected, since justification of this kernel is *ipso facto* justification of the Transcendental Project; as the Scholastic logicians would famously have it, *ab esse ad posse valet consequentia* (idiomatically translated: 'from what is assertorically the case, we may validly infer what is possibly the case'). In effect, the Transcendental Project is possible precisely because there *are* actual examples of Transcendental Argument which appear to be sound and which appear to stand up against critical scrutiny.

As this volume intends to reflect upon and celebrate Whitehead's Harvard lectures, I shall put a special focus upon various passages in the lectures which are relevant to the two connected themes of the possibility of the Transcendental Project and the precise nature of the special relationship between Whitehead and Hartshorne. With these basic themes in mind, in the following essay, I wish to argue that Whitehead's Harvard lectures display a philosopher who is convinced of the following positions – each shared by Charles Hartshorne – that could be unified under the banner of the 'Ontological Approach' to fundamental questions of philosophy:

1) 'Something exists' is a necessary, or, as Whitehead puts it, 'eternal' truth. This is Hartshorne's 'Principle Zero' (P-Zero). This truth is a precondition for all coherent thinking, a position corroborated by the doctrine of *Principia Mathematica* that the universe of discourse cannot be empty.

2) Because P-Zero is a precondition of all coherent thinking, it follows that ontology precedes epistemology, not vice versa as in the apparently prevailing opinion at Harvard in 1924–25. Philosophy *begins*, for Whitehead, with the ontological, with the encounter with something given.

3) However, any adequate ontology must coherently 'make room' for a plausible epistemology. In the Harvard lectures, Whitehead develops this motif by suggesting the main theme of his work on *Symbolism*, namely, the important distinction between prehension in the mode of causal efficacy and in the mode of presentational immediacy. Here the doctrines of Hume and Kant are taken as foils for Whitehead's epistemological outlook. In effect, Whitehead presents a reversal of Kant's 'Copernican Revolution'. Parallel to this, Charles Hartshorne's later synthesis of 'realism and idealism', while in some respects anticipated in his Harvard dissertation, requires the crucial addition of Whitehead's event (as contrasted with substance) ontology. Consequently, if the Principle of Universal Objectivity (in particular) is to be preserved, an event ontology is logically *required* for the systemic coherence of his (Hartshorne's) synthesis. Thus, the interpretation of Hartshorne as standing in 'preestablished harmony' with Whitehead is here profoundly qualified, since, in at least the case of Universal Objectivity, Whitehead *is* its ultimate source.

4) Correlated with the above, Whitehead's Harvard lectures present a critique of Kant's crucial distinction between the noumena or things-in-themselves altogether outside the Categories of the Understanding and the *a priori* forms of intuition and the phenomena which are subject to the Categories and the *a priori* forms. It will be argued that this critique is sound, and thus a principal objection to P-Zero, an objection advocated by Richard Rorty, is undermined. *Contra* Rorty, there are no noumena to be taken as pure existential surds, and thus P-Zero remains unscathed by Kant's doctrine of noumena.

5) Whitehead's Harvard lectures present us with a philosopher who possesses a 'global' approach to philosophical problems, an approach characterised by 'balanced definiteness' in Hartshorne's felicitous expression. In effect, in doing metaphysics or speculative philosophy in any adequate way, philosophers *must* avail themselves of the resources of formal logic and mathematical analysis, balanced by appeals to phenomenological and intuitive considerations, as well as the aesthetic sensibilities of poets and novelists. The appeals to *all* of these components are thus never merely adventitious to the endeavour of philosophy.

In course I shall offer various defences of these theses against some important potential objections, but will also offer some corroborating arguments from philosophers outside the ambit of process philosophy (wittingly from James F. Ross and unwittingly from W. V. Quine) – thus illustrating the indispensability of P-Zero as a precondition of rational thought. In effect, I not only wish to offer an interpretation of Whitehead in the early Harvard period (HL1, SMW, RM and PR included) which emphasises his agreement with Hartshorne on a broad Ontological Approach to philosophy, but also to argue that both Whitehead and Hartshorne are in fact correct in this approach, and that consequently the detractors of metaphysics or 'a priori ontology' or the Transcendental Project are patently wrong. Thus, the focus here is not only on historical interpretation, but on considerations of much contemporary relevance. The latter focus represents an important philosophical contention in an era still dominated by anti-metaphysical tendencies among large swaths of philosophers and humanities scholars generally.

## The Primacy of Metaphysical/Ontological Inquiry Over Epistemological Inquiry

Given the evidence provided by Victor Lowe and by reports of many of Whitehead's graduate students attending his early Lowell lectures and seminars in metaphysics and philosophy of science,[5] the intellectual atmosphere at Harvard was strongly influenced by C. I. Lewis's focus upon epistemology and Kant's critical philosophy, and by the so-called New Realism of Ralph Barton Perry, which was fundamentally oriented towards epistemological questions. Epistemology was primary and metaphysics (if engaged at all) was secondary. Whitehead's fundamental inclination was, as it were, to swim against the Harvard tide. This is, of course, not to say that, for Whitehead, epistemological inquiries were unimportant or unnecessary, since, for instance, his earlier *Principles of Natural Knowledge* was preoccupied with questions concerning the foundations of empirical scientific knowledge. In fact, in his first year Harvard course he asserts at HL1, Lecture 76, Bell's Notes, 5 May 1925, 363 that '[The] test of self-consistency of any ontology is in its possibility of giving a place to epistemology.' However, epistemology defined as inquiry into how knowledge is possible is not 'the first step in Philosophy' (HL1, 363). Ontological inquiry is first: 'You can't express yourself until you have a minimum of ontological doctrine – i.e. a certain general description of what is known. . . . That's ultimately based on your apprehension of the immediate occasion' (HL1, 363). Here the encounter with reality, with the actual occasion, is the starting point. This affirmation of the primacy of encounter with the actual occasion is logically connected to Whitehead's aversion to Kant's phenomenalism and doctrine of noumena (see discussion below).

This also clearly seems to be Hartshorne's orientation from the dissertation through the mature works, and surely counts as an important part of the 'pre-established harmony' with Whitehead. For, in the PhD thesis, being and knowledge are coincident, and every experience is by virtue of its very constitution an encounter with being; this is also to say that every experience is somehow, however obliquely or subliminally, an experience of God (cf. the chain of arguments regarding the interconnectedness between being, value, knowledge and God (OD, 210–81)). The latter doctrine becomes a mainstay of Hartshorne's metaphysics throughout his career, although it later receives a technical Whiteheadian refinement as the 'total prehension' of the divine consequent nature with its cues, impulses or desiderata for the temporal and contextual situation (cf. DR, 142). Moreover, a phenomenological insight that Hartshorne embraces from the 'Unity of Being' thesis to his essays on Husserl and most complete statement on phenomenology in his 'My Eclectic Approach to Phenomenology' (CRE, Ch. 5) is another way of stating Whitehead's 'ontological minimum': every experience is 'experience *of*' something that is not itself identical to the experience, and so all experience has an immediately social structure. This is clearly in line with Whitehead's declaration of an 'ontological minimum' that involves immediate apprehension of the objective occasion. This 'first step' in philosophy, I suggest, evades all the modern epistemological anxieties about external realism, subjective idealism, solipsism and the Husserlian need for an *epoché*. As Hartshorne would more fully articulate this perspective when responding to the transcendental idealism of Husserl's *Ideen* and *Cartesian Meditations*: Every experience is already contact with reality *extra mente*, since every experience is analysable as involving bodily occasions, indeed neuronal occasions, as data of the experience. In effect, a full account of 'experience *of*' requires the positing of a *content* of the experience which is really independent of the experience. For consider: 'No experience is merely "of" that very experience, nor even merely of an earlier moment in the same stream of experiences [it would then simply be indistinguishable from that earlier moment], nor can merely "intending" an object that may not exist constitute the "of" in "experience of" [because the projection of possibilities is grounded *somehow* in *actual* objects of experience]' (IO, 275).

It is also to be noticed that Whitehead's insistence upon the primacy of the ontological, yet within the context of an ontology that has 'room for' or logically accommodates an epistemology, is well illustrated by Hartshorne's brilliant and now classic essay on synthesising epistemic realism and ontological or 'objective' idealism ('A Synthesis of Realism and Idealism' reprinted as chapter 8 of ZF). Here Hartshorne argues that ontological and epistemic

theses of certain types are not only logically compatible, but are mutually complementary; respectively, the Principle of Objective Independence (objects
exist outside the knowing subject), the Principle of Subjective Dependence
(every subject derives some of its character from entities of which the subject
is aware), the Principle of Universal Objectivity (any entity must be or be
destined to become an object for some subject or subjects), and the Principle
of Universal Subjectivity (any concrete entity is a subject or set of subjects
such that any other concrete entity or entities of which it or they are aware is
also a subject). Importantly, Whitehead is explicitly listed as the one philosopher who upholds all of these doctrines (see ZF, 138–9). I would suggest that
through his emphasis on the 'coming together' of entities and ideal forms in
process and the development of the concept of prehension in the first year of
Harvard lectures (examine, e.g., HL1, 162–5, 243, 473, 487 and also SMW,
69, 148), Whitehead enfolds all of these general 'core' doctrines of process
philosophy. For prehension as the mechanism of causal influence involves
internal relatedness to or dependence on data being prehended by the subject of prehension, but involves external relatedness to or independence of
the subject of prehension on the part of the data prehended. This logically
enfolds all four principles, by definition. Thus, Hartshorne's synthesis here
is a thoroughly *Whiteheadian* one. But I point out that it is not at all clear
how at least the Principle of Universal Objectivity could be embraced by the
monistic substance philosophy of the dissertation, since Universal Objectivity
*requires* a notion of unit events or occasions and a clear notion of prehension
as the fundamental concept of causal influence (substances are what they are
over time and only accrue accidental properties externally), but both of these
notions (unit-events and prehensions) are absent from the dissertation. With
the loss of Universal Objectivity, as with any other of the four principles, the
systematic character of Hartshorne's ontological-epistemic synthesis would be
suborned. Thus, the exposure to Whitehead in achieving this synthesis is critical and transformative. This is a profound qualification of the 'pre-established
harmony' thesis.

## The Starting Point of Metaphysics: 'Something Exists'[6]

### The Argument from Logical Foundations[7]

Let us consider Hartshorne's central tenet of neoclassical metaphysics, held
at least as early as the thesis on 'The Unity of Being', namely, the proposition
that 'something exists'. For Hartshorne, this proposition is *necessarily* true;
consequently, Kant and Hume were wrong in their widely held doctrine that

'"something exists" and "nothing exists" are both contingent propositions', implying the *possibility* of an absolutely empty universe. Hartshorne holds that this often uncritically examined 'dogma' of modern philosophy is in fact incoherent and self-defeating upon careful reflection. For 'something exists' passes the two critical tests for genuine metaphysical status: 1) by definition, the proposition is *verified* by every conceivable *state* of affairs or *state*-description, and 2) it cannot be *falsified* by any conceivable state of affairs or state-description. For consider: 'nothing exists' – the logical contradictory of 'something exists' – cannot be verified in principle since any attempt at verification would posit a verification-event which would in turn falsify 'nothing exists'.[8] This result in turn entails that the contradictory of 'nothing exists' cannot be falsified. Yet, further, this 'something' cannot be fundamentally abstract, since the abstract is always *in* the concrete not vice versa, that is to say, all abstraction is intelligible only as abstraction *from* the concrete. For instance, where virtually any illustration will do, the abstraction 'redness' refers to a class of red hues instantiated in red perceptual objects. (Hartshorne is prepared to defend this Aristotelian principle against numerous objections.) Thus, 'necessarily, something exists' becomes quickly ramified into what Hartshorne calls 'the essential argumentative kernel of the ontological argument', namely, the proposition that 'necessarily, something actual exists' or that God (or more minimally the Universe) is always *somehow actualised*, reflecting the very title of Hartshorne's *Anselm's Discovery*, Part I.

Whitehead likewise holds that 'something exists' is an 'eternal' truth. In fact, this was a position prepared for even as early as *Principia Mathematica* (PM). For Whitehead and Russell confront the question of whether the PM universe of discourse can be empty, can make no assumption of objects or entities with certain properties. Their decision was that any such supposition of emptiness would be incoherent, as it would make certain logical principles of the quantificational calculus potentially falsified, as in the case of Universal Instantiation: $(\forall x) (Px) \rightarrow (\exists x) (Px)$, where $\rightarrow$ is so-called Russellian or material implication. Thus, they adopt the following provision as axiomatic for the PM universe of discourse: $(\exists x) (Fx \vee \sim Fx)$ where $F$ is a one-place predicate. In effect, there must be at least one object that either has or does not have some arbitrary predicate $F$. The incoherence would occur in this way: with an empty semantical domain, $(\exists x) (Fx)$ would be falsified, as there simply would be no $x$, but the provisional *assumption* of $(\forall x) (Px)$ would then yield a truth-value scenario where the antecedent is presumed T and the consequent F, which in turn falsifies the theorem of Universal Instantiation. (In fact, this result would occur whether we are employing Russellian implication or Lewisian strict implication: it can never be logically consistent to draw a false consequent from a true antecedent.) Not incidentally, Hartshorne echoes this argument in the following passage in *Anselm's Discovery* (283) where he is commenting on the work of German logician Heinrich Scholz:

> logic can admit the notion of existential necessity in the form, (x) fx ➔ (Ex) fx; properties universally instantiated cannot be uninstantiated, or in other words, logic cannot deal with a simply empty universe. The widest class cannot be empty. The case for this contention, which Scholz himself accepts, seems to me conclusively made by two recent authors, Jonathan Cohen and William [and wife Martha] Kneale.[9]

It is important to notice also that PM logic is a system designed to have cognitive import as a method for formalisation of propositions across scientific domains and ordinary language arguments concerning 'how the world is'. Since I would concur with Whitehead's basic realist epistemological stance, and I would argue, with Kripke, that *de re* modality with quantification is perfectly intelligible, I see no credible hindrance to the inference from what is required of logic to what is required of 'the scaffolding of the world'.[10] Logical systems which seek freedom from the constraints of systems with existential import, as in the case of free logics, encounter difficulties in explaining exactly what cognitive import (if any) they have, and exactly how to make their semantical domains clear (see the discussion of free logics below).

I want to consider the 'argument from the foundations of logic' in much further detail. For I submit that one of the most powerful counter-arguments against the contemporary Neo-Pragmatist refusal of the Transcendental Project is to show just how, from a number of angles as shown in the following three corroborating arguments (thus providing a strong unifying *cumulative* case), P-Zero displays pragmatic credentials as it is arguably doing real intellectual work. It does real intellectual work because, as each of the following arguments explicate, its assumption is a *presupposition* of rational discourse, while its denial seems to be a case of 'language idling' in Wittgenstein's famous expression.[11] As it were, the Transcendental Project is pragmatically efficacious, because at least one proposition – Whitehead and Hartshorne's Principle Zero – provides a transcendental condition for having theses, and is thus not itself a mere thesis among other happenstance theses. As Umberto Eco once insightfully put it, we must eventually face not only the question *terminus a quem*, 'What are we talking about?' but also the deeper pre-linguistic question *terminus a quo*, 'Why do we make signs? Why do we even talk at all?' We make signs, we talk, says Eco, precisely *because there is something*.[12] Leibniz's question, 'why is there something rather than nothing?' – if not shorthand for the question, 'Why does a universe of finite entities in space-time exist even if God would exist?' – is to be immediately dissolved, for the *only* answer there could be is, 'there is something rather nothing, *because there is something*'. As the only answer to such a question, and since being is the 'amniotic fluid' in which all thought takes place, this answer is neither circular nor trivial.[13]

## Three Corroborating Arguments: Ross's Quantificational Deduction of Existential Necessity, Quine's Curious Affirmation of Non-Emptiness, and Bergson's Thought-Experiment with General Non-Being

*Ross's Deduction.* It is interesting to notice James F. Ross's reduction to absurdity proof of precisely Whitehead and Russell's 'axiomatic' existential quantification in his treatise on *Philosophical Theology*. If correct, Ross's argument brings out the 'logical necessity' of the existentially quantified formula with particular clarity and force (within standard quantificational logic which assumes Universal Instantiation). In the context of showing the demonstrable falsehood of both David Hume's and Alvin Plantinga's often repeated principle that 'no existential statement has a logically contradictory denial', Ross presents the following argument.[14] I re-state it here with some alterations of format and with a fuller explication of the proof-step justifications:

| | |
|---|---|
| 1: $(\exists x)\ (Fx \lor \sim Fx)$ | Assertion to be proven by Indirect Proof |
| 2: $\sim (\exists x)\ (Fx \lor \sim Fx)$ | Assumption of the denial of (1) for Indirect Proof |
| 3: $(\forall x) \sim (Fx \lor \sim Fx)$ | Quantifier Replacement from (2): $\sim (\exists x) = (\forall x) \sim$ |
| 4: $(\forall x)\ (\sim Fx\ \&\ \sim \sim Fx)$ | DeMorgan's Theorem from (3) |
| 5: $(\forall x)\ (\sim Fx\ \&\ Fx)$ | Double Negation from (4) |
| 6: $\sim Fy\ \&\ Fy$ | Universal Instantiation from (5) |
| 7: $Fy$ | Simplification from (6) |
| 8: $(\exists x)\ (Fx)$ | Existential Generalisation from (7) |
| 9: $\sim Fy$ | Simplification from (6) |
| 10: $(\forall x) \sim Fx$ | Universal Generalisation from (9) |
| 11: $\sim (\exists x)\ (Fx)$ | Quantifier Replacement from (10) |
| 12: $[(\exists x)\ (Fx)\ \&\ \sim (\exists x)\ (Fx)]$ | Adjunction from (8) and (11) |

Since step (12) is a direct contradiction, it follows that the denial of the assumed assertion at step (1) is absurd; thus, step (1) is as logically necessary as the *reductio ad absurdum* theorem of the propositional calculus. Under

Ross's interpretation of the predicate F as the 'disjunction of all possible properties and combinations thereof' (104), it is clear that the assumed denial
of the Indirect Proof at step (2) is 'equivalent to the assertion that nothing
exists at all'. Thus, by Indirect Proof, there is at least one existential assertion that is necessarily, not contingently, true. This, of course, means that the
proof is directly relevant to Whitehead's non-emptiness assumption in PM,
Whitehead's later submission of the Ontological Principle (see below), and
Hartshorne's similar arguments for the essential argumentative kernel of the
Ontological Argument.

*Quine.* It is indeed difficult for philosophers to escape commitment to the
'non-emptiness' requirement of the *Principia*, even philosophers who appear
to attack the very distinction between necessary and contingent propositions
such as, in particular, W. V. Quine, who recall went to Harvard specifically to
study the *Principia* with Whitehead. For instance, Franklin Gamwell, in his
important essay 'On Transcendental Argument' (see endnote 4), provides
a compelling critical discussion of Quine's arguments on the untenability
of the necessity-contingency distinction. As Gamwell perceptively notes,
Quine's underlying idea that purported necessary propositions (upon analysis
of the act of defining their constituent terms) cannot succeed in making non-
circular appeals to 'analyticity' is simply insufficient for showing that such cir-
cularity renders a constituent term or proposition 'senseless'. To the contrary,

> The circumstance that a term cannot be defined except by using other
> terms that presuppose it does not, so far as I can see, make the term sense-
> less. Indeed, the Transcendental Project not only concedes but also insists
> that any transcendental condition of human thought has this character,
> since transcendental conditions are presupposed by all thought.[15]

Quine is thus merely asserting, rather than properly arguing for, the impossibility of a transcendental argument for 'something exists'. What I think could
have been further argued at this precise juncture is that, not only does Quine
fail to give a proper argument for the impossibility of the Transcendental Project, but he also in fact explicitly commits himself to the very proposal that
Gamwell has submitted as an exemplar of necessary propositions (thus my
earlier reference to the difficulty of escaping 'the "non-emptiness" requirement of the *Principia*'). It is interesting and important that, in his classic essay
'On What There Is', Quine declares that there is one decision about what
there is which cannot be a merely 'ontic' one, namely, that we *must* admit
some object or another into our universe of discourse. In effect, for Quine,

*what* objects exist is relative to and contingent upon the natural or theoretical language we happen to speak, but *that* we must speak of objects in speaking a natural or theoretical language is inescapable.[16] Even for Quine, then, logic and language commit us to *that much* ontology, since we cannot speak sensibly of nothing at all. As Ilham Dillman notes in his tightly reasoned (but for my tastes too polemical) treatise on *Quine on Ontology, Necessity and Experience*, Quine commits himself in this instance to an ontological or non-ontic claim, but then drops it from his philosophical purview altogether and fails to comment upon its significance for the question of existential modalities.[17] Thus, Dillman is indeed correct in claiming that Quine's overall position in modal theory is self-contradictory: he affirms at least one necessary proposition, namely, the non-emptiness assumption of the *Principia*, yet also holds that all propositions are contingent or they are nothing at all. This bears witness to the presuppositional necessity of 'something exists', and *ipso facto* issues a forceful objection to the view that all propositions are contingent.

*Bergson on 'General Non-Being'.* Another important corroborating argument is suggested by Henri Bergson in his classic *Creative Evolution*,[18] an argument explicitly endorsed by Hartshorne (cf. CS, 245) and implicitly congenial to Whitehead's references to 'not-being' in SMW. Bergson contends that the concept of *general non-being* is a 'false problem' generated by an unwarranted abstract opposition to all being; in fact, meaningful specific 'negations' are always upon analysis expressions of a 'need of substituting for an affirmative judgment another affirmative judgment'.[19] If I say, for instance, that 'we did *not* win the game', I do not assert some absolute privation, but rather imply that other or alternative affirmative states of affairs (for example, that 'the other team won the game', or 'we forfeited the game', or 'the game was cancelled', or perhaps even 'the result was a tie', etc.) are to be asserted in place of the affirmative judgement that 'we won the game'. Negations make coherent sense as functions presupposing and logically attached to affirmative states of affairs. While Whitehead does not explicitly discuss this matter in HL1, he implicitly agrees with Bergson in the 1925 Lowell lectures, for at SMW, 162–3, he speaks of 'not-being' as *attaching to* actual occasions: While no occasion can include an eternal object A in *all* its determinate relationships, some being contraries, an actual occasion will include some relationships in A and exclude others; thus, an occasion is to be described as a synthesis of being and not-being ('not-being' is Whitehead's actual expression). But, for Whitehead, there is only contextualised or relative not-being – not-being as related to a particular occasion – while there is no reference to absolute not-being or privation. Whitehead is here groping towards the doctrine of negative prehensions developed in PR.

However, asks Bergson, what are we thinking when we posit absolute or general non-being? We could only be thinking of being as an abstract collection that then has a complete or total opposition in general non-being, but this presupposes being in its very conception. In effect, general non-being requires a background context of being (taken as noun), and thus it cannot be asserted without contradicting that very background. This is not coherent, and as such is a 'false problem' as famously declared by Gilles Deleuze in his arresting lectures on *Bergsonism*.[20]

We could gloss Bergson's contentions about general non-being as the negation of being in the following more logically precise way: The conceptual intention involved in invoking a concept of absolute non-being or emptiness is tantamount to presenting an indefinitely long list of *negated* states of affairs. Symbolically, we could render this as statement N1, where '*nth*' represents the continual repetition of distinctive negated states through an absolutely unlimited range, indeed, throughout the entire universe of discourse:

N1: { ~A & ~B & ~C . . . *nth*}

The conjunctivity of the negated states of affairs is required, since even a single affirmation would be *logically sufficient for establishing the counter-thesis that* '*something exists*'. Thus, an unlimited range of affirmative statements must *each* be denied if we are to express the notion that truly 'nothing exists'. Moreover, it is extremely interesting to notice what occurs when we apply De Morgan's Theorem to N1. We see that the formula is rendered:

N2: ~ {A V B V C . . . *nth*}

Since N2 expresses a series of disjunctions *without any limits whatsoever throughout the entire universe of discourse, and by the standard law of association includes any and all combinations of disjunctions*, it is clear that this is tantamount to denying *alternativeness itself*. But this result is absurd, as it would deny all contingent *and* all necessary states of affairs (necessity being defined in the modern modal logical sense of 'what is in common with all alternatives or possibilities').

It is to be granted that not all philosophers agree that Bergson's argument establishes the conceptual absurdity of 'nothing exists', although such distinguished figures as Hartshorne and Gilles Deleuze (at least as I interpret him) hold that it does. For instance, Donald Viney has called attention to the criticism that Bergson's argument commits the fallacy of composition:[21] since each state or attribute is denied, it is a fallacy of composition to say that the composed whole of states or attributes is to be denied. However, this is a mis-application of the fallacy of composition. While it is true that, in the normal case, each class member's possession of an attribute does not allow imputing that attribute of the composed whole or class, there are notable exceptions where causal relationships are involved – as in, for instance, 'each particle of this piece of chalk has mass, therefore, the whole piece of chalk has mass'. Likewise, the negation of all members of a class does entail the negation of the class as a whole. If no tigers existed in any particular locale *whatsoever*, there would be no compositional class of actual tigers. The fallacy of composition does not apply where sheer denials of membership in classes are involved, as in the case of Bergson's argument.

Perhaps a more challenging objection is posed by Richard Gale. Gale analyses Bergson's argument in the light of the 'at least one object' commit-ment of *Principia Mathematica*, and argues that it involves a subtle begging of the question. Consider the proposition that 'Every object has some property incompatible with unicornness' (labelled E5 by Gale).[22] A proposition such as E5 could be asserted, says Gale, but it would not require that there be at least one object in the universe of discourse, and this shows that Bergson's reason-ing is circular. Writes Gale:

> if there were Nothing, no objects, E5 would be true – vacuously true (to use a pun). Bergson might counter that a system of quantificational logic must presuppose that there exists at least one object in the domain over which its bound variables range: without this assumption the rule of uni-versal instantiation faces counter-examples. But why must Bergson's oppo-nent grant that this is a necessary presupposition?[23]

I want to object to this that 'nothing exists' as *the semantical presupposition* for E5 would in fact render E5 as neither true nor false. Rather E5, under such a semantical presupposition, is simply *unassertable*. For consider: if the semantical domain of the language in terms of which E5 is expressed were completely empty, we should in fact understand E5 as the mere schema: 'Every _____ is incompat-ible with _____.' For 'object' and 'unicornness' are already 'somethings'; more charitably, at the very least, they involve oblique references to 'somethings', and in the case of 'unicornness', oblique references to actual objects and attributes such as 'horns' and 'white equines'. Such oblique references are quite impossible if the semantical domain is *sheerly* empty. *Pace* the claims for various so-called free logics (see below), a language system does require, as Richard Martin once put it, a 'non-logical ontology' in the modern formal semantical sense of an ontology as a domain of entities taken as the values for variables and attributes or predicables of variables.[24] Indeed, how is it possible to explicate the grammatical function of general terms, individual constants, or predicates in a logical language without reference to non-logical values for the semiotic units we take to represent general terms, individual constants, or predicates? A general term is a different sort of linguistic entity from an individual constant, and rules of quantificational logic involved with, for example, restrictions on proper existential and universal generalisations break down if we fail to note the difference. Indeed, how can term difference matter in the case of a truly empty semantical domain? There is an essential matter of *content* to be discerned in making the distinction between general term and constant.

Gale might well respond that his notion of 'Nothing' in the citation above refers to the notion that the semantical domain contains 'no actual objects' as the value for the variables present in the existential quantifications that may be included within the scope of N1. If you remove actual objects from the semantical domain of the language expressing E5, E5 would be vacuously true, since, to state the logically equivalent obverse of E5, there would simply be no actual objects that possess some property compatible with 'unicornness'. However, while this is perfectly legitimate so far as it goes with such a restricted domain, I do not see that it represents a principled refutation of Bergson's doctrine that the concept of general or absolute non-being collapses into incoherence. This is because it is a logically contingent matter as to whether E5 is true or false if we allow actual objects into the semantical domain; it is true when the semantical domain is restricted to actual objects, but not true in other possible worlds whose semantical domains include, for example, creatures whose DNA instructions include horn sites on the noses of white equine bodies (there is nothing logically impossible about this combination, indeed, some such mutations might have existed in this actual world – I certainly would include a 'unicorn' as a possibility 'accessible' from the actual world, which can thus be modelled in terms of Kripke semantics for quantificational S4). What I find to be unintelligible, what Bergson finds to be unintelligible, is a truly empty semantical domain that simply does not have *any* objects or attributes – whether actual or 'potential'; in effect, a semantical 'domain' that really is not a domain containing some kind of content, a domain which represents the sheer absence of a 'non-logical ontology'. But such a situation is what we are presented with on the supposition that 'nothing exists' in the absolute sense considered by Bergson; to say otherwise is, it seems to me, not to take into account the metaphysically strong conceptual intention embodied in the supposition that literally 'nothing exists'. This is why I contend that a truly empty semantical domain at best allows for empty schemas with mere rhemes for object and attribute positions. (And even this would be questionable, e.g., how does one explain 'compatible

with' in E5 without objects or attributes as presuppositions for making conceptual connections of 'compatibility' or 'incompatibility'? Note that any example
that might be employed to explicate 'compatibility' or 'incompatibility' would
require at least a dyad of objects that would stand in a relation of compatibility
or lack of it.) Again, mere rhemes are simply not assertable.

Free logics, of course, are designed to operate with so-called 'empty
domains', and consequently such logics are constructed in ways that alter the
usual quantification rules. (Thus, for example, universal generalisation [UG]
in free logic will include a two-step process, where a provisional assumption
for free UG is made followed by application of a free UG rule containing three
conditions that include the appropriate discharging of provisional assumptions.) However, as I see it, the existence of free logics does nothing to address
the properly philosophical issues involved here. This is, again, because their
semantics do not represent truly empty domains in the strong metaphysical
sense attacked by Bergson, even in cases where we have a so-called 'null
Leblanc-Thomason (LT) structure', where both the inner and outer semantical domains are assumed to be empty. While the null LT case assumes that
the inner domain D is empty, as well as the outer domain D' (D' is normally
taken to be empty in the non-null LT structures), the way in which D and D'
are described – their 'nullness' – comes from the fact that they 'contain non-
existent [i.e., non-actual] *objects*'. They still reference content as in free logic
quantificational representations of such sentences as 'Batman is a super-hero'.
The concepts involved in such sentences are rich with oblique references to
actual entities or attributes, in the case of this example – 'bats', 'men', 'courage', 'crime fighters', etc. In fact, we might present a dilemma to anyone wishing to employ free logic as a counter-example to true non-emptiness of the
semantical domain. If a free logic FL has any cognitive import, i.e., can be used
to formalise fictional scenarios, then FL ought to assume fictional objects that
obliquely reference actual states of affairs. In that case FL is not truly empty.
If FL has no cognitive import, then FL is meaningless (comparable to allowing 'I ate nothingness' or 'nothingness is wigwam') precisely because it has no
semantical domain. In that case, free logics have no point. So, either free logics make oblique references to actual states of affairs and are not truly empty,
or they are entirely pointless from a cognitive point of view.[25]

## The Argument from the Ontological Principle

Whitehead shows his commitment to the non-emptiness thesis, at minimum
inchoately but discernibly, in among his very first public expressions of metaphysical doctrine in the Harvard lectures. At page 60 of HL1 (Lecture 17,

Bell's Notes, 1 November 1924), in the context of discussing the 'prime puz-zle' of the relation between the dipolar concepts of the Eternal and the Con-tingent, we find Whitehead stating: 'You're always pushing the Contingent back and back, but never get quite rid of it. If there's no Eternal in this sense there's nothing to be said, no Metaphysics, no Science, etc., etc. It's because there's something Eternal that we keep going at all.' Later in HL1 (Heath's Notes, 4 November 1924, 446), Whitehead broaches the notion that is cen-tral to process metaphysics, i.e., the creative advance as an *Eternal* process of enrichment. The Eternal is a 'general envisagement' that is always 'relevant to a particular occasion' and integral to each occasion that demands a 'solu-tion' (in the later vocabulary of PR a 'satisfaction'), and with this 'solution' an 'extrusion of irrelevant detail' (PR's 'negative prehension' contrasted with 'proximate prehension'). Once realised, the occasion stands as an 'eternal enrichment of [the] eternal ground of becoming' (HL1, 446). The very notion of an eternal ground of becoming relevant to occasions clearly posits P-Zero as 'necessarily, something actual exists'.

In the language of PR, this assumption of ontological non-emptiness will be codified in the eighteenth Category of Explanation, the so-called 'Onto-logical Principle' (PR, 24). Perhaps we should say more cautiously, 'necessarily, something actual exists' is an obvious corollary of the Ontological Principle, since, as Whitehead says when defining the principle, to search for any *reason* is to search for an actuality or some character of an actuality, and, of course, an actuality counts as 'something'. Put obversely, 'utter absence of actuality' could never serve as a referent for any rational inquiry or discourse because all reference requires reference *to* something.[26]

A more refined expression of a Whiteheadian modal or ontological type argument for an Eternal something as ground of contingency is articulated by Hartshorne when drawing upon Whitehead's later utterance at PR, 72 (Hartshorne is using the original pagination): 'The general *possibility* of the universe must be *somewhere*' (my emphasis). Drawing out this passage's sev-eral logical implications, Hartshorne writes:

> If possibility is meaningless without existence, then it cannot be that all existents are contingent; for this is to say that the *being of possibility* is also contingent, that it might have been that nothing was possible ... The conclusion of this argument is that there is a primordial power whose nonexistence is not a possibility, since possibility presupposes its existence. (WP, 80; first italics my emphasis, second italics Hartshorne's)

Put another way, given, by definition, the eternity of the domain of eternal objects – a view held by Whitehead from the very first introduction of this vocabulary at HL1, Bell's Notes, 8 January 1925, 161, where Whitehead also says they are 'Existences' but are 'not real', which I take to mean not instantiated in an event or actual occasion – any proposed absolutely otiose condition of such domain would be entirely counter-intuitive, like proposing a 'possibility' that *could never* be actualised, yet haunts reality (does 'it' then deserve the name 'possibility'?), and thus there must be a primordial actuality that serves as ground of such potential.

It should be noticed that, if this interpretation of Whitehead is correct, then it follows that, in addition to the other kinds of theistic argument that might be located in Whitehead (surveying the Lowell lectures through *Modes of Thought*, Hartshorne locates five strains of argument, see WP, 78–83), an 'ontological type argument' – that is to say, an argument that turns on logical requirements relating to concepts of modality – must be included. At least at face value, this seems contrary to such treatments of Whitehead's natural theology as David Griffin's, which explicitly reject ontological arguments and claim that Whitehead concurs.[27] But that the above ought to be classified as an ontological type argument would appear to be borne out by comparison of the line of thought encoded in PR, 72 with Paul Tillich's argument for an 'Ontological Approach'[28] to philosophy of religion: like Whitehead's contentions regarding an aboriginal actual ground of potentiality, the power of being[29] cannot itself be non-existent because this would entail that *potentiality itself* could emerge from nothing, from no potentiality at all. (Thus, in effect, as Tillich says repeatedly, God defined as the power of Being-itself is the *presupposition* of the question of God.) The latter consequent of the above entailment seems conceptually absurd or incoherent, and thus by *reductio ad absurdum*, the power of being is a presupposition of, a *prius* of, coherent thinking. The structure of Tillich's reasoning as given here, where P = 'the power of being exists' and $x$ = 'something exists', might be symbolised in modal propositional logic as follows:

◊ ~ P ➜ ( ~ ◊ $x$ ➜ ◊$x$ ), but the consequent is a contradiction (where ➜ is strict implication as seems required by the *de re* context of ontological transition from non-being to being), and so by the rule of *reductio ad absurdum* it follows that ~ ( ~ ◊ $x$ ➜ ◊$x$ ), which in turn by *modus tollens* ensures that ~ ◊ ~ P, which by modal definition is equivalent to □ P. Note, again, that the consequent of the original proposition is contradictory in any Lewisian modal system employing strict implication. By modal definition, the use of strict implication in the consequent shows it to be logically equivalent to □ ~ (~ ◊ $x$ ^ ~ ◊$x$) – as such this is equivalent to denying the tautologous law of Repetition in every possible world, which is absurd.[30]

## Whitehead, Hartshorne and the Return to Pre-Kantian Modes of Thought[31]

Whitehead's famous declaration in *Process and Reality* that the philosophy of organism represents a return to pre-Kantian modes of thought was expressed as early as the first year of the Harvard lectures. At HL1, Bell's Notes, Lecture 27, 24 November 1924, 113, it is noteworthy that Whitehead begins with the suggestion of a counter-revolution to Kant's Copernican one: 'Whitehead trying to turn Kant on his head – without Kant's "Copernican Revolution"'. This utterance makes complete sense in the light of notions Whitehead is expounding in this and the several subsequent lectures on the role of objects in 'the coming together' constitutive of processive events and the concomitant denial of the modern assumption of 'simple location' that undergirds the problematic 'bifurcation of nature'. For Kant's sharp distinction between the noumena and phenomena is the very embodiment of such bifurcation; as Kant himself realised, if left unqualified, the critical philosophy exposes itself to the charge of unwitting commitment to subjective idealism, or even worse, solipsism.

Kant's mature doctrine of noumena as developed in the B edition of the first *Critique* does not in fact provide a coherent example of 'existential possibilities which are yet strictly inconceivable', such putative existential possibilities standing as a clear objection to the necessity of the ontological non-emptiness thesis. The argument against the possibility of Transcendental Argument inspired by Kant – as endorsed by Stephan Körner and Richard Rorty[32] – is such that, even if 'nothing exists' turns out to be inconceivable, it would not establish that 'nothing exists' is logically impossible. This allegedly follows from the general principle that what is in fact conceivable does not exhaust the possible, as exemplified by Kant's notion of noumena. However, upon careful analysis, I argue that Kant's noumena do *not* provide coherent examples of the general principle that certain putative existential possibilities outstrip our capacity of conception. Thus, if Körner and Rorty wish to defend the general notion of existential possibilities which are yet inconceivable, they cannot find support for it in Kant's doctrine of noumena. I also find that, as early as the Harvard lectures, Whitehead had already anticipated or was committed to the particular objections regarding the intelligibility of Kant's 'revolution' to be explicated below (see my documentation of Whitehead regarding items 1–3 below).

As mentioned earlier, after the original A edition of the *Critique* had been published for some years, Kant came to realise that the critical philosophy was vulnerable to the charge that it collapses into 'subjective idealism' –

the doctrine that no real things exist outside the knowing subject, and that consequently only subjects and their phenomena or 'ideas' exist. In answer to this charge, he added to the revised B edition a section entitled 'The Refutation of Idealism'. Kant's all-important distinction – the core idea of his 'Copernican Revolution' in philosophy – was the distinction between, on the one hand, the noumena or things-in-themselves beyond sensibility, intuition and the categories of the understanding, and, on the other hand, the phenomena or the objects that we can know through the faculty of sensibility and applications of the categories and the forms of intuition. However, if this distinction is left unqualified and the noumena are strictly 'unknowable', why postulate their existence at all? What justification is there for even invoking the existence of noumena? To answer this, Kant argues in the 'Refutation' that we can know that the noumena exist, because if they did not, there would be nothing to appear. The manifold of sense has an 'objective' side which is the very ground for the existence of appearances. In effect, without noumena, our percepts would be empty. As such, Kant wants the following metaphysical scenario: The noumena exist, but only their mere existence as ground of phenomena is knowable. At the same time, the noumena are entirely outside the application of both the categories of the understanding and the *a priori* forms of intuition – the noumena are thus outside 'conceptualisation', yet they exist and are possible.

This metaphysical scenario is hiding subtle incoherence. In fact, it is not possible to be a consistent Kantian, that is to say, one cannot maintain the sharp divide between noumena and phenomena (where no categories or forms of intuition have application to the noumena), and at the same time resist subjective idealism or solipsism. For by providing a reason for the existence of noumena, Kant opens the door to categorical and intuitive conceptualisations of the noumena. In fact, I would argue that the noumena are not 'mere Xs', but must be positively conceived in four distinctive ways. The Whitehead of HL1 concurs:

1) What Kant does not adequately account for in his system is that, by holding that the noumena are grounds for the appearances, he is in fact committed to the idea that noumena are causes. As such the category of causality cannot be strictly confined to the domain of phenomena. Noumena are thus describable as causal agents. To be sure, if we grant Kant the notion that our cognitive apparatus constructs phenomena, noumena are necessary causal conditions for appearances, rather than sufficient conditions, but they are causal conditions nonetheless. This difficulty was observed as early as F. H. Jacobi's 1787 essay 'On Transcendental Idealism'.

As Körner has expressed Jacobi's insight: 'Kant assumes without qualification that perception is in part *caused by the action of* things-in-themselves
on the perceiving self . . . The assumption that things-in-themselves act
upon the senses is thus contradictory.'[33] In the Harvard lectures, Whitehead also pinpoints this issue with things-in-themselves or objects *extra
mente* as problematic for Kant. As he says at HL1, Hocking's Notes, 23
October 1924, 432, where he is commenting on Edward Caird's interpretation of Kant: 'Whenever therefore we can make any universal assertions
as to objects presented through sense . . . our assertions must be based
on [the] nature of our own sensibility*, and not on [the] nature of the
object affected * [Whitehead] does disagree on negative statement after.'
So, then, for Whitehead, the nature of our sensibility or cognitive apparatus does affect our resultant perceptual experience, but the nature of the
object outside that apparatus also has an essential role to play – here in
germ is Whitehead's important distinction between perceptual modes, i.e.,
initial causal efficacy of the object, and physiological-cognitive processing
towards the end of presentational immediacy.[34]

  2) In an important sense, there cannot be the ontological distinction
between the noumena as grounds of phenomena and the phenomena themselves if the noumena are not co-existents with the phenomena. While perhaps the self is noumenal (as Kant suggests in the discussion of the Third
Antinomy of reason), there must be at least some noumena extrinsic to the
noumenal self on pain of collapsing into solipsism. As such, the noumena
must be 'outer' in relation to any self. The very difference between noumena
as ground of phenomena and the phenomena themselves thus posits space as
real separation between subjects constructing appearances and noumena as
grounds of appearances. For consider that space, as Leibniz famously pointed
out, is the order of discriminable co-existents, whatever else it may be. Thus,
the noumena must be describable as 'spatially other' than the subjects that
entertain appearances. Again, Whitehead, who famously defended a relational theory of space as part and parcel of his defence of a revised theory
of relativity, acknowledges Leibniz's contribution. At HL1, Bell's Notes, 17
March 1925, 269, Whitehead asserts: 'Leibniz says [that] space is relation
between bodies in space. Then the point is a logical . . . construct from two
or more [presumably bodies].' But space, on the Leibnizian criterion, exists
as a relation between co-existents not as a pre-existent fixed matrix, and
any Kantian escape from compression into solipsism must also posit a spatial
distinction between knowing subject and object known. Space as relational
in this manner thus transcends its characterisation as an *a priori* form of intuition imposed upon the objects of perception. Related to this, Whitehead

also sees Kant as infected with a Newtonian Absolute conception of the 'point-moment' as a least unit of extensive quantity, which carries with it the paradox of an *occupied* point whose 'pointiness' is incompatible with occupation of content (cf. HL1, 305). Whitehead adds that, 'Now, no respectable person' – that is, any person acquainted with relativity theory – can abide by an Absolute Theory of space-time (HL1, 305f). Kant's thinking about space is illicit, as its framework is Absolute rather than Relational; indeed, Kant's spurious commitment to the *necessity* of Euclidean geometry is precisely countermanded by the very non-Euclidean geometry that opens the door to relativistic considerations.

3) Noticed as early as Schopenhauer's *Criticism of the Kantian Philosophy*, the category of quantity is applicable to the noumena on pain of violating the law of non-contradiction. For the noumena cannot be 'neither one nor many'. What would it mean to say otherwise? Kant cannot say that they 'correspond to zero' or 'there are zero noumena', for this is not distinguishable from saying 'there are no noumena', a proposition which Kant is anxious to deny in the 'Refutation'. On the other hand, how can the cardinality of the noumena be, say, one-and-two or one-and-ten simultaneously? As S. F. Barker says similarly when critically examining intuitionism in his operculum on *The Philosophy of Mathematics*, the claim that something is beyond the very domain of quantity – is neither one nor many – 'is too close to contradiction to be plausible'.[35] Thus, in order to maintain intelligibility, the noumena must again cross the chasm into the realm of categories to become describable as at least 'either one or many'. I argue that Whitehead concurs in principle with Barker, as he (Whitehead) is in no way committed to L. E. J. Brouwer's *classical* intuitionism that would ultimately reject the law of excluded middle in the analytic sense of propositional bivalence. While, granted, Whitehead rejects excluded middle insofar as it is wrongfully applied by Aristotle in a rigid way to the notion of *transition* where some S as not qualified by P transitions to S as qualified by P – a transition of 'jumping' from one state to another as in the flicker of a cinematic tape (HL1, Bell's Notes, 48–9) – Whitehead never dismisses excluded middle in the analytic sense of $A \lor \sim A$ that can be applied to the description of *actual* states, to realised or satisfied occasions, in effect, to states of being. Whitehead's philosophy of mathematics is indeed a complicated affair that, again granted, does involve an element of constructivism and finitism, but not without retaining a strong element of realism that would countermand any defence of Kant here based on Brouwer's principles. The definitive case for this interpretation of Whitehead has been made, in my view, by my late friend James A. Bradley.[36]

4) Most obviously, in asserting that the noumena exist, Kant is committed to the notion that they share two modal features with phenomena, namely, possibility and actuality (phenomena are actual when we are actually having experiences). The noumena are not mere possibilities, for otherwise the phenomena would be merely possible and not actual.

All told, then, if Kant is to preserve the law of non-contradiction while fending off subjective idealism (or, stronger still, solipsism), then the noumena are not sheerly inconceivable, but are co-existent and actual, spatially other, causal agents, subject to quantification. Thus, Kantian noumena do not represent entities which are possible and yet are *strictly* inconceivable. Even on Kant's own epistemic criteria and admissions, there is a good deal we can say descriptively and a good deal we can know about noumena beyond and precisely because of the very positing of their existence. Summarily, we might say that Kant's own 'Refutation' deconstructs the doctrine of noumena taken as pure existential surds. For the reasons provided above and their textual correlations in the Harvard lectures, Whitehead concurs that Kant's standpoint and its entanglement with subjective idealism and solipsism is to be strongly rejected (also cf. HL1, 57, 83, 311, 313, 337, 339, 425, 441).

In addition to the *critique* of Kant's view, Whitehead provides a coherent and intelligible alternative. The quest for contact with reality outside the human knower and its organising faculties that gets us beyond Kant's epistemic 'prison' is found in what Victor Lowe and Hartshorne have deemed the 'truly revolutionary' aspect of Whitehead's philosophy, namely, the notion of initial physical prehension, or in the technical language which we first encounter in *Symbolism*, 'perception in the mode of causal efficacy'. In the light of this construct, the problem which Kant faces concerning the necessity of affirming the causal role of noumenal objects in order to give rise to phenomena in the first place is not a problem which *can* occur within the Whiteheadian framework. The problem of 'external realism' which so occupied 'modern' philosophy from Descartes to Hume and Kant is simply outside the ambit of the Whiteheadian conceptuality from the 1924–25 Harvard lectures onward – this alone justifies the now common characterisation of Whitehead (and Hartshorne) as a constructive *post*-modernist. Here Whitehead joins C. S. Peirce's doctrine of the primary icon and related critique of Cartesian methodical doubt; Heidegger's analysis of *Dasein* as always and inescapably *Mitwelt* or being-in-the-world; and Merleau-Ponty's roughly equivalent notion of human existents as *l'etre au monde*. None of these thinkers have any preoccupation with the problem of external realism in the important sense that, within their respective philosophical frameworks, the question of *epistemic grounding* of access to external reality does not arise.

## Coda: The Use of Formal Logic and Mathematical Analysis as a Necessary Component of Philosophical Reasoning/The Necessity of Their Limitations/The Aesthetic Dimension

Whitehead's international fame first came from his collaboration with Bertrand Russell on the multi-volume *Principia Mathematica*. The publication of this work became one of the hallmark, indeed founding, events in the history of Cambridge analytic philosophy, as the power of first order quantificational logic to elucidate language and the logical structure of argumentative reasoning became quickly evident. But it is often assumed that, after Whitehead dropped his focus on philosophy of physics, as well as his still influential developments of topological mereology, his approach to philosophical problems that employs rigorous appeals to formal logic and mathematics was essentially over; consequently, the gap between PM and PR is wide and yawning. Even a Whitehead scholar as knowledgeable as Victor Lowe casually makes the claim that Whitehead dropped the use of mathematics and logical formulae in his later published work since the beginning of his Harvard period. While this is evident in a large number of Whitehead's later publications, there are very important exceptions. The difficult chapter on 'Abstraction' in SMW, while not employing the notation of PM logic, does include considerable use of variables (such as A for eternal object, *a* for actual occasion, and R for relation); here we see ideas explicated in a quasi-formal manner reminiscent of the light formalism found in, say, F. H. Bradley's *Principles of Logic*, Vol. II. Part IV of PR in the chapters on extensive connection, loci and strains is also rigorously formalistic and diagrammatic as would be required in any sophisticated discussion of the theory of extension. The later *Essays in Science and Philosophy* contains technical mathematical discussions such as the important chapter on 'Indication, Classes, Numbers, Validation'. One of the most important revelations of the newly discovered Harvard lectures is the fact that Whitehead the logician and mathematician is very much alive in the development of his ontological and epistemological ideas, as even the most cursory review of HL1 will show. Consider, for example, just the short stretch of lectures from 15–17 February 1925, where Whitehead employs twenty-six formulae of propositional and quantificational logic (HL1, Heath's Notes, 474–7); or note the employment of twenty-nine diagrams in the stretch of lectures from 17–30 March 1925 when discussing relativity theory (HL1, 494–503); or the casual provision of six Larmor invariance equations compared with the 'regular Newtonian system' (HL1, Hocking's Notes, 408). This is a mere sampling used to illustrate; an inventory of the entire volume would yield an enormous number of formulae, equations and formal diagrams. In the light of this, the community of process scholars owes the editors, Paul Bogaard and Jason Bell, a great debt of gratitude for the painstaking way in which the various notes were transcribed and reproduced, including this wealth of technical logico-mathematical and diagrammatic material. This material clearly indicates that, while Whitehead the profound metaphysician of the opening Lowell lectures was mystifying to many, HL1 reveals that he was also every bit the logician and technical scientific mind that the audience had expected from the author of *The Concept of Nature* and the *Principia*.

Perhaps a deeper consideration is that it is arguable that the Categoreal Scheme of PR is throughout undergirded by the quantificational principles, axioms and deductions of the *Principia*. This is the overall thesis of John Lango's neglected *Whitehead's Ontology*, which accordingly challenges the standard view that there are disconnected or bifurcated periods in Whitehead's career that are alienated from the 'Mediterranean clarity' of PM (to use Russell's characterisation). As Lango asserts concisely in his Preface: 'although Whitehead's career is often divided into periods, there is no hiatus between his later metaphysical speculation and his earlier writings in mathematics, logic, physics, and the philosophy of science. In short, this indicates that the Whitehead of *Principia Mathematica* is at work in *Process and Reality*.'[37]

Despite the complexity (and granted some considerable obscurity[38]) in the literary exposition of PR, the Categoreal Scheme *is* arguably logically coherent, like a system of axiomatic mathematical notions, as Lango attempts to demonstrate with a set of eighteen formal quantificational Definitions and four deducible Theorems (important alternative formalisations have been developed by R. M. Martin and Lucio Chiaraviglio).[39]

Let me briefly illustrate this last comment concretely by providing an exposition of some selected items in Lango's PM-based account of Whitehead's Categories of Existence: actual entities, eternal objects, subjective forms, prehensions, contrasts and nexus (plural). Each of these Categories, argues Lango, is definable in terms of the formal properties of a basic and all-pervasive relation in PR (also pervasive in the Harvard lectures, cf. the repetitive references to 'togetherness' of entities in processes of realisation) that Lango deems 'synonty'. Synonty is the fundamental relation such that '$x$ is synontic to $y$ when $x$ has being for $y$' (WO, 76). It is immediately suggested by Whitehead's central metaphysical intuition, expressive of the very essence of creative process, that 'the many become one and are increased by one' (PR, 32), that is, since the many actual occasions have 'being for' the new occasion in its process of becoming. Put another way, synonty expresses the relation of ontological 'togetherness' which is found across the Categoreal Scheme; for example, to take only two of numerous instances, the many entities in the actual world are said to be 'together with' (prehended by) the actual entity in its process of becoming, and eternal objects are said to be 'together with' (ingress into) the actual entity in its process of becoming. (Formally, 'synontic to' can be rendered '➔' as distinguished from the *Principia* material conditional.) Given this, such basic notions as, for instance, eternal object, subjective form, prehension and created mental entity can be quantificationally formalised as follows:

> Since any eternal object (Whitehead's 'forms of definiteness') is synontic to every *other* entity and all other entities are synontic to it, in contrast to God who is synontic to every entity (including self) and every entity to God, an eternal object can be precisely defined as follows, where *EO* abbreviates 'eternal object' (*D14*):
>
> $(\forall x)$ $(EOx$ *iff* . $Ex$ . $\sim x$ ➔ $x)$
>
> Given *CM* for 'created mental entity', *SF* for 'subjective form', *PR* for 'prehension' and $\Delta$ for 'compresent with', we can formulate quantificational definitions for subjective forms and prehensions respectively as follows (*D15* and *D16*):
>
> $(\forall x)$ $[SFx$ *iff* . $CMx$ . $(\forall y)$ $(x \neq y . x \Delta y . \supset . x$ ➔ $y . y$ ➔ $x)]$
>
> $(\forall x)$ $\{[PRx$ *iff* . $CMx$ . $(\exists y)[ x \neq y . x \Delta y . (\sim x$ ➔ $y$ V $\sim y$ ➔ $x)]\}$
>
> In effect, something is a subjective form 'if and only if it is a created mental entity such that it is synontic to every other entity with which it is compresent and every other entity with which it is compresent is synontic to it'. On the other hand, something is a prehension 'if and only if it is a created mental entity such that it is not synontic to any other entity with which it is compresent or some other entity with which it is compresent is not synontic to it'.[40] From these two definitions the theorem logically follows that, if something is a created mental entity, then it is a subjective form if and only if it is not a prehension:
>
> $(\forall x)$ $(CMx \supset . SFx$ *iff* $\sim PRx)$

While this illustration is necessarily quite terse, the point is to show that an important subset of items in the Categoreal Scheme, namely, the Categories of Existence, has, much akin to a mathematical system, a discernible structure that admits of precise PM-based quantificational definition. Moreover, these Categories arguably exhibit a relational *unity* as found in their universal involvement with formal properties of synonty. While even this subset of Categories is quite complex (far more so than this brief summary can convey), its undeniable features of precision and unification under a common relational motif strongly argue against any quick dismissal of the Categories as simply 'muddleheaded'. On this reading of Whitehead, Russell's earlier assessment of Whitehead's Harvard metaphysical work as 'mystical' and 'muddleheaded' is simply off the mark.

Charles Hartshorne is also a philosopher who employed and explicitly insisted upon both the use of formal logic and mathematical analysis in the work of speculative philosophy (in particular, see the section on 'Formal Logic' in 'Some Principles of Method', CS, Ch. V). Again, this counts as a signifi-cant element in Hartshorne's perception of his 'pre-established harmony' with Whitehead. While Whitehead certainly reinforced this belief, especially given the use of logic and mathematics in the Harvard lectures which Hartshorne attended and transcribed as his assistant (as of Fall 1925), there is no direct evidence that Hartshorne derived his specific uses of formal logic from White-head. Rather, his primary influences on this score were his Harvard teach-ers of advanced symbolic logic, namely, C. I. Lewis and H. M. Sheffer. Also, C. S. Peirce's *Exact Logic*, which Hartshorne co-edited with Paul Weiss, was further reinforcement of Hartshorne's position on the uses of formal logic.[41] I demonstrate immediately below with brief accounts of some of Hartshorne's highly original uses of formal approaches to philosophical issues: i) use of Peirce's position matrices, ii) use of and reflection upon modal logic and modal theorems for insight into the logical structure of metaphysical concepts, iii) reflection upon the defining power of asymmetrical Sheffer functions and its implications for metaphysics, and iv) a formal triadic solution to the tradi-tional problem of future contingents:

Importantly, through exposure to Peirce's matrices, Hartshorne's so-called 'mathematical analysis of theism' published in *Philosophers Speak of God* as his 'Epilogue: The Logic of Panentheism' (a revision of his earlier 1943 article 'A Mathematics of Theism') details a six-fold table of logically possible positions on modes of being relating to reflexive and nonreflexive notions of the relations 'superior to' or 'inferior to' (PSG, 507–8). This was a first published warm-up for his later development and employment of Peirce's doctrinal position matri-ces.[42] Hartshorne's approach here – using the logically exhaustive quantifiers (all, no, and some) on the modal contrasts of necessity and contingency in application to God and world, thus arriving at sixteen possibilities – represents a genuine advance in metaphysical or philosophical theology, since it provides a matrix that may well suggest *missed* possibilities in traditional or conventional ways of thinking. Indeed, the position matrix is arguably necessary, since, until all possibilities are exhaustively exhibited, the *complete* rational adjudication of a metaphysical issue simply cannot occur. Furthermore, Hartshorne's method can be extended: similar sixteen-fold matrices can be made for other polar metaphysical contrasts such as infinite/finite, eternal/temporal, and so on. If any two matrices are combined (16 X 16) the number of formal alternatives leaps to 256. More generally, if $m$ equals the number of contrasts one wishes to include in talking about God and the world, then $16^m$ is the number of formal alternatives available. There is no apparent antecedent in the history of metaphysics for Hartshorne's specific and revised doctrinal matrices.

A later influence on Hartshorne was the work of Rudolf Carnap, especially his *Meaning and Necessity: A Study in Semantics and Modal Logic*. As Hartshorne makes clear in his autobiography, Carnap was helpful in assisting his (Hartshorne's) formal reduction to absurdity proof of the incoherence of the ensemble of classical theistic attributes regarding omniscience, foreknowledge and world contingency as found at DR, 12–14 (really a formalisation of Spinoza's famous argument for such incoherence in the *Ethics*, Part I, prop. 33, scholium). Moreover, the technically competent discussion of 'Relativity and Logical Entailment' owes much to Carnap as any examination of its text and footnotes will reveal (see DR, esp. 100–1, n 2). The direct influence of Lewis and Sheffer is also significant. Hartshorne's famous and much discussed modal formalisation of the Ontological Argument – again the first in the history of philosophy – as found in *The Logic of Perfection*, employs C. I. Lewis's S5 and includes use of Becker's Postulate or the Strong Reduction Principle (i.e., the Principle that the modal status of a proposition is always itself necessary – a postulate I find with A. N. Prior to be intuitively convincing, but which if judged problematic can be avoided altogether in a simpler formation of the argument such as we find in Hartshorne's 'Foreword' to Goodwin and elsewhere).[43] Similarly, Hartshorne reflects on the significance of various theorems of modal logic as a key to understanding, for example, how contingency includes necessity rather than vice versa, as reflected in the theorem that $[(\Box p \ \& \ \Diamond q) \ \rightarrow \ \Diamond \ (p \ \& \ q)]$: The conjunction of necessary and contingent propositions logically entails the contingency of the conjunction of the same propositions taken assertorically. On the other hand, one of Hartshorne's most important arguments for the basicality of Peirce's asymmetrical notion of logical implication is his (Hartshorne's) metalogical reflection on the defining power of the asymmetrical Sheffer functions as contrasted with symmetrical equivalence (cf. 'The Prejudice in Favor of Symmetry', CS, 205–26). Here, after explicating in detail the sixteen propositional-function possibilities encompassed by Sheffer's asymmetrical monary stroke and daggar operators, he announces that, although Peirce's asymmetrical logic of relatives has been 'with us for nearly a century', nonetheless 'philosophers for the most part have yet to realize the importance of this logic for metaphysics or speculative philosophy' (CS, 205). In effect, the important general point is that, for Hartshorne, there has been insufficient recognition of the fact that 'some rather simple, though neglected, truths of formal logic as it now stands seem to me quite *relevant* to traditional philosophical problems' (CS, 82). Somewhat similarly, Whitehead envisions an expanded Symbolic Logic that will be of important use to aesthetics, ethics and theology (see ESP, 99).

A perfect illustration of Hartshorne's adage at CS, 82 is the simple but neglected application of the traditional quantifiers of classical syllogistic (all, some, and no) to causal conditions of future events. By such application Hartshorne shows the fallacy in the Stoic Master Argument for fatalism (also apparently held by Russell during his University of Chicago sojourn where he discussed the issue briefly with Hartshorne) that our choices reduce to 'All causal conditions at *t* are such that *x* will occur' and 'No causal conditions at *t* are such that *x* will occur'. This excludes by omission the available common-sense notion that at *t* it is *indefinite* whether *x* will occur as embodied by the sub-alternative assertions that 'some causal conditions at *t* are such that *x* will occur and some at *t* are such that *x* will not occur'. The Stoic dichotomy of propositions is guaranteed to yield fatalism, and this begs the question. What is needed to exhaust the possibilities is a triad of propositional schemes: *x* will occur, *x* will not occur, or *x* may-or-may-not occur.[44] This triadic formulation can be displayed as a perfectly consistent modal-tense version of the square of opposition that will preserve both the law of excluded middle and the law of non-contradiction.[45]

Thus, while Whitehead encouraged Hartshorne's employment of formal logic in a general way especially through the exposure at Harvard, Hartshorne developed his own distinctive formal devices owing more to the four-fold influences of Peirce, Lewis, Sheffer and Carnap. At the same time, it is to be noted with some emphasis that Hartshorne, like Whitehead, was quite cognisant of the limitations of formal approaches to philosophical problems. Intuition is an indispensable aspect of philosophy no matter how thorough and systematic the use of formal logical analysis (WP, 112). *Adequate* philosophising involves far more than achieving clarity and precision in the formulation and analysis of concepts. Recall here Whitehead's famous qualification that, while 'Logic is a superb instrument', when taken as an *adequate* analysis of the advance of human thought, it is a 'fake', indeed 'exactness is a fake' (ESP, 74). The question *terminus a quem*, '*what* are we talking about?', when probed to its depths, compels an encounter with qualitative dimensions of experience that are uniquely accessible to artists, novelists, poets and musicians. The imaginative exploration of aesthetic possibilities, phenomenological description and the voices of poets and litterateurs are *mandatory* to philosophical adequacy. In Hartshorne's pithy expression, ideally 'philosophers ought to be poets and logicians' (CS, xvii). As Whitehead says similarly and again famously, literature is 'the laboratory of philosophical ideas' as it explores the heights and depths of human experience.

For this reason concerning adequacy and the need for aesthetic depth, Hartshorne suggests (WP, 6) that Whitehead did not explicitly employ, in the main, formal logic or mathematics in his later philosophical master-pieces, although (assuming Lango's thesis) I do not see that Hartshorne was sufficiently aware of just how extensively the logic of the *Principia* was at work, albeit tacitly, in the formulation of the Categoreal Scheme. Above all, however, for both philosophers, philosophy requires a balanced approach where logic, mathematics, reflections on the best results of empirical science, fine arts, poetry, music (and even, in Hartshorne's case, given his scientific work on birdsong, bio-musicology), literature and reli-gious studies all work together towards a coherent, comprehensive world-view narrative – the goal being what might be called 'global thinking' or 'thinking with the whole brain'. Whitehead was Hartshorne's archetypical model for such global thinking and integrated 'balance with definiteness' (CS, 92–8 and WP, 112). I emphasise here that the Harvard lectures clearly exhibit this ideal of enormously wide and balanced erudition, and such erudition is in fact one of their most impressive overall features. Standing alongside the many explorations of the history of philosophy from Plato and Aristotle to medieval Scholastics to Spinoza to Hume and Kant to Hegel to Russell and Dewey, experimental psychology, geometry both Euclidean and non-Euclidean, relativity and quantum theory, Newtonian mechan-ics, and epochs in the history of science, are the manifold references to poets and novelists – for instance, Dante, Milton, Shelley, Tolstoy, Virgil and Wordsworth (see HL1, 41, 47, 108–9, 136, 530, 533). This depth of erudition and concomitant appeal to aesthetic dimensions of experience will, of course, become a hallmark of Whitehead's later published work.

In summation, Whitehead and Hartshorne call philosophers to the highest and most daunting aspirations of philosophy as the 'appetite for *every* kind of learning' (Plato); as such philosophy is nothing less than the audacious aspira-tion to the grand narrative of the University.

## Concluding Remarks

What all the above analysis and argument shows, I think, is that Whitehead and Hartshorne were united in the Transcendental Project and its defence through meta-logical reflection on the universe of discourse assumed in first-order quantificational logic, and through what could be called the 'Ontologi-cal Approach' to the most basic fundaments of metaphysical theory (necessity of existence, the ultimacy of creativity and its embodiment in an 'aboriginal actuality', the eternity of the domain of potentials, God). This emphasis on the Ontological Approach provides an important qualification of Sessions' account in 'Hartshorne's Early Philosophy', which, while quite correct in envisioning many specific elements of the 'pre-established harmony', altogether lacks the logico-ontological dimension I have presented here. This unity of approach is also clearly reflected in Whitehead's Harvard lectures, as I have attempted to document throughout. I have also attempted to argue that the commitment to the necessity of ontological non-emptiness in both philosophers stands unscathed against a number of important potential objections, including Rorty's argument from an appeal to Kant's doctrine of noumena as existential surds. If this is correct, the Ontological Approach is strongly plausible and demands to be taken seriously. Embracing this Approach, Whitehead and Hartshorne stand as exemplary twentieth-century defenders of a *philosophia perennis* tradition that extends back to Parmenides.[46] Further, I have shown that Whitehead and Hartshorne are united in understanding the importance of the use of formal logic and mathematics in assisting the philosopher, while at the same time they envision the limits of this use and observe the requirement that there must be other kinds of consideration both aesthetic and phenomenological in order to achieve adequacy. Wisdom demands nothing less.

## Notes

1. Lowe, *Alfred North Whitehead, Volume II*, 142.
2. Lowe, *Alfred North Whitehead, Volume II*, 142.
3. Sessions, 'Hartshorne's Early Philosophy', 34.
4. See Gamwell's important treatise, originating from his University of Chicago seminar on 'Foundations of Ethics' with Paul Ricoeur, *The Divine Good: Modern Moral Theory and the Necessity of God*, esp. chapter 4, 'On Transcendental Argument', 85–126. Also see his analysis of Apel's 'transcendental pragmatic' approach to moral norms and its lack of success without a metaphysical framework in 'Metaphysics and the Moral Law: A Conversation with Karl-Otto Apel'.
5. Lowe, *Alfred North Whitehead, Volume II*.
6. For obvious reasons of space, I will be unable to treat here all relevant objections to the necessity of P-Zero. I have instead focused attention on issues and objections more directly relevant to Hartshorne and Whitehead's Harvard lectures. However, for supplementation of my perspective, consult William L. Reese's thorough and competent examination of conceptions of non-being ranging from Plato's *Sophist* to Sartre's neantising in his classic 'Non-Being and Negative Reference'. Also see my 'Appendix: Hartshorne's Ontological Argument and Continental Doctrines of "Nothingness"' in the forthcoming *The Mind of Charles Hartshorne*, co-authored with Don Viney (manuscript, chapter VI, 54–68). Here

we consider conceptions of non-being in Barth, Berdyaev, Heidegger, Moltmann, Sartre, Tillich and the Japanese Buddhist philosopher Nishida. We argue that the intelligible conceptions of non-being are equivalent to Berdyaev's non-being as meontic potency, which correlates with process conceptions of 'creativity' (Heidegger, Moltmann, Nishida and Tillich, we argue, all advocate meontic conceptions). The other conceptions are either contradictory or unintelligible (Barth's 'impossible possibility' of *das Nichtige*) or present us with thought-experiments that result in the description of possible worlds with mere differences of content (Sartre's neantising and mental acts in 'the imaginary'), thus reducing to Platonic 'othering'. Nowhere in these Continental and Buddhist thinkers is there an intelligible conception of or successful analogue for 'absolute nothingness'. It should also be noted in this context that Deleuze stands with Bergson on this issue (see note 19 below).

7. Although I have here used the vocabulary of 'foundations', I do not hold that this entails any commitment to classical epistemic foundationalism. (Nor do I hold that either Whitehead or Hartshorne are foundationalists.) While I am making the *claim* that Whitehead and Hartshorne are correct in contending that P-Zero is necessary and presuppositional, this does not in and by itself entail that such principle is an *absolutely, epistemically incorrigible foundation*. If it were so, there would be no point in engaging the potential 'defeaters' of P-Zero, ranging from considerations of the implications of non-classical free logics to considerations of the ontological status of a primordial quantum vacuum to considerations of the status of *sunyatta* in Buddhist metaphysics, etc.

8. Some philosophers who are sympathetic to Hartshorne and process philosophy generally, such as Eugene Peters, have expressed doubts about the necessity of bringing in the notion of observers into the primordial situation (see Peters, 'Methodology in the Metaphysics of Charles Hartshorne', 9–10. However, his objection can be circumvented by arguments for existential necessity that are confined to strictly logical 'class membership' considerations as in Gamwell's quasi-formal presentation of a Transcendental Argument in the previously referenced Ch. 4 of *The Divine Good*. Gamwell's argument is parallel to Hartshorne's observation that 'nothing exists' cannot be true of any *state of affairs*.

9. Cohen, *The Diversity of Meanings*, 255–64; W. and M. Kneale, *The Development of Logic*, 706.

10. See Goodwin, *The Ontological Argument of Charles Hartshorne*, chapter IV; Kripke, 'Semantical Considerations on Quantified Modal Logic'; see my discussion of Goodwin's interpretation of Kripke and Quine's objections to *de re* modality in *Process and Analysis*, 21–3.

11. In a neglected but important commentary on the early Wittgenstein by John Moran entitled *Toward the World and Wisdom of Wittgenstein's Tractatus*, it is argued that there is an implicit Ontological Argument in the *Tractatus*. For Wittgenstein is contending that an absolutely empty domain for the universe-class is impossible for logic. The argument can be found by ruminating on passages

2.021 through 2.0212. 'Objects make up the substance of the world (2.021) . . .
If the world had no substance [and thus no objects by virtue of 2.021], then
whether a proposition had sense would depend on whether another proposition
was true . . . In that case we could not sketch *any* picture of the world (true or
false).' The assumption of objects (of some sort) – in effect, the non-emptiness
of the universe of discourse – is thus a *precondition* for logical coherence in picturing the world.

12. Eco, *Kant*, 49.
13. Eco, *Kant*, 18.
14. Ross, *Philosophical Theology*, 104; this refers to the earlier Plantinga of *God and Other Minds*, not the Plantinga of the later *The Nature of Necessity*. In the latter work Plantinga develops what he calls a 'victorious' version of the Ontological Argument. For a discussion see my biographical essay 'Alvin Plantinga' in *American Philosophers, 1950–2000*, 215–25, esp. 220–1.
15. Gamwell, *The Divine Good*, 96, n4.
16. Quine, 'On What There Is', 12.
17. Dillman, *Quine on Ontology*, 81–3.
18. Bergson, *Creative Evolution*, 296–324, see esp. 304–5.
19. Bergson, *Creative Evolution*, 314.
20. Deleuze, *Bergsonism*, 17–23, 44–7, 101–3.
21. Viney, *Charles Hartshorne*, 63.
22. Gale, *Negation and Non-Being*, 113, more generally see esp. 105–16.
23. Gale, *Negation and Non-Being*, 112.
24. Martin, 'Ontology, Category Words, and Modal Logic', 27.
25. An excellent primer on free logics is to be found in Priest, *An Introduction to Non-Classical Logic*, chapter 13, 'Free Logics', 290–307. On the surface, and on the basis of non-classical free logic, Priest would seem to disagree with my argument from the existence assumption of the *Principia*, which is a form of classical logic. As he puts it plainly, '[in free logic] particular generalization fails, since a constant can denote a non-existent object; and the logic is not committed to the logical truth that something exists, for there are interpreta-tions where E [the inner semantical domain] is the empty set' (293). But what I am after in defending Bergson's argument concerns the meta-linguistic (or perhaps pre-linguistic) consideration about the conceptual origination of and ultimate referent for the *objects* of the inner domain E. Note that the examples Priest provides for members of E are 'Sherlock Holmes' and 'Pegasus'. While I understand their description as 'non-existent objects', I ultimately object to the use of the vocabulary of 'non-existence' for the purposes of the *appropri-ate metaphysical context* of Bergson's argument. There is a sense in which such objects exist *as* potentialities or as a combination of potentials, otherwise we could not countenance the *truth* of such sentences as 'In the novels by Arthur Conan Doyle, Sherlock Holmes lived in Baker St' (to use a sentence which Priest agrees is true and constitutes one of his 'philosophical objections' to the

Negativity Constraint Rule of certain free logics, see 275). In effect, again, free logics with empty inner domains are not truly relevant to the properly onto-logical issues at stake. For one could well agree with the employment of free logics for the quantificational formalisation of sentences involving Sherlock Holmes, and yet agree with Hartshorne's assertion that the domain of 'pos-sibility' is not to be contrasted with the domain of 'existence' (or the real), but rather with the domain of 'actuality' (RSP, 52). In effect, I hold with White-head and Hartshorne that potentialities of actual states are not 'unreal' or 'in every sense absent'; if they were we could not meaningfully refer to them. A linguistic entity with a truly *metaphysically* empty inner domain such as '_____ lives in Baker St' is not a proposition that can be asserted. Such examples as Sherlock Holmes make my point that free logics involve oblique references to actual states of affairs since Holmes is some sort of composite of actual proper-ties in non-realised combinations.

26. It is uncanny how close this is to Parmenides' reasoning about the utter futility of 'the way of non-being'; see reference below on Milton Munitz's interpretation of Parmenides.

27. See Griffin, *Reenchantment without Supernatualism*, 171. Griffin cites RM, 68 as the textual basis for holding that Whitehead rejects ontological type arguments. However, my own examination of this text and the ensuing discussion through RM, 69–70 shows that Whitehead describes the 'Ontological proof' of Anselm and Descartes as the 'only possible' proof because arguments from the actual world cannot get beyond the metaphysical principles inherent in the actual world to infer a transcendent God. Rather, he says, and we are left presumably to infer his agreement, Christianity has taken neither Anselm's nor Descartes' approach, nor presumably the so-called *a posteriori* approaches of Aquinas and Neo-Thomists. Contrary to these alternatives, he says that the 'genius' of Chris-tianity is found in the subordination of religious metaphysics to its traditional 'religious facts', which he then identifies as the spiritual internalisation of the 'Kingdom of Heaven' and the invocation of St John that 'God is love'. But none of this precludes Whitehead from appealing in the same course of lectures to an argument much in line with Hartshorne's and Tillich's very similar modal reasoning. At RM, 146 (my emphasis), he holds that 'the whole process itself . . . requires a definite entity, already actual among the formative elements, an *antecedent ground for the entry of the ideal forms* [potentialities] into the definite process of the temporal world'. Thus, that Whitehead might affirm a more gen-eral modal argument to God as 'the primordial power' – the 'complete aborigi-nal actuality' in Whitehead's vocabulary (RM, 146) – is by no means prohibited. Perhaps this is partly a semantic issue as to how we differentiate and classify types of theistic argumentation. But there certainly *is* a plausible tradition of interpretation which sees such reasoning as Hartshorne outlines above as of the properly ontological sort that trades in *a priori* or conceptual rather than restrictively empirical concepts.

28. I challenge those who wish to dismiss this approach in a facile way with fashionable slogans like 'ontologism'. Philosophers enamoured with Heidegger should be cautious here. For there is a strong case to be made for the position that Heidegger's 'The Nothing' is to be equated with Being as No-thingness, as infinite meontic potency, as that which is 'most void' (because it is *ontically* empty, it is not a 'thing' or aggregate of 'things' which exists or 'stands out' in space-time) and yet as potency is 'most abundant' and is 'being-er (*seinender*) than the beings'. The point of Heidegger's Postscript to the 4th edition of *Was ist Metaphysik?* was in fact to correct the 'nihilistic' interpretations of his talk about 'the Nothing' (*das Nicht*) which he explicitly disassociates from *das Wesenlose*, the 'merely nugatory', or that which lacks essence or potency (Brock trans., *Existence and Being*, 46). Moreover, if we follow up on Heidegger's own famous footnote suggestion for philosophical theology – his suggestion of God as infinitely temporal rather than as the timeless *nunc sans* of the tradition – we see direct implications for an affirmation of ontological non-emptiness. See *Sein und Zeit*, 427, n. 1. On the other hand, for a staunch critique of Heidegger's claim that his way of thinking radically transcends the metaphysical tradition which allegedly fails to grasp the 'ontological difference', see Puntel, *Being and God*, 99–112. Puntel directly approaches the issue of ontological emptiness and argues, in agreement with Whitehead and Hartshorne, that the concept of the *possibility* of absolute nothingness is a 'pseudo-concept', see esp. 227–30. He reformulates and then rigorously defends a version of Aquinas's 'Third Way' to the conclusion that there must be what Puntel calls an 'absolute dimension of Being'. He presents the argument as a simple *modus tollens* syllogism (a reformulation which avoids the quantifier-shift fallacy of Aquinas's original): 'If everything – that is, Being as such and as a whole – were contingent, then absolute nothingness would be possible, but absolute nothingness is impossible; therefore, not everything is contingent.' This affirms Whitehead's notion in his Harvard lectures that 'it is because something is Eternal' that coherent thinking in science and metaphysics is even possible. In general, Heidegger is roundly taken to task by Puntel for confused, deficient and logically spurious modes of thinking. See *Being and God*, chapter 2, 'Heidegger's Thinking of Being: A Flawed Development of a Significant Approach'.

29. See Tillich's discussion of the 'Ontological Approach' in his celebrated essay 'Two Types of Philosophy of Religion' in *Theology of Culture*, esp. 27, where he asserts that the power of being is 'the power in *everything* that has power' and where being-itself is taken as a *prius* of all thought, is 'first in the intellect', citing St Bonaventure. He also regards as 'more consciously ontological' Whitehead's conception of the primordial nature of God and Hartshorne's efforts at resurrecting the Ontological Argument while combining elements of the contingent in God (21–2). Also see Tillich, *Systematic Theology*, Vol. 1, Part II, Section II, B 'The Actuality of God', 235–41. I would suggest that Tillich's concept of the 'power of being' is to be correlated with Whitehead's concept of Creativity, but

is not identical to it. Perhaps it is arguable that it would be more accurate to say that 'power of being' correlates with all three of the primordial Formative Elements of RM taken together (Creativity, the Eternal Objects and God). Yet, the issue is complicated. For although Whitehead's God arguably includes the 'power of being', nonetheless, for Whitehead, God is literally and univocally a 'personal' entity, and consequently is more than the 'power of being'. Tillich's doctrine that the power of being 'includes' the personal or is 'the ground of everything personal', and thus God is personal in some metaphorical sense, is essentially unclear. Whitehead's doctrine straightforwardly conforms with Richard Swinburne's criterion for attributing personality to an entity by virtue of possessing at least one high-order P-predicate (or higher-order mental property, following P. F. Strawson's vocabulary of classes and sub-classes of P-predicates and M-predicates); *a fortiori* God as consciously envisioning eternal objects, evaluating their relevance and value for particular historical contexts, and then providing ideal subjective aims for the guidance of finite entities, is to possess numerous high-order P-predicates (cf. Swinburne, *The Coherence of Theism*, 101). However, Tillich is right, I think, to hold that both Whitehead and Hartshorne are mixing or synthesising ontological and cosmological approaches by offering a theistic model in which there are properly *a priori* ontological and *personal* monotheistic elements (*Theology of Culture*, 26–7), an ideal that Tillich himself wants, although I think dipolar panentheism more clearly achieves. Of course, these statements require much more clarification and qualification than I can provide here.

30. An important potential objection to ontological non-emptiness comes from 'empirical' cosmological inquiry based on interpretations of quantum mechanics. Some recent cosmologists have advocated notions of *creatio ex nihilo* purportedly without any pre-existent agent or agency. Such cosmological scenarios are sometimes described by professional physicists and by some popular science authors as events in which 'something comes from nothing' – the idea being that rules of quantum mechanics ranging over a primordial quantum vacuum would allow some probability of an event which 'tunnels' out of the vacuum analogous to the behaviour of virtual particles popping out of quantum foam. Self-proclaimed 'new atheist' physicist Lawrence Krauss has offered such a proposal under the revealing title *A Universe from Nothing: Why There is Something Rather Than Nothing*. Cosmologists A. Vilkenkin, Stephen Hawking, James Hartle and Y. B. Yel'dovich have also boldly suggested that, based on principles of quantum physics, there is some probability that the universe could have 'appear[ed] from nothing' (Hartle and Hawking, 'Wave Function of the Universe'; for references to Linde, Vilenkin, Yel'dovich and related literature, see my bibliography in Shields, 'The Wider Design Argument and the New Physics', 192–6). An adequate reply to this potential objection could well occupy an entire monograph, and for obvious reasons of space I cannot provide this here and now. However, I can quickly suggest a couple of lines of argument which support my (and no doubt Whitehead's) strong

objection to any such proposal. 1) The 'vacuum' which is postulated is clearly a 'something' with a quite substantial physical description as a 'diffuse energy field'. As John Gribbin puts it rather explicitly in an entry on 'vacuum' in his encyclopedia of particle physics: 'In quantum physics, the vacuum is not nothing at all, but seethes with activity . . . the vacuum is a superposition of states for many different kinds of field' (Gribbin, *Encyclopedia*, 418). 2) Consider the following 'fundamental equation of quantum mechanics': p q | q p = h (divided by 2π) / i (where p is the matrix variable for the momentum parameter, q is the matrix variable for the position parameter, h is Planck's Constant and i is the square root of -1). To what are these terms referring in application to nothing whatsoever? *What* constitutes or plays the role of, say, the momentum parameter or position parameter or Planck's Constant (inherently involving *energy* measurements in terms of joules per second), when the formula must purportedly function on the posited primordial *absolute* emptiness? I simply do not know what any such *ex nihilo* theory could *mean* when there is no referent of any sort for the mathematical terms of the quantum formalism. For some suggestions regarding 'origins of cosmic epochs' that are purportedly congenial to both Whitehead's thought and recent cosmological physics, see Griffin, *Panentheism*, chapters 2–3. See also my chapter (with Don Viney) on 'Dipolar Theism and Cosmology' in our *The Mind of Charles Hartshorne* (manuscript, chapter 8, forthcoming).

31. This section invites comparison with the chapter by Bell and Iyengar, 'Whitehead and Kant at Copenhagen', included in this volume. At first glance our approaches to the relationship between Whitehead and Kant would seem to stand in stark contrast. But I would suggest that I am simply articulating in a concrete way Whitehead's specific rejection of Kant's view of noumena as existential surds, leaving open the possibility of a special sense in which Whitehead offers a kind of 'Kantian' way forward toward a 'future metaphysics' that coalesces with quantum mechanical philosophy, as developed by Bell and Iyengar. They themselves acknowledge, of course, that Whitehead offers a critique of Kant's perspective in the Harvard lectures; I am articulating important elements of that critique. But so far as I can see, this does not preclude Whitehead's recognition of Kant's genius nor does it preclude other qualified senses in which there can be 'Kantian' elements in Whitehead's perspective.

32. Körner, *Understanding Philosophy*, 215–16; Rorty, 'Transcendental Argument', 82–3.

33. Körner, *Kant*, 41, my emphasis.

34. Compare Hartshorne's quite similar rejection of the noumena/phenomena distinction in his commentary on Kant at PSG, 147.

35. Barker, *Philosophy of Mathematics*, 77.

36. Bradley, 'Whitehead and the Analysis of the Propositional Function', 139–51. Also see the section on 'Anti-Realism and Excluded Middle' in my paper 'A Logical Analysis of Relational Realism' in *Physics and Speculative Philosophy*, 127–40.

37. Lango, *Whitehead's Ontology*, ix.

38. Leemon McHenry and I agree that there is some validity to the complaint of some analytic philosophers that the literary exposition of PR lends itself to obscurantism, but there is little merit in the perception that Whitehead did not give good reasons for his views. Indeed, a number of analytic philosophers have made their way full circle to embracing some central tenets of the philosophy of organism, including its panexperientialist-physicalist standpoint. See our 'Analytical Critiques of Whitehead's Metaphysics'; also available online at <http://journals. cambridge.org> (August 2016 issue). For what it is worth, Galen Strawson, whose perspective in his contemporary classic on 'Realistic Monism' is discussed in this paper, has expressed enthusiasm for our project.

39. See Martin, *Whitehead's Categoreal Scheme*, esp. 1–26, for an extensionalist event-logical formalisation; Chiaraviglio, 'Extension and Abstraction', 205–16 for a set theoretic formalisation.

40. Lango, *Whitehead's Ontology*, 95.

41. While Hartshorne often downplayed his expertise in this field, it is not often enough noticed that, because of his Harvard training in advanced logic as well as his editorial experience with Peirce's logical papers, Hartshorne was tasked with teaching Symbolic Logic at the University of Chicago until Rudolf Carnap's arrival. I venture the comment here that, for many professional philosophers, being assigned to teach logic at such a prestigious institution would be an imprimatur of one's competence in the discipline.

42. Don Viney and I have articulated Hartshorne's mature doctrine of matrices, tracking the history of its revisions, in our forthcoming volume *The Mind of Charles Hartshorne* (manuscript, chapter III, 14–17); see also our article 'Hartshorne: Neoclassical Metaphysics', in *The Internet Encyclopedia of Philosophy* <www.utm. edu> the section on 'Position Matrices'.

43. Hartshorne, 'Foreword' in Goodwin, *The Ontological Argument*, xv. See also the simple modal syllogistic presentation at CRE, 107. This version likewise dispenses with Becker's Postulate. For A. N. Prior's defence of Lewis's S5, which includes Strong Reduction, see his *Formal Logic*, 2nd edition, esp. 198–206, section on 'Iterated Modalities'. Because it concerns the abstract notion of necessary existence or 'universal existential tolerance', not concrete actualities, I submit that Hartshorne was correct to employ S5 as the appropriate modal system for the Argument's presentation.

44. See CRE, 81–92 for a full explication.

45. For a defence of Hartshorne's doctrine of future contingents against the objections of Steven Cahn, see my article on 'Fate and Logic', 369–78; for an elaboration of the modal square of opposition for future tense propositions see my essay with Don Viney on 'The Logic of Future Contingents', in *Process and Analysis*, 216–21.

46. For a profound defence of Parmenides' rejection of the possibility of sheer ontological emptiness, and one that shows that it is naïve and implausible to assume that Parmenides rejected deep common-sense notions of a world of plural entities which move and change, see Munitz, 'Making Sense of Parmenides' in his *Existence and*

*Logic*, 19–41. Also, see my paper 'The *Esti/To Eon* Distinction in Parmenides' *Proem*: A Defense of the Munitz Interpretation' presented at the March 2016 annual meeting of the Metaphysical Society of America, Annapolis, MD. (This paper has not yet been submitted for publication but is available by request via email at emeritus. shieldsg@kysu.edu.)

# Bibliography

## *Abbreviations of Works Cited by Charles Hartshorne*

AD      *Anselm's Discovery: A Re-examination of the Ontological Proof for God's Existence* (La Salle, IL: Open Court, 1965).

BH      *Beyond Humanism: Essays in the Philosophy of Nature* (Chicago: Willett, Clark & Company, 1937). Republished in 1975 by Peter Smith.

CAP     *Creativity in American Philosophy* (Albany: State University of New York Press, 1984).

CRE     *Creative Experiencing: A Philosophy of Freedom*, ed. Donald Wayne Viney and Jincheol O (Albany: State University of New York Press, 2011).

CS      *Creative Synthesis and Philosophic Method* (La Salle, IL: Open Court, 1970).

DL      *The Darkness and the Light: A Philosopher Reflects Upon His Fortunate Career and Those Who Made it Possible* (Albany: State University of New York Press, 1990).

DR      *The Divine Relativity: A Social Conception of God* (New Haven: Yale University Press, 1948).

EA      John B. Cobb, Jr. and Franklin L Gamwell (eds), *Existence and Actuality: Conversations with Charles Hartshorne* (Chicago: University of Chicago Press, 1984).

IO      *Insights and Oversights of Great Thinkers: An Evaluation of Western Philosophy* (Albany: State University of New York Press, 1983).

LP      *The Logic of Perfection and Other Essays in Neoclassical Metaphysics* (La Salle, IL: Open Court, 1962).

OD      *An Outline and Defense of the Unity of Being in the Absolute or Divine Good* (PhD Dissertation, Harvard University, 1923).

PCH     Lewis Edwin Hahn (ed.), *The Philosophy of Charles Hartshorne*, The Library of Living Philosophers, Volume XX (La Salle, IL: Open Court, 1991).

PSG     *Philosophers Speak of God*, with William L. Reese (Chicago: University of Chicago Press, 1953). Republished in 2000 by Humanity Books.

RSP     *Reality as Social Process: Studies in Metaphysics and Religion* (Boston: Beacon Press, 1953). Republished in 1971 by Hafner Publishing.

WP      *Whitehead's Philosophy: Selected Essays, 1935–1970* (Lincoln: University of Nebraska Press, 1972).

ZF      *The Zero Fallacy and Other Essays in Neoclassical Philosophy*, ed. Mohammad Valady (Peru, IL: Open Court, 1997).

## Other Works Cited/Consulted

Barker, Stephen F., *The Philosophy of Mathematics* (Englewood Cliffs: Prentice-Hall, 1964).

Bergson, Henri, *Creative Evolution*, trans. Arthur Mitchell (New York: Random House, 1931).

Bogaard, Paul and Jason Bell (eds), *The Harvard Lectures of Alfred North Whitehead, 1924–1925: Philosophical Presuppositions of Science* (Edinburgh: Edinburgh University Press, 2017).

Bradley, James A., 'Whitehead and the Analysis of the Propositional Function', in George W. Shields (ed.), *Process and Analysis: Whitehead, Hartshorne, and the Analytic Tradition* (Albany: State University of New York Press, 2003), 139–56.

Carnap, Rudolf, *Meaning and Necessity: A Study in Semantics and Modal Logic*, 2nd Edition (Chicago: University of Chicago Press, 1956).

Chiaraviglio, Lucio, 'Extension and Abstraction', in Eugene Freeman and W. L. Reese (eds), *Process and Divinity: The Hartshorne Festschrift* (LaSalle, IL: Open Court, 1964), 205–16.

Cohen, Jonathan, *The Diversity of Meanings* (London: Routledge, 1962).

Davies, P. C. W., *God and the New Physics* (New York: Simon and Schuster, 1983).

Deleuze, Gilles, *Bergsonism*, trans. Hugh Tomlinson and Barbara Habberjam (New York: Zone Books, 1991).

Dilman, Ilham, *Quine on Ontology, Necessity, and Experience* (Albany: State University of New York Press, 1984).

Eco, Umberto, *Kant and the Platypus: Essays on Language and Cognition* (New York: Harcourt, 2000).

Gale, Richard M., *Negation and Non-Being* (Oxford: Basil Blackwell, 1976).

Gamwell, Franklin I., 'Metaphysics and the Moral Law: A Conversation with Karl-Otto Apel', in George L. Goodwin and Philip E. Devenish (eds), *Witness and Existence: Essays in Honor of Schubert M. Ogden* (Chicago: University of Chicago Press, 1989), 200–27.

Gamwell, Franklin I., *The Divine Good: Modern Moral Theory and the Necessity of God* (Dallas: Southern Methodist University Press, 1990).

Goodwin, George L., *The Ontological Argument of Charles Hartshorne*, AAR Distinguished Dissertation Series (Missoula, Montana: Scholars Press, 1978).

Gribbin, John, *Q is for Quantum: An Encyclopedia of Particle Physics* (New York: Touchstone, 2000).

Griffin, David Ray, *Reenchantment without Supernaturalism: A Process Philosophy of Religion* (Ithaca: Cornell University Press, 2000).

Griffin, David Ray, *Whitehead's Radically Different Postmodern Philosophy: An Argument for Its Contemporary Relevance* (Albany: State University of New York Press, 2007).

Griffin, David Ray, *Panentheism and Natural Science* (Claremont, CA: Process Century Press, 2014).

Hartle, James and Stephen Hawking, 'Wave Function of the Universe', *Physical Review*, D 28 (1983), 2960–75.

Heidegger, Martin, *Sein und Zeit* (Halle: Max Niemeyer Verlag, 1927).

Heidegger, Martin, '"What is Metaphysics?" (with 1943 4th edition "Postscript")', trans. F. C. Hull and Alan Crick, in W. Brock (ed.), *Existence and Being* (Chicago: Henery Regnery, 1965), 353–94.

Kant, Immanuel, *The Critique of Pure Reason*, trans. Norman Kemp Smith (New York: Macmillan, 1965).

Kneale, William and Martha, *The Development of Logic* (Oxford: Oxford University Press, 1962).

Körner, Stephan, *Understanding Problems of Philosophy* (Sussex: Harvester Press, 1969).

Körner, Stephan, *Kant* (Harmondsworth: Penguin Books, 1970).

Krauss, Lawrence, *A Universe from Nothing: Why There is Something Rather Than Nothing* (New York: Free Press, 2012).

Kripke, Saul, 'Semantical Considerations on Quantified Modal Logic', in Leonard Linsky (ed.), *Reference and Modality* (Oxford: Oxford University Press, 1971), 63–72.

Lango, John, *Whitehead's Ontology* (Albany: State University of New York Press, 1972).

Lowe, Victor, *Alfred North Whitehead: The Man and His Work*, Vol. II (Baltimore: Johns Hopkins University Press, 1988).

Martin, Richard M., 'Ontology, Category Words, and Modal Logic', in Eugene Freeman and W. L. Reese (eds), *Process and Divinity: The Hartshorne Festschrift* (LaSalle, IL: Open Court, 1964), 271–84.

Martin, Richard M., *Whitehead's Categoreal Scheme and Other Essays* (The Hague: Martinus Nijhof, 1976).

Moran, John, *Toward the World and Wisdom of Wittgenstein's* Tractatus (The Hague: Mouton & Co., 1973).

Munitz, Milton, *Existence and Logic* (New York: New York University Press, 1974).

Neville, Robert, *Creativity and God: A Challenge to Process Theology* (Albany: State University of New York Press, 1995).

Neville, Robert, *Realism in Religion: A Pragmatist's Perspective* (Albany: State University of New York Press, 2009).

Peters, Eugene H., 'Methodology in the Metaphysics of Charles Hartshorne', in John B. Cobb, Jr. and Franklin I. Gamwell (eds), *Existence and Actuality: Conversations with Charles Hartshorne* (Chicago: University of Chicago Press, 1984), 1–11.

Plantinga, Alvin, *God and Other Minds* (Ithaca: Cornell University Press, 1967). Revised edition, 1990.

Plantinga, Alvin, *The Nature of Necessity* (Oxford: Oxford University Press, 1974).

Priest, Graham, *An Introduction to Non-Classical Logic*, 2nd Edition (Cambridge: Cambridge University Press, 2008).

Prior, Arthur N., *Formal Logic*, 2nd Edition (Oxford: Oxford University Press, 1962).

Puntel, Lorenz, *Being and God: A Systematic Approach in Confrontation with Martin Heidegger, Emmanuel Levinas, and Jean-Luc Marion*, trans. Alan White (Evanston, IL: Northwestern University Press, 2011).

Quine, W. V., 'On What There Is', in *From a Logical Point of View* (Cambridge, MA: Harvard University Press, 1961), 1–19.

Reese, William L. 'Non-Being and Negative Reference', in Eugene Freeman and W. L. Reese (eds), *Process and Divinity: The Hartshorne Festschrift* (LaSalle, IL: Open Court, 1964), 311–324,

Rorty, Richard, 'Transcendental Arguments, Self-Reference, and Pragmatism', in Peter Bieri et al. (eds), *Transcendental Arguments and Science* (Dortrecht: D. Reidl, 1982), 77–103.

Ross, James F., *Philosophical Theology* (Indianapolis: Bobbs-Merrill, 1969).

Russell, Bertrand, *Portraits from Memory and Other Essays* (London: Unwin & Allen, 1958).

Sessions, William Ladd, 'Hartshorne's Early Philosophy', in Lewis S. Ford and David Ray Griffin (eds), *Two Process Philosophers: Hartshorne's Encounter with Whitehead* (Tallahassee, FL: American Academy of Religion, 1971), 10–34.

Shields, George W., 'Fate and Logic: Cahn on Hartshorne Revisited', *The Southern Journal of Philosophy*, 26:3 (Fall 1988), 369–78.

Shields, George W., 'The Wider Design Argument and the New Physics: Ruminations on the Thought of P. C. W. Davies', in Mark Shale and George W. Shields (eds), *Science, Technology, and Religious Ideas* (Lanham and London: University Press of America, 1994), 77–96.

Shields, George W., 'Alvin Plantinga', in Phil Demattise and Leemon McHenry (eds), *American Philosophers, 1950–2000*, Dictionary of Literary Biography, Vol. 279 (New York: Gale-Thomson Publishing, 2003), 215–25.

Shields, George W. (ed.), *Process and Analysis: Whitehead, Hartshorne, and the Analytic Tradition* (Albany: State University of New York Press, 2003).

Shields, George W., 'A Logical Analysis of Relational Realism', in Timothy Eastman, Michael Epperson and David Ray Griffin (eds), *Physics and Speculative Philosophy: Potentiality in Modern Science* (Berlin: DeGruyter, 2016), 127–41.

Shields, George W. and Donald W. Viney, 'Charles Hartshorne: Neoclassical Metaphysics', in *The Internet Encyclopedia of Philosophy: A Peer Reviewed Academic Resource*, July 2015 <www.iep.utm.edu>

Shields, George W. and Donald W. Viney, *The Mind of Charles Hartshorne: A Critical Exploration* (Claremont, CA: Process Century Press, forthcoming 2019).

Shields, George W. and Leemon McHenry, 'Analytical Critiques of Whitehead's Metaphysics', *Journal of the American Philosophical Association*, 2:3 (Fall 2016), 483–503.

Swinburne, Richard, *The Coherence of Theism* (Oxford: Oxford University Press, 1978).

Tillich, Paul, *Theology of Culture* (New York: Oxford University Press, 1964).

Tillich, Paul, *Systematic Theology*, Vols I–III (Chicago: University of Chicago Press, 1965).

Viney, Donald Wayne, *Charles Hartshorne and the Existence of God* (Albany: State University of New York Press, 1985).

Whitehead, Alfred North, *An Enquiry Concerning the Principles of Natural Knowledge* (New York: Dover Publications, [1919] 1982).

Whitehead, Alfred North, *The Concept of Nature* (Cambridge: Cambridge University Press, [1920] 1971).

Whitehead, Alfred North, *Science and the Modern World* (New York: The Free Press, [1925] 1967).

Whitehead, Alfred North, *Religion in the Making* (New York: Fordham University Press, [1926] 1996).

Whitehead, Alfred North, *Symbolism: Its Meaning and Effect* (New York: Fordham University Press, [1927] 1985).

Whitehead, Alfred North, *Process and Reality: An Essay in Cosmology* (New York: The Free Press, [1929] 1978).

Whitehead, Alfred North, *Adventures of Ideas* (New York: The Free Press, [1933] 1967).

Whitehead, Alfred North, *Modes of Thought* (New York: Free Press, [1938] 1966).

Whitehead, Alfred North, *Essays in Science and Philosophy* (London: Philosophical Library, 1948).

# 13

## Footnotes to Plato

### Aljoscha Berve

It would be a commonplace to claim that the philosophy of Alfred North Whitehead was deeply influenced by Plato. This statement is as true as it is trivial. There is no doubt that by far the most famous quotation from Whitehead's work is his contention that '[t]he safest general characterization of the European philosophical tradition is that it consists of a series of footnotes to Plato' (PR, 39). In German philosophy alone, there have been two monographs entitled *Footnotes to Plato*.[1] However, it is much more difficult to state precisely what the importance of Plato for Whitehead's thought is. The first volume of *The Edinburgh Critical Edition of the Complete Works of Alfred North Whitehead*, entitled *The Harvard Lectures of Alfred North Whitehead, 1924–1925*, has brought to light new material that helps to determine the exact nature of Plato's influence on Whitehead.

In order to contextualise these transcripts within the larger framework of Whitehead's philosophy, in a first step it is necessary to provide a short overview of the different forms in which Whitehead takes up Plato in his writings published thus far. In order to keep the focus of the discussion on the Critical Edition, these influences will be limited to specific topics that are relevant for the points Whitehead makes in the Harvard lectures. Therefore, some wider implications of Platonic influence upon Whitehead's philosophy, such as the notions of 'substance' and 'dynamis', have to remain outside of this paper's scope.[2] In a second step, it will be possible to have a look at the how the first volume of the Critical Edition has provided additional grounds for clarification in this matter.

There is good reason to distinguish four aspects of Plato's influence on Whitehead's philosophy. First, it is surprising to realise that the only deep discussion of a Platonic concept by Whitehead is the adoption of Plato's notion of *chorá* into the highly sophisticated theory of the extensive continuum in the infamous fourth part of *Process and Reality*. This topic has received due attention, but it remains a special field within Whitehead scholarship.[3] Beyond that, Whitehead's main grappling with explicit positions of Plato takes place in 'Discussions and Applications', the second part of *Process and Reality*, especially the comparison of Plato's *Timaeus* and Newton's *Scholium* (PR, 93ff). Here, he also refers to his own concept of the eternal objects as 'Platonic forms' (PR, 44). While this connection is obvious, it would not suffice to prove a deep connection between Whitehead and Plato on its own. A reason to suggest caution would be Whitehead's habit of expropriating great thinkers' positions from time to time to support his own theory. For example, when he talks about the concept of value as the 'hyle', the abstract matter of an event, he conceives of the process of realising possibilities of value as its 'substantial activity' (SMW, 165). We are, therefore, tempted to see a strain of Aristotelian thought as having an influence on *Science and the Modern World*.[4] However, in *The Aims of Education*, Whitehead models his cycle of learning in explicit reference to Hegel's dialectical method – while later, he conversationally mentions that he had read exactly one page of Hegel's philosophy in his entire life (AE, 17ff / ESP, 88). As this example shows, to the surprise of any scholar well-trained in philosophical method, it is dangerous to take Whitehead's invocation of other philosophers at face value because it can occupy any position on a plastic scale between sound structural dependency and mere allusion. Obviously, Whitehead's discussion of the extensive continuum, his adoption of Plato's ideas and his recourse to the *Timaeus* in *Process and Reality* result from genuine interest, but we should be wary of putting too much emphasis on that factor. This caution is reinforced by the fact that Whitehead relies heavily on A. E. Taylor's commentary on the *Timaeus* in *Process and Reality* as well as in *Adventures of Ideas* and admits as much (AI, viii).

A second aspect of Plato's influence on Whitehead is the obvious discussion of seven general notions of Plato in *Adventures of Ideas*, namely The Ideas, The Physical Elements, The Psyche, Eros, The Harmony, The Mathematical Relations, The Receptacle (AI, 158). More to the point, the entire book is a reflection on the legacy of Plato's thought in the tradition of Western philosophy. Interestingly, Whitehead might reasonably be considered an unabashed Platonist in *Adventures of Ideas*, although the book is more a reflection on the historical realisation of general ideas within human societies than a methodically rigorous philosophical treatise. It is the juxtaposition of Aristotle as the main proponent of scientific systematisation and Plato as the speculative thinker throughout the book that provides a clue as to why Whitehead holds Plato in such a high regard. Looking beyond rigid structural argument, *Adventures of Ideas* articulates the conviction that 'philosophic systems . . . are the way in which the human spirit cultivates its deeper intuitions' (AI, 144). As we shall see, Whitehead quotes Plato as a witness for these deeper intuitions on a number of other points as well.

Even further removed from detailed analysis is a third aspect of Plato's influence on Whitehead's thought. In *The Function of Reason*, Whitehead decides to introduce personifications for the two main modes of reason he discusses. Ulysses represents practical reason, while Plato embodies theoretical or speculative reason. The description becomes even more metaphorical: 'The one shares Reason with the Gods, the other shares it with the foxes' (FR, 10). Again, he connects Plato to speculation. There is yet another facet to Whitehead's understanding of speculation, and it connects to Plato as well. If we accept Lucien Price's records of his dialogues with Whitehead as an at least somewhat authentic portrayal of his positions, then it seems that the speculative openness of Plato's philosophical outlook specifically appealed to him: '[Plato] seems to me to have been the one man in the ancient world who would not have been surprised at what has happened, because his thought constantly took into account the unpredictable, the limitless possibilities of things.'[5]

It seems prudent to assume that the decision to utilise Plato as a representative for theoretical reason conforms to Whitehead's statement about the European philosophical tradition consisting of a series of footnotes to Plato. However, the symbolic importance of the identification of Plato with theoretical reason goes further. While Whitehead opens *Function of Reason* with a description of practical reason as a fundamental power of the universe whose sheer scope is reminiscent of Goethe's description of cosmological processes of nature in the opening of *Faust*, speculative reason occupies an entirely different place in the world. Whitehead is adamant that speculative reason is a product of human civilisation, an anthropological rather than a cosmological phenomenon. However, he is not interested in social explanation, but in scientific theory. Within the development of civilised societies, he feels confident enough to determine a specific point of origin of speculative reason: 'But the critical discovery which gave to the speculative Reason its supreme importance was made by the Greeks. Their discovery of mathematics and of logic introduced method to speculation. . . . The Greeks produced the final instrument for the discipline of speculation' (FR, 40f).

The identification of speculative reason with Plato further reinforces its plausibility by this statement. Whitehead cherishes Plato as not only a Greek philosopher, but more than that as a crosser between philosophy and mathematics in the formative phase of both disciplines. Since he defines theoretical reason as retaining more than a mere tinge of speculation, the person of Plato is far better suited than Aristotle.

The last aspect of Plato's influence on Whitehead concerns Whitehead's ideal of philosophical communication. Thus, we are dealing with nothing less than the fundamental question of the identity of philosophy. Even in his time as a mathematician, Whitehead was renowned for his capabilities as a teacher. It comes as no surprise then that he was interested in philosophy beyond the mere question of truth. In fact, we might assume that his shift to philosophy was motivated at least in part by his sound conviction that the quest for final truths is ultimately futile – dogmatic certainty commits the 'fallacy of misplaced concreteness' (SMW, 51). This is where Plato becomes relevant. In the preface to his *Principle of Relativity* from 1922, Whitehead explicitly states that he regards his audiences as 'silent interlocutors' with whom he has to manage a dialogue, reacting to their questions and demands rather than giving a monolithic presentation (R, vii). Price relates a discussion in which Whitehead ascribes this perspective explicitly to Plato: 'He was at pains *never* to mean anything exactly. He gave every side of a question its due. I have often done the same, advancing some aspect which I thought deserved attention, and then in some later work, presenting its opposite.'[6]

In effect, with his allusion to Plato, Whitehead turns the scepticism towards ultimate truth into a virtue. He regards the subjective standpoint of every discussant as an irreducible element of philosophical discourse, so that the process of undertaking a discussion takes precedence over a mere look at the results. Again, he locates this approach to conceiving of philosophy as a speculative process distinctly with Plato: 'Everybody has had his say, the subject has been examined from many sides, some of the aspects are more persuasive than others, but it is erroneous to identify Plato entirely with one of them. . . . We do fairly well with half-truths so long as we remember that they are half-truths.'[7]

On the one hand, Whitehead's emphasis on the persuasiveness of arguments connects back to his conviction that all discourse must be based upon a shared environment of common sense. That every 'classification depends on the current character of importance' (MT, 15) has a direct equivalent in his cosmology: his concept of propositions explicitly claims that 'in the real world it is more important that a proposition be interesting than that it be true' (PR, 259). On the other hand, it points towards his understanding of Plato in yet another way. In *Adventures of Ideas*, he argues that the progress of agents in the world is one from force to persuasion. In a chapter named likewise, he claims Plato's authority to say that '[t]he creation of the world . . . is the victory of persuasion over force' (AI, 83). There is an obvious consequence of this notion of persuasion, now understood to be a metaphysical factor rather than a mere factor in philosophical debate, in *Process and Reality*, when he claims that God 'is the poet of the world, with tender patience leading it by his vision of truth, beauty and goodness' (PR, 346).

As we have seen, Whitehead relates to Plato on different tiers of argument. The most important discussion of Plato within the context of the theory of the extensive continuum is a rather specialist topic. Other than that, there is some immediate relevance of some philosophical concepts of Plato, although the implicit kinship is obvious. Much more apparent is Whitehead's dealing with what he calls the seven Platonic notions in *Adventures of Ideas*. True to his characterisation of Western thought as a series of footnotes to Plato, he tries to both claim Plato's authority and align himself with a strong philosophical tradition. While at first glance the idea of making Plato the representative of speculative reason in *The Function of Reason* seems to be a strange form of symbolism, upon closer inspection it becomes apparent that Whitehead's understanding of Plato as a historical person indeed overlaps to a substantial degree with his concept of scientific theory. However, there seems to be sufficient ground to contend that the most relevant influence of Plato on Whitehead's concept of philosophy stems from the shared speculative reach of thought, a common perspective on the limits of philosophical theory-crafting and, consequently, the emphasis on the process of discussion itself.

The first volume of the Critical Edition provides material to suggest that this interpretation of the influence of Plato on Whitehead's thought ought to be expanded upon. The Harvard lectures show a surprising degree of coherence in Whitehead's perspective on Plato. Most importantly, the transcripts demonstrate a surprising understanding of Plato – Whitehead conceives of him mainly as a mathematician, whose metaphysics is a result of his dealing with eternal forms. Repeatedly, Whitehead insists that starting your metaphysical design with the topic of eternity, as Plato did, necessarily results in '[t]he Metaphysics of the Geometer, the Logician, of the Arithmetician [the pure Mathematician]' (HL1, 139, 460, 505). Whitehead claims on two occasions that another metaphysical position of Plato ultimately was a mathematical argument. When Plato insists that mathematical points without extension are mere 'geometrical fiction', Whitehead takes this to be an argument for an interrelated world, comprised of facts extended in time and space (HL1, 254, 305). The dependency of Plato's metaphysical speculation on mathematics is, as Whitehead makes abundantly clear, not a mere fancy, but demonstrates the ultimate localisation of Plato's thought:

Plato was a mathematician, Aristotle son of a doctor – and that is essence of difference between the two. Plato was considering complex abstractions – and how actual presupposed the idea. Aristotle was classifying – brought up to see the ideal <u>after</u> the example. Plato studied (equivalent of Euclid) and then looked about and saw – 'Here and here they find their realization'. For Aristotle it seemed that Universals sprang out of the actual – the redness of plumage of stuffed bird, etc. A mathematician is bound to be Platonic. (HL, 341)

The connections between mathematics and philosophy Whitehead is so anxious to emphasise in his *Philosophical Presuppositions of Science* make it abundantly clear that he regards Plato to be a *structural* precursor to his own philosophy. We are justified in maintaining that Whitehead himself carried important structural aspects from mathematics over to philosophy. For example, from a purely philosophical standpoint it is baffling that in *Process and Reality* the second part is called 'Discussions and Applications', while the comprehensive 'Theory of Prehensions' is only laid out in Part III. However, the solution is that this layout is a direct structural heritage from his work as a physicist. In *The Principle of Relativity with Applications to Physical Science*, Whitehead uses exactly the same exposition to demonstrate a strictly physical argument (R, vi).[8] We can therefore assume that even during his time at Harvard, his self-perception remained that of a philosopher heavily indebted to mathematical thought and practice. It is important, however, not to draw the conclusion that his role as a mathematician had turned Plato into a thorough scientist in Whitehead's estimation. Instead, for a long time the obvious perception of Whitehead's attitude towards Plato by most scholars would have been that Plato holds a much more ambivalent position, again invoking Price:

Philosophers verbalize and then suppose the idea is stated for all time. Even if it were stated, it would need to be restated for every century, perhaps every generation. Plato is the only one who knew better and did not fall into this trap. When ordinary methods failed him, he gave us a myth, which does not challenge exactitude but excites revery.[9]

The connection between this statement and Whitehead's idea that the ultimate aim of human experience is not knowledge per se, but a maximum of emotional intensity, is obvious. Even in his concept of propositions Whitehead famously grants precedence to emotional intensity over logical judgement: 'But in the real world it is more important that a proposition be interesting than it be true. The importance of truth is, that it adds to interest' (PR, 259). The passage from Price pretty much assigns Plato's concept of myth the same quality, namely that it speaks to the fundamental structure of our experience: 'Have a care – here is something that matters!' (MT, 116). While the assertion of Price's Whitehead about the function of myth in Plato aligns pretty well with the general philosophical perspective of Whitehead's philosophy, it is only now that the Harvard lectures allow us to see first-hand that White-head ascribes structural importance to the Platonic concept of myth. If we remember Whitehead's statement that Plato's system of dialogues lets every-body have his say until a subject has been exhausted sufficiently, we take it first and foremost to be a statement about conversation techniques. However, in extension it also makes some strong commentary about the limited faculty of language to solve any philosophical problem, due to the inherently dynamic and ambivalent nature of terminology. In the Harvard lectures, this limitation of philosophical language is taken to be a structural limitation of metaphysics at large: 'Any metaphysics is a good metaphysics which takes you a good long way without its metaphors breaking down' (HL1, 384). In addition to that, Whitehead's statements in the lectures make it clear that he considers the concept of Platonic myth to be a structural parallel to the narrative design of his dialogues. This parallel amounts to more than simply stating the obvious – 'Plato has recourse to myth' (HL1, 85). Whereas the limitations of language are considered within the context of scientific method, the Harvard lectures show that Whitehead seems to discuss the concept of myth not as a mode of knowledge – building on Plato's distinction between *doxa* and *episteme* – but as a mode of *approaching* philosophy. Instead of a Platonic hierarchy of knowledge, that would order truths into the ranks of *eikòs mythos*, *eikòs lógos* and *alethès lógos*, Whitehead regards the Platonic notion of myth as the cul-mination of one approach to philosophy. The praise is obvious: 'Plato is the culmination with the primitive element still there. That's the charm of Plato' (HL1, 56f). The welter of students' notes taken during Whitehead's Harvard lectures allows us to conclude that this strong wording must pretty much have been what Whitehead actually said, because another set of notes uses almost the same phrasing: 'Always two sides to a culmination – Side looking to the primitives (Plato) & looking toward a long development (Aristotle)' (HL1, 441).

We are left to speculate about the nature of the primitive element pres-ent in Plato's philosophy, but the answer is obvious. Extending the argument about the need of propositions to elicit emotional interest, Whitehead's remarks in the lectures make it clear that he regards Plato's concept of myth as a prime philosophical instrument for doing precisely this – providing a state-ment of reasonable speculation beyond the point of provability. Following his statement that metaphysics is basically a comprehensive phrasing of a number of key metaphors, Whitehead insists that 'Metaphysical philosophy stands as near to Poetry as to Science, and needs them both' (HL1, 5). This is, of course, immediately reminiscent of the famous closing sentences of *Modes of Thought* in which he insists that 'Philosophy is akin to poetry, and both of them seek to express that ultimate good sense which we term civilisation. In each case there is reference to form beyond the direct meanings of words. Poetry allies itself to metre, philosophy to mathematical pattern' (MT, 174). Within the context the Harvard lectures provide, we have good reason to infer that the function of poetry – in *Modes of Thought* considered without any connection to specific philosophers – bears heavy structural similarity to the function Plato's myth performs for Whitehead's concept of philosophy. It is the junction of myth and mathematics that best defines Plato, because he 'took into account the unpredictable, the limitless possibilities of things'.[10]

As the Harvard lectures show, there is yet another aspect of Whitehead's use of Plato: The most prevalent situation Plato appears in during the lectures is in combination with Aristotle, whereby both function as antitheses to each other. This opposition of the two thinkers is not as prevalent an occurrence in Whitehead's main oeuvre; in addition to a number of references in *Adventures of Ideas*, in *Modes of Thought* he contrasts 'Aristotle's analysis into genus, and species, and sub-species' – the method of classifying worthy of a biologist – with Plato's doctrine of division, which he deems 'an anticipation, vague and hazy' (MT, 15). In *Modes of Thought*, we perceive this contrast as merely episodic. As the Harvard lectures show, Whitehead uses the combination of both as a much more fundamental ideal-typical antagonism of opposing scientific and, in consequence, philosophical positions. Indeed, the antinomian character seems to be of such importance to Whitehead that he fills it with a number of complements. Plato's role as a mathematician, starting with potentiality abstracted from particularity, is contrasted with Aristotle's role as a biologist – again Whitehead stresses that Aristotle was the 'son of a doctor' – who is interested mainly in the flux of things, the actual. As a result, 'Plato rather put the flux into the ideal – Aristotle vice-versa' (HL1, 310). The complements Plato and Aristotle embody – idea and actual, speculative division and analysis into genera, potentiality and particularity – provide a good overview over some main problem areas Whitehead saw his own philosophy concerned with. We may speculate as to why Whitehead chose Ulysses and not Aristotle as the embodiment of practical reason in *The Function of Reason* in contrast to Plato. In all probability, Whitehead wanted a person completely outside of philosophy to emphasise the radically pre-scientific importance of practical reason as a method of life pertaining to all agency in the universe, not only to scholarly debate. It comes as no surprise that he deems the approaches of Plato as well as of Aristotle equally valid, because the interplay between both perspectives is the fundamental activity of philosophical realism:

Philosophy of the Greek civilization culminated in Plato and Aristotle –
dual side to the culmination. Plato is the culmination with the primitive
element still there. That's the <u>charm</u> of Plato. Aristotle might have been
one of his own <u>followers</u>. (The difference between them). They do sum
up and express fundamental elements of any philosophy founded upon a
naïve objectivism. And this is implicit philosophy of Scientist when he's
really doing science. . . . Any really thorough-going Realism must have
faced that question. That, Whitehead supposes, why Aristotle and Plato
classed as once and thorough-going <u>Realists</u>; because they <u>did</u> face that
question. (HL1, 98f.)

As Whitehead continues to explain, realism in the sense he uses it means
limitation and, following from that, processes of selective transition. With
this interpretation of Plato and Aristotle as proponents of the same 'naïve
objectivism' implicit in any scientist who is doing science, he manages to turn
both of them into systematic precursors of his own approach to philosophy.
With this fresh perspective from the Harvard lectures, we see much deeper
systematic implications in Whitehead's statement at the very beginning of the
preface to *Process and Reality* that he considers his philosophy to be indebted
to 'the two founders of all Western thought, Plato and Aristotle' (PR, xi).
Indeed, his appreciation of the primitive element in Plato and the naïve objectivism underlying both Plato's and Aristotle's thoroughgoing realism, as we
have seen, seems to be the very thing that enables Whitehead to follow this
commentary with the statement that 'the philosophy of organism is a recurrence to pre-Kantian modes of thought' (PR, xi). This interpretation lines up
quite well with the famously programmatic chapter, 'Romantic Reaction', in
*Science and the Modern World*, where Whitehead rejects what he sees as a deep
inconsistency in Western thought, namely a bifurcation between a scientific
and an aesthetic approach to reality. When he determines his own position to
be a 'provisional realism' (SMW, 91), he specifically traces back to the fruitful vagueness and speculative reach of Plato's philosophy, in effect returning
not only to pre-Kantian modes of thought, but to what he deems the Platonic
essence of philosophical dialogue itself.

In conclusion, the Harvard lectures shed light on the importance of Plato
for Whitehead's thought in a number of areas. While Whitehead's published
philosophical works contain various points of contact with Plato, these often-
times remain out of context and unconnected. The transcripts of the Harvard
lectures do not add entirely new aspects to the debate, but support us with
further evidence in areas where Whitehead's *magnum opus* remained vague. Up
until now, every analysis of Whitehead's appreciation of Plato's openness for

philosophical discourse had to accept the authority of Lucien Price's *Dialogues of Alfred North Whitehead*. More importantly, the lectures manage to present the structural importance of Plato as a mathematician not only for Whitehead's philosophy, but also for his identity as a mathematician-turned-philosopher. In effect, Whitehead's concept of a 'provisional realism' and his return to 'pre-Kantian modes of thought' both stem from his long-held perspective on Plato and Aristotle as the ideal-typical embodiment of the fundamental contrast of organised thought that informs both his concept of scientific theory and his speculative cosmology.

## Notes

1. Cf. Kann, *Fußnoten zu Platon* and Beierwaltes, *Fußnoten zu Plato*.
2. For a more detailed discussion of the notion of 'substance' in Whitehead's philosophy cf. Berve, 'The Notion of Substance in A. N. Whitehead's Cosmology'.
3. Cf. Mingarelli, *'Chora* and Identity', Brennan, 'Alfred North Whitehead: Plato's Lost Dialogue' and Brennan, 'Whitehead on Plato's Cosmology'.
4. Interestingly enough, in the Critical Edition, the transcripts show Whitehead making exactly the same point, identifying value with *hyle* and claiming that they were non-transcendent compared to forms, which were transcendent. Thus, Whitehead concludes, he felt more at home in the Platonic than in the Aristotelian tradition of *hyle*. Cf. HL1, 86, 89.
5. Price, *Dialogues of Alfred North Whitehead*, 344.
6. Price, *Dialogues of Alfred North Whitehead*, 306.
7. Price, *Dialogues of Alfred North Whitehead*, 302.
8. In this instance, Whitehead makes abundantly clear that in his mind this structure is the best approach to present the argument: 'The order in which the parts should be studied will depend upon the psychology of the reader. I have placed them in the order natural to my own mind, namely, general principles, particular applications, and finally the general exposition of the mathematical theory of which special examples have occurred in the discussion of the applications. But a physicist may prefer to start with Part II, referring back to a few formulae which have been mentioned at the end of Part I, and a mathematician may start with Part III. The whole evidence requires a consideration of the three Parts.'
9. Price, *Dialogues of Alfred North Whitehead*, 368.
10. Price, *Dialogues of Alfred North Whitehead*, 344.

## Bibliography

Beierwaltes, Werner, *Fußnoten zu Plato* (Frankfurt am Main: Klostermann, 2011).
Berve, Aljoscha, 'The Notion of Substance in A. N. Whitehead's Cosmology', in R. Faber, J. R. Hustwit and H. Phelps (eds), *Beyond Superlatives: Regenerating*

*Whitehead's Philosophy of Experience* (Newcastle upon Tyne: Cambridge Scholars Publishing, 2014), 18–30.

Bogaard, Paul and Jason Bell (eds), *The Harvard Lectures of Alfred North Whitehead, 1924–1925: Philosophical Presuppositions of Science* (Edinburgh: Edinburgh University Press, 2017).

Brennan, Joseph Gerard, 'Whitehead on Plato's Cosmology', *Journal of the History of Philosophy*, 9:1 (1971), 67–78.

Brennan, Joseph Gerard, 'Alfred North Whitehead: Plato's Lost Dialogue', *The American Scholar*, 47:4 (1978), 515–24.

Kann, Christoph, *Fußnoten zu Platon: Philosophiegeschichte bei A. N. Whitehead* (Hamburg: Felix Meiner Verlag, 2001).

Mingarelli, Eleonora, '*Chora* and Identity: Whitehead's Re-Appropriation of Plato's Receptacle', *Process Studies*, 44:1 (2015), 83–101.

Price, Lucien, *Dialogues of Alfred North Whitehead* (Boston: Little, Brown and Company, 1954).

Whitehead, Alfred North, *Science and the Modern World* (New York: The Free Press, [1925] 1967).

Whitehead, Alfred North, *The Aims of Education and Other Essays* (New York: The Free Press, [1929] 1967).

Whitehead, Alfred North, *The Function of Reason* (Boston: Beacon Press, [1929] 1958).

Whitehead, Alfred North, *Process and Reality: An Essay in Cosmology* (New York: The Free Press, [1929] 1978).

Whitehead, Alfred North, *Adventures of Ideas* (New York: The Free Press, [1933] 1967).

Whitehead, Alfred North, *Modes of Thought* (New York: Free Press, [1938] 1966).

Whitehead, Alfred North, *Essays in Science and Philosophy* (London: Philosophical Library, 1948).

# Part V

# Metaphysical Reflections

# 14

# Diagrams and Myths

## George Allan

During his first Harvard lecture, on 25 September 1924, and in nearly identical language two days later in the Radcliffe College version of the same lecture, Whitehead says that 'Metaphysical Philosophy', the kind of philosophy he is for the first time formally attempting, is 'not the mere handmaiden of Science', but rather 'stands as near to Poetry as to Science, and needs them both' (HL1, 5). It's a puzzling claim. Why should metaphysics be near to, much less in need of, poetry, that most personal and emotive form of human discourse, an endeavour far distant from the maximally impersonal study of Being Itself? And why should metaphysics be thought in need of the empirically rooted sciences, since the task of metaphysics is to articulate the first principles upon which those sciences depend?

The aim of this chapter is to remove this initial puzzlement, and by doing so to uncover more interesting ones, puzzles crucial to Whitehead's metaphysical insights as expressed in his 1924–25 lectures at Harvard University. Through these insights, I will towards the end of the chapter attempt to explicate an approach to how we can understand the world that is rooted in Whitehead's views but that departs from them in ways he would have rejected in the 1920s but maybe not by the 1930s.

## Simplicity

Whitehead's apparent answer to the question of why metaphysicians needs to use both scientific and poetic methods is because 'metaphysics is [the] critical appreciation of [the] whole intellectual background of man's life' (HL1, 413). It leaves nothing out, because it seeks a critical appreciation of the whole. Hence everything is its subject matter, from one extreme to the other, from the humanities to the sciences, from poetry to mathematics. That's true enough, but it's too trivial a reason. It's not just that metaphysics deals with everything, but that everything is an interdependent whole: 'Togetherness of things is fundamental. "Organization" (in Biology) exists only in Relationships. There can't be any one thing (a horse, e.g.) except in certain circumstances. Its happiness too, a further dependence' (HL1, 5). The togetherness of things is not a unitary lump; nor is it a heap of separable things, not even a well-ordered heap. Rather, it is a process of events internally related to all other events, 'a flowing process of becoming – of realization' (HL1, 5), where all else is the environment for whatever is. 'Every entity', says Whitehead, 'expresses itself in [the] whole of reality & [the] rest of reality is patient of it' (HL1, 416). Everything is distinctively individual but nothing self-sufficient. The world is a boundless process of emergent structures that are transitions to other structures. It is not just any whole, but an unimaginably dense whole, too dense ever to fully grasp.

The reason that poetry and science are so crucial to metaphysics is that they offer the tools, the methods, by which it can grasp the ungraspable. What these methods are is captured in Whitehead's remark that a 'diagram is [the] mathematicians' analogue to Plato's myth'. Whitehead says he prefers a diagram to a 'long verbal statement' because he 'can't make up myths!' (HL1, 172), but it would be more accurate to say that he prefers diagrams to complex mathematical formulae and myths to long verbal statements. Since myths and diagrams are analogues, however, it's not just to diagrams but to myths as well that we can have recourse. To either, as a way to gain access to a world otherwise too dense to be understood.

Whitehead sometimes speaks of a diagram as a picture. It's not, however, in the sense of being a reproduction of some region of reality, because it leaves a lot out. It's a sketch, not a replica. A roadmap is a diagram that excludes everything about an area except its roads, which are enlarged and the details of their shape smoothed for easier recognition. The diagrams Whitehead draws on the blackboard are extreme in what they omit: only a few lines remain, indicating relationships relevant to what he is discussing, along with letters that name them.

For instance, his diagram of the congruence of particles p and q from a moment $M^1$ to the next two moments, $M^2$ and $M^3$, has three vertical M lines all crossed by a p and a q horizontal line. At each intersection of M, p and q have the same relative location: if p crosses $M^1$ at the 6 inch mark, it crosses $M^2$ at 6 inches and also $M^3$; and if q crosses $M^1$ at the 10 inch mark, it crosses $M^2$ and $M^3$ at 10 inches as well. Hence, for each M, p and q are the same distance apart and at the same relative location. That is, p and q are at rest. This illustrates what relativity theory means by congruence: 'Two particles mutually at rest in

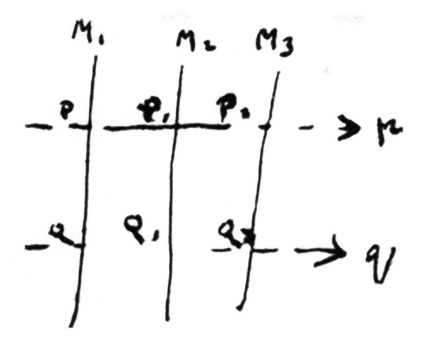

any <u>one</u> Space-Time remain at the same distance in any <u>other</u> Space-Time'
(HL1, 284).

Note that congruence is not something one 'discerns' or 'intuits'; it is a
relation that can be geometrically demonstrated as applying or not to any two
or more specified time systems. 'Silly little diagram', Whitehead remarks, but
'don't be afraid of being silly sometimes' (HL1, 130). Besides, it's '<u>equally</u> silly
to go agitate air with noises and tell people to <u>understand</u> them. Make <u>another</u>
noise and say "that's what I <u>mean</u>"' (HL1, 328). The advantage of a diagram
is that it '<u>does</u> preserve that scheme of relationships which are relationships
<u>among</u> the internal relationships' (HL1, 328). It discloses the form of the
internal relationships of a complex reality while stripping away the confusing
details not relevant to the analysis.

The same is true of myths, which can be thought of as verbal diagrams
that 'give you an easier picture', a way 'more convenient, psychologically,
to reason' about some particularly complicated things (HL1, 26). This is
especially so with respect to what Whitehead calls 'ultimate presuppositions'
(HL1, 24) such as, in science, electrons or quanta. 'Electrons are mere myth',
he says, 'a way of stating things' (HL1, 425). Calling an electron a myth, however, isn't saying it's a useful fairy tale about something that isn't there. It is

useful only if grounded in verified facts and subject to a formal analysis which gives rise to further verified facts. Electrons refer to objective features of the world, but ones best dealt with in mythic terms. An electromagnetic field is a flux of energy that we can take as having a vibratory 'character with a focal centre', which we call an electron. This electron is not a concrete thing, however, but 'that type of vibration with that focal location' (HL1, 26). It's a useful way of talking about something very complicated – like using graphs in dealing with unemployment data. The graphs are a helpful way to clarify complex trends, but they would be worthless 'if there were no such thing as Unemployment in the Nation', if there were no unemployed people whose numbers were actually being totalled (HL1, 26). Myths require facts but are not reducible to them, for like diagrams they make visible what the facts in their millions obscure.

## Thinking with Surrogates

'We habitually reason and think with surrogates' (HL1, 26), of which diagrams and myths are important examples. Nor should we distinguish them too carefully. In drawing a diagram of how things grow through a process of retentive endurance, Whitehead points to his chalk marks and calls them 'a myth drawn on the blackboard' (HL1, 89). Such surrogates are our way of making sense of things, interpreting them in ways we find meaningful. We do this by abstraction: isolating a particular fact from its environment, and identifying, by how we select it, its value for us, its relevance to our aims.

Abstracting a fact from the intertwined complexity of the world is not an arbitrary process. It is not, as Locke or Hume would claim, simply a matter of a mind observing 'sense-data and spatio-temporal relations between them'. Nor is it, as contemporary science would have it, 'energies' that 'are nothing but' their 'Spatio-temporal adventures' (HL1, 24). These approaches lose sight of their point of departure, substituting what they have abstracted for what they abstracted from. Whitehead wonders what has become of 'ordinary entities, which in ordinary life we "observe" – Sounds and Sights, bars of iron and green trees and birds, bodily feelings of wide gradations, watches etc.' (HL1, 24). He proposes a different approach, one that remains connected to the complexity of things, suggesting that there are 'three types of entity' we need 'to play with' in order to give an adequate account of 'Observability': Firstly, 'Observers', but not in a passive sense, for 'we don't feel [ourselves as] mere Observers – we feel ourselves taking a hand in the game, too – in various ways'; secondly, 'Things observed', which is the 'Field of Display'; and thirdly 'the Physical Field' which is the 'Field of Control' (HL1, 24–5). We must note, however, that these are 'very neat abstractions . . . only got at <u>by</u> high degree of abstraction' (HL1, 25). So we should use them with care.

These three types of entity are related: 'The Display <u>is</u> what it <u>is</u> now; but . . . is always <u>for</u> something else. <u>For</u> an Observer', and because of conditions that have led to the Display and to its likely consequences (HL1, 27). These conditions are the Field of Control, composed of '"observed" entities – but with a particular function with regard to [Display] entities' (HL1, 27). They constitute the background context for both Display and Observer, accounting for how what is displayed came to be so displayed and to what end. There is an ontological aspect to this triadic relation that I will return to later, but the relation is also epistemic. It explicates abstraction by calling attention to how an abstraction is made: by an Observer, who distinguishes the immediate perceptual Display of an object from the contextual Controls that justify singling out that object and explaining its character. Attention to the Control provides an insight into the concrete whole from which the Observer has abstracted the Display.

Understanding this to be how an abstraction is accomplished raises the important question of its value. Why focus on certain features of experience rather than others? Because doing so is an effective tool with which to further some purpose – like validating a scientific hypothesis or exhibiting a valuable work of art. Thus, Devices like myths and diagrams can be thought of as Controls for determining how data are selected and how organised. And if they illuminate our sensory and cognitive capacities effectively, they will have furthered our knowledge and its usefulness, its truth and its value, by allowing our imagination to see possibilities that can provide better controls and better aims while recognising their unavoidable imperfections, the need for constant revision. Thinking with surrogates is not merely a useful habit, it's a necessary one. 'With man', says Whitehead, 'it is not possible to deal with [the] universe without abstraction' (HL1, 219).

A clear example that Whitehead discusses at length is the concept in geometry of a point-instant. We understand the notion of something being right here just now, but it's a quite vague notion, ambiguous as to how it might be taken. The mathematician eliminates 'the prolixity and pitfalls of ordinary language' (HL1, 211) by abstracting from the concrete notion of 'here' until its ambiguity is purged: a point is a spatial location that has no length, breadth or depth. It can be uniquely defined by three spatial coordinates x, y, z. The notion of 'now' adds a fourth coordinate, t, indicating the point's temporal location. Point-instants are 'very high abstractions' (HL1, 267), achieving 'exactment' by an 'enormous simplification of thought' – by what Whitehead calls 'cognitive gelding' (HL1, 197).

Exactment has an additional virtue, an emotional one. It 'calms the air of excited mystery' that often surrounds things that because of their complexity or beauty or novelty are felt to be marvels beyond our ken, uncanny mysteries of overwhelming significance. Scientists are trained to see things in terms of abstractions, permitting them to remain unexcited in their pursuit of what is objectively the case. In Sergeant Friday's immortal words: 'Just the facts, Ma'am.' Or as Whitehead puts it, 'The Scientist doesn't want his heart to "leap up" when he beholds the rainbow.' Instead, he 'gets out his spectroscope' (HL1, 56). Consider the discovery of irrational numbers like $\sqrt{-1}$, which seemed to the Greeks an uncanny kind of number, but it was useful and so was used, though with a certain unease. When mathematicians finally worked out its exact meaning within a theory of numbers, its mystery was toned down, so that scientists – and metaphysicians – would know exactly what they were thinking about and so could deal with its ontological importance without confusion (HL1, 266).

Exactment comes at a price, however. If a line is defined as a sequence of points, and a volume as a sequence of lines, then space-time is a fixed four-dimensional volume composed everywhere of points. As I noted with Whitehead's diagram of congruence, something is said to be at rest if its spatial location at moment $M^1$ is the same as at $M^2$ and at $M^3$. The condition of something being at rest, however, is not simply a matter of a congruence pattern. Such an analysis misses something fundamental: duration. We don't perceive a thing at rest as being a static replica of a pattern at a number of contiguous locations, but rather as an enduring object with its enduring pattern. To be at rest is to retain basic features throughout a temporal duration. Accounting for change by means of changeless point-instant patterns is obviously incoherent, an endeavour that blatantly exhibits its own inadequacy.

## Ragged Edges

The problem for Whitehead is not exactment. Not only does he insist that the precision gained by abstraction is necessary in order to understand our experiences, but also that it is useful, and most importantly so with respect to the high-level abstractions of mathematics utilised by scientists in developing and testing their hypotheses. Abstraction is both necessary and useful, but it can also be dangerous if its limits are not recognised. We are familiar with what Whitehead calls the 'Fallacy of Misplaced Concreteness', the problem that results from confusing abstractions with the concreteness from which they have been abstracted (HL1, 43). But Whitehead notes as well the parallel problem of excessive effort to achieve exactment, the attempt to be more precise than our interpretation requires: committing the 'Fallacy of Misplaced Abstractness' (HL1, 473). The 'Art of reasoning' is to arrange our abstractions 'so they bring out by their very nature' what is important about what is being investigated, fashioning a sort of picture of the logical relations in their formal side (HL1, 199). Effective reasoning requires being master of our techniques, exploiting them as far as appropriate, but knowing and respecting their limits. It means knowing how much exactness is worth putting in, not letting technique obscure the aesthetics of our subject matter, but also not letting the aesthetics obscure the formal relationalities involved. Mathematical precision and emotive significance are 'intense' ways of interpretation. Whitehead recommends, instead, 'the Peacock's way' (HL1, 211): distributing the intensity, as a peacock does when spreading its tail, so that contrasting or even mutually exclusive features are harmonised rather than one of them dominating and the other being discarded.

The aim of science may be at theories verified by established fact, but its key tool is the use of hypotheses, which are effective insofar as they offer what Whitehead calls a 'vague apprehension of a vague sort of relationship' (HL1, 242). A hypothesis pushes out '<u>beyond</u> what is clearly and obviously fact', beyond exact data and tested theories. It directs attention to possibilities of connection not previously explored, ones offering thereby a wider although fuzzier grasp of things (HL1, 241). A habit of formulating promising hypotheses cultivates the 'vividness and delicacy of appreciation' that prepares the mind for imagining what was assumed to be unimaginable, for noticing what otherwise would go unnoticed. 'You do not perceive what you're not prepared to perceive.' Even what proves to be a false hypothesis, Whitehead adds, can lead to a 'right type of observation' (HL1, 242).

This is what poetry gladly does and that science needs to do as well. A great poem evokes a feeling that the poet 'has gone beyond [his or her] own direct experience'. We may eventually forget the details of the poem, but our 'apprehension of wonder' that it kindled remains. Whitehead, having just said that the scientist should avoid the wondrously befuddling excitement of seeing a rainbow in order to focus on identifying its cause, now applauds experiencing the wonder of a rainbow or a skylark's song at dawn (HL1, 242). But as always, it's the middle way to which we are directed. On the one hand, hypothesising can be little more than fantasising, a matter of imagination run wild. We need to be able to identify and 'to have firmness of mind to discard what won't hold water' (HL1, 248). On the other hand, 'lazy assumption[s]' (HL1, 249) about the adequacy of familiar truths are to be avoided, the habit of constantly criticising new ideas, of avoiding speculative adventure because of the risk of failure.

> You can't get a fundamental connection . . . of ideas of one Science without considering their connection with others. It is in their irrationality that you'll find best ground for revision. In trying to get Concepts of allied Sciences into harmony, you point the way to a reorganization within each branch of science. You will not get something you Know is true. But you will get [a] 'well-grounded' hypothesis; and you've taught yourself to be imaginative without any danger of running wild. (HL1, 248)

When doing science, but also when doing metaphysics, our aim should be creative and critical, not merely utilitarian. There is a danger in both science and philosophy of engaging in 'detailed subtlety without a broad view', pursuing 'a lot of little niggling investigations that lead nowhere', that have 'no relevance to anything' (HL1, 250). It's not that there is anything wrong with detailed subtlety, but when it becomes an end in itself, when it fails to serve a wider purpose, it has limited value because it is unaware of other investigations with which it is incompatible. Its results confirm a narrow purpose while ignoring or ignorant of conflicting purposes. The conflict needs to be taken seriously, which means widening one's perspective. You 'can't get a correction' to the clash of established theories 'without trying for a wider harmony', without a hypothesis that reaches beyond what has been rationally justified and empirically verified. 'You need to have something behind your symbols which when elucidated leads to something' (HL1, 250).

It is in the 'irrationality' of scientific or metaphysical knowledge 'that you'll find [the] best ground for revision' (HL1, 248). For 'when you've got hold of your Concept', your working hypothesis, 'you'll find some things it doesn't explain – rough edges' (21). Get up against the rough edges of thought, Whitehead advises, although it 'depends on how rough as to what you do'. For instance, 'Quantum vs. Wave Theory on face of them quite contradictory. But each explaining so much that you can't believe either quite wrong' (HL1, 21). One has to use 'Common sense about judging your rough edges', how in this case to reconcile fundamental differences in fundamental theories, or somehow to affirm them both despite that incompatibility (HL1, 22). And sometimes those detailed subtleties and niggling trivialities, freed from narrow-visioned understandings, can be 'Minute Clues' to a needed rethinking of the truths we think self-evident. 'Very trivial facts' can have 'enormous importance', as for instance the '<u>slight</u> difference of atomic weights in isolating Nitrogen' that led to the discovery of Argon, or the 'silly little shifting' in the orbit of Uranus that led to the discovery of Neptune (HL1, 22). A good hypothesis, in other words, 'must always allow for ragged-edges' (HL1, 488).

It is a boon to our attempted mastery of abstractions when the tools we use are able to reveal their own limits, to display not only the features they are designed to emphasise, but also their boundaries, the perimeter of their expertise – thereby revealing their beyond. Diagrams and myths do this fairly well because they are so obviously partial. A diagram is a sketch, calling attention not only to a formal pattern otherwise easily overlooked, but also acknowledging by its sketchiness that there are all sorts of other things that obviously had to be excluded in doing so – some of which might nonetheless justify being seriously looked at afresh. A myth is a story, a verbal account of something that begins with some event, from which it moves along to other events until it comes to the one where it ends. The story conveys more than it says, however, pointing not only to truths about those events that might otherwise be overlooked, but also conveying a realisation that the story goes ever on, towards unexamined consequences and further unmentioned episodes. To put it in a slightly different way, diagrams and myths are open-ended. They point beyond themselves, revealing that there is more than what they are equipped to articulate.

Towards the end of his 1924–25 lectures, having gone on for a considerable time sketching the metaphysical schema that would become his Gifford lectures and then *Process and Reality*, Whitehead pauses to remark that 'any neat schema of this sort is entirely and absolutely foolish'. Familiar metaphysical assertions, however, if 'repeated long enough don't <u>appear</u> silly', although they are, and fresh ones will always seem silly, as of course they are. Because in doing metaphysics 'your language will <u>always</u> be <u>metaphorical</u>' and so if taken literally will be silly. Yet many of these silly sentences survive and are used with serious intent. Surely they 'wouldn't have been used if there weren't <u>something</u> in it' (HL1, 372).

I've been arguing for the value of diagrams and myths, which although silly provide useful controls for abstracting from experience meaningful interpretations – ones, that is, that are both understandable and fruitful. In light of what Whitehead says about metaphorical language, I think it appropriate to understand diagrams and myths as kinds of metaphor. I want now to underscore a feature of metaphors in general, and hence of diagrams and myths in particular, that the Whitehead lectures don't touch on, but that is crucial to an appreciation of how abstractions can foster open-ended thinking without succumbing either to idle speculation or to unimaginative closure.

Metaphors are not analogies. An analogy asserts a similarity between two different things: x is *like* y. Whitehead uses analogies frequently. The essential nature of an electron, he reports, is like having 'tentacles stretching out throughout all space & all time' (HL1, 416). Attempting to justify the congruence of two space-time systems by saying we 'discern' it, that we intuit it directly, is for Whitehead like forecasting the actions of the Republican Party 'by going to Africa and studying elephants' (HL1, 284). In contrast, a metaphor asserts the identity of two incompatible things: x *is* y. We are asked to understand that light is both a wave and a particle, that Romeo really means it when he says that Juliet is the sun. An analogy compares two different things in a way that illuminates one or more features of one or both of them. A metaphor turns two different things into one thing. It claims not a similarity but an identity.

Logical contradictories, and all other sorts of incompatibles, held together in a metaphor, require constant attention because they are constantly bubbling over their container. We can try to release the tension by turning the metaphors into analogies: Juliet is like the sun with respect to her radiance; light under certain conditions is a wave but under other conditions a particle. These escape strategies don't work, however. It's like all those people, says Whitehead, who 'burned each other through [the] ages' as heretics in order to smooth away the rough edges in their moral beliefs (HL1, 21). By eliminating those who believe otherwise, they think those beliefs no longer possibilities and so blind themselves to what in fact continues to hover just beyond the edges of their sense of moral adequacy. Metaphors help with this sort of open-ended thinking because the essence of a metaphor is its unsettling ragged edges, by means of which, if we have the courage, we may venture into the beyond it discloses. Because they insist on the tension they create, because they refuse to burn the heretics or sanctify the believers, metaphors force us to face up to the limitations of our established ways of abstractive thinking.

## Niches

The creative tension of rough edges, of unsettling contradictions simultaneously affirmed, is ontological as well as epistemological. It applies not only to how we think but to how the world works, how it can be a continuum of atomic individuals. On the one hand, the world is composed of finite actualities, emergent momentary events, unique particulars that are 'mere flashes in the pan' (HL1, 140). Now this flash; now that one; now yet another. On the other hand, the world is marked by things that are not atomic, things that endure, that are systemic, stable, well-ordered complexes that persist over time. These enduring entities remain a unified whole even as they grow or shrink or oscillate, move about and pursue ends, adapt to changing conditions or disintegrate: electrons and molecules, organisms and environments, planets and galaxies. The world is fundamentally oxymoronic: an atomic continuum, a momentary stability. A reality, in short, that can only be expressed adequately with metaphors.

The scientific myth that can help us explore the incompatible features of this metaphysical metaphor of atomic durations is the one about the evolution of our cosmos. For in the beginning, there were the mere flashes, the momentary achievements: emerging and perishing in bursts of actualisation. Slowly, however, these kinds of entities became 'self-propagating', replicating themselves in successors that in turn did likewise, fashioning links between bursts that served as a 'basis for Endurance' (HL1, 140). These linkages made possible longer and more expansive forms of enduring that came eventually to comprise a stable 'Environment', an 'order of Nature' that augmented the likelihood of entities successfully enduring and propagating successors similar to themselves, 'an order growing in its achievement of Value by its achievement of Endurance' (HL1, 140). The stability of an environment is what made possible 'this evolution of <u>Similar Things</u>!': early on, an 'enormous number of Electrons' were propagated, and then protons, which 'evolve[d] into higher types', combining in complex ways that eventually resulted in ninety-two basic kinds of molecules, and after billions of years in stars with planets, and on some of those planets millions of species of organisms, and on our planet a very few 'types of <u>men</u>!' (HL1, 141).

Enduring entities are dependent on their environment and it on them. 'Each entity <u>takes account of</u> [its] surrounding field and vice versa . . . The Entity then isn't the Entity in itself alone but in interaction with [its] Environment' (HL1, 93). The atom, in other words, is not actually isolated. Its relationship to other atoms is not, as atomists from the Greeks to Newton contended, only external. Its relations are internal, such that 'apart from its Environment, Entity has lost individuality'. Abstract it from its 'particular Spatio-temporal root', from its 'anchorage in the Environment' (HL1, 115), and it has lost its uniqueness, lost that which makes it 'this' entity and not a place holder for any entity with similar characteristics. The emergence of a momentary atomic achievement depends on what its environment allows, what the stability of its context makes possible. Yet since that context is composed of enduring entities which are composed of momentary ones, and since its emergence is the achievement of value, then 'the whole of what there is in realization is things becoming of Value to one another' (HL1, 71).

Environmental stability is relative, not absolute, an 'Evolution toward Stability' through a slow 'modification' of the environment to the benefit of the kinds of things already adapted to it (HL1, 141). Were this the whole story, however, there could never be novelty because novelty requires instability – although it requires stability as well. To express this in a metaphysically appropriate metaphor, the becoming requires being which requires becoming. The emergence of new kinds 'takes place at an Edge between two Environments – between two fair stabilities with just enough Instability there' (HL1, 141–2) for novel things to be formed, yet with just enough stability for them once formed to reproduce sufficient others like themselves to comprise a flourishing new kind of thing. 'Creative Activity', says Whitehead, is 'not an independent Substance but <u>emergent</u> upon occasions from <u>possibilities</u> of relationship. – It emerges by reason of the niche which is there for it in the Universe' (HL1, 356). Niches, rough edges, or simply Edges: they are Whitehead's many names for pathways into the beyond. They are faults in the stable order of things through which new possibilities arise, opportunities for new variations, or versions, or even new kinds of achievement.

The relationship of two different kinds of stable environment with their differing kinds of stable entities creates a minor instability along their adjacent edges, a niche chipped away from the continuity of their shared boundary, a slight breach creating an openness that is neither one environment nor the other. A crack of some sort in the established order of things can offer an opportunity to escape the repression of unsuitable possibilities, to be free to achieve something different, to create a novel variant that until then had been impossible or even inconceivable. Or alternatively, it can offer an opportunity to escape any such variant if it is taken as a threat to the established order of things, avoiding it long enough to multiply enough to be able to fashion a suitable environment for itself. 'Translating the niche <u>qua</u> Potentiality to niche <u>qua</u> Actuality' requires the 'Creative Energy' of achieving definite novel individual embodiment of that energy (HL1, 361). It creates an environment 'with a patience for reiteration of that Character' (HL1, 362). By such inventiveness are new species of organism born, new kinds of actions taken, new physical or cultural worlds created, a Universe transformed.

## The Eternal

But how is all of this possible, the evolution from momentary atoms to enduring environments? We need, argues Whitehead, 'some <u>ground</u> of things by virtue of which they are what they are'. We need an 'eternal principle which carries with it the solution (from within!) of these questions. Something self-explanatory' (HL1, 55). A flash in the pan has no awareness of any flashes occurring before it or after it. It is the present emerging out of the resources available to it, without any awareness (in the generic sense of prehension) of the specific source of any resource or even any awareness that there are such things as sources. Self-propagation, however, requires a sense of there being the possibility of more than present achievement, namely a repeat of that kind of achievement. It is not the particular flash-in-the-pan fact that recurs, because it's not possible that what is uniquely this determinate moment can reoccur. Rather, it is the kind of fact that recurs, a fact similar to the achieved fact, a successor very much like itself. This entails an efficacy of generalities: the constitutive functioning of moments as a kind, of which the present emerging moment is an instance. Achievements as a kind must be possible, moments as members of a sequence of instances of a kind. 'Wherever you get anything general you've got something that lies beyond [any] particular occasion' (HL1, 57). There must be something else beyond the temporal now and the particular fact therein achieved, beyond what come to be and perish, that makes possible their transformation into kinds and thereby environments and worlds. When you talk of such a reality, 'you're essentially presupposing the Eternal' (HL1, 57).

The reason Whitehead calls this source of generality 'the Eternal' has to do with what its nature must be in order to carry out its function. It cannot be an entity or occasion, nor an environment of interlocking enduring things, because such things are finite, bounded by a particular location at a particular time, no matter how extensive or enduring. Whereas what is needed is something that is a feature of every emergent occasion and hence every enduring complexity. Something that is 'The "Static Basis" which gives the character to the process of Realization' because found in all occasions. 'We can know nothing which is not embodied in the occasion that we are apprehending', but what we see that is general 'in making that occasion what it is . . . must turn up in any other occasion what is relevant to that one'. If an occasion 'is in any way connected with' another occasion, 'then the Eternal of the one must be [the] Eternal of the other' (HL1, 58). Furthermore, emerging entities are not points at instants but moments with spatial and temporal volume. Because this is so, they can be organised into systems that sustain a pattern of value with spatial breadth and temporal duration adequate enough to support the coming to be and perishing of those momentary components. But the Ground that makes it possible for particular things to emerge and for patterns of their achievements to form and endure cannot be spatio-temporal because it is what they presuppose. The Eternal is therefore not immortal or everlasting, not 'always enduring but something out of Space and Time' (HL1, 59).

Obviously, the only way 'The Eternal' can be characterised is metaphorically – appropriately so, given Whitehead's insistence that all genuinely metaphysical statements are metaphors. 'Always enduring' but 'out of Space and Time' is the simultaneous affirmation of contradictories, for to endure is to be essentially temporal, but to be eternal is essentially not to be temporal. Let's embrace this metaphor, refusing to rush to any satisfying harmonisation of its oxymoronic meaning, rubbing close to its rough edges and seeing where that leads us.

The Ground of the momentary events that comprise the world must be a general rather than a specific reality if it is to make them relevant to each other. It must be omnipresent if the world is to be one cosmos, an interdependent unity of finite components. But how does this account for the emergence of stable systems, of a cosmic environment, an order of nature characterised by long-enduring laws? Whitehead's answer is that how the Eternal functions is by 'Conditioning the processional Realization. To condition is to impose limitation', which 'means essentially the reference to alternatives inherent in that particular occasion of Realization' (HL1, 61). Alternatives are possibilities realisable on a given occasion, and what is not realisable on that occasion is, for that occasion, impossible. 'All reference to Possibility is a reference to some ground which is in the Occasion but which is not occasional – Same holds for Impossibility' (HL1, 60).

Emergent moments are not arbitrary achievements, random possibilities realised while others are ignored. Such a helter-skelter process would not be processive; it would be chaotic, not cosmic. For there to be an ordered process of coming to be and perishing, there must be a limit on any nascent occasion to what is possible for it, within the confines of which a unique new moment can be made. 'The how of limitation is the Eternal. How fact does come before us in a plurally monadic form.' The procession of the world is plurally monadic because the Eternal limits what is possible but does not determine what can be done with those possibilities that remain. 'The "how" of limitation' is 'also the transcendence of limitation' (HL1, 60). The moment made is self-made within constraints inherent in its situation. 'Each [occasion] emerges in respect to its own grounds' (HL1, 93). What Whitehead will later call the Creative Advance is 'not managed from Without by a stage-manager' but is 'all-inclusive/self-explanatory'. 'It embodies in itself its own conditions', includes its own 'motive which can therefore be conceived as the reason for the passing, and its "How"' (HL1, 92).

The Eternal is not a stage-manager because it is not an agent. Doing something is an action, a behaviour, which involves orientation towards realising a possibility. For Whitehead, telic behaviour is a feature not only of any organism but of any entity whatsoever. To be is to have been made, and making is a process directed by an agent towards the realisation of a possible outcome. The Eternal is the Ground of created things, but not their creator. Whitehead's Eternal is not a Divine Creator, not a Demiurge, not even the God of *Process and Reality*, all of which are agents shaping the world as best they can towards ends they envision. But if the Eternal cannot choose the possibilities that are to be available for what emerges each moment, how does it function? The Eternal limits not by choosing but by disclosing, and what is available for disclosure yet not within the inherit capacities of an emerging moment is the fact of what has proceeded it, the context of the prior achievements that comprise its environment – that is, its past.

An event occurs, and then is no more, but if what has passed away were simply gone, then there would be no limits to what in the emerging moment was possible. So the limitation of possibilities is necessary to there being a cosmos, and therefore it must be the case that what perishes does not pass away. And, Whitehead insists, our intuitions confirm this ontological fact, for we all have a 'Sense of Intrinsic permanence of the Value that has been achieved' (HL1, 72). Whitehead references Keats, the last stanza of 'Eve of St. Agnus' which begins:

> And they are gone: aye, ages long ago
> Those lovers fled away into the storm.

Gone, yes, but not forgotten. Fled away, yet passionately remembered, memories always there to be recalled. 'The irrevocable Past as yet the relevant past' (HL1, 72). So how the Eternal shapes the course of things without being an agent is as the receptacle for actualities that were present in their moment of achievement but are now no longer present. Their actuality is nonetheless relevant to their successors because retained by the Eternal, included in the emerging of new actualities as limitations on what could possibly emerge. 'Every definite occasion points beyond itself by enriching the Eternal' (HL1, 74), thus taking 'its place as an eternal truth' (HL1, 75). The truth of what is past, the value of definite achievement, is a fact that cannot be avoided, that must be taken account of. The heritage of the new is the irrevocable condition for what it can become. It is a constraint, but in the form of a structure. A limit is not only a barrier eliminating opportunities for what might be realised; it is also a channel affording opportunities previously not possible. The pathway through a dense forest constrains us to walk between narrow boundaries, but those constraints offer us a way to reach a destination that otherwise would not be possible. 'A Structure is a definite limitation amid an unbounded . . . ocean of possibilities.' It's the shape of the process by which something can be realised – its framework liberating by limiting. It's the 'How' of emergence, the mode of 'becoming in this particular and definitive way!' (HL1, 91).

Whitehead has been elaborating a concept of the Eternal as a timeless ground necessary for a world where coming to be and perishing can lead to stable environments capable of supporting enduring forms of achievement, including limited forms of novel achievement that make possible the stabilisation of some of those novelties, the emergence of different enduring forms of achievement. He calls this ground 'The Eternal' because it is timeless and is thus the obvious contradictory of whatever is temporal and therefore changing. But Whitehead is also arguing that the Eternal changes and that it does so because of what is temporal. The Eternal cannot change on its own initiative, but because of the temporal. Not because of the temporal as such, but because of each particular temporal individual's influence. 'Value as shaped and particularized upon any finite occasion is the Eternal captured by the finite. But that's all the Eternal can do: – to become so captured' (HL1, 71), because only agents can act and only actual entities can be agents. 'Emergent Value is "The Capture of the Eternal" – What has been is an eternal fact that nothing can blot out', but it is an eternal fact 'held and captured there and now' by a temporal fact in the making (HL1, 87).

But how can what perishes change what is not perishable? By perishing, says Whitehead. Because 'as the Eternal is now for us the total nature of the past belongs to it' (HL1, 74), and so the Eternal gets altered because it is constantly enriched by new facts. The total nature of the past changes each moment it is augmented by a present achievement perishing, so the conditions by which the Eternal limits the emerging present are constantly changed by the specific achievements of its predecessors. When we remember some past event, the truth of what it once was influences our remembering, changing our general sense of the past because of its particular relevance. As with memory so with all else: 'Each fact of realization takes its place as an eternal truth' that influences whatever happens, altering in some way the character of its influence. Indeed, the 'very laws of Nature are relevant to the past', and so altered under its influence (HL1, 75).

Whitehead then draws an even more radical conclusion: 'The eternal is nothing but the Unity of its limitations' (HL1, 76). Truth is fundamentally about realisation, the truth of a fact is its realisation, the eternal truth of this realised fact is its alteration of the Eternal. In short, change in the Eternal is the impact on it of realised particular fact. But furthermore, because a truth is a particular realisation, the value achievement of an atomic fact, the How of its realisation is 'always a <u>particularized</u> How – having relevance to the particular' (HL1, 87). The character of the Eternal is thus always particular to the current situation, always changing in specific ways as specific new realisations become specific new eternal facts. These are not general changes, but they are context-sensitive, always located within an environment because of which their influence can endure, and thereby contribute to the preservation and growth of temporal value.

A radical consequence of this radical claim is that change is boundless. 'As Nature arose, it may decay.' We need to recognise the possibility, says Whitehead, of 'an Evolution of the very order of Nature', that the 'Spatio-temporal system and the Sensibles' that comprise the 'static ground of being in <u>this</u> order of Evolution', may be the 'actual product of other orders of Evolution' (HL1, 136). 'Cosmology is itself an issue from something else' (HL1, 461). This is not to imagine some kind of linear progression originating at 'a time before there was time – which is nonsense' (HL1, 138). We cannot start the evolution of the Cosmic Order from some ex nihilo 'arbitrary starting point' or from some aboriginal 'arbitrarily given stuff' (HL1, 136). Instead, we need to think in terms of expansions. 'The Cosmic Order presupposes an Expansion which stands behind (beyond) it.' But not simply one expansion. There are '<u>various</u> stages' of expansion such that our 'Cosmological Stage presupposes other stages that provide [the] very ground of <u>Becoming</u> for [the] Cosmological stage' (HL1, 136). Whitehead knows he is going beyond what can be observed, but 'not beyond what has been found necessarily . . . to give any rational account of Cosmological order' (HL1, 136). Metaphysicians are too apt to embrace a 'World-Elephant-Tortoise philosophy', but we 'mustn't stop with [the] Tortoise just because [our] brain doesn't want to go further' (HL1, 143). Reality is an evolutionary process, without beginning and without end.

What is temporal captures the Eternal, and as completed fact becomes itself eternal, thereby changing the Eternal. The eternal is temporal and the temporal eternal. Having said these things, and drawing a little diagram of how it works, Whitehead notes that '<u>this</u> is a <u>myth</u> too. – drawn on black board' (HL1, 87). We can see why metaphors are so important for metaphysics, for thinking creatively and hence for understanding a world restlessly changing, inherently evolutionary. For both metaphors and worlds create instability, by virtue of which new possibilities emerge that give rise to novel achievements – achievements initially individual but eventually collective, achievements initially a threat to the stability they eventually secure by altering it. A metaphor is a paradox, a cognitive contradiction held together because of the fresh possibilities it discloses, and thereby fosters. The cosmos is an ontological paradox, a constant clash of conflicting actual stabilities that foster the fresh possibilities from which is fashioned the creative advance that makes our actual cosmos an ongoing adventure. 'What an extraordinarily odd fact definiteness of achievement is', exclaims Whitehead (HL1, 361): a particular individual, momentary or enduring, emergent from a particular contextual disunity without which it could not be; a collective whole, cosmic or cultural, emergent from a radical plurality of incompatible particulars, without which it could not be. No wonder only metaphors can express metaphysical truths adequately.

## The Shadow of Truth

I will end my essay by examining a particular phrase that Whitehead uses in two of his November lectures, but never explicates: the 'shadow of truth'. I think it gives us a crucial insight into Whitehead's metaphysics, exposing a niche that opens that metaphysics to new and enhancing possibilities. 'The shadow of truth' is, of course, a metaphor; and like any metaphor it harbours a destabilising contradiction. Shadows are created by opaque objects intercepting a field of light, leaving a dark area behind them in an outline of their shape. A shadow is an absence. Truth is a primary feature of any fact, a feature without which it is not fact, without which it has no intrinsic value. Truth is a presence. Whitehead's metaphor says that this absence is a presence, because it makes a difference for what has presence, and in doing so makes a difference for what is absent because yet only possible.

At first glance, Whitehead's statements about the shadow of truth are like those we have already considered. Truth is about the process of making a unique fact. The truth of that fact is its realisation, how its possibilities have issued in a particularised moment, how a specific actual matter-of-fact has been achieved. The Past is the irrevocable totality of those facts which, because of features of the Eternal ingredient in each new process of making, limit its possible outcomes. In this sense the Truth which is the Past is the shadow that falls on the emerging present, shaping its particularity, and that likewise falls on the Eternal, shaping its character also. 'The shadow of truth' is a metaphor, however, and metaphors have difficulty holding their concepts firmly within boundaries. Unintended new possibilities keep bubbling up. The interpretation I will sketch explores one of those possibilities.

Whitehead uses the phrase 'shadow of truth' on three occasions. The first time is eye-opening. After stating that 'every definite occasion points beyond itself by enriching the Eternal', he adds that this involves 'enrichment of realm of "Existents" (= "Platonic Ideas")', which is an 'Essential attribute of [the] Eternal' (HL1, 74). The whole realm of ideas 'itself alters in its reference to the particular occasions as they flow by. How it gets altered: – the shadow of truth falls on it . . . and affects it' (HL1, 74–5). What is meant by 'affecting' is clarified: 'The shadow of truth falls on the ideas (makes them particular – in enriched envisagement), & as such are taken up into memory' (HL1, 77). Truth is a matter of realisation, so it is definite fully realised occasions that in their perishing cast a shadow of the truth of their reality on the realm of ideas, on the realm of the totality of possibilities for realisation, altering some of those possibilities by making them no longer merely generic but rather particular envisagements. That's *how* the Past influences the Present: by the shadow of prior achievements transforming pure possibilities into relevant ones by particularising them. The particularisation of a possibility narrows its scope, limits it to a possibility that is possible in the specific context of a newly emerging successor occasion.

Almost all pure possibilities are impossible for the emerging entity, given the massive constraint imposed by its widespread and long-enduring stable environment. But there are always a few possibilities about which that environment, as Whitehead puts it, will be patient. How the shadow functions is by tailoring those few possibilities to the entity's particular context, sharpening them into opportunities for realisation. The particularisation of a possibility gives it value for the emerging occasion, a way by which to unify its myriad constraints and options. By valuing that particularised possibility and further particularising it, or by disvaluing or even eliminating it, and similarly for all other real possibilities and impossibilities, the emergent thereby achieves realisation as a fact. The final integration of fixed limitations and viable possibilities is the occasion's work, but the shadow of things fled away into the storm heightens the value of certain possibilities rather than others, suggesting ways by which that integration might be achieved.

Whitehead's second use of 'shadow of truth' emphasises its particularising function: 'The process of Realization is a process of Garnering in. You have "The Shadow of Truth". Therefore the How is always a particularized How' (HL1, 87) resulting in 'a particularized value' (HL1, 89). The shadow of truth is 'how' the constraints and opportunities are garnered in, by which the results of prior realisation are able to afford a transition to new realisation. It is because of the shadow cast by the fading past that the transition is effected. A truth is always particular; it is what a fact is. The term 'truth' can also be an abstraction, a useful way to generalise, to refer to multiple particular truths with respect to some common feature. Concretely, however, a truth is always a specific fact and its shadow is therefore always particular. What influences the emergence of a novel occasion is not The Past, understood generically as the totality of things gone, ages long ago. What influences its emergence is each of a number of particular achieved occasions contiguous to it. Yet not those occasions, for they have perished, but rather the particular shadows they cast, that confront the nascent succeeding moment with what it must accept, with what it can alter, and with the value of each altering. The past occasions and all that they have achieved are what cannot be altered. The niches among them are what point a way to some possible alterings in their successors. The shadows the past occasions cast are what provide their nascent successors with the information they require to become actual occasions. And in turn, they in their own perishing will cast new particular shadows influencing their successors' emergence into an already different world.

A past occasion has its own past, of course. The conditions its shadow imposed on each of its nascent immediate successors were shaped by the shadows its immediate predecessors imposed on it, and similarly for the predecessors of those predecessors, ad infinitum. Much like, at the macro level, as we influence our children, so our parents influenced us, and so they were influenced by their parents, and so on back generation after generation. Each moment perishes and is no more, but what it became in becoming that moment influences in some way its successors. It is not only its vital presence that perishes, but also most of the content of that presence. Its shadow is simply an aspect of what it had become, a nudge or a suggestion. This aspect usually grows more and more vague as its influence becomes increasingly indirect, an aspect of an aspect of an aspect. That young couple we once knew (or were) are still fondly recalled, but they themselves have fled away into the storm, gone forever, even their importance for us obscured by the swirling ravages of change.

Whitehead calls this sequential transmission of influence a 'strain of control'. My examples have been of thin sequences, lacking any similar parallel sequences, as though I was the only one my grandmother influenced, the only one remembering the young couple. Whenever my siblings and I recall something our grandmother did or said, the impact of her life increases. The impact of the young unnamed couple is considerable thanks to Keats's poem. The impact of George Washington much greater, that of Jesus or Mohamed even more so. The impact of trillions of momentary achievements replicating themselves and the patterns of influence they have inherited over millennia and across vast spaces has an impact that leaves no room for their successors to do more than pass on what they have received. Although bacteria mutate, species evolve, mountains push up and wear down, stars are born and disintegrate, and modes of cosmos are supplanted, due to the accumulation of opportune niches in the widespread intransigence. An event of any sort is a 'pattern of aspects. And this pattern is nothing but the aspect in this event of the mutual determination of Events'. An event 'is an essential unity of a pattern of Aspects and these <u>include</u> "Aspect of Control" – mutual determination of events' (HL1, 168). 'Science is the study of point of view (side) of control' (HL1, 471), of the strains of aspect inheritance that create the continuities, the stable patterns, we count on, 'just that connection of Events on which our whole life is based' (HL1, 168). Whitehead uses a number of times the same concrete example of a 'school-boy catching a cricket-ball in an important game' (HL1, 427). The boy sees the ball batted into the air, and runs towards the point where he predicts he will need to be in order to catch it. The ball he sees includes 'data appearing as issuing from a strain of control', the 'Perceptual object' (HL1, 325), and the pattern of that data is a parabola that in his mind's eye guides him to the crucial location at the proper time.

'Activity . . . is what makes process of realization possible', and therefore we should pay attention to 'Entities discerned as setting the conditions satisfied by concrete procession of reality itself'. That is, we should look for 'strains of self-conditioning process, . . . strain[s] of conditioning (of control)', which involve 'an insistent localization of control' (HL1, 31). I take 'self-conditioning' to mean the strains conditioning the process of the realisation 'of reality itself': the momentary entities, the actual occasions, that come to be and perish. The evolution from flashes in the pan to massive strains of the environmental stability necessary for both the flourishing of enduring entities and for continuing diversity in such entities is the work of those entities themselves, from the very simple to the very complex. The ontology of our cosmos is built up from a base of particular moments of achievement, without an underlying primary ground or overarching primary control.

Whitehead's third reference to the shadow of truth widens the horizon of relevance from the procession of achievements in our particular cosmos to any and all other modes of cosmos. For the 'Order of Nature is in a sense a <u>particular</u> entity; and defines <u>particular</u> facts' (HL1, 144). It is that Order, that systematic framework for endurance and change, that is key to a cosmos, its 'particular limitation in this particularity of being realized'. It is the mode of a particular cosmos's realisation, therefore 'having the processional, transitional character which relates it to [a] <u>wider</u> community of modes' (HL1, 144). The ordering framework for our mode of cosmos is the three dimensions of space and the dimension of time. Whitehead speculates about what there might be in our cosmos that points beyond it to something else, something that might comprise the defining character of another mode of cosmos. He mentions 'those data of Rationality which insistently refuse to put [them]selves under spatio-temporal guise (Arithmetic; Logic; Minds themselves)' (HL1, 145). There is nothing contingent about the fact that $2 + 2 = 4$, that if p is true and q is true then p & q is true, and that an idea exists independently of any time when or place where it is thought. Because they are not plausibly reducible to actualities defined by a physical location, it can be argued that they 'are emergent entities that have their roots in a wider cosmos, and simply their aspects in the [our] order of nature' (HL1, 147).

Thus, not only can we theorise abstractly about modes of cosmos other than our own, with their distinctive orders of nature, but some of those 'potentialities for the order of nature have already on them the shadow of actuality of another cosmos' (HL1, 147). What is strikingly different in what Whitehead is saying here is that modes of cosmos other than our own actually exist, and we are aware of them because the shadow of their actuality can be found in entities in our cosmos that are not actual, in the sense of being particular achievements that come to be and perish. Whitehead also mentions, referencing Bergson's *Matter and Memory*, 'the idea of S̲p̲i̲r̲i̲t̲' (HL1, 144).

These three uses of the metaphor of the shadow of truth have implications for how we can interpret Whitehead's metaphysics, both as it is expressed in his 1924–25 Harvard lectures and as he formulates it in *Process and Reality*. The Past was posited by Whitehead as a mode of being so that past entities could have the ontological standing that seemed needed for them to have the impact they clearly have. They must *be* in some sense, even though they have perished as actual beings. But this Past, with its ever-changing content, then needs to be somewhere from which it can exert an influence. Whitehead's solution is to ground it in an Eternal receptacle, a reality that is not itself temporal but is able to sustain the things of the past, and to do so in a way that makes it possible for them to have an impact, to perish and yet to live forevermore. Such a Past is an Everlasting Past in contrast to an Ephemeral Present, a Past retained for ever and ever in the Eternal, whereas actual present achievements are momentary flashes, here and gone, their subsequent sequential nature a feature not of themselves but of the Past to which they are transported.

The temporality of things, the fact that the world is composed of momentary achievements that perish and are no more, is lost, replaced by a reality the endurance of which is not a contingent achievement but an ontological necessity, the contingent achievements of actual occasions everlastingly preserved. So moments are not moments but instead elements of what is everlasting, and so become themselves everlasting. Nor is eternity eternal but instead forever changing, changing not temporally but timelessly. Despite my attempt to interpret these contradictories as metaphysical metaphors, rich in interpretive possibilities, I have to conclude they are not. Whitehead's ontology of an everlasting past grounded in the eternal is simply incoherent. And quite unnecessary.

We should understand The Past as an abstraction, a useful bit of mythmaking that we ought not fallaciously think concrete. There is no actual past, it has no being. All facts, all things that are true, come to be and, realised, perish and are no more. But as each vanishes into the storm, its shadow is cast on newly concrescing facts in the form of particularised conditions influencing but not fully determining what they can realise. That influence is not solely on its immediate successors, for it in turn becomes, strongly or faintly, a feature of the shadows its successors cast on their successors. To understand our cosmos metaphysically as through and through contingent, because composed in all its complexity and evolving stability of momentary events, is to do what I thought Whitehead said we should: to take time seriously.

Whitehead eventually dispenses with The Eternal, replacing it in *Process and Reality* with God. God's Primordial Nature functions as the receptacle for pure possibilities, which he now calls eternal objects, and also as the agency needed to tailor those possibilities to the specific situational constraints confronting concrescing actual occasions. These tailored possibilities comprise the options from which each occasion selects its initial aim, by means of which it shapes the physical and conceptual content of its direct prehension of the predecessors comprising its past. God's Consequent Nature is the receptacle for the Past, for the achievements of past actualities, but here also as the agency that orders them valuationally so that they can be used to influence their successors over the long run. So the Eternal is divided into two components – an Eternal aspect that houses all possibilities, and an Everlasting aspect that houses all actualities. The Eternal aspect, rather than the Past, is the agency for shaping pure possibilities into initial aim options; the Everlasting aspect is the agency for translating the achievements of the past into resources for devising better aims and effecting better ends. No such transcendental receptacle and agency is needed, however, if the shadows cast by perishing occasions can provide the requisite relevant possibilities and firm necessities, each with their relative value, to account for the creative advance.

## Concluding Summary

The take-aways from this chapter are these. Whitehead in 1924–25 has a robust notion of internal relations as fundamental to the world we experience. Such a world is too interwoven to be intelligible except by the use of abstract surrogates, by leaving a lot out in order to exhibit a few important things. Some of these abstractions, such as those developed by modern science, have, despite their virtues, one great fault: the fallacy of misplaced concreteness.

Diagrams and myths, hypotheses and stories, analogies and metaphors, are all excellent ways to avoid this fallacy because they are obviously not concrete, obviously incomplete.

Appropriately, this essay is no more than a silly sketch, a verbal diagram of what I think Whitehead was arguing. I think Whitehead would agree that metaphors are an especially useful mode of abstraction, because they force a reader beyond what they say, due to their unstable unification of systemic incompatibles. I illustrated this claim with Whitehead's metaphor 'the shadow of truth', developing one of the possibilities it bubbled up into the suggestion of a worldview that finds no need for the two ontological realities which in 1924–25 he thought central: The Past and The Eternal. By indicating how the coming to be and perishing of interdependent fact-events provides a fully adequate basis for a mode of Whiteheadian process metaphysics, I have been spinning a story about how not only our world but all there is and can ever be is intractably temporal. It is a story that finds strong roots in Whitehead's first year lectures at Harvard, including the resources for purging his ideas of the nontemporal realities of a God both eternal and everlasting, and of an everlasting past – ideas that at that time he thought crucial.

## Bibliography

Bogaard, Paul and Jason Bell (eds), *The Harvard Lectures of Alfred North Whitehead, 1924–1925: Philosophical Presuppositions of Science* (Edinburgh: Edinburgh University Press, 2017).

# 15

# How 'Eternity' Got 'Thrown Forward' Into 'Perishing'

*Jude Jones*

Eternity haunts the Harvard lectures of 1924–25. Sometimes as the spectre of Spinozistic substance, sometimes as a vague indication of the most beyond of 'beyonds' that might lurk behind what is 'here', Eternity seems never to have been far from Whitehead's mind in his seminars, and hovers as an incompletely formed idea, or as an idea that gestures towards a completeness that insinuates itself in every effort to conceptualise things holistically. And this manifests one of Whitehead's explicit claims, as he works through his thought process with his students, which is that from the humblest gesture of indication, through the most practicable inductive reasoning, along the shores of memory, and in the aspirations of metaphysical speculation, Eternity is implicit in most of our mental operations (HL1, 60).[1] These lectures, which simultaneously lay out the conditions of scientific/philosophical explanation and the facts of perceptual experience from which such explanation might begin, welcome the Eternal into their wanderings as their logical ally and their necessary Muse.

Along with Eternity, the other 'spectre' in these lectures for me is the notion of 'Superject'. As noted in Bogaard's 'Introduction' to the Harvard lectures, it is not the 'subject' but the 'superject' that is introduced as one of the few key novel concepts as Whitehead deepens his commitment to systematic metaphysical explanation (HL1, xliv). While the linguistic dominance of the 'subject' as seat of concrescence did unfortunately come to shape the discussion of becoming in *Process and Reality*, even as Whitehead warns us that it is always an abbreviation for the subject-superject construction (PR, 88, 222), it is almost always as 'superject' that events or things realised in process are referenced here in the early seminars.

In one lecture we meet the claim that 'The concrete fact is eternal substance emerging in a plurality of superjects' (HL1, 77–78) and that the Superject 'is in itself an envisaging Eternal' (HL1, 76). So the connection between the spectres of Eternity and Superject is very tight. Alluding to the metaphor of 'throwing forward' that Whitehead uses when addressing the emergent achievements of process as they 'impress' themselves on other processes, I want to make some suggestions about how the notion of 'Eternity' that haunts these lectures is inflected or 'thrown forward' into the doctrine of 'perishing' that might be said to haunt the mature metaphysics of *Process and Reality*. Recently I've been considering the implications of a strong reading of 'perishing' for my approach to interpreting Whiteheadian actualities as 'ecstatic intensities' that pervade process, since on the ecstatic reading one has to confront the question of what, in terms of the satisfied occasion, 'does not remain' in its superjective ecstatic self-insinuation in subsequent entities; that something must *not* remain seems essential to avoiding a processive version of a block universe or extreme monism, and so the type of 'perishing' Whitehead ascribes to the temporal reality of occasions must be taken seriously. But more fundamentally than this, an understanding of the very notion of 'process' requires – both systematically and in the application of the system to experience – consideration of notions involving endings, closures, loss and other factors of radical contingency. So my goal will be to connect Eternity and Perishing in part through the mediation of the concept of the ecstatic Superject, as it seems to me that some of the work that Eternity does in these lectures actually helps us understand what 'perishing' means in the later work, and vice versa. I will end with some reflections on finitude and contingency suggested by the conceptual intersection of Eternity and Perishing.

As noted a moment ago, Whitehead seems to have been describing the emergent Superject as one of the plurality of such by which 'eternal substance' attains actuality, and that the Superject is, as Bell reports, 'itself an envisaging eternal' (HL1, 76). In the lectures in which Eternal Substance is discussed in this way, Whitehead is in many respects prefiguring elements of the primordial nature of God, which is the fundamental actuality whose inner dynamic is the envisagement of forms of potentiality indifferently relevant to *all* processes of becoming, and *particularly* relevant in *particular ways* to specific instances of becoming (as they arise) by way of 'subjective aim' (PR, 85), or as tantalisingly framed in these lectures, as a 'niche' arises for them (HL1, 359–60). In other (though of course not unrelated) respects he is describing aspects of what would become the 'substantial activity' of *Science and the Modern World*, the notion that captured what was required of the 'internal relatedness' that was of the essence of any emergent organism in nature: 'The event is what it is, by reason of the unification in itself of a multiplicity of relationships' (SMW, 123), and the underlying activity is fundamentally activity towards individuation in such events as, we can say with the help of these lectures, a 'niche' arises for such individuations. There is also of course the allusion to what will become the role of 'eternal objects' that are forms of definiteness in abstraction from their temporal realisation in the finite organisms of actualising processes. In this sense Eternality is met in these lectures as that which is not, from one perspective, temporally real but is a condition of all such realisation by way of modes of potential definiteness of form, and which nonetheless has no actuality unless thus realised (cf. HL1, 59). I want to acknowledge these important prefigurings in order to create a broad intellectual context for readers, and to acknowledge that Whitehead's purposes are not limited to those on which I wish to concentrate. But having said this, I now pass on to other aspects of the description of the Eternal that are more germane to my present speculative purposes.

Despite being 'the Ground exhibited in every Occasion of Realisation' or 'the Substance of which the Occasion is a limited affection or the Substance which requires all occasions' in a dynamic (i.e. non-passive) sense (HL1, 59),[2] the Eternal that is met with in these lectures is capable of enhancement and enrichment. This is a curious Eternal indeed: it is tolerant of enrichment by individual events that are realised in time, and all the more so insofar as Whitehead claims that Occasions are *necessary* to it. In Lecture 19 as reported by Bell we find: 'The general how of Becoming is "the Eternal". But value as shaped and particularised upon any finite occasion is the Eternal captured by the finite. But that's all the Eternal can do:– to become so captured. The Eternal as captured by and in the "Impress" – the Impress is then also a substance:– the Eternal particularized in this finite mode' (HL1, 71). 'Impress' seems here to be a prototype for 'feeling', a way to designate the internal relations by which things make a difference to one another existentially and valuatively, and as Bogaard notes, this verbiage eventually does give way to the language of 'prehension' as the lectures develop (HL1, xliv). As relationships among actualities are achieved, the Eternal is 'captured' and 'particularized' as having grounded such relational potential, but it is also somehow expanded. In a way that helps underscore Whitehead's departure from Spinoza in terms of the passivity the lectures attribute to the Eternal, in a subsequent discussion of these moments of impress/relational becoming, Bell notes:

> It's individuality shown as a definite enrichment of the Eternal. All the "Static" has to take account of what "happens." The "Eternal" is particularized into particular occasions. Enters into occasions with access of Value owing to definite station of that occurrence within the whole. That

condition of things which is enriched by whole Past. The past transitory emerges into permanent Value – part of static condition of all subsequent occasions. (HL1, 74)

The entire past is, for any occasion, part of the standing condition of valuative potential (what he refers to in this quote as the 'Static') out of which that occasion will emerge. In other words, for any occasion, the 'Eternal' as expressing value potentials includes not only abstract forms of possibility but also the specific, located realised Value (with a 'definite station') in every occasion that has realised Eternity in specific form already. Eternity's role as condition of value is enhanced by the realisation of value in particular, non-eternal things or processes which nonetheless have standing value as expressions of and relations to that Eternal. One can almost hear the refrain, 'The many become one, and are increased by one' (PR, 21) in this description of enhanced eternity.

What interests me in this discussion is that what this enhancement means is that each individual realisation does not simply express Value achieved but is itself, as already quoted, a bit of 'envisaging Eternal'. Envisaging seems to be the fundamental activity of valuation in the metaphysical scheme as here described, and it certainly retains that meaning in the mature system (though it is not so openly applied to entities which are rather described as potentials via 'objective immortality' and the like). To envisage is most basically to 'take account of' in these lectures (HL1, 54), but in the sense conveyed by its association with the Eternal substance/activity, it is the taking account of that points always forwards, towards value to be achieved in others, and away from definitive location and the 'definite station' of what already is. It is what is later described as being a 'lure for feeling' that draws any entity into its process of self-realisation that issues in the superject (PR, 85).

At this point I should briefly sketch the sense of ecstatic intensity that I have developed elsewhere,[3] as I think what Whitehead is describing in these lectures in terms of the enhancement of the Eternal by individuated value achievement does in fact endorse the ecstatic reading of Whitehead's ontology of individuals. As we know, the 'subjective aim' of any entity is at intensity of feeling in the present and in the relevant future (PR, 27). The internal telic growth of the entity is a present-and-future-directed appropriation of the past and of the possible as relevant to that present-future construction, and the appropriation of the past happens only because a direction into the future has become possible. On my view this means that in some sense the 'individuality' and 'identity' of any entity includes any locus of becoming in which its intensive unity of feeling might be or is realised, fully or in part. Since the emergent superject is what is actually aimed at in the subjective immediacy of feeling (PR, 69, 241), there is no reason to think that a 'subject' is not present just because its quantum of temporalising concrescence is completed. To locate the activity or agency of an entity exclusively in its subjective process of becoming in *its* present is fairly common in describing the model of process Whitehead lays out, but I find such a view hard to describe as a model of 'internal relatedness', and much more troublingly akin to the fallacy of 'simple location' that the philosophy of organism was designed to undo.[4] Preoccupation with merely present subjective process is a blinding truncation of the subject-superject structure of actuality whereby things are really, and not merely virtually or ideally, connected (i.e. are present *in* other things) via their repetition of intensive patterns of feeling. I call my reading of Whitehead's ontology an 'ecstatic interpretation' despite the fact that no such terminology appears in his texts in order to purge the description of the real actuality of a thing as belonging only to its subjective standpoint of concrescence, as if that meant anything at all in abstraction from all the other standpoints of realisation that might, or which eventually do, take account of that standpoint of feeling. In place of the model of exclusive actuality-location as merely 'present', I think a model of 'multiple effective location' across temporal modes better captures the basically intensive structure of reality as vibratory (PR, 163) and genuinely relational feeling-activity. The language of ecstasis, in the sense of something existing in multiple non-collapsing, non-reducible and non-totalisable temporal modes[5] – existing outside of itself, in other words, which of course deliberately strains but also redefines the very notion of 'itself' – captures the sense in which a given entity is wherever and to whatever extent its unity of feeling is operating as lure or as realised anew in transcendent process. An entity in its individual activity of being literally, and not just formally or figuratively, 'pervades the continuum' (PR, 67) of other entities that can and do 'take account of it' in manners influenced by its 'taking account of' other things, and so forth. In the language of these lectures inventing Whitehead's view of how value grows, an entity is an 'envisaging' implicated in all subsequent envisagings.[6]

An ecstatic view in all but name seems to be what is developing in the Harvard lectures. In Heath's notes covering Whitehead's discussion of the 'capture of the eternal by some passing circumstance', which capture 'enriches the eternal', we find the following:

The eternal is nothing but the eternal <u>how</u> of its limitations. There is not one eternal substance – its unity is the organic unity of its limitations. The plurality of individuals is an eternal either (?) but which is of its very essence . . . Concrete fact is the eternal Subject emerging with a plurality of Superjects. That which emerges is a realization of particularized fusion & valuation from determination. (HL1, 447)

It is important to point out the intriguing fact that in the broader context of this quote Whitehead is carefully distinguishing the kind of Eternity-enhancing individuation of the Superject from the notion of 'Endurance' which is 'entirely different from eternality' (HL1, 447; also HL1, 59; PR, 77). Endurance is the sense of spatio-temporally spread definiteness that constitutes the possibility of the lasting things of ordinary experience. What 'Eternality' captures is not the enduring profile of achieved value as spread out in some of our apprehensions of a space-time of 'things', but the *activity of envisaging* values. The activity of envisaging (of how things may be or are to be felt together) is associated with Eternality rather than with Endurance. The Superjects enhance the Eternal by adding to the range and intensity of potential for feeling in process beyond any act of realisation – by adding to envisaging as such as the evaluative energy of process. It is in this sense that the 'Superject *is in itself* an envisaging Eternal' (HL1, 76, emphasis added). The emphasis is not on static endurance but on contribution to active, creative possibilities for fresh valuations. And the literal sense of superjects reappearing *as themselves* in other things in the ecstatic interpretation seems to be hinted at here: 'Every definite occasion points beyond itself by enriching the Eternal – the very ground of Becoming. – Here the essential distinction between Past and Future. The Past is relevant to us by how the Eternal has been enriched by those occasions with reference to us here. So the Individuality of an occasion is in one sense eternal' (HL1, 74). If we take this assertion of Individuality as 'in one sense eternal', we have to give up any attachment to a notion of atomic individuation as meaning some sort of simplistic numerical oneness located exclusively in anything like a simply located subjective process of concrescence that somehow ceases to be upon satisfaction, as we also surrender any static version of Eternality as well. Instead of measuring an entity's becoming by its non-endurance, which nonetheless figures it as virtually and impossibly enduring in some exclusive 'present' of its vanished becoming, we are invited to consider it fundamentally in light of its plunging forward into and as new envisagings. In other words, even in these early lectures Whitehead's model is demanding the surrender of conceptualities that privilege overtones of 'enduring being' in favour of more evanescent modes of capturing the energic and self-transcendent heart of process.

Since being an Eternal requires that something *not be* an Endurance, it seems to me that the notion of Eternity points sharply to the sense of reality Whitehead advanced later when he said that an entity 'never really is' (PR, 85). And since this phrase arises in a discussion that involves the concept of perishing, it would be wise to finally throw forward our reflections on 'Eternality' into that very notion of 'perishing'. It is my contention that by 'perishing' Whitehead did not mean the disappearance of the entity as individual, active process of feeling, but something nearly the opposite that will reflect back into the discussion of the Superject as 'envisaging Eternal' and as 'Eternal individual' here in the Harvard lectures. Our first order of business is to bring 'perishing' into clearer focus.

In *Process and Reality*, several of Whitehead's actual references to 'perishing' have to do with his wish that Locke had better understood the implications of his calling time a 'perpetual perishing' (PR, 29, 147, 210). In these instances Whitehead takes the opportunity to note that actual entities 'perish, but do not change' and to advance the idea that actuality must be construed as consisting of atomic occasions rather than enduring substances. He writes, 'If he [Locke] had grasped the notion that the actual entity "perishes" in the passage of time, so that no actual entity changes, he would have arrived at the point of view of the philosophy of organism' (PR, 147). In these contexts it is clear that we should see 'perishing' as a relative contrast term to 'change' in the sense that the two notions are incompatible as descriptions of actuality in process. Becoming is not change, as there is no actuality present until the process of concrescence is completed – but on completion it is there in the mode of being-appropriated and as active in the appropriator. The subject does not underlie concrescence, but emerges from that process as superject; it is *aimed at* rather than being that which does the aiming (PR, 222–3; also HL1, 93). In this sense, 'perishing' might be understood as the *condition of becoming-superject*, or becoming-feeling-to-be-felt; a name for the transition from concrescent immediacy to aspect of conformation for and in subsequent actualities. And insofar as a present actuality 'feels the feelings' of prior actualities, perishing is also the *condition of appropriation and reappearance* for superjects. It is not the condition of absolute disappearance as active individual, in other words, but of the reappearance of particular dynamics of active, feeling reality from and in the standpoint of yet another locus of reality, and so on.

So what exactly perishes when a nonetheless *repeatable* intensive unity of feeling qua actual entity perishes, if this perishing is, as I think Whitehead means it to be, the radical basis of his description of actuality in the incantatory phrase from Plato's *Timaeus*, 'it never really is' (PR, 85)? Whitehead variously ascribes perishing to the 'immediacy', 'unrest' (PR, 29), 'indetermination' (PR, 212) and 'individual absoluteness' (PR, 60) of concrescences. In a sense, these are strongly coordinate notions, as 'immediacy' could be described precisely as the phase of 'indetermination' and 'unrest' that express the 'individual absoluteness' of the process of self creation out of which the subject-superject emerges, considered abstractly in analysis. It is important to not ascribe exaggerated ontological implications to any of these notions to which perishing is applied, as the only reality emerging in process is the intensive unity of the superject. It's not like individual actuality is disappearing when an entity perishes; in fact, quite the opposite: 'an actual entity has "perished" when it is complete' (PR, 81–2). What perishes is simply some structural character of 'privacy' attending experience (that is, its unavailability to the public or 'other'). The intensity of feeling achieved via concrescence not only does not disappear, its projection from the past into the future was in fact an inherent part of the telic end of the process to begin with, as set forth in the Categoreal Obligation in which intensity and subjective aim are introduced (PR, 27). The 'aim' that originates the conceptual feelings that prehend together the physical feelings projected in from prior entities is at intensity in the 'immediate subject' and the 'relevant future', and Whitehead is clear that these aims are not divided, as anticipatory feeling for the entity's role in the future, as well as some feeling of what the relevant future might in fact be, 'are elements affecting the immediate complex of feeling' (PR, 27). The projection of an entity into relationship – constitutive relationship, at that – with other entities ensconces the futural role of the intensive satisfaction in the ontological centre of our sense of that 'individual' entity per se.

Thus the 'private' character of subjective concrescence cannot be understood to exhaust the creative activity of process itself (which is important, since privacy is ultimately what perishes) if relationship (referred to in the quote below as 'real unity') is supposed to be more than the sham or impossible reflection 'here' of what is really only 'privately' there. Whitehead notes that the 'origins' of feelings in the vector influx of feelings that belong to prior actualities *are not lost* even as the new concrescing entity experiences the supplementation of the given by the influx of new possibilities constitutive of its own subjective aim:

> [T]he reason why the origins are not lost in the private emotion is that there is no element in the universe capable of pure privacy. If we could obtain a complete analysis of meaning, the notion of pure privacy would be seen to be self-contradictory. Emotional feeling is still subject to the . . . principle, that to be 'something' is 'to have the potentiality for acquiring real unity with other entities' . . . In more familiar language, this principle can be expressed by the statement that the notion of 'passing on' is more fundamental than that of a private individual fact. (PR, 212–13)

If passing on is a more fundamental notion than that of a private fact, I am tempted to assert that perishing is not only not disappearance, but the very ground of the appearance and reappearance (feeling and repetition of feeling) that is 'creative advance' per se in the fundamentality of 'passing on'. In fact, one key objective in Whitehead's elaboration of the Theory of Extension in Part IV of *Process and Reality* was to describe the conditions of systemic relationship that make possible the vectoral character of the transmission of feelings, and in service of this goal he is insistent about breaking down our bifurcatory tendencies when we are thinking about the contrast between the 'private' and the 'public' (PR, 289, 290, 309). Perishing is thus a functional description of the possibility and the fact of multiple location of intensive feeling – a fundamental descriptor of active, non-enduring vectoral, vibratory process, rather than a reference to the ending of a *res vera* as an ontologically active being.[7]

The price of perishing – the question of what is lost as an entity in its completion achieves the status of 'never really being' – is not the absence or death of the activity achieved in satisfaction, but its attenuation arising from the conditions of contrast that cannot help but spell loss across time. The price of perishing is also the perpetual lack of self-coincidence or undifferentiated persistence, a lack I attempt to capture here in the language of 'ecstasis'. In the Harvard lectures, Whitehead refers to such loss at the fringes and at the core of achieved actuality as 'omission'. There is the omission that comes from what is not included in a new process of realisation, omission in the sense of selectivity given the other items in the 'past' of a process that have to be prehended together (HL1, 63, 93, 121); and there is omission that is a necessary correlate of the sheer fact that all process is at its heart projection into the future such that what becomes is superseded. In this sense omission is a way of denying endurance, undifferentiated persistence, or even those conditions of persistence that would allow things to change in themselves. Insofar as to be actual is basically to lend character to other (subsequent) things, certain possibilities are omitted from what an entity can ever 'be' – this I think is what Whitehead captures in the following note by referring to the Occasion as a 'limitation within Procession' rather than a fulfilment of some kind: 'There's also the reaching forward – the putting in the Actual. The Occasion is therefore a limitation within Procession. The Occasion has an internal processional nature itself. Always going on to Otherness, than itself' (HL1, 61). 'Going on to Otherness' is very clearly here seen as part of the 'internal' nature of the dynamic Occasion itself, not as some extraneous adventure of a dead objectivity. This seems to speak clearly to the fact that by 'internal nature' we cannot mean something univocally located within the concrescent process itself, but must always include the 'reaching forward' of the satisfaction as it insinuates itself and is actively repeated under whatever the conditions of (new) limitation might be.[8]

So perishing might be understood in the language of these lectures as the necessary fact of 'going on to Otherness' that is nevertheless the telic aim of the process of coming to be in the first place – entities in their telic arising are meant to 'never really be'. Perishing is the condition of the 'throwing forward' of a reality, and 'This throwing-forward is the protension of present into Future' (HL1, 61). 'There is . . . a reaching forward – The occasion is [a] limitation within procession always reaching forward – otherness – never get away from this' (HL1, 64). It is important to bear in mind that this reaching forward into otherness is nothing but the 'envisaging' activity at the heart of what Whitehead means by 'Eternity' in these lectures. Thus we are faced with the interesting observation that what 'perishing' facilitates in the metaphysics of *Process and Reality* – the ecstatic intensive recurrence of active individual superjects feeling together conditions of value – is strongly associated with what Eternality (in one of its aspects) accomplishes in the Harvard lectures: the envisaging of value that is the energy (HL1, 145, 154, 361) of relentless throwing forward into Otherness.

It is difficult to conceive of a single individual occasion of experience in a way that does not either actively or inadvertently collapse into the notion of a 'one' that is a merely numerical unity occupying the privacy of the quantum of concrescent becoming and then evaporating. To think the identity of an individual actuality as ecstatically located outside itself as well as in the occasion of its emergence is to explode the non-relational privacy of the numerical unit. If the activity of envisaging value for the sake of creative procession is what both Eternity and the individual emergent superject essentially are, then the activity of being that constitutes the identity of any individual is always directed *away from* privacy to the transcendent public otherness of process as such. Whitehead describes the 'me now' of the present as necessarily referent to other beings: 'The present . . . has transition within it. There is otherness within it. The otherness is not *me and the other things*, but *the otherness*' (HL1, 336, emphasis added). Not me AND the other things, but *otherness per se* is the transition that constitutes the 'present' in its processive character. But further, 'It has transition from otherness which lies without it – from an otherness which is past. The present doesn't represent itself as a complete entity . . . Also transition to otherness which is future. So the present exhibits itself as with internal relations to that which is beyond it' (HL1, 336). Internal to anything that is to be thought of as the 'present' is the transition (dynamic envisaging of valuative possibility that spurs and expresses the 'passing on' which is the most fundamental fact) that is its inclusion of past envisaging eternals and future envisaging eternals. Internal relations are described here as belonging to the entity in itself even as these relations also situate the entity in terms of other things which will include *it* (i.e. internal relations in the relatively unproblematic sense of including the other in oneself). Intriguingly it seems that internal relatedness – feeling the feelings of other things – cannot be thought of exclusively in terms of any one concrescent occasion, even if individuated concrescences are implied by the fact of there being entities available for relationship and mutual qualification. Being serious about thinking of the activity of feeling as fundamentally 'envisagement' rather than private enjoyment helps us purge the vestiges of simple location in our conception of the individuality of any entity. Envisagement vibrates across temporal modes in expressing any process of individuation that has helped 'spray' those modes out into being; ecstatic intensive feeling is the electricity of envisagement that is many places at once and never all at once. For me somehow the conceptual intersection of Eternity and Perishing captures the non-numerical-unity and non-self-coincident character of the intensity of feeling that is the active envisioning of value and not its private clutching into a solipsistic particularity that could not underwrite the internal relatedness demanded in the philosophy of organism. Neither that which is Eternal nor that which is Perishing 'endures', but all that Eternity and Perishing encompass is repeatedly 'thrown forward' into new moments of realisation.

To think together Eternity and Perishing as mirror conditions of nonenduring but individuated feeling is to cast all becoming in a light of a radical and what Whitehead calls 'haunting' contingency (HL1, 64). Repeatedly in the Harvard lectures Whitehead invokes Spinoza's definition of finitude as a thing's capacity to be bounded by another of its own kind (e.g. HL1, 61, 63, 70, 71, 73, 445). In fact he relates Spinozistic 'finitude' to the internal and external transition to which we were referring above (HL1, 445), though whether Whitehead's usage can be said to adhere to Spinoza's own thinking is dubious. Be that as it may, in these lectures being bound by another of one's own kind is the essential transitoriness of process as an envisaging hurled out of a past and thrown into a future – not so much 'bound' as in circumscribed, but as in *connected* in the *vibratory* sense of plunging forward into appropriatable repetition of envisaging potential. Finitude is the radical contingency of the 'it never really is' where self-coincidence is surrendered to an always-perishing but always-reappearing Envisaging individuality that is at the same time Eternity. Perpetual perishing is more than just perishing cum evanescence or evaporation. Treatments of perishing in the literature have neglected the perpetuality of perishing by seeing it as a one-and-done ending to the exclusive actuality/individual activity of 'the present'.[9] The ecstatic reading takes the perpetuality of perishing seriously: by locating the activity of intensive feeling ecstatically across temporal modes (and therefore never fully collapsed into temporality), it asserts that any given individual is *perishing all the time*, in every time-epoch in which it appears and as envisaging activity in eternal non-self-coincidence. This reading means that as entities don't cease their action just because they are in some 'other', they also don't cease perishing either. This is the anguish of finitude – that the subject-superject *is always being lost because it is always showing up again*. This is, or should be, the core of the organic philosophy as a model of finite achievement of relational value against eternal conditions of value that require radical finitude in the form of realised limitation in order to be real.

Anguished finitude is one in which the mirroring relation between Eternity and Perishing in their co-definition of finite actuality recognises the precarious contingency of any value realised. If value is recognised in the envisaging activity as it throws itself forward evermore, it is precisely non-enduring in the technical sense. It is what George Allan has described as a 'perishable good': 'Situated contingently and governed by conditions that are situated contingently, any being and its degree of goodness is necessarily a contingent being contingently as good as it is.'[10] And such goods or values are all the more perishable the further up the scale of fineness of good or value we may go: 'Because of its greater degree of uniqueness – and hence its greater complexity and intensity – a greater good is more difficult to sustain, much less to enhance, than is a less complex, a less distinctive, achievement.'[11] In another project not devoted to the Harvard lectures per se, it would be instructive to relate such precarious goods to the human experiences that to my mind best illustrate the feeling of contingent finitude that pervades ecstatic individuality – the experiences associated with grief.[12] In grief we recognise the intersection of abrupt disappearance and recurrent, intensive, felt connection. The presence-in-absence and absence-in-presence that characterise felt grief are an exquisite rendering of the mirrored concepts of Eternality and Perishing which define finite achievement, finite achievement which is nevertheless the only path to realisation in an ontology of that which never really is. The only path to realised value is the path of ecstasis, the path of perpetual perishing and an appearing-again that is also an always-being-lost of what is precious. The Superject as 'envisaging eternal' is simultaneously a perpetual perishing that renders the Eternity of the value-dimension the condition of radical contingency and loss. The gift of value is the gift of grief, and vice versa. In this paradox lies the nature of ecstatic individuation, as well as its experiential manifestation. As illustration it is more Etch-a-Sketch

than Sistine Chapel ceiling, and yet in the contrast between the trivial evanescence of the former's sandy determinations and the important permanence of Michelangelo's great work lies the intensive truth of most of how we
live and die as mere mortals.

## Notes

1.  Brian Henning calls our attention elsewhere in Chapter 17 of this volume to the
    ways that the Harvard lectures may inflect our sense of the consistencies and
    changes in Whitehead's systematic thought over time. Henning is particularly
    insistent that the approach Whitehead takes in the classroom is not of the master-
    lecturer who already knows what he thinks, but one where he is often working
    out his ideas 'in real time' with his students (see below, p. 341), in a process of
    discussion, hypothesis and elaboration.
2.  Here of course we are hearing the Spinozistic dimension of Whitehead's specula-
    tive development, explicitly embraced in these lectures despite the sharp devia-
    tion from pure Spinozism that these lectures also evidence in the notion of an
    Eternal that is capable of enrichment.
3.  See e.g. Jones, 'Provocative Expression', and Jones, Intensity.
4.  For example, Sherburne describes process in the following manner: 'The key
    point for a Whiteheadian is that in this moment of transition from past to pre-
    sent, from the preceding actual occasion to subsequent actual occasion, the
    decision, the power, the reality, the spontaneity of response is all located in the
    present; it is located in the concrescing, becoming occasion that is organizing its
    own affirmation, denial, or creative transformation of its inherited initial condi-
    tions' (Sherburne, 'Some Reflections', 10). No activity or power is accorded here
    to the entities felt into this concrescent unity; but unless we accord such power,
    they cannot actually be said to be contributing feeling in the new concrescent
    entity. I argue that since an entity either contributes as itself or not at all in a
    genuinely 'relational' ontology, we must ascribe some kind of genuine presence
    to an entity (even as past) in light of its active influencing of a present/future
    successor.
5.  We see something of a model like this in Nobo's interpretation in Whitehead's
    Metaphysics of Extension and Solidarity.
6.  It is possible that the conceptualities emerging in the biological sciences were
    steering Whitehead in this direction in the Harvard lectures, as explored in
    Chapter 5 of this volume by Dennis Sölch. As modes of conceiving the plural-
    ity and unity of things in the universe in the terms of pure physics had hit, as
    Sölch explores, a 'dead end' (see above, p. 102) as insufficiently dynamic, White-
    head was doubtless more open to the possibilities afforded by close attention
    to relationships between organisms and environments in describing the funda-
    mental natures of things metaphysically. The conceptual centrality of 'environ-
    ments' is also crucial in Paul Bogaard's treatment in this volume of Whitehead's

likely instruction by the work of L. J. Henderson as to the kinds 'mutualism' and 'co-evolution' that rival 'competition' as the core of evolutionary thinking (see Chapter 3, p. 80 and passim).

7. It is interesting to note that Whitehead contrasts perishing with 'everlastingness' (PR, 347) in a manner that seems to echo the contrast of Eternity and Endurance in the Harvard lectures.

8. I realise that there is some straining of available language and concepts to make this point stick. This is undoubtedly one of those places where philosophy might reach out to poetry to articulate or 'grasp the ungraspable', as George Allan discusses in this volume (Chapter 14, above, p. 284). I recognise that I have engaged in leaving 'ragged edges on one's hypotheses', as Allan (pp. 288–92) describes the speculative process of trying to conceive wholes and integrations 'vividly', but hope that these formulations at least 'throw us forward' in creative directions by giving us the kind of 'contrast' (Eternity and Perishing) through which such rough edges do in fact create. That I am dealing with concepts in Whitehead's own gropings that lead Allan to these cogitations in the first place helps reassure me that I am on legitimate, if 'ragged', grounds here!

9. See Flynn, 'The Importance of Forgetting Perishing'; Simmons, 'Antinomy of Perishing'.

10. Allan, 'Perishable Goods', 10.

11. Allan, 'Perishable Goods', 11.

12. See for example the reflections in Halewood, 'Death, Entropy', 664–7, though Halewood *contrasts* 'perishing' and 'creativity' in a manner that is to some extent in tension with my objectives here.

## Bibliography

Allan, George, 'Perishable Goods', *Review of Metaphysics*, 54 (2000), 3–26.

Bogaard, Paul and Jason Bell (eds), *The Harvard Lectures of Alfred North Whitehead, 1924–1925: Philosophical Presuppositions of Science* (Edinburgh: Edinburgh University Press, 2017).

Flynn, Mark, 'The Importance of Forgetting "Perishing" in Whitehead's Cosmology and Epistemology', *Interchange*, 36 (2005), 85–93.

Ford, Lewis, 'Can Whitehead Rescue Perishing?', *Personalist*, 54 (1973), 92–3.

Halewood, Michael, 'Death, Entropy, Creativity and Perpetual Perishing: Some Thoughts From Whitehead and Stengers', *Social Sciences*, 4 (2015), 655–67.

Jones, Judith, *Intensity: An Essay in Whiteheadian Ontology* (Nashville: Vanderbilt University Press, 1998).

Jones, Jude, 'Provocative Expression: Transitions in and From Metaphysics in Whitehead's Later Work', in Roland Faber, Brian G. Henning and Clinton Combs (eds), *Beyond Metaphysics: Explorations in Alfred North Whitehead's Late Thought* (Amsterdam: Editions Rodopi, 2010), 259–79.

Nobo, Jorge Luis, *Whitehead's Metaphysics of Extension and Solidarity* (Albany: State University of New York Press, 1986).

Sherburne, Donald, 'Some Reflections on Sartre's Nothingness and Whitehead's Perishing', *Review of Metaphysics*, 48:1 (1994), 3–17.

Simmons, James, 'An Antinomy of Perishing in Whitehead', *Personalist*, 50 (1969), 559–66.

Stengers, Isabelle, *Thinking With Whitehead*, trans. Michael Chase (Cambridge, MA: Harvard University Press, 2011).

Whitehead, Alfred North, *Science and the Modern World* (New York: The Free Press, [1925] 1967).

Whitehead, Alfred North, *Process and Reality: An Essay in Cosmology* (New York: The Free Press, [1929] 1978).

# Part VI

# Reinterpreting Whitehead

# 16

# Uncovering a 'New' Whitehead

*George R. Lucas, Jr.*

When Brian Henning began a decade ago to organise a Scholarly Editions project focused on the works of A. N. Whitehead, the principal goal was to collect, correct and publish a uniform edition of Whitehead's previously published works, alongside some minor *Nachlass* (such as Whitehead's personal correspondence). The principal expectation was to shed greater light on how Whitehead had developed his mature metaphysical thought, as expressed in his formally published works during his lifetime.

That goal has been dramatically met in the first volume of previously unpublished lecture notes, which illuminates important details of Whitehead's initial metaphysical synthesis in 1924–25. This first volume is already helping to resolve longstanding controversies regarding the degree to which Whitehead may or may not have subsequently deviated from this initial comprehensive metaphysical vision – one that he had long bottled up while teaching mathematics at Cambridge and the University of London, and hoped finally to express during a tenure at Harvard teaching philosophy for the first time in his career.

But the copious notes, newly discovered in the papers of Whitehead's postdoctoral colleague, Winthrop Bell, reveal a very different image of his tentative, wide-ranging and 'experimental' approach taken in the classroom, as opposed to the more systematic and literarily sophisticated views published in works like *Science and the Modern World* and even *Process and Reality*. The classroom lectures also reveal the marked difference between Whitehead's highly technical philosophical thought, and the content of his popular lectures delivered to a general audience for eventual publication. The latter are without exception considerably less technical and detailed than the intricate discussions of physics, logic and philosophy presented principally to graduate student specialists in Whitehead's classroom.

Henry Sheffer's famous but disparaging characterisation of Whitehead's initial Harvard lecture was that it consisted of little more than 'pure Bergsonianism'.[1] Had Sheffer attended some of the eighty-four subsequent lectures during Whitehead's initial academic year at Harvard, accompanied by equations and detailed diagrams never before seen by subsequent generations of scholars, he might well have reached a different opinion about Whitehead's thought. For these lecture notes reveal a keen analytical and scientific mind – arguably far surpassing that of Bertrand Russell, and more in keeping with the eminent philosopher of science and logician whom the Harvard faculty initially thought themselves to be recruiting.

The classroom lectures appear to offer little support for speculative claims (like those of Lewis S. Ford) of sudden discoveries (like 'epochalism' or 'temporal atomism') or other dramatic revelations or 'turnings' (*Verkehren*: I deliberately invoke the Heideggerian term) that might signal some radical discontinuity between the earlier and later Whitehead.[2] Likewise, the lectures serve to refute claims based upon 'arguments from absence' in the published works – including some of my own, decades ago, regarding Whitehead's knowledge of and interest in evolution – based solely on the relative absence of such discussion in the contents of the published works.[3]

The lectures do reveal new and tell-tale absences of their own, however, as the Edition's Executive Editor, Brian Henning, discusses in his chapter for this volume. They appear devoid of any treatment of topics like God, panpsychism, panentheism or other novel theological insights, so intriguing to subsequent Whiteheadian scholars. Rather, the lectures contain little other than purely mainstream, but revolutionary, extraordinary, cutting-edge philosophy of science, with discussions of relativity and quantum mechanics far surpassing anything seen in North America prior to this time. As such, I find that they turn traditional Whiteheadian scholarship 'on its head', inverting (*Verkehrte*) or re-balancing subsequent decades of mythologisation, wishful thinking and misplaced emphasis, as I now hope to demonstrate.

## Of Mythology, Steel Traps and Know-it-Alls

This subheading is drawn directly from Joe Petek's remarkable introductory chapter for this volume, particularly from the section describing notes taken by several students in 1930, including W. V. O. Quine, and the textual difficulty Petek encountered in those notes regarding both the date of Philo's birth and Augustine's city of residence at death ('Hippo'). Whitehead himself, like many of us in the lecture hall, often relied a bit too much on his own vague recollections, rather than careful advance fact-checking, in summarising the history of philosophy. Petek's points are now both to assert the value of comparative and multiple note-taker texts to determine just what was going on, and also to offer an aside about Quine, whom Joe describes as having a mind like a steel trap, but also seeming to be something of a know-it-all.

There is much that can be said in response, about Whitehead, about Quine, and about the Edition's methodology. To begin with the last of these: it has been my own position that we have inadvertently and fortunately come across multiple variant transcripts of Whitehead's actual lectures. I immediately think both of multiple canonical Gospel accounts and their differences, and the technique of 'Gospel Parallels', putting them side by side to determine overlap and consistency.

We would scarcely be in a better position if instead we had early versions of Edison-cylinder recordings, all in deteriorated condition (although the latter might shed light on the ancillary question Petek raises regarding the possibility of Whitehead having a speech impediment). Regardless, our goal would be, from whatever sources, to produce as faithful as possible a transcript of each lecture *as Whitehead himself had delivered it*. That is to say: the ultimate goal would always be to recover a faithful version of Whitehead's lecture, and never simply to collect and publish as many variant lecture notes taken by students as we could discover. Petek's account reveals the value, but also the difficulty of using these multiple sources, while raising the question of repetition and redundancy, should we simply decide to edit and publish all the extant lectures for a given year, rather than (as I advocate) trying to generate a faithful and accurate transcript of Whitehead's remarks from them. We are, after all, seeking answers pertaining to what Whitehead himself said, rather than what various students heard or wrote down. But (as Petek demonstrates with his case studies of Augustine and Philo) these are not easily disentangled.

What is revealed by these transcripts, moreover, is not always flattering to the note-taker. If you are a disciple of Quine, it can hardly prove reassuring to see how, on one hand, Quine does not hesitate to caricature and denigrate Whitehead sarcastically, in asides and in his notes. But we also have a set of Quine's own notes of an office session he scheduled with Whitehead, in order to show to Whitehead (and presumably seek his approval of) some of the work that Quine himself was doing on logic proofs. Quine reports in this 'memo to himself' that Whitehead seemed very impressed, describing Quine's work as 'a very pretty proof, my boy! I wish we had had this for the *Principia*'. The overall account is, frankly, a sharp contrast to the attitude revealed in the note-taking in class: in this case, sycophantic and self-serving, as well as kind of 'kissing up' to the famous professor whom he secretly holds in contempt.

The transcripts also add further credit to the remarkable work that Leemon McHenry was able to do in gaining Quine's confidence and forcing him to reckon more authentically at the end of his life on just how significant a figure Whitehead himself was, and what a positive influence on Quine's own philosophy Whitehead had proven to be, despite Quine's subsequent decades of unflattering, ungrateful and disparaging remarks.[4]

So now let me turn from criticising Quine to criticising Victor Lowe. Again, the archival materials coming to light cannot but serve to diminish a considerable portion of Lowe's own intellectual biography of Whitehead. The Whitehead family itself (as grandson George Whitehead reported to me in our first phone conversation) secretly made fun of Lowe, treated him shabbily, and sometimes deliberately and unkindly withheld from him information that Lowe was persistently seeking for his project. George Whitehead's mother and grandmother found Lowe (George reports) to be something of a pest.

Lowe thought himself to have assembled the largest and most complete collection of *Nachlass* available, but we now know he had, at best, only a partial realisation of what was actually available. Of course, the materials that Jason Bell discovered and recognised the monumental significance of in the Mount Allison University archives, and that Paul Bogaard subsequently took the lead in editing, are probably the singularly most remarkable case in point. Ironically Lowe had, over the decades, attempted to discount the stories he heard from Hartshorne and others concerning the existence of these materials, to the point of nearly denying that Winthrop Bell even existed, let alone that he or anyone else had ever taken the copious notes we have now published in Volume 1 of the Critical Edition.

Petek is characteristically diplomatic in describing Lowe's account of Whitehead's 'Logic seminary' in this volume. In fact, he (Lowe) did not seem to be intellectually up to it, or even up to the rigours of the PHIL3b class, which Lowe inexplicably dropped mid-year, early on, and only completed a decade later (see Paul Bogaard's account of these events in his Introduction to Volume 1). I knew Victor pretty well during his last years in retirement at Johns Hopkins, through the mediation more of Jerome Schneewind than Lewis Ford (for whom Lowe himself had scant regard).

It is perhaps time to excise some of the saintly aura that surrounds his reputation: not that he was especially venal, nor that he did not usually behave like the gentleman he was by reason of birth, but that he was not quite the historical master scholar he immodestly portrayed himself as being, especially as this opportunity was afforded to him largely by default. That is true of Ivor Leclerc as well, when you turn your eyes more critically than I did as a youth on his books, from *Whitehead's Metaphysics* (1954) to his final, singularly unimpressive *Philosophy of Nature* (1987) that Jan Van der Veken arranged to publish at Leuven, all of which content themselves with fairly pedestrian comparisons of Whitehead to Aristotle, while utterly ignoring Whitehead's most complex, revolutionary and utterly essential doctrines (like conceptual reversion, 'symbolic reference', and 'perception in the mixed mode of causal efficacy and presentational immediacy'). But all those are observations not connected to this project directly, and best left for another time.

Finally, let us consider Lewis Ford's earlier examination of the W. E. Hocking class lecture notes from this same academic year. Gary Herstein, in an online review of Volume 1 of the Critical Edition, roundly denounces 'the riot of untethered speculation' exhibited in Ford's work in particular, as the sort of inexcusable excess likely to arise in the absence of any grounding in archival evidence (such as Whitehead apparently ordered destroyed).[5] Paul Bogaard (in his introduction to HL1) and myself[6] likewise raise questions concerning the plausibility of Ford's 'emergence' thesis in the light of findings in the now more complete lecture notes from this period. Ronny Desmet's essay in this volume, however, supports the overall conclusions of that early work by Ford, even if the evidence and argument upon which it was originally based were incomplete or flawed.[7] What is clearly the case is that the publication of Volume 1 of the Critical Edition has re-opened some old wounds, while generating substantial new controversy surrounding the development of Whitehead's eventual, mature metaphysical views.

I would say, at bottom (with respect to Ford, at least), we have a recap of Socrates' problem in the *Laches*: 'do you get full credit for being right "by accident", either for the wrong reasons (Ford, Laches), or in the absence of any clear underlying substantive reasons other than gut intuitions (Nicias)?' Most Whitehead scholars agree that there is a shift from the continuity of Spinozism (creativity as a continuous underlying substrate, quantised in its 'nodes' or 'modes') in *Science and the Modern World*, and the more Leibnizian epochalism/atomism of *Process and Reality*. Ford traced the shift to the March 1925 lectures. But that shift is more subtle, as Desmet demonstrates, for the right reasons. His (Desmet's) recognition of 'primates' as standing waves in the EM continuum is Spinozistic, and compatible with Einstein (an avowed Spinozist). But then there is the divisible/indivisible contrast, and the 'discovery' by Whitehead that 'becoming' is not divisible (surely a conclusion with which orthodox Whiteheadians will agree), while 'extension' (time as 'transition', or what would come to be called transition, the flux of indivisible occasions?) is divisible.

So, in fact, there is a lot to unravel here. There seems to be a background of widespread agreement among Whitehead scholars that Whitehead's early

Spinozism is replaced by a more Leibnizian approach in *Process and Reality*. Our question is both when this occurs, and how sudden or gradual is the transition. I think Desmet is able to provide a more nuanced and fine-grained analysis than any I have seen before. His is a remarkable account of the discovery and the shift. And it does tend to rehabilitate Ford from the criticisms that Paul and I levelled at his 'finding' (along with his method). I am pleased that this volume has made this debate public, which helps to make this matter clearer to all of us, and our understanding of how Whitehead continuously wrestled with the 'continuity/atomicity' problem is afforded even greater nuance.[8]

## Self-flagellation

Since neither Ford nor Lowe is here to defend themselves, rendering my comments somewhat cowardly and ungracious, let me turn my attack on another guilty party, namely, myself. Paul Bogaard has already called attention to what is, in retrospect, my clearly mistaken inference drawn from Whitehead's published works that he really didn't focus much on Darwin and evolution. *Mea culpa*. The new puzzle, given the extended discussion of both Darwin and evolution more generally during Whitehead's classroom lectures in 1924–25, is *why* these same discussions did not figure more prominently in *Science and the Modern World*, let alone in Whitehead's subsequent published works. That puzzle is even more extraordinary than the one I thought (mistakenly) that I had discovered in the 1980s.[9] But to be absolutely clear: the first volume of class lecture notes from 1924–25 demonstrates the compatibility of Whitehead's philosophy *with* evolutionary development, change and novelty, as well as a far more detailed and careful reading of and reference to viewpoints from Darwin to Bergson, C. Lloyd Morgan and others whom Bogaard names in his second chapter for this volume than I had ever realised. That connection cannot be gainsaid.

So, in sum: if Ford was wrong about temporal atomism as a 'discovery', then I was equally wrong to infer from a lacuna in Whitehead's published works that he really didn't focus much on Darwin and evolution. 'Poor old Victor' (as the Whitehead family regarded him) wasted a great deal of his time and made a lot of mistakes.[10] Meanwhile, Quine often seems little more than a nasty, venal, self-serving narcissist . . . what other 'sacred cows' remain to be gored?

Allow me to focus on what turn out to be my own highly mythologised accounts of Whitehead's importance during his own lifetime, for one thing. In his chapter for this volume, Petek mentions Paul Weiss's speculation that Whitehead would not have been a particularly effective administrator. In sharp contrast, some of my earlier work has Whitehead portrayed historically as an incipient administrative genius, and as having (in essence) been summoned upon leaving Cambridge by a search committee headed by no less than Prince Albert himself (who had of course been deceased for decades) to join the faculty of the brand-new Imperial College of Science and Technology in 1910 as Dean of Faculty (the College was in fact founded in 1907, without Whitehead's presence or contribution), and which he then proceeded to build up during the ensuing decade, from a virtual 'vocational-technical' school for London's lower classes into one of the premier scientific research institutions in the world at the time of his summons to Harvard in 1923 – all while authoring many of the major works that made him the darling of analytic philosophy in the early twentieth century.

Embarrassingly, my accounts were badly garbled partial truths blended with outright nonsense. Petek and Henning discovered my exaggerations as we prepared our editorial introduction for the volumes of the Critical Edition. My claims made a compelling case for Whitehead's importance while attempting to justify his receiving an NEH grant (which our Scholarly Editions project has thus far not obtained).[11] But the details are little more than 'alt-facts' and 'fake news', to my utter shame and mortification. The philosopher Joseph Brennan at Columbia, whom Petek quotes in another context, summarises Whitehead's importance in a similar manner, although Victor Lowe's facts of the matter seem more correct, that Whitehead was in fact merely an unemployed mathematician living on some kind of stipend and book royalties during his first year in London, and only subsequently taken on as an adjunct mathematician at King's College, and only coming to Imperial College in 1914, and finally serving as Dean of the Science faculty considerably later still, right around the time of his letter of invitation from President Lowell at Harvard.

In my defence, Whitehead's own son, North, has an account somewhat more like mine in his unpublished autobiography concerning the home life of the Whiteheads in Grantchester and Bloomsbury.[12] Neither of which, by the way, were wealthy or desirable neighbourhoods at the time that the Whiteheads resided there; followers of the BBC series *Grantchester* know that this little lower-middle-class suburb of Cambridge only went further downhill since North's description of the inebriated postman and other downtrodden locals who lived there during his pre-college days.

I've heard and seen many other Whiteheadians offer something like my own inaccurate biographical account. Am I channelling them, or they me? I don't know. But this narrative is seriously in error. Lowe's account, and Petek's in *Wikipedia* (he rewrote the article in late 2013), are probably the most accurate, and the most deflating of the 'myth' of Whitehead – although where

Lowe got his facts is beyond me, since the family, including North, apparently believed something closer to my mythologised account. What we all agree upon is that Whitehead definitely did *not* chop down any cherry trees at Sherborne, nor did he throw a one-pound note across the Thames.

Mythologising our revered historical and philosophical figures, and endowing them with almost superhuman powers or endearing charms, is not without precedent. It is what fans and disciples do. I'm sure readers of this volume have heard the oft-told tale regarding Charles Hartshorne, at the University of Chicago, encountering a student on the quad, engaging in spirited conversation for an hour, and then asking the student to remind him of the direction he had been going at the time of their encounter! The trouble is, students of Rudolph Carnap repeat exactly the same anecdote about their beloved teacher, at exactly the same school. And I have heard this anecdote ascribed to other great scholars. It's less 'bogus' than affectionate, and perhaps indicative of the character of absent-minded intellectuals (ever since Thales fell into that hole while pondering the heavens).

Yet another piece of 'fake news', however, redounds more to Whitehead's character and importance than to undermining it. We have Whittaker's account of the Giffords recorded by Lowe, now contrasted in Petek's chapter to Whitehead's own account of how they went. Even more objectively, we have the famous story that Lowe recounts of Henry Sheffer walking out of Whitehead's initial Harvard lecture in September of 1924 and muttering in disgust, 'Bergsonianism, pure Bergsonianism'. In pawing through the archives, however, Paul Bogaard and I discovered notes of the Harvard department's repeated attempts, through the auspices of President Lowell and Prof. W. E. Hocking, to secure Bergson himself, and giving up only after the end of the First World War. We looked over those letters with awe and amazement. Meanwhile, while digging around for some other records at Petek's behest, I myself discovered an edition (from Fall 1924) of the *Harvard Crimson* which I immediately forwarded to the Whitehead Archives, in which Sheffer (well after that initial lecture of Whitehead's) was interviewed and asked to comment on the importance of bringing Professor Whitehead to the university.[13] His response to the student journalist consisted of unequivocal praise for the kind of philosophy and scientific insight Whitehead was adding to campus, and for what a 'catch' he was. And that, unlike Lowe's 'viva voce' remark, is in print.

North wasn't prone to exaggerate, or even focus particularly on his father's prowess or accomplishments. There is little of that in his autobiography. He complains (surprisingly) about the lack of intellectual rigour at Cambridge, and praises American students at Harvard by contrast for their focus and drive. His comments on his father and his family life are perfunctory and polite, lacking in much detail. I would therefore accord more weight to his account of their life and transition to London (undertaken exactly at the year North matriculated in Cambridge) than I would to anything Lowe dug up, especially in the absence of archival evidence, and given the (behind his back) disdain of the Whitehead family themselves, who were his main alternative source of information.

## Re-thinking Whitehead

I do not doubt, either, Petek's account of Whitehead's own estimation of the success of his Giffords, and especially his own estimation of the final lecture.[14] No one who reads *Process and Reality* Part V can gainsay the eloquence and profound insight of that chapter. But it was a requirement of the Giffords that such an evaluation of science and theology be offered in conclusion. That leaves unanswered, then, the role of these ideas as central to Whitehead's broader thought. It seems to me that the day-to-day lectures, over many years, bear more witness to the relevant importance of themes than do a set of one-off lectures, written with boundary constraints, for a popular audience. For that is what *Process and Reality*, and indeed, almost all of Whitehead's published works, are. And in those, by contrast, there is scant mention of God in any serious, let alone theological fashion.

The ultimate demythologisation, then, is to claim that Whitehead's own desire that his published lectures be permitted to stand alone without further secondary commentary is gravely paradoxical. It is the daily and yearly classroom lectures for serious students, not the occasional popular talks for general audiences, that should define his thought. If so, the blunt truth is that we really don't know the true Whitehead, unless and until we delve into these lectures more deeply. They are not to be characterised as secondary interpretive materials, or even *Nachlass*. They are primary archival source materials that take us deeper into the real Whitehead than anything he formally published. While he was certainly a brilliant lecturer and essayist, he was also, after all, barely a better researcher and editor than he was a correspondent. All of that subsequent work for publication was done in haste – sloppily, carelessly, quickly and inconsistently – in part to satisfy editors and the public, and in part to pay the bills, as Evelyn Whitehead herself often bore witness.

As Bogaard beautifully portrays it in his introductory essay to HL1, by contrast, we have in Whitehead's classroom lectures a direct window into his mind at work, which I have characterised, in turn, as his laboratory. In these classroom settings, on a weekly basis, Whitehead experimented, tested ideas and concepts, bounced them off his students, listened to their reactions, reflected, changed, expanded and further developed his nascent metaphysical ideas. His classroom was his sounding board for his own fledging ideas.

And those experiments go *far* beyond anything we have in his relatively truncated public, published works. We discover in his classroom a far greater knowledge of and reflection on Darwinian evolution, for one thing. Also, we find a greater knowledge of post-Copenhagen quantum mechanics, for another.[15] Likewise we find a dialectical back and forth on Einstein's relativity, absent in his published work, where Whitehead is seemingly willing to accept, later, doctrines concerning the inseparability of space and time that he rejected outright in his *Principle of Relativity* in 1922. We also find diagrams and equations, never seen by us before, for which we have had to substitute purely speculative illustrations composed by Lowe, Sherburne, Ford and others over the years – disciples who lacked his own command and prowess in mathematical physics.

## Conclusion

Nevertheless, it remains the goal of the new Critical Edition to restore something of the original reputation Whitehead enjoyed when he was first hired into Harvard's venerable philosophy department in 1924, as well as to call attention, through recent discoveries of these lecture notes and papers long thought missing or destroyed, to what he actually taught to students and faculty at Harvard. It is remarkable to see how revolutionary, even now, was the work he was doing at the time on the philosophical foundations of relativity theory, the 'universal algebra' of quantum mechanics (later championed by Paul Dirac), and non-Euclidean geometries in the 1920s and 1930s. 'Whitehead's axioms' are routinely invoked as the foundation of contemporary projective geometry by mathematicians with little knowledge of or interest in his philosophy, while Russell himself credited Whitehead with devising the symbolic notation and conventions that now are commonplace in standard textbooks on formal symbolic logic and predicate logic.

The discovery of some of these long-missing archival materials and *Nachlass* is a fascinating detective story in itself, which the individual volume editors' remarkable prologue to Volume 1 relates and interprets in detail. The notes on Whitehead's lectures taken by the likes of W. V. O. Quine and the young Harvard postdoctoral fellow, Winthrop Bell (the first North American student to write his doctoral dissertation under Edmund Husserl, Bell was subsequently imprisoned in Germany during the First World War as a British spy) reveal a logician and mathematician hard at work on some of the most intricate details of, for example, nuclear structure and the geometry of space-time, in close dialogue with Einstein and other major contributors to these scientific revolutions of the day, while drawing out the epistemological and ontological implications of these discoveries with a technical capacity far exceeding that of his philosophical contemporaries, including even Bertrand Russell. All of this occurred during a time at which these new concepts in physics had just been published in Europe, and were only beginning to make their way (and their influence felt) across the Atlantic. As I have stressed in this chapter, none of this is really evident in his published works, which were largely based upon lectures to the general public – difficult enough, to be sure, but (apart from Part IV of *Process and Reality*) not really indicative of the difficult and close technical work that Whitehead was simultaneously undertaking with students and specialists at Radcliffe and in Emerson Hall.

When we began the Critical Edition, we expected to shed greater light upon how Whitehead had originally formulated and subsequently developed the ideas found in his published works. We are now in the midst of discovering, somewhat to our shock and awe, that we are for the first time observing an entirely different scholar, one much closer to the figure that the Harvard department originally thought it was hiring as an acceptable alternative to Russell or Bergson. That is certainly a more intricate and complex Whitehead than the traditional view supports. I myself am convinced that this is the true and authentic Whitehead, one markedly different, more complex, and even more deserving of our respect than the public, published figure we have long admired.

## Notes

1. Lowe, *Alfred North Whitehead, Volume II*, 142.
2. See the debate between Herstein and Desmet on this issue (Chapters 9 and 10 in this volume).
3. See Bogaard's 'Whitehead and His Philosophy of Evolution' in this volume.
4. Cf. Quine, 'Response to Leemon McHenry'. See also the extended discussion of and with Quine in McHenry's extraordinary work, *The Event Universe*.
5. Herstein, 'Reading Between The Texts'.
6. Lucas, 'The Emergence of Whitehead's Metaphysics'.
7. See Desmet's 'From Physics to Philosophy, and From Continuity to Atomicity', in this volume.
8. Again, see Chapters 9 and 10 in this volume.
9. See Lucas, 'Evolutionist Theories and Whitehead's Philosophy'.
10. Brian Henning has unearthed a scathing review of both volumes of Lowe's Whitehead biography by Nicholas Griffin, one of our editorial board members, that reaches even more devastating conclusions. See Griffin, 'Lowe's Whitehead'.

11. See Henning's preface to this volume.
12. Whitehead, *Now I Am An American*.
13. 'New Harvard Philosophy Professor is Well Known'.
14. See Petek's introduction to this volume, p. 19.
15. See Desmet's 'Whitehead's Highly Speculative Lectures on Quantum Theory' in this volume for a detailed account of Whitehead's command of both Copenhagen and post-Copenhagen interpretations of quantum theory.

## Bibliography

Griffin, Nicholas, 'Lowe's Whitehead', *Russell*, 6:2 (1986), 172–8.

Herstein, Gary, 'Reading Between the Texts', *The Quantum of Explanation* <https://garyherstein.com/2017/11/01/reading-between-the-texts>

Lowe, Victor, *Alfred North Whitehead: The Man and His Work, Volume II: 1910–1947* (Baltimore: Johns Hopkins University Press, 1990).

Lucas, George, 'Evolutionist Theories and Whitehead's Philosophy', *Process Studies*, 14:4 (1985), 287–300.

Lucas, George, 'The Emergence of Whitehead's Metaphysics', *Process Studies*, 46:1 (2017), 52–62.

McHenry, Leemon, *The Event Universe* (Edinburgh: Edinburgh University Press, 2014).

'New Harvard Philosophy Professor is Well Known', *Harvard Crimson*, 14 October 1924 <https://www.thecrimson.com/article/1924/10/14/new-harvard-philosophy-professor-is-well>

Quine, W. V. O., 'Response to Leemon McHenry', *Process Studies* 26:1–2 (1997), 13–14.

Whitehead, T. North, *Now I Am An American: Habit and Change* (unpublished manuscript, 1966).

# 17

# Whitehead in Class: Do the Harvard-Radcliffe Course Notes Change How We Understand Whitehead's Thought?

*Brian G. Henning*

In large part, this entire volume is an attempt to answer the question posed by my subtitle: Do the Harvard-Radcliffe course notes change how we understand Alfred North Whitehead's thought? Each author considers a version of this question from the perspective of her or his own philosophical interests. Whether the question is answered affirmatively or negatively likely depends much on each author's own standing interpretations of Whitehead's thought. For my part, I would say that there is no 'smoking gun', no passage that fundamentally contradicts my previous understanding of Whitehead's thought. However, it would not be correct to conclude from this that the first volume of Harvard lectures are insignificant. Indeed, I would go so far as to suggest that these new materials will permanently change how we understand Whitehead's thought.

Characterising the nature of this impact reminds me of a passage from the lectures themselves. On 2 October 1924, Whitehead said to his Radcliffe students: 'New theories [are] always turning up which don't fit in. To say [that the] earlier forms are wrong is not as good as to say that they are lacking in richness of conception. [There is] modification rather than overturning. Real change is a gain in richness' (HL1, 416, interpolations added). This is how I understand the impact of the 1924–25 Harvard lectures. It is not so much that they 'overturn' previous understandings. Rather, by providing insight into the development of Whitehead's project, the Harvard lectures deepen the 'richness of [our] conception' of his thought.

Now, there are many ways of approaching my central question. When sitting down to explore this topic I considered returning to some of my earlier work to evaluate whether and how these new materials change – whether weakening or strengthening – positions I've staked in the Whiteheadian terrain. I hope to do this in time, but for now I've decided to take a broader perspective of the first volume of the Critical Edition. Thus my goal in this chapter is to take a slightly wider view from a higher altitude, as it were, in order to discern some of the key features and landmarks that immediately stood out to me in this new intellectual landscape.

First I consider three ways in which the Harvard lectures clarify and deepen our understanding of the *development* of Whitehead's thought. What we gain is greater understanding of 1) his views of his own pre-Harvard published works and other philosophical positions and philosophers, 2) some of the sources and inspirations for certain of his ideas, and 3) technical terms that he introduces but subsequently abandons and which therefore do not appear in his published works. I conclude with a reflection on what does not much appear in these lecture notes and what we might look for in subsequent volumes of the Critical Edition.

## Whitehead's Comments on His Pre-Harvard Work and on Other Philosophical Positions and Philosophers

As Aljoscha Berve notes in his chapter for this volume, one of Lowe's lasting contributions to Whitehead scholarship lies in the periodisation of Whitehead's work. As is often the case, it is likely that subsequent philosophers are as much to blame for the ossification of these boundaries as Lowe. After all, Lowe himself is careful to note that 'From what Whitehead said in his first lectures, it appears that most of the key ideas of his mature philosophy were in his mind when he arrived from England; they needed precise verbalization, review, and further development into a system.'[1] Now that we have the Winthrop Pickard Bell notes and a complete edited transcription of the Hocking notes, one thing that the 1924–25 lectures collectively demonstrate is that those who think there is a sharp break in Whitehead's thinking from Cambridge/London to Harvard are mistaken. Not only is there a clear continuity from his earlier published works, one can also already see many of the key features of what would become his Gifford lectures and *Process and Reality*.

Beyond the moderation of Lowe's periodisation, we also learn a bit more about how Whitehead thought about his own pre-Harvard work. Rarely in print did Whitehead significantly comment on, or even reference, his own previously published works. But in these lectures his students capture him frankly, if often in passing, assessing the shortcomings of *Principles of Natural Knowledge* (1919), *The Concept of Nature* (1920) and *The Principle of Relativity* (1922). We can now see more precisely the ways in which this is and is not true, as evidenced by the following quotations:

in *Principles of Natural Knowledge* [I am] under of influence Class theory –
continuously expressing [myself] in ways, though, that don't jibe with
this. – Was in a muddle. (HL1, 31)

Whitehead: *Principles of Natural Knowledge* Ch. VI, VII (frightfully confused chapters). (HL1, 69)

[I] was in a great muddle about (in first book, and better in second or in
*Principle of Relativity*) – to get quite clear as to what is to be substituted for
'Simple Location'. (HL1, 167)

Ingenuity in refining original ideas to get rid of these. You'd say aKb
to allow as special case here a and b coincide. b a 'proper' part of a in
*Principles of Natural Knowledge*. – Silly. In avalanche of new symbols in
*Principia Mathematica*. Trying to get as few special cases as possible. One
or two assumptions in aKb. The relation is transitive. If you're thinking
exactly you are bound to get to symbols. aKb . bKc . ⊃ . aKc. (HL1, 198)

In *Principles of Natural Knowledge* [I] let [myself] be fooled on point concerned with this. (HL1, 267)

Read chapter on Time in *Concept of Nature* [Had not full theory of
Mentality then. Talking there only of the Experient Occasion – not the
Cognizant one] Time enters Thought in a clearer way than Space does.
(HL1, 354)

In *Principles of Natural Knowledge*, I was confused. (HL1, 187)

Details of what lecturing on worked out somewhat clumsily in 3rd Part of
*Principles of Natural Knowledge* and throughout *Concept of Nature* and 1st
Part of *Principle of Relativity*. Not so concerned now in following systematic
details as in pointing out confusion etc. in those books as in pointing out
what lies behind ideas there. (HL1, 195)

In many ways these are merely more evidence of Whitehead's well-known
modesty. However, they are also more than that. They reveal a bit about what
he was not satisfied with in his earlier work and, therefore, what he wanted to
do in his future work. These passages at once illustrate the development and
strong continuity of his thought. In particular, I find it helpful to learn that
he sees himself not working out the earlier claims in 'systematic details', but
trying to 'point out what lies behind [the] ideas there'.

Although I do not have time to do more than list them here, it is interesting to note that we also learn more about what Whitehead thought about specific *positions*, such as vitalism. It is reassuring to see, for instance, Whitehead explicitly rejecting vitalism, a position with which his own work has at times been erroneously associated.[2]

> The problem of vitalism is wrongly stated – It assumes mechanism as prevailing throughout inorganic, then ask whether vitalism supervenes, with an organism of material – If put in that way, the mechanists have it all the time. (HL1, 158)

> On point of methodology, the vitalist has too easy a solution;– he has only to say 'This is what the whole wants' – reintroduces final causes, whereas the whole of modern science has been built up on the Baconian basis – Mechanists have here a strong point If you are going to bring in organism you must do so, so as not to disturb the whole procedure of modern science. (HL1, 159)

It is too bad he didn't make some of these explicit claims in his published works.

We also learn more about what Whitehead thought about specific *philosophers* and *scientists*, such as Aristotle, Kant, Bergson, Alexander, Einstein, Russell and James. For instance, regarding his student and collaborator, Bertrand Russell, Whitehead says

> Other theories:– Lump of chalk is merely classes or groups of sense-data [Whitehead poked Russell up to re-adopt this after his excellent little *Problems of Philosophy*.] Whitehead's only objection to this theory is that he doesn't think it true. (HL1, 28–9)

> Whitehead regards Realism that's <u>not</u> quite naïve as in a quite impossible position – Then a public world becomes a dream <u>inside</u> a private one – once you've <u>got</u> the private world. Whitehead thinking of Bertrand Russell here. Whitehead thinks Russell makes a concession here that bowls him over. If you once admit private images [Depends on <u>how</u>!?] you can never get beyond this. (HL1, 81–2)

For me, among the more interesting references is the discovery that Whitehead had a much more positive view of Aristotle than implied by his published works.[3] He defends to his students spending so much time in class on Aristotle 'because of <u>his</u> seeing what really <u>is</u> the problems of Metaphysics' (HL1, 55).

And he cites mostly approvingly Newman's claim that 'To talk sense is to talk with Aristotle' (HL1, 321). Another example concerns Kant. Although Whitehead still believes we must 'throw Kant over somewhere or other' (HL1, 305),[4] in the same class Hocking records (but Bell does not) the tantalising comment 'Whitehead's delight in Kant. One of the reasons he turned to philosophy' (HL1, 307). All of these scattered references reveal more about how he understood his own work and the work of others, which in turn helps us better understand the meaning of his thought. This leads me to my second subsection on what the lectures reveal about some new influences on and inspiration for Whitehead's thought.

## Influences and Inspiration For His Thought

On the first day of his second semester at Harvard (10 February 1925), Whitehead notes to his students in Emerson Hall: '[I] only know three ways of getting up a subject: (1) to be "taught" it; (2) to write a book on it; (3) to lecture on it. ⟨The⟩ Advantage of lecturing is that your pupils teach you as much as you them' (HL1, 195). What we have in these notes is Whitehead working through these problems in real time with his students in the classroom. The Harvard lectures capture the development of Whitehead's thought in the classroom with his students. As Bogaard notes in his introduction to HL1 and in recurring footnotes in the text, contrary to Lowe's claims, Whitehead was not sitting behind his desk reading out his notes. He was working from a prepared outline for sure, but the note-takers capture a person thinking through the expression of his thought in real time. This is further confirmed by comparing the recently discovered 'First Lecture', which is for the first time published in this volume, with what he said (or at least what was recorded by Bell and Hocking) in that first class.[5] He is 'getting up' the subject by lecturing on it. The course notes help us better understand what motivated his project and how it developed in his first year at Harvard.

One of the things that we learn in this first volume of the Harvard lectures is more specifically from where Whitehead derived some of his ideas. In his published works Whitehead was frequently not good about citing his influences. Here in the Harvard lectures we learn more about those figures with whom he thought and from whom he learned. We learn the genealogy or patrimony, as it were, of several concepts that become important as Whitehead strives to express his views. I'll consider just three examples.

First, as Bogaard explores more fully in Chapter 3 of this volume, the work of Whitehead's Harvard colleague Lawrence J. Henderson (1878–1942) had a profound influence on his understanding of the role of 'environment'. As

Bell and Hocking record it 11 December 1924, Whitehead says he was 'put on to' the central role of the environment by reading two of Henderson's books, *The Fitness of the Environment* (1913) and *The Order of Nature* (1917) (HL1, 135).[6] It is helpful to know specifically that Henderson was the inspiration for his thought, though of course he goes far beyond Henderson's work in the use to which he puts it. Whitehead takes Henderson's eco-biological concept from evolutionary biology and then applies it to his own problems in physics. Consider this lengthy passage from Bell's notes:

> Each organism to some extent creates its own environment – Previous life of organism has stamped itself somehow on whole present environment. How to account for <u>enormous</u> stability of Electrons etc. and for evolution of things in this order of Nature? . . . [B]y survival of fittest. You go back to where within order of Nature you had fitful stretches . . . of emergent enduring entities. . . . An Environment i.e. created by a Society of entities producing an Environment favourable to existence of them all. Environment has evolved as an Environment which secures selection of definite types. . . . Whole theory of Evolution considered largely from other point of view – as if Environment given and Organism had to adapt <u>itself to</u> this. . . . think of Brazilian Forest. – No individual tree could have grown without its environment. <u>The[y] produced</u> an <u>environment favorable to each other</u>. That's really the Key! Those animals die out which passively fit themselves to environment. The great lizards e.g. [It's the restless ones that survive]. Physical Science gives us an environment not unlike outside view of great <u>Societies</u>. Electrons, Protons etc. – two or three kinds – large numbers – There builds up higher organisms from these. Here you have cases of Emergent Entities which fit environment to each other. Electrons, Protons, etc. is just as much social being as rest of us are. (HL1, 135)

You get in passages like this a discussion of the extrapolation from the biological account of macroscopic organisms and their environment and the way that Whitehead translates this to the physical account of electrons, something which he'd considered since at least his dissertation on James Clerk Maxwell's theory of electromagnetism.[7]

Whitehead's reference to 'survival of the fittest' relates to a second philosophical figure who was not previously known to be an influence on Whitehead's thought. Both Bell (HL1, 141) and Heath (HL1, 461) record Whitehead as saying that he realised the importance of cooperation upon reading the Russian anarchist philosopher Peter (Prince) Kropotkin's (1842–1921) *Mutual Aid* (1902). Heath captures Whitehead putting it this way:

[The] Social side of evolution is important to keep in mind – natural selection as ruthless competition has been very much run[.] Other aspect put by Prince Kropotkin – called 'Mutual Aid' – evolution impresses idea of mutual aid quite as much as competition. 'Philosophic' Basis of 'mutual aid' is that it is creation of environment. (461)

Whitehead's references to Henderson and Kropotkin put into a new light some of the claims at the end of *Science and the Modern World*. In particular I have in mind his discussion of the same 'Brazilian Forest' which is not merely a violent evolutionary scene red in tooth and claw, but *also* an example of species which 'mutually assist each other in preserving the conditions for survival' (SMW, 206). Mutual aid is one of the means by which stable environments are created. Or as he puts it, 'Every organism requires an environment of friends, partly to shield it from violent changes, and partly to supply it with its wants' (SMW, 207).

As a brief aside I would note that, if Eugene Hargrove is correct, Whitehead's reference to an 'environment of friends' in SMW may itself have had an unexpected impact on the development of environmental philosophy. Hargrove, one of the founders of the field of environmental ethics and a historian of the movement, has argued twice in print that this particular passage in Whitehead's Lowell lectures might have been the source of inspiration for Aldo Leopold's notion of the 'biotic community', which itself became a chief inspiration for the founding of environmental ethics in America.[8]

A third concept whose genealogy becomes more clear with the help of the Harvard lectures is the notion of 'speculative philosophy'. In the opening pages of *Process and Reality*, Whitehead famously defines speculative philosophy as 'the endeavor to frame a coherent, logical, necessary system of general ideas in terms of which every element of our experience can be interpreted' (PR, 3). What the Lectures make clear is that Whitehead at least partially arrived at this concept from C. D. Broad (1887–1971), whose work *Scientific Thought* – which had just been released the year previous to his class starting (1923) – we now know was an assigned text in Whitehead's class and serves as a frequent source for the presentation of Whitehead's ideas during the course.[9]

A quick reading of the first pages of Broad's book makes it clear why it was a good choice for Whitehead's class on the 'Philosophical Presuppositions of Science'. 'I shall devote this introductory chapter to stating what I think Philosophy is about, and why the other sciences are important to it and it is important to the other sciences.'[10] As Bell records in his notes in November, Whitehead discusses Broad's division of philosophy into Critical Philosophy and Speculative Philosophy. To quote Broad directly, the former is an attempt to 'take the concepts that we daily use in common life and science, to analyze them, and thus to determine their precise meanings and their mutual relations'.[11] Broad sees this as 'the most fundamental task of philosophy'.[12]

The other approach to philosophy, speculative philosophy, is the reason why, according to Broad, many in the 'general public' have an 'unfavorable opinion' of philosophy. It differs from critical philosophy, he claims, in both object and method, attempting to use not only science, but also ethics and religion to come to 'general conclusions as to the nature of the Universe, and as to our position and prospects in it'.[13] A key problem is that, he contends, 'At the best Speculative Philosophy can only consist of more or less happy guesses, made on a very slender basis'.[14] Thus, he explains at the conclusion of his introduction, 'The present book deals wholly with Critical Philosophy . . . It is concerned almost entirely with an attempt to clear up some of the concepts used in the natural sciences.'[15] It becomes clear that Whitehead is not satisfied with Broad's approach.

Heath records Whitehead as putting it this way: 'Broad suggests that [I have] deserted the safe Critical Philosophy & embarked in Speculative Philosophy. [I] question whether this distinction is so sharp' (HL1, 449). Of course Whitehead's rejection of Broad's false dilemma is not surprising; Whitehead never met a bifurcation he didn't question. For his part, Whitehead tells his students he is more interested in the view of philosophy given by R. F. Alfred Hoernlé that the 'Object of philosophy is the synoptic vision' (HL1, 79). Another point of contention with Broad is captured by Heath, who notes that Whitehead takes issue with Cambridge philosophers' tendency 'to suspect ethics religion aesthetics & be bored by them' (HL1, 449). Though he had not delivered any of his famous lectures at this point, we now know that Whitehead is dedicated to a more thoroughgoing or radical empiricism than many of his Cambridge colleagues. While neither of these things is surprising, given his disagreement with Broad's characterisation of the two approaches to philosophy (critical and speculative), it is interesting that Whitehead later chooses to adopt one of these (speculative) to define his own project starting in the Gifford lectures, which of course are later published as *Process and Reality*.

What one is not likely to notice in the Harvard lectures until having also read Broad is that some of Whitehead's richest statements about the purpose of philosophy seem to be unstated but nevertheless direct responses to Broad's project. For instance, in his introduction, Broad explains 'I shall therefore begin by stating the case against philosophy as strongly as I can, and shall then try to show that, in spite of all objections, it really is a definite science with a distinct subject-matter.'[16] Contrast this with Whitehead's claim as recorded by Heath in February: 'Philosophy is not another science with its own limitations, but is the intellect standing back & criticizing & harmonizing – asking reason of it all' (HL1, 484).[17] Of course Broad is not the only person to have made the claim that philosophy is a science, but it seems likely that it was Broad's claim that provoked Whitehead's statement. It appears quite likely that Broad was an important foil for Whitehead in this first year of lectures.

While I am still piecing together the relationship between Broad and Whitehead, in researching this chapter I found that, on the occasion of Whitehead's death, in 1948 in *Mind* Broad wrote a lovely and quite comprehensive essay appraising Whitehead's life and work. It opens with the following: 'When Alfred North Whitehead died on 30th December, 1947, in his eighty-seventh year, the English-speaking world lost one of its deepest and most constructive thinkers.'[18] His treatment of Whitehead's earlier work, often ignored by later philosophers, gets the lion's share of Broad's analysis. Whitehead's Harvard works are only briefly discussed, partly because Broad says he 'understands it so imperfectly'.[19]

> *Process and Reality* is one of the most difficult philosophical books that exist; it can vie in this respect with the works of Plotinus and of Hegel. I cannot pretend to understand much of it, and I cannot help thinking that many of its enthusiastic admirers must simply be counted among those who 'wonder with a foolish face of praise'.[20]

It seems that Whitehead might have been as much or more of an influence on Broad than the reverse. I look forward to continuing to explore this relationship. For now, to summarise my conclusion in this section: as the examples of Henderson, Kropotkin and Broad illustrate, the lectures provide new or more detailed information about some of the intellectual inspirations for Whitehead's thought, which thereby shed new light on the genealogy of his ideas.

## Whitehead's Terminological Experimentation

One of the most exciting aspects of the Harvard lectures is seeing Whitehead struggle to express his ideas in different ways. Part of this process is the trying on of certain technical terms to express various insights. We know, for instance, that in these lectures we find Whitehead introducing for the first time terms that will later become central to his published works, such as: 'superject' on 23 October (HL1, 47), and both 'eternal object' (HL1, 161) and 'prehension' on 8 January (HL1, 216). It is helpful to see how and when he introduces these key terms. Regarding the first, 'superject', for instance, we learn in Bell's notes from October 1924 that Whitehead derived the term from his reading of Pliny and Virgil, who use the Latin term *superjacio* in the sense of 'lying over' (HL1, 47). I was excited to see these first uses and to learn more about how Whitehead came to them. What I did not expect to find is a great many technical terms that were subsequently abandoned by Whitehead, never to appear in print as technical terms. To give a sense of the number and diversity of these, I thought it would be helpful to present a list of them and then to consider a few in a bit of detail.

- Aspect 162, 168
- Beyond; Beyondness 47, 49, 65, 76, 433, 438, 448
- Different versions of 'objects'
  - Basic object 172
  - Emergent object 98, 163
  - Pure object 468
  - Social object 97, 451, 468
- Display 115, 120, 155, 162, 429, 431, 447
- Effectiveness 155
- Emergent entity 46–7, 91–2, 134, 528
- Experient Occasion 354, 396, 401–2
- Expansional 62, 63
- Formula 154
- Fusion 93, 113–18, 153
- Impress 70f, 87, 88
- Niche 356–64, 379–84
- Primates or prime entity 93, 95
- Processional 61, 443
- Protension 39
- Occasional and Praeter Occasional 45, 435, 462, 144
- Translucency 53, 152, 311, 314, 347–9, 354, 374, 400, 401, 518, 521
- Shadow of truth[21] 75, 87, 103, 328, 446–7, 452

Given that many already bemoan the number of neologisms in Whitehead's published works, it is remarkable to realise that the published terms are but a fraction of those that he *considered* adopting. But *why* did he abandon these terms? And what does it tell us about the development of his thinking? Granted more time, what we will find is that these linguistic cul-de-sacs are illuminating both in their own right and of the terms he ultimately adopts. These terminological experiments can help us better understand how Whitehead thought about and struggled with the problems he was addressing, which in turn can help us better understand the philosophical problems themselves. Let's look at a few of these in a bit more detail.

## a) Formula, Formulation and Environment

To start, let us continue the discussion of the role of environment started above. In late November 1924 Whitehead is exploring the role of pattern and environment. As we know, part of what he got from Henderson and Kropotkin was the fact that organisms are affected by and affect their environment, that organisms are better conceived as organisms-in-an-environment. That is, the relationship between the organism and its environment is internal and constitutive, not external and accidental. The environment is not a container in which the organism lives and moves and has its being. Rather, the pattern of the environment is an *essential* part of what the organism is, whether we are talking about a wolf in a forest, a cell in my hand, or an electron in an electromagnetic field.

Whitehead is so keen to emphasise the importance of this that he introduces what he calls the 'principle of the necessity of the environment' (HL1, 115). To my recollection, though the concept is retained, the principle does not later appear. Bell captures him explaining it in this way: 'The very first principle of description of what we find in real entities is that the Concreteness of finite emergent entity is compatible with, and requires the conditioning by its environment. Apart from its Environment, Entity has lost individuality. Unity in something more than itself is exactly what you're always talking about' (HL1, 115).

To further explain this point, Whitehead introduces a contrasting pair of terms: formula and formulation. Bell captures Whitehead putting it this way: 'If you try to get [the] Individual out of the process you get only a formula' (HL1, 118). Several classes later Whitehead explains further: 'Thus if you tear it away from its Environment, it simply degenerates into a formula, which will tell you the type of pattern which will be the outcome of the Electron in any conceivable environment. It's the most abstract formula possible. – Simply the type of outcome 'pattern' which would be the outcome of any Environment' (HL1, 154). If we properly see the constitutive relationship with the organism as *a part of* its environment, we have a full 'formulation'. If on the other hand you take an organism *apart from* its environment, you do not have a concrete occasion, but a mere 'formula' (HL1, 113). 'Formulation is the environment as patterned. Formula is science – concept of formulation' (HL1, 116). Too often scientists are satisfied by studying the formula – the 'concept of formulation' – and not the concrete formulation. I find myself rather liking this notion of an organism as a mere formula. It is regrettable that he decided not to retain the term explicitly.

## b) Object

One of the most vexing problems Whitehead is considering in this first year of lectures is how to account for endurance within a thoroughly processive metaphysics. What he is experimenting with here is the use of the concept of an 'object'. It is well understood that he will, even in these lectures, arrive at the concept of 'eternal objects'. However, especially in the early months of the course, he is using the concept of an object to cover a wider philosophical terrain than that later covered by eternal objects. Let's dive into the way that he describes 'objects' in general and their various species.

In his third lecture of the year, Bell records Whitehead as saying that he conceives an object as that which is 'identical through process'. It is what explains 'Recurrence . . . Sameness – Identity. – "There it is again"' (HL1, 11). Months later, in January 1925, Hocking records Whitehead as briefly considering the term 'existences' instead of 'objects'.[22] These 'objects' are both like and unlike our usual understanding of eternal objects as pure possibilities. What immediately jumps out as different is that Whitehead has a great many different divisions of kinds and types of objects, and that many of them do not seem to bear much similarity to eternal objects. For instance, in late November, when he is struggling for several days with the concept of objects, he introduces a division between two different kinds: 'primary objects' and 'emergent objects'. He gives 'greenness' as an example of a primary object (HL1, 96). This would seem to make primary objects much like eternal objects as we normally understand them.

He further divides these primary objects into two subclasses: 'pure objects' and 'social objects' (HL1, 97).[23] Whitehead is concerned in many of these lectures with understanding the 'togetherness' of reality. Pure primary objects seem to function like what he will later call eternal objects. Pure primary objects are not the 'concept' of an occasion because they cannot be realised on their own. 'Realization is a togetherness – a mutuality' (HL1, 97). On the other hand, social primary objects are the 'concept of an occasion' because they involve the 'structural relation between [pure] primary objects' (interpolation added). Thus, he explains,[24] 'Social primary objects are social in that they involve a pattern of pure primary objects' (HL1, 450–1). If I understand this properly, pure primary objects can never be realised by themselves. You never have greenness per se, but some aspect of greenness in relation to other pure primary objects, which together make a social primary object.[25]

The second major species of objects he calls emergent objects. What is odd, from the perspective of eternal objects, which term he does not introduce for another two months (8 January), is that emergent objects are 'actual'. 'Whole essence of an emergent object is:– it emerges as being actual. The fact of Actuality in Realization is the emergent object . . . The very essence of an emergent object is that it is actual. You've got the stuff of reality in it' (HL1, 98). We know for certain that eternal objects are real but not actual,[26] so something different is going on here. As 'actual' and 'emergent', it is tempting to wonder if these 'emergent objects' are what he will eventually call 'actual occasions' or 'actual entities'. This interpretation seems to be supported by his introduction of a particular form of emergent object called a 'basic object'. Whatever basic objects are, they are 'Fundamental type of object of which everything is built. . . . Basic objects are very final ultimate groundwork of everything' (HL1, 107).[27] However, I'm not entirely certain that it is correct to see emergent objects or basic objects as a version of actual entities for the reason that emergent objects are of different 'grades', and that a basic object is simply an emergent object 'of zero grade' – that is, Whitehead goes on to explain, 'an emergent object whose ingredients are pure objects' (HL1, 98). He introduces the concept of basic objects to avoid an infinite regress (HL1, 98), that much is clear. However, his concern here is that we 'Can't always try to explain in terms of lower object – else infinite regress – finally have to come to a basic object which we will describe simply in terms of social objects. i.e. in terms of patterns of pure objects which are eventually realized' (HL1, 451–2).[28] It seems that a basic emergent object corresponds not to a pure primary object, but to a pattern of social primary objects. At any rate, if I'm understanding him correctly, and it is not clear that I am, 'emergent objects' are actual, but they are not to be confused with what he elsewhere in the lectures calls a 'primate' or an 'emergent entity'. It is emergent entities, not emergent objects, which are the real concrete actualities. 'The "Ideas" never are real but what is real is the emergent entity, their relations etc.' (HL1, 437).

This interpretation is supported by an example captured by Heath. Whitehead gives the example of 'ancient Rome' as an emergent object that 'has both an endurance in time and an eternal actuality'. It was actual and will always be an 'eternal actuality'; it is an 'eternal fact' (HL1, 451–2). Given this example and characterisation, it seems that perhaps 'pure objects' are what will later become eternal objects, and that 'emergent objects' are what he sometimes calls in these lectures 'actual potentiality' (e.g., HL1, 119,

121, 124), or will in later published works refer to as the past or the 'actual world'.[29] But it just isn't quite clear, because he also seems to describe human beings as a particular 'emergent object of high type' (HL1, 452). And in later published works he will describe humans in terms of socially ordered structured societies.

To be honest, Whitehead's discussion of objects seems rather muddled, a claim which I think Whitehead himself would not hesitate to admit. And that is part of the point. He is working through these things, slicing a distinction thinner here, introducing a new one there, in order to get at a way of correctly expressing his fundamental concerns about realisation and togetherness. Bell captures Whitehead admitting how difficult the topic is: 'The almost insuperable difficulty of that first start – always getting cloaked in our minds because we start <u>further on</u> – Reality emerging into something <u>more</u> than itself. But transition from <u>Platonic ideas</u> to reality that's the problem. [I] can't get more than a ghost of a glimmer of light here' (HL1, 98).

With more time and space it would also be fruitful to examine in some detail other failed terminological experiments such as: 'impress', 'beyondness', 'translucency', 'aspect', 'display', 'praeter-occasional', 'pretension', and perhaps most interesting, 'shadow of truth', a concept quite closely related to Whitehead's discussion of objects. I don't have time to do more than quote a few intriguing passages on this final term.[30]

> Viewed in the <u>pale apartness</u> from any reference to what happens, there's nothing true or false – There can be logical and illogical ideas. But Truth – what has to do fundamentally with question of Realisation. And shadow of this falls on Realm of Ideas and affects it. Its that shadow of truth that we comprehend in Memory. (HL1, 75)[31]

> Truth has to do with the act of realization. The shadow of truth falls on the ideas, (makes them particular – in enriched envisagement), & as such are taken up into memory. (HL1, 77)

> 'The Shadow of Truth' The object as past is a <u>living</u> past. (HL1, 103)

Finally, in addition to what Whitehead does discuss, it is also important to consider what he does not discuss much or at all, and what might be inferred from that absence. For instance, he doesn't much discuss God, and when he does (HL1, 4, 52, 86) it is not to argue for any metaphysical role for a God. Indeed, on 4 April Hocking records Whitehead as saying that a particular position is the 'business of theology to explore', to which he is said to have added 'not my business' (HL1, 312). It is important to not read too much into this absence, but given the dominance of theological God-talk in process thought in the second half of the twentieth century and the ongoing debate about the role of God in Whitehead's thought,[32] it does seem noteworthy. It is also important to remember that Whitehead was to give his second Lowell lectures on the topic of religion the following year (1926) – published as *Religion in the Making*. Whitehead obviously had such topics on his mind. Yet, at least in his class, he does not seem to have been looking to solve any of his metaphysical problems with recourse to God. It will be interesting to see at what point the primordial and consequent natures of God appear in his courses, if in fact they do.

It is also potentially noteworthy that several other central concepts are absent, such as 'concrescence', 'satisfaction', 'intensity' and even 'creativity'. Indeed, the term 'creativity' does not appear until 14 May, though in March he discusses the 'creative activity' of the intellect. The term 'actual occasion' appears at times, but to my reading it does not yet seem to function as a technical term. On the other hand, 'actual entity' does not appear at all, with Whitehead preferring instead 'primary entity', 'primate' or 'emergent entity' (not to be confused with 'emergent object', discussed above). Closer to my own philosophical interests is the complete absence of a metaphysical role for 'beauty', which comes to be a dominant feature of his work in the 1930s. It is true that aesthetic value plays a role in these lectures, and that is reflected in his *Religion in the Making* as well. Still, as with the lack of God, I'm left to wonder what future volumes of the Edition might reveal about when beauty becomes an important metaphysical concept for him.

We are well underway on the second volume of the Critical Edition, which will cover two academic years (1925–27). Obviously, this is a critical period in the lead up to Whitehead's Gifford lectures, which were delivered in Edinburgh in 1927–28. We will have to wait to see what the next volume reveals about the development of his thought. If this first volume is any measure, it seems likely that it will once again deepen our understanding of the meaning and development of Whitehead's thought.

By way of conclusion, I'd like to quote the final paragraph of C. D. Broad's 1948 remembrance of Whitehead:

> It is, perhaps, fortunate for most prophets that, unlike Whitehead, they have been without honour in their own countries and times. A lesser man than he might easily have been spoiled by the adulation which his later work received and by being treated as a kind of Messiah by many of his more foolish admirers. Nothing of the kind happened. He remained simple, natural, modest, humorous, and intensely human. He was equally

great in intellect and in character, and one of the finest products of that very fine civilisation and culture which have perished in England's two Pyrrhic victories over Germany.[33]

## Notes

1. Lowe, *Alfred North Whitehead: The Man and His Work, Volume II*, 146. Of course we know that Lowe did not have access to Whitehead's first lectures, since Hocking's notes don't start until October. Nevertheless, Lowe did an admirable job with the materials available to him. That said, it is now clear that his bio-graphical conclusions were based on necessarily limited documentary evidence. We also now know that some materials were withheld from him by Whitehead's heirs. As we know, with the passing of Harriet Whitehead, T. North Whitehead's second wife, the intellectual property of Alfred North's estate came to his grand-son, George Whitehead. In the first phone conversation that I had with George Whitehead he mentioned that he thought his mother had treated Lowe unfairly, going so far as to intentionally withhold some materials from him. It is hard to square this claim with Lowe's acknowledgement in the first volume in which he expresses his gratitude to 'Mrs. T. North Whitehead for her constant moral support and infinite patience' (ix). Regardless, George Whitehead expressed his interest in helping us, in part out of a desire to compensate for the way that his mother treated Lowe.

2. See, for instance, Bell, 'A Dog's Life'.

3. See, for instance, PR, 30, 50; AI, 132–3, 276; MT, 15.

4. See also, 'Whitehead trying to stand Kant on his head; – without Kant's 'Coper-nican Revolution' (HL1, 113).

5. For more on this, see Bogaard's chapter on the 'First Lecture' in this volume.

6. We also know from his course gradebook that that in the 1930s Whitehead listed both of these books as assigned reading for his PHIL3b class (e.g., Whitehead, Alfred North, 'Student Record Book for Harvard and Radcliffe Classes', HUG 4877.10, Papers of Alfred North Whitehead, 1924–1947, Harvard University Archives <http://oasis.lib.harvard.edu/oasis/deliver/~hua10017> 299).

7. It is a terrible thing to realise that Whitehead's dissertation does not seem to have survived.

8. Hargrove, 'The Historical Foundations of American Environmental Attitudes', 238–9. Yet, at the same time, as I've argued elsewhere, this claim is not based on any identifiable documentary evidence and should not be overstated. See Hen-ning, 'Unearthing the Process Roots of Environment Ethics'.

9. As an aside I would note that the Whitehead Research Project has obtained about seventy-five pages from the Trinity College Cambridge Archives of what appear to be C. D. Broad's notes from 1919–20 on Whitehead's books. It seems possible that Broad was doing research for his 1923 book, which Whitehead then uses in his class.

10. Broad, *Scientific Thought*, 11.
11. Broad, *Scientific Thought*, 16.
12. Broad, *Scientific Thought*, 16.
13. Broad, *Scientific Thought*, 20.
14. Broad, *Scientific Thought*, 21.
15. Broad, *Scientific Thought*, 25.
16. Broad, *Scientific Thought*, 11.
17. Cf. 'Guard against impression that metaphysical philosophy is <u>merely</u> handmaid of science. Metaphysics is critical appreciation of whole intellectual background of man's life. As near to poetry as science' (HL1, 413).
18. Broad, 'Alfred North Whitehead', 139.
19. Broad, 'Alfred North Whitehead', 144. On the whole, he remained positive: 'Still, from my knowledge of Whitehead and of those of his writings which I think I can understand, and from the occasional gleams and glimpses which have been vouchsafed to me in struggling with *Process and Reality*, I feel fairly certain that there is something important concealed beneath the portentous verbiage of the Gifford Lectures.'
20. Broad, 'Alfred North Whitehead', 144. This phrase is from line 212 of Alexander Pope's 'Epistle to Dr. Arbuthnot', but it might have come to Broad from Emerson's more famous essay 'self-reliance': 'I mean "the foolish face of praise", the forced smile which we put on in company where we do not feel at ease in answer to conversation which does not interest us. The muscles, not spontaneously moved, but moved by a low usurping wilfulness, grow tight about the outline of the face with the most disagreeable sensation.'
21. For more on this particular concept and its role in HL1, see George Allan's chapter in this volume.
22. 'There are beings, existences, objects which stand outside. As merely outside they might have no relation to the process, in which case we should know nothing about them. But let us take them as parts of the machinery – as such we might call them existences, But prefer the term object – as what stands firm' (HL1, 170).
23. Bell records Whitehead as briefly offering 'simple objects' instead of 'pure objects', but says he is a 'bit afraid' of this formulation (HL1, 97). Whitehead tries to describe to his students the difference between pure objects and social objects in this way: 'A pure object is purely an object. Its only relevance to any occasion is either that it's ingredient in it or has a relation of potentiality. You can't look on it as the concept of an occasion. It's never the whole concept of the occasion. Thus it doesn't achieve any further status than that of being discerned in an occasion; whereas "Social" Object is a concept of an occasion – is the structural relation between primary objects. Primary objects allow such and such relational structures between themselves. This external (to their individual essences – Same e.g. for red or green or brown as to their status in it) structural relation stands in potentiality of their relational essences; but viewed merely as Social object there's no reality about it' (HL1, 97). Heath records something very close to this, which

should give us more confidence in the recording: 'To explain this further we must divide primary objects into two kinds:– "Pure" objects and "Social" objects of "Situations". "Pure"; or "Simple"?? A bit afraid of "Simple". A pure object is purely an object. Its only relevance to any occasion is either that it's ingredient in it or has a relation of potentiality. You can't look on it as the concept of an occasion. It's never the whole concept of the occasion. Thus it doesn't achieve any further status than that of being discerned in an occasion; whereas "Social" Object is a concept of an occasion – is the structural relation between primary objects. Primary objects allow such and such relational structures between themselves. This external (to their individual essences – Same e.g. for red or green or brown as to their status in it) structural relation stands in potentiality of their relational essences; but viewed merely as Social object there's no reality about it. Only trace of reality is as it stands in this envisagement of the Eternal principle. It's equally "potential"' (HL1, 97).

23. 'But has this difference from a pure object that you can ask if this is being realized. "Pure" object – Nonsense to ask whether it alone is being realized. Realization is a togetherness – a mutuality A social object is the concept of a togetherness – even if only as standing within the potentiality of a relational essence. It's the concept of a realized togetherness – out of Space, out of Time. Social object presupposes therefore "pure" objects. "Situations" can be realized' (HL1, 97).

24. A social primary object 'presupposes therefore "pure" objects' (HL1, 97).

25. See, 'The event beyond is always ingredient in my bodily event. Then you get the conception of the event as a pattern of aspects. Then you have pattern . . . qua concept is social object, i.e. a situation' (HL1, 468).

26. See, for instance, Category of Explanation seven: 'That an eternal object can be described only in terms of its potentiality for "ingression" into the becoming of actual entities; and that its analysis only discloses other eternal objects. It is a pure potential' (PR, 23).

27. 'Whitehead doesn't think that "basic" object is the one first turning up in time. Logically prior. No temporal priority. Whole stuff of reality comes on together. Its vigour of realization may differ from time to time' (HL1, 99).

28. See, 'When you come to basic objects, (otherwise infinite regress. Whitehead thinks this regress would be vicious) you must start with one in which all ingredients are primary objects. A 'basic' object is essentially – has no accent of reality in any of its ingredients. So we're up against difficulty – (pure initial difficulty) of what we mean by realization' (HL1, 98).

29. See, for instance, PR, 65.

30. Most fortunately, George Allan does engage with this intriguing concept in his chapter for this volume.

31. 'The process of Realization is a process of Gathering in. You have "The Shadow of Truth". Therefore the How is always a particularized How – having relevance to the particular – The irrevocable Past is there and what becomes has to become, in relation to what is actual. So you get this constant modification of eternal

ground of Becoming. – Very Laws of Nature themselves have a quality of pass-ingness in them. So Emergent Value is not merely general; but is a particularized Value – Emergent Value has Endurance – I.e. this Value is qualifying. (The individual notes of a tune – passing along, each – But only with the retention do you have a growing of Value and get the Tune)' (HL1, 87). 'The Actuality means that in the emergent object we find a delegation or limited embodiment or exhibition of the "eternal underlying principle". It (this ground of becoming) is itself only through this embodiment in emergent objects. Whitehead thinks the very foun-dations of Time are to be found in "Actuality". Take "Subsequent" in broad sense. – Means that the Eternal becomes stamped with "a definite limitation which is that object" the impress of that object – takes account of that Object – "The Shadow of Truth" The object as past is a living past. By the word "Subsequence" of an object means that Spatio-temporal region throughout which Eternal is so stamped' (HL1, 103).

32. See, for instance, Cobb, 'Whitehead, God, and a Contemporary Rift Among Whiteheadians'. For a representation of the 'Whitehead without God' position, see Allan, 'A Functionalist Reinterpretation of Whitehead's Metaphysics'.

33. Broad, 'Alfred North Whitehead', 145.

## Bibliography

Allan, George, 'A Functionalist Reinterpretation of Whitehead's Metaphysics', *The Review of Metaphysics*, 62:2 (2008), 327–54.

Bell, Jeffrey, 'A Dog's Life: Thoughts, Symbols and Concepts', in Roland Faber, Jeffrey Bell and Joseph Petek (eds), *Rethinking Whitehead's* Symbolism: *Thought, Language, Culture* (Edinburgh: Edinburgh University Press, 2017), 147–69.

Bogaard, Paul and Jason Bell (eds), *The Harvard Lectures of Alfred North Whitehead, 1924–1925: Philosophical Presuppositions of Science* (Edinburgh: Edinburgh University Press, 2017).

Broad, C. D., *Scientific Thought* (London: Kegan Paul, Trench, Trubner & Co, 1923).

Broad, C. D., 'Alfred North Whitehead (1861–1947)', *Mind*, 57:226 (1948), 139–45.

Cobb, Jr. John B., 'Whitehead, God, and a Contemporary Rift Among Whitehead-ians', *Process Studies*, 45:2 (2016), 132–42.

Ford, Lewis, *The Emergence of Whitehead's Metaphysics, 1925–1929* (Albany: State University of New York Press, 1985).

Hargrove, Eugene, 'The Historical Foundations of American Environmental Attitudes', *Environmental Ethics*, 1 (1979), 209–40.

Henderson, Lawrence J., *The Fitness of the Environment: An Inquiry into the Biological Significance of the Properties of Matter* (New York: Macmillan, 1913).

Henderson, Lawrence J., *The Order of Nature: An Essay* (Cambridge, MA: Harvard University Press, 1917).

Henning, Brian G., 'Unearthing the Process Roots of Environment Ethics: Whitehead, Leopold, and the Land Ethic', *Balkan Journal of Philosophy*, 8:1 (2016), 3–12.

Kropotkin, Peter, *Mutual Aid: A Factor of Evolution* (London: William Heinemann, 1902).

Lowe, Victor, *Alfred North Whitehead: The Man and His Work, Volume I: 1861–1910* (Baltimore: Johns Hopkins University Press, 1985).

Lowe, Victor, *Alfred North Whitehead: The Man and His Work, Volume II: 1910–1947* (Baltimore: Johns Hopkins University Press, 1990).

Pope, Alexander, *Imitations of Horace, with an Epistle to Dr Arbuthnot and the Epilogue to the Satires*, ed. John Butt et al., Vol. 4 (London and New Haven: Methuen, 1961).

Whitehead, Alfred North, *Science and the Modern World* (New York: The Free Press, [1925] 1967).

Whitehead, Alfred North, *Process and Reality: An Essay in Cosmology* (New York: The Free Press, [1929] 1978).

# Notes on Contributors

**George Allan** is Professor of Philosophy Emeritus at Dickinson College, where he taught for thirty-three years and was also its senior academic officer for two decades. His publications are mainly on topics in social philosophy and philosophy of education, influenced by the metaphysical ideas of process philosophers such as Whitehead and Langer, and of the American pragmatists. His most recent book is *Modes of Learning: Whitehead's Metaphysics and the Stages of Education* (SUNY Press).

**Jason Bell** is Assistant Professor of Philosophy at the University of New Brunswick. He has taught in the graduate programme at the Higher Institute of Philosophy at the Catholic University of Leuven in Belgium and at Mount Allison University in Canada, and has served at the University of Göttingen as Fulbright Professor, as scholar-in-residence at Boston University, as Onderzoeksfonds Research Fellow at the Husserl Archives, and as d'Alzon Fellow at Assumption College. He was awarded the doctorate in philosophy at Vanderbilt University. His research focuses on ethics and the relation of American and phenomenological philosophy.

**Aljoscha Berve** is Assistant Professor of Philosophy at the Heinrich-Heine-Universität and Executive Director and Vice-President of the European Society for Process Thought. The author of a book and various articles on Whitehead, his fields of research include process philosophy, metaphysics, philosophy of psychology, and German philosophy at the turn of the twentieth century.

**Paul A. Bogaard** retired from teaching after forty years at Mount Allison University, having published on the philosophy of chemistry, history of science in Canada, ancient philosophy and (since retirement) the local history of the Chignecto area of Maritime Canada. He is a founding director of the Tantramar Heritage Trust, the Sackville Waterfowl Park, the Cape Jourimain Nature Centre and the UNESCO-designated Fundy Biosphere Reserve. He is lead editor of the first volume of the *Edinburgh Critical Edition of the Complete Works of Alfred North Whitehead*.

**Ronny Desmet** became a master of mathematics in 1983 with a dissertation on the mathematics and philosophy of quantum mechanics. After a career in the private sector, he left a position at Sun Microsystems in 2002 to study philosophy. He became a Master of Philosophy in 2005 with a dissertation on the decline of the mechanistic worldview, and obtained a PhD in 2010 for his study on Whitehead's theory of relativity. Currently, he is a postdoctoral researcher of the Fund for Scientific Research Flanders, and is affiliated with the Centre of Logic and Philosophy of Science at the Free University of Brussels. Among his publications are a collection of essays, co-edited with Michel Weber, *Whitehead: The Algebra of Metaphysics* (Les éditions Chromatika, 2010), and another collection, *Intuition in Mathematics and Physics: A Whiteheadian Approach* (Process Century Press, 2016).

**Brian G. Henning** is Professor of Philosophy and Environmental Studies at Gonzaga University and Director of Research and Publication for the Whitehead Research Project. He is author or editor of seven books and more than thirty articles and chapters. His book *The Ethics of Creativity* (University of Pittsburgh Press, 2005), won the 2007 Findlay Book Prize from the Metaphysical Society of America for the best work of metaphysics published between 2001 and 2006. He is founding co-editor of the *Contemporary Whitehead Studies* book series through Lexington Books and founder and executive editor of the *Edinburgh Critical Edition of the Complete Works of Alfred North Whitehead*.

**Gary L. Herstein** began his career in the computer and networked PC industries, where he worked for almost twenty-five years. During this time he completed an MA in Interdisciplinary Studies at DePaul University, writing his thesis on the group-theoretic structures underlying the concept of identity. Dr Herstein completed his PhD at Southern Illinois University at Carbondale, writing his dissertation on Whitehead's criticisms of the logical presuppositions of Einstein's general theory of relativity. He has taught full-time at Merrimack and Muskingum colleges and part-time at Harper College, where the courses presented included Ethics, Logic, Critical Thinking, American Philosophy and Philosophy of Science. He is currently an independent scholar working on various projects relating to the philosophy of Alfred North Whitehead, the logical forms and presuppositions of measurement, and the connections between spatial reasoning and metaphysics. His publications include *The Quantum of Explanation* (with Randall Auxier, 2017), *Whitehead and the Measurement Problem of Cosmology* (2006), 'Alfred North Whitehead' (*The Internet Encyclopedia of Philosophy*) and 'Davidson and the Impossibility of Psychophysical Laws' (*Synthese* 145:1, 2005).

**Seshu Iyengar** is a PhD student in the University of Toronto Department of Physics where he holds a C. David Naylor University Fellowship. He has received a Bachelor of Science in Biology-Physics and a Bachelor of Arts in Philosophy from the University of New Brunswick. His graduate research focuses on the physical and mathematical principles of modelling biological processes related to organism lifespan and aging. He is also interested in physics education research and philosophy of science in the German idealist and phenomenological traditions, alongside their historical influences on physics.

**Jude Jones** joined the faculty at Fordham University in 1991, where she has served as teacher, programme director, mentor, faculty senator and happy alumnus. She received her BA in Philosophy and English from Fordham in 1985, earned her MA and PhD from Emory University in 1993, then returned to New York, which has always been home. Her chief work is *Intensity: An Essay in Whiteheadian Cosmology* (Vanderbilt University Press, 1998). Her philosophical interests and graduate teaching centre on Whitehead's metaphysics and philosophy of experience, as well as related issues in Classical American thought (especially Dewey and James). She has a lifelong affliction with trying to figure out what constitutes the 'individuation' element in ontology and in the stream of thought, and in finding ways of construing 'agency' in a meaningful way.

**George R. Lucas, Jr.** is Professor Emeritus at the US Naval Academy. A past president (2016) of the Metaphysical Society of America, he current serves as the society's Secretary-Treasurer. He is the author of a number of books and articles on Whitehead, including *Hegel and Whitehead* (SUNY 1986) and *The Rehabilitation of Whitehead* (SUNY 1989).

**Joseph Petek** is a doctoral candidate in Process Studies at Claremont School of Theology. He is the Chief Archivist of the Whitehead Research Project, Assistant Series Editor for the Critical Edition of Whitehead, and co-editor (with Brian Henning) of the second volume forthcoming in that series, devoted to Whitehead's Harvard lectures and seminars from the period 1925–27.

**George W. Shields** is the 2000–2001 University Distinguished Professor, Professor of Philosophy, and Chairperson of the Division of Literature, Languages and Philosophy at Kentucky State University in Frankfort, Kentucky. He also serves as Professorial Lecturer in Philosophy at the University of Louisville, where he has taught graduate level health care ethics and law at the Health Sciences campus. He holds a PhD from the University of Chicago, where he wrote a doctoral dissertation on the philosophy of Charles Hartshorne. He has done further study at Oxford University, England. He has published some 100 articles, reviews and critical studies in a wide variety of scholarly books and peer-reviewed professional journals, including (among many others): *The American Journal of Theology and Philosophy*, *International Journal for Philosophy of Religion*, *The Modern Schoolman*, *Process Studies*, *Religious Studies*, *Sophia* and the *Southern Journal of Philosophy*. He is co-author and editor or co-editor of six books, including *Process and Analysis: Whitehead, Hartshorne, and the Analytic Tradition* (SUNY, 2003) and *Science, Technology, and Religious Ideas* (University Press of America, 1994).

**Dennis Sölch** is Assistant Professor of Philosophy at Heinrich-Heine-Universität Düsseldorf and Executive Director and Vice-President of the German Whitehead Society. In 2016 he was the William James Scholar in Residence at the William James Centre in Potsdam, Germany, and held visiting professorships in Tampere, Finland, and Klagenfurt, Austria. He has authored and edited three books on Whitehead, including a translation of Whitehead's *The Aims of Education* into German, as well as published various articles on Process Philosophy, Pragmatism, Nietzsche and American Transcendentalism.

**Maria-Teresa Teixeira** holds a PhD in contemporary philosophy from the Faculdade de Letras da Universidade de Lisboa. She is a researcher at Universidade de Coimbra, Portugal. She is the author of two books: *Being, Becoming and Perishing: Creativity in Whitehead's Philosophy* and *Consciousness and Action: Bergson and Neuroscience*. She has translated Whitehead's *Process and Reality* into Portuguese. She is the executive director-elect of the International Process Network.

# Index

Abraham, Max, 166
abstraction
    and the art of reasoning, 289
    critical examination of, 141
    exactment and, 288
    geometry of a point-instant example,
        287–8
    of individual entities, 49–50, 66
    method of extensive abstraction, 143
    and open-ended thinking, 289–91
    philosophy's role and, 132
    process of, 286–7
    subject-predicate relationship, 136–7
    surrogates and, 286
    of temporal points, 207
    and the three types of entities, 286–7
    through mathematics, 215–16
    *see also* fallacy of misplaced
        concreteness
actual entities
    atomisation and, 148
    emergent objects as, 349, 351
    mutual dependence with eternal
        objects, 111, 250–1
    as perishing over time, 313–14
    purpose and valuation of, 91–2, 94
    relationship with their environments,
        75, 112
    society as a nexus of, 95, 96, 97
actual occasions
    the process of becoming and, 147–8
    realisation of, 302, 303, 304, 305

as a synthesis of being and not-being,
    237, 250
actuality
    actualisation of organisms, 85
    of emergent objects, 349–50
    of noumena, 248
*Adventures of Ideas* (AI)
    Poynting Flux of Energy, 159–60
    seven Platonic notions in, 270–1, 273,
        276
    victory of persuasion over force, 272
analogies, 292
anthropic principle, 81–2
archival materials
    challenges of, 19–21
    challenges of transcription, ix–x
    destruction of Whitehead's personal
        papers, xii, xvi, xvii, xviii, 56, 329,
        334
    impact of digitisation, xii
    and knowledge of Whitehead's
        thought, 337
    multiple sets of notes from individual
        lectures, 21–9, 327–8
    searches for, xii
    typescript of the first Harvard lecture,
        xviii, 56–60
    and US copyright laws, x–xi
    Victor Lowe collection, 19
    *see also* First Lecture: September 1924;
        Harvard lectures
Aristotelian Society, 142